COLETTE'S REPUBLIC

COLETTE'S REPUBLIC

Work, Gender, and Popular Culture in France, 1870–1914

Patricia A. Tilburg

Berghahn Books
New York • Oxford

Published in 2009 by

Berghahn Books
www.berghahnbooks.com

©2009, 2010 Patricia A. Tilburg
First paperback edition published in 2010

Library of Congress Cataloging-in-Publication Data
Tilburg, Patricia A.
Colette's republic : work, gender, and popular culture in France, 1870-1914 / Patricia A.
Tilburg.—1st ed.
    p. cm.
Includes bibliographical references and index.
ISBN 978-1-84545-571-2 (hbk) -- 978-1-84545-789-1 (pbk)
1. Popular culture—France—History—19th century. 2. Popular culture—France—History—
20th century. 3. Secularism—France—History—19th century. 4. Secularism—France—
History—20th century. 5. Education—Social aspects—France—History—19th century.
  6. Education—Social aspects—France—History—20th century. 7. Sex role—France—
History—19th century. 8. Sex role—France—History—20th century. 9. Performing arts—
Social aspects—France—History—19th century.   10. Performing arts—Social aspects—France—
History—20th century. I. Title.
  DC33.6.T55 2009
  306.0944'09034—dc22

                                                    2009012946

British Library Cataloguing in Publication Data
A catalogue record for this book is available from the British Library

Printed in the United States on acid-free paper

ISBN: 978-1-84545-571-2 Hardback, 978-1-84545-789-1 Paperback

To my mother and father,
Kathleen and William Tilburg

CONTENTS

List of Figures

ACKNOWLEDGMENTS

I am deeply indebted to the friends, family, and colleagues without whom *Colette's Republic* could not have been realized. Several generous teachers guided this book from its earliest stages, and thus it seems appropriate to begin with them. I was tremendously fortunate to find in a doctoral advisor that too-rare combination of an exceptional scholar and concerned teacher. Debora Silverman trained me in the métier of the cultural historian; her methodological originality, penetrating eye, and scholarly rigor shaped this project from its conception, and continue to stimulate my teaching and research to this day. Lynn Hunt and Edward Berenson gave their time, formidable knowledge, and insight to this project, and their seminars have been a pedagogical model for my own teaching.

Numerous scholars have provided perceptive readings and advice on portions of the book, including Emily Apter, Barry Bergen, Lenard Berlanstein, Sally Charnow, Vivien Dietz, Steven Hause, Carolyn Johnson, Cheryl Koos, John Mangum, Ben Marschke, Kelly Maynard, David Meyers, Marie-Laurence Netter, Robert Nye, Karen Offen, Jared Poley, Mary Louise Roberts, David Sabean, Pierre Simoni, Lynn Sharp, Catherine Slawy-Sutton, Stacey Sloboda, Leon Sachs, and Mary Lynn Stewart. The late Eugen Weber and his wife Jacqueline enabled me to write some parts of this book while cat-sitting in their splendid home for several months. Robert Baker's historical imagination, scholarly mettle, and friendship fortified this project from its inception. Warm thanks to Britta McEwen, Andrea Mansker, Amy Woodson-Boulton, and Claudia Verhoeven for their analytical shrewdness and nourishing feminist fellowship. This book owes Andrea a special debt, as her study of fin-de-siècle gender provided a vital complement and occasional foil for my research, from seminars in Los Angeles to coffee breaks at the BN. I am particularly beholden to Jean Pedersen, Diana Holmes, and Elinor Accampo, who offered suggestions on the entire manuscript. Elinor has been an exceptionally rich source of critical analysis, encouragement, and professional guidance.

I had the pleasure of developing the ideas for this book in a variety of fruitful intellectual environments, including the Western Society for French History, the Society of French Historical Studies, UCLA's European History Colloquium, the

American Historical Association, the UCLA Center for the Study of Women, and the History of Education Society. The early years spent on this project were funded through the immense generosity of the University of California Los Angeles, including the Graduate Division, the UCLA Center for the Study of Women, and, most especially, the UCLA Department of History. Davidson College has supplied not only financial support, but also a stimulating and collegial interdisciplinary space in which to work and think. I am especially appreciative of my colleagues and students in the Department of History.

This book would not have been possible without the resources and efficiency of numerous libraries and archives, including the Bibliothèque nationale de France; the Bibliothèque Marguerite Durand; the Archives nationales de France; the Bibliothèque historique de la ville de Paris; the Bibliothèque de l'Arsenal; the Bibliothèque de l'Opéra; the Archives Départementales de l'Yonne; the Mairie of Saint-Sauveur-en-Puisaye; and the Musée Colette. I am grateful to Hugues de Jouvenel for assisting me in accessing some of Colette's correspondence at the Bibliothèque littéraire Jacques Doucet. For their assistance and generosity in helping me acquire the images for this book, I thank the Centre d'études Colette, especially Samia Bordji, as well as the Conseil général de l'Yonne and the Bibliothèque nationale de France. Stateside, I benefited greatly from the librarians and collections at UCLA's University Research Library, and from the assistance of Shela Patel and Barbara Bernstein. The final stages of this project have been facilitated by the staff of Davidson College's Little Library, especially Joe Gutekanst and Susanna Boylston, as well as Margaret Sprinkle. I also thank Ann Przyzycki, Melissa Spinelli, and Marion Berghahn for their invaluable support during the production process, and Lori Rider for her masterful copyediting. As this book deals in part with the impact of public education, I think it also appropriate to mention the extraordinary public schools that formed me, namely those in my *ville natale* of Needham, Massachusetts, and my undergraduate home, the College of New Jersey.

Many treasured friends and family members have made certain that the years spent writing this book have been joyful ones, including Michael Farnan, John Ryan, Tara Dailey, Stefani Alessandrini, and Carolyn Stawicki. For more than a decade, Sheila Callaghan and Kirstin Ohrt provided a succession of feasts, roadtrips, and all-night conversations; I thank them for never accepting my excuse that I had too much work to do. Deanna Kreisel and Scott MacKenzie allowed me take shameless advantage of their erudition, culinary skill, and wanderlust, serving double duty as editors and dear friends. In France, I found warm meals and ready sounding boards from countless friends and family to whom I can never fully express my gratitude: Loïc LeGuerhier and Céline Clavel, Laura de Souza, Olivia and Antoine Chateau, César Sanint and Karine David-Sanint, Sébastian Legon, and Ludovic and Emmanuelle Portois. I especially thank the Nozal, Vedel, Barzani, and Ricard clans for welcoming me into their circle, especially Sarah, Jean-Pierre, and Deborah Ricard—who inexplicably embraced this strange American so enamored with their country. I thank my grandparents, William and Elsie Tilburg, and Jack and Mary Reilly, for the value they placed on education. Will and Karen Tilburg have helped keep my sarcasm well-honed, no matter how far I stray from the family dinner table. My parents, William and Kathleen Tilburg, have been the sustaining force behind the years spent on this project and all the years that came before it. They have spoiled me with their boundless encouragement, generosity, and love. Their irrepressible *joie de vivre* and engaged compassion have shown me the meaning of a life well lived. I dedicate this book to them.

The greatest serendipity of this project was meeting Thomas Ricard as it began. Before he knew that doing so would have him moving across an ocean, he introduced me to the peculiar nuances of contemporary French culture, making France at once more legible and delightfully more strange for me. His humor, curiosity, knowledge, and humanity nourish and inspire me every day. It has been my unfathomable good luck that he has agreed to come along with me down a road which has taken us from Paris to Los Angeles to North Carolina. As tour guide, translator, chef, teammate, and *compagnon de route*, he has made the researching and writing of this book a rare adventure. His partnership and love have ensured that it was never even close to everything.

INTRODUCTION

A line of poetry does not always have to be beautiful to adhere to the
deepest recesses of our memory and slyly occupy the same space that
certain loathsome but indelible melodies have already invaded.

—Colette, *Le Fanal bleu* (1949),
regarding a poem she memorized for school in 1885

Histories of secularization inevitably pale alongside those of religious crusades.
The convert and zealot, with their preternatural faith and drive to pull away
from the worldly, are the visionaries. The secular, by contrast, begins as a nega-
tion, a removal of God from the public square. And so it has been with histories
of the Third French Republic. In the fin de siècle the most entertaining figures,
historically speaking, were those who, while not necessarily religious, embraced
the immaterial. In studying everyone from Baudelaire to Huysmans, historians
have been drawn to those prophets of modernism who mocked and disdained the
grasping commercial interests and aesthetic flatness of the new secular middle-
class man—the bourgeois with his dull black frock coat and sensible devotion to
science. Avant-garde art and culture were those delightfully unreasonable realms
that rebelled against modernization with the primitive, and against democratization with the marginal. And yet the Third Republic, with all of its pragmatic
smoothing over of the supernatural edges of Catholicism, engendered its own
fantastical ways of seeing, its own iterations of the devotee's experience that embraced observation, corporeal dynamism, and imaginative introspection.

This book reassesses the meaning of secularization by way of a cultural history
of French republicanism at the turn of the twentieth century. France in this period was a nation riven by a ferocious culture war. In the course of just ten years,
the Republic born in 1870 conducted an all-out campaign against the forces of reaction and superstition, in an aggressive effort to rid the newly secularized nation
of Catholic influence. Since essentially all education in France had previously
been directed by the Church, the new secular school was at the center of a political battlefield upon which science and reason warred with faith, and materialism

warred with mystical devotion. Secularism in France in the final decades of the nineteenth century was, for its adherents, a new faith, a civic religion founded on a rabid belief in progress and the Enlightenment conviction that man could remake his world. Though such beliefs captivated many Europeans in this period, only in France did a secularized state attempt an uncompromising implementation of a new laic moral system in the course of just one generation. The principal weapon of the Republic's positivist ambitions was a nationwide secular school system, created from scratch in only a decade.

Historians have studied the attempts by republican officials to sacralize the Republic and science, to recreate the quasi-religious fervor of the first French Revolution of 1789 with festivals, monuments, and the *14 juillet*.[1] But the Third Republican program produced reverberations far beyond the political sphere. One of the most intriguing but underanalyzed of these reverberations was the interplay between republican secular morality, or *morale laïque*, and belle époque popular culture. Indeed, the social philosophy of the republican program frequently interacted with and even transformed audience expectations and artistic emphases at the turn of the century. The end result was a culture of popular entertainment that treated the human body in new ways, reimagined respectable femininity, and sought aesthetic and narrative structures that could order all of this troubling innovation. Most important, perhaps, secular reforms helped engender a subversive and yet culturally attractive version of the New Woman, which found spectacular articulation in belle époque popular entertainment. Thus, while republican initiatives placed enormous stock in the power of *morale laïque* to create from whole cloth a unified republic in which each class and gender attended cheerfully to its prescribed social role, this was by no means the sum cultural impact of these efforts.

How can one access such an explosive laic mental framework? This study uses as a point of entry a number of fraught cultural episodes at France's turn of the century: a village's battle to secularize feminine education, a titillating novel that engendered a new type of French girl, a vaudeville smash hit featuring a nude Parisian celebrity, a craze for female boxing, a heated journalistic exchange between two respected mimes. As unlikely as it may seem, these episodes all shared an attachment to the potent moral and aesthetic directives of the Third French Republic and heralded the often unintended cultural effects of democratization and secularization, particularly for women.

Many scholars have catalogued the efforts of the Third Republican hierarchy to institute their renewed social vision, especially through the establishment of a radically secular public school system for French children. Others have turned their attention to the period's Bohemian avant-garde, those artists and writers who sought refuge from the very positivist reason that characterized republican rhetoric. Yet cultural historians have largely ignored the impact of the republican pedagogical revolution on popular culture, rarely linking the frenetic rhythms of the music hall and the lessons of the laic school.[2] Thus, the student of history is left with the impression of a strangely bifurcated France—a country at once plodding through positivist reforms and reveling in avant-garde experimentation and irrationalism. This book, in reevaluating the popular entertainment of the belle époque, probes the startling connections between republican thought and cultural innovation.

My study allies these two seemingly disparate realms of French history by means of a woman who was involved with all of the episodes under scrutiny, and who was also a graduate of the new secular school system: Sidonie-Gabrielle Colette (1873–1954). An author, performer, and cultural icon, Colette most often has been depicted by scholars as a charming eccentric: the vivacious chronicler of delights both rural and urban, the incurable gourmand, the incestuous stepmother, the *grande dame* of French letters. She has been treated as an anomaly: one biographer writes lyrically of Colette as one of those women who is "impervious . . . to History," another as a "freakishly sound" exception to the fin-de-siècle artistic rule of pessimism and excess.[3] Without a doubt, Colette conformed poorly to the model of the decadent fin-de-siècle artist, her literature and life a striking contrast to the world-weary, metaphysically troubled work of the artists and poets of turn-of-the-century Paris's elite cultural circles. In searching out the sources of Colette's eccentricity, I became interested in a striking detail of her life history which has too often served as a picturesque side note to her long career: unlike most of her literary contemporaries in France, educated in private and often Catholic schools, Colette attended a secular public school as part of the first generation of girls formed by the laic instructional revolution of the 1870s.

Gabrielle Colette was born in 1873 in the village of Saint-Sauveur-en-Puisaye (Yonne) in an unremarkable corner of Burgundy. She was the youngest child of Captain Jules Colette, a dashing war veteran and the town's tax collector, and his wife, Sidonie Robineau-Duclos née Landois, a wealthy widow who married the captain just months after the (possibly suspicious) death of her first husband. Thanks to her mother's substantial property, Gabrielle enjoyed an eminently bourgeois childhood as the family's cosseted youngest child. However, while her three older siblings attended private schools, Gabrielle was educated in Saint-Sauveur's public *école laïque*, where she studied alongside girls who hailed from more modest peasant or petty bourgeois families.[4] She found herself in this somewhat unusual position because of a downturn in her family's fortunes, but also, as we shall see, because of her parents' political convictions and a galvanizing moment of innovation in the village's secular schools. Gabrielle began attending the girls' public school in Saint-Sauveur in 1879, at the age of six, and continued there until the end of her schooling at seventeen—her entire education taking place during a decade of sweeping educational reforms that animated political culture in her hometown and across France.

In assaying the republican culture of Colette's childhood, as well as her adult life, literature, and work during the belle époque, I found that the Third

Republic's *morale laïque* could be intellectually problematic, even subversive, for children growing up in this period. Indeed, Colette's tension-ridden treatment of the body, labor, and art in her adult life reflected the values of her republican educational formation in the 1880s. Rather than representing an anomaly in prewar culture, the fin-de-siècle "freak" of Judith Thurman's description, Colette (it turned out) also embodied the intellectual and moral contradictions of a generation of French children raised in a period of revolutionary pedagogical reform. Thus, more than an eccentric, Colette provides an opportunity to unpack the gender and aesthetic implications of the grand if flawed republican project. An author, entertainer, and cultural icon, Colette developed new performative styles and new literary emphases just as French audiences began to require these same novelties from popular entertainment. The professional and artistic tensions that marked her music-hall and literary careers exposed the unpredictable frustration and promise of the republican laic ideal. Though other figures play key roles in this study—vaudeville stars, teachers, art critics, philanthropists, and politicians—Colette's life and celebrity serve as an intimate guide through the various ways in which Third Republicanism may have transformed feminine norms, artistic practices, and even the workings of the imagination.

The Third Republic's secularization initiative, an ambitious political program sometimes dismissed by historians as a rather bland social project, endowed a generation of French men and women with potent aesthetic directives—directives that called for the union of art and craft and for an effacement of class discord. It is the argument of this book that the belle époque saw the rise of forms of modern popular entertainment that were imprinted with these same values—a republican aesthetic forged primarily but not exclusively in the laic schoolhouse. Colette and her experience of the republican school provide a template with which historians can read the cultural effects of secularization and better understand precisely how the cultural resources of her childhood informed her life, literature, and social transgression. Julia Kristeva has recently characterized Colette as having had "no moral sense than that of following her desires . . . an art of living that goes against the teachings of the Church and of its secular successors."[5] One might have said as much about belle époque popular entertainment. But such a statement misses the cultural importance of both Colette and the popular entertainment spaces in which she performed and prospered. I propose that knotted republican values of moral decency, physical health, and the imaginative life played a substantial role in the birth of the New Woman and the modernization of French popular culture at the turn of the twentieth century.

The book is divided into two parts. The first reconsiders the educational culture of the 1870s and 1880s; the second scrutinizes belle époque cultural milieus in which a markedly republican aesthetic took hold. While providing some biographical insight, the chapters that follow are organized according to thematic areas: republican pedagogical culture, the turn-of-the-century music hall, popular representations of workingwomen, the belle époque physical fitness craze, the literary genre of republican school memoirs, working-class arts initiatives, and debates over the modernization of art forms such as pantomime. This study's chronological focus—the early period of Colette's life and career in the decades leading up to World War I—encourages a reappraisal of belle époque France (approximately 1900–14).[6]

Rather than merely a boisterous precursor to the cultural upheaval of the interwar period, the first decade of the twentieth century was a crucial moment in the shaping of modern French popular culture and female identity. It was, as Carrie Tarr and Diana Holmes point out, a historical moment characterized by a "fundamental contradiction" between French society's "extreme gender conservatism" and "the impetus towards women's emancipation provided by both republican principles and socio-economic progress towards modernity."[7] In achieving this vexed transition from domestic angels to *femmes nouvelles*, women such as Colette called upon intellectual resources supplied by the secular primary schools of the new Republic. The republican *morale laïque* not only enforced social discipline and reaffirmed republican values; it also, inadvertently, helped organize and make palatable the social and sexual rebellion of bourgeois women such as Colette. Though her racy novels, nude performances, and scandalous private life seemingly set her far outside the bounds of the Third Republican feminine ideal, Colette embodied the intellectual negotiations that characterized this charged moment of cultural change in France. When the silent film actress Musidora described Colette's appeal for the generation of French girls growing up in the first decade of the twentieth century, saying that her novels were "so like us," she signaled the forceful resonance of Colette's words, subjects, and style with French audiences seeking a popular entertainment that quite literally spoke their language.[8]

* * *

Countless book-length biographies have explored the events of Colette's life, often reproducing the same colorful anecdotes of her provincial childhood, her love affairs, and her carnivalesque sorties into Bohemian Paris.[9] Because of her work's often semi-autobiographical nature, many studies of Colette slip seamlessly between her fiction and her lived experience, despite much critical attention to this issue.[10] As Joan Hinde Stewart affirms, Colette's life was "so rich in anecdotal material that biography threatens to submerge the works."[11] While attentive to her fictional works as invaluable texts, my study offers a multilayered reading that asserts the frequently tense relationship between her life and her often highly autobiographical fiction, and draws upon other crucial sources, such as letters, journalistic accounts, and archival material.

Throughout her career, Colette was encased within a myth of entertaining subversion that began with the defiant eroticism of her first novels, the *Claudines*—a myth that Colette and her first husband gleefully manipulated during her early years in Paris. As she and her reputation aged, Colette was saddled with the slightly sanitized mythic equipage of the fetching, ultrafeminine doyenne of French culture. Succeeding scholarly treatments often replicate this view of the author as an archetypal French Woman—a phenomenon that Claude Pichois and Alain Brunet have referred to as the "cult of 'Saint Colette.'"[12] Mona Ozouf began her 1997 essay on Colette with just such an image of archetypal femininity: "When you walk into Colette's house, the first thing to strike you is the smell, the wonderful smell of chocolate, wax, ripe peaches, toast. The walls echo reassuring domestic sounds. . . . By day or by night, the light is soft. . . . You sense right away that here, someone is absorbed in indispensable and frivolous activities."[13] This insistence on treating Colette as a charming, timeless French figure reduces a complex writer to a "frivolous" hodgepodge of sensual delights and "reassuring" domestic bliss.

During her lifetime and for most of the twentieth century, Colette's work was often devalued by critics due to its perceived stylistic simplicity and lack of concern for contemporary sociopolitical events.[14] Anne Poskin notes that Colette's early literary work was hounded by the label "littérature féminine"— literature written instinctively, without systematic thought.[15] While Poskin suggests that Colette spent the first decade of her literary career trying to shed this label, secondary literature on the author in the decades since her death often reproduces this contemporary assessment. Jennifer Waelti-Walters, for example, writes that in Colette's literature, "whatever is or appears to be happening, the heart of the matter is love" and that Colette "continually created versions of the eternal feminine victim . . . not for her the emancipated . . . 'new' women of her feminist peers."[16]

Indeed, Colette sometimes referred to female political participation and feminist action with amused condescension, and she rarely took sides on political issues.[17] For this reason, historians and biographers understandably have not regarded her as an exemplar of feminist activism. I do not disagree, nor do I offer a triumphal tale of how the Third Republican curriculum unwittingly liberated French women. Rather, I suggest that the measure of the curriculum's influence on women, and on gender roles in general, cannot be only the degree to which republican ideology did or did not support feminist political participation. The école laïque provided students with a novel set of mental resources that, while maintaining gendered notions of citizenship, opened up a conflicted intellectual space in which women such as Colette could forge reasonable identities as public, productive, and creative individuals. As the chapters that follow will demonstrate, this was not, for Colette and her generation, an effortless endeavor.

With the reevaluation of the literary canon beginning in the 1980s, Colette too has undergone a reappraisal. Feminist literary theory in particular has provided new perspectives, examining crucial issues of gender, writing, and identity in Colette's work.[18] Such readings, however, tend to limit their analysis to the "feminine" and/or feminist qualities of Colette's writing while slighting other aspects of her work, at times reducing her significance to well-worn tropes of the Eternal Feminine (i.e., her strong identification with nature and her crucial bond with her mother).[19] While analyses of this sort demonstrate that Colette's experience of sexual difference was not, as some have indicated, unproblematic, such readings often preclude an extensive investigation of Colette's work within a distinct social milieu. Diana Holmes points toward such an investigation by emphasizing the "creative contradictions" of Colette's childhood, and by decrying the "highly selective" scholarly vision of Colette as "an intimately personal writer whose work is apolitical and whose only relevance to social history lies in her quaint evocations of the belle époque."[20] Michèle Hecquet proposes that Colette's writing needs to be taken as part of a *devoir démocratique* in the era's literature, and that historians "have not remarked enough that she was, alone amongst the great writers, formed exclusively by the school of the Third Republic. . . . She whose optic is so resolutely laic, belongs to the generation of the '*école laïque*' that emerges between 1890 and 1914."[21] As an immensely popular and prolific writer, Colette can be used to gain entry to this laic "optic" and to the Third Republic's conflicted handling of gender and class. Thus, my study of Colette and her celebrity, while illuminating from a biographical and literary perspective, is more useful as a means of studying republicanism itself.

* * *

For, if Colette has been somewhat misunderstood by biographers, the Third Republic has suffered a similar and more consequential fate. Bertrand Taithe commends a recent historiographical "coming of age" for the Third Republic, moving from a "simplistic portrayal of a society drifting leaderless towards the abyss" to a "more sophisticated understanding of a complicated society experiencing complicated changes."[22] In joining the scholarly reassessment of the Third Republic, the first half of this book offers a concentrated analysis of the education Colette's generation received in the primary schools created by the republican pedagogical revolution of the 1870s and 1880s. France in that period was experiencing the problematic and incomplete democratization of culture, leisure, and politics. In the face of this tumult, the leaders of the precarious new French Republic, shaken by a humiliating defeat by Prussia in 1870 and the subsequent civil insurrection of the Paris Commune, recognized the urgency of forging a population of engaged, reasoning citizens. To this end, they enacted a series of legislative acts that sought to end Catholic influence in education and in its place establish a nationwide network of free, secular primary schools. While pedagogical reform had been incubating for some time, the birth of the Third Republic provided a state organ for the practical implementation of this reformist spirit.[23] Some four million French children attended the state's public primary schools in the 1880s, nearly two million of them girls.[24]

The early years of the Third Republic were contentious ones, as conservative, moderate, and leftist factions vied for a commanding role in the construction of the new state. In this context, pedagogical ideas took on national political significance, and the content as well as the methods of primary education became the subject of passionate and politicized debates from the corridors of power in Paris to provincial villages. The year 1879, in which Colette started school, marked the end of the Republic's most uncertain period and saw the establishment of a solidly republican administration that made secular education one of its chief goals. Indeed, the school laws, in the words of Gordon Wright, "dwarfed other political issues" in the 1880s.[25] Republicans were convinced that a sound modern state depended on teaching French men and, especially, women to participate in society as rational citizens freed from religious superstition.[26] This zealous republican ideological battle with the Catholic Church resulted in a far-reaching overhaul of the nation's primary-school system. The best known of the republican reforms were the so-called Ferry Laws (1881–82), which declared primary school mandatory for children between the ages of six and thirteen, and also made public school free and secular for children of both sexes.[27] Girls' education was particularly targeted. In 1879 every French department was ordered to construct a secular teacher's training college for women. In 1881 primary-school teachers were required to have a *brevet élémentaire*, and clerical teachers were gradually removed from public posts in many places. In order to fill secular reading lists, publishers produced a flurry of laic textbooks written especially for the new schools by ardently republican pedagogues, teachers, and government officials. By way of this educational program, which, according to Linda Clark, served as "the basic outline" for France's primary education system until after World War II,[28] the liberal factions of the early Third Republic promoted an often underestimated moral and social philosophy: the *morale laïque*.

A number of studies have provided detailed accounts of the Third Republican pedagogical revolution.[29] Several historians have scrutinized the axioms of patriotism, hard work, and clearly defined gender roles contained within the laic curriculum of the 1880s.[30] These superb studies, however, seldom connect the curriculum to broader cultural movements. Likewise, the Third Republican pedagogical revolution has often been overlooked by cultural historians who dismiss the initiative as either an overly optimistic moment of liberal experimentation or a calculated ploy by the bourgeois leadership to better control the laboring classes. While attentive to these facets of the republican curriculum, I reevaluate this educational initiative in order to expose several important if underanalyzed pedagogical and curricular shifts. The first two chapters interrogate the themes and concerns of the national curriculum, using Colette's region of the Yonne as a case study. Republican educational reforms maintained traditional gender and social relations but also embraced a radical new approach to the body and the self. Even the reformulation of traditional messages, such as the benefit of hard work, carried a new intonation within the moral philosophy of the republican school. The architects of the Third Republic also made a central place for the imagination within their renovated vision of French society by fusing labor and creative production in new ways.

Many historians of the Third Republic echo the claim of Robert Gildea that "much of what the republican leadership said about education remained at the level of rhetoric, if not of hypocrisy."[31] Such a contention is complicated by a consideration of the curriculum in the context of republican instructional culture as a whole, including study of new pedagogical methods, how and where classes were taught, and extracurricular activities that linked school and village. Echoing historian James Lehning's appeal for scholars to give as much attention to the "cultural identities" engendered by Third Republican civil society as "the institutions in which they are employed,"[32] I propose that a rich local associative culture turned what might otherwise have remained a sterile imposition of an official political philosophy onto an unreceptive rural community into a powerful social initiative. More than passive auditors of republican oratory, girls such as Colette could be intimately connected to the pedagogical revolution through parents, teachers, and community.

The republican curriculum has been especially underestimated as regards girls' education. While republican pedagogues sought to end the *divorce des esprits* between devout wives and their secular husbands by means of a more reasoned girls' education, they were also concerned about the nation's falling birthrates and the specter of New Womanhood. The republican educational program attempted to resolve this dilemma by establishing a school system that removed women from the clutches of the Church while at the same time reinforcing the traditional ideal of the private, maternal woman. Historians consequently criticize the system for promoting gender roles that differed little from those of Catholic instruction.[33] Françoise Mayeur insists that "all that which had to do with girls' education, in the pedagogy of the 1880s, [was] linked to the principal of educational maternity."[34] More recent scholarly assessments, while agreeing that the republican program was deeply conservative and even misogynist in much of its vision of girls' education, have noted that calls to obedient and fecund motherhood were not the complete experience of the new school system for many French girls.[35] Public schoolgirls did not learn exclusively from those textbook passages that referred to women's social role but rather came to understand such lessons in conjunction with broader coeducational curricular directives that could have as much force as those most intended for young women.

This study thus engages, at its heart, the relationship between French republicanism and the emancipation of French women.[36] Philip Nord has shown that although middle-class republican politics in late nineteenth-century France was founded on the exclusion of groups such as women and labor, these groups were not "enemies" of the regime; in fact, the republican system was fundamentally adaptable and hence "contained within itself an emancipatory moment."[37] Katherine Auspitz agrees that Third Republicanism's contradictions speak to its "larger inclusiveness"; the republican agenda sought the active support of workers and women and thus "depended upon internalization, not upon surveillance."[38] Auspitz attempts to refute Theodore Zeldin's allegation "that only rather odd people took its slogans seriously" by suggesting that the power of republican thought is best understood as a "sensibility" that "could accommodate many dispositions and tendencies."[39] Thus, the republican curriculum needs to be scrutinized at its pedagogical level in order to ascertain both its meaningful contradictions and its radical, if unintended, emancipatory potential.

This study of the Third Republican program owes much to a methodological approach exemplified by scholars such as Michael Baxandall and Carlo Ginzburg , which focuses on the particular conceptual equipment of a historical age and place—a "period eye" or mental "grill" through which individuals selectively digest the ideas to which they are exposed.[40] By fusing intellectual biography and microhistorical practice, Carl Schorske and Debora Silverman have demonstrated the importance of examining the connections between the cultural productions of a particular epoch and contemporary conceptions of the self and society as a whole.[41] Silverman's work on Vincent van Gogh and Paul Gauguin illustrates the crucial relationship between educational formation and the production of modernism.[42] I probe early Third Republican educational culture in order to ascertain connections between this institutional initiative and the prevalence of certain republican themes and intellectual techniques in belle époque popular fiction and entertainment. I am interested in the definition of a particular cognitive style, created by both individual considerations unique to Colette and a more generalized moral structure unique to the Third Republic. This methodological approach is attractive because while it insists on a critical attention to the historical ingredients of cultural production, it also leaves considerable room for, in Ginzburg's words, the "aggressive originality" of an individual interpretation,[43] thus providing historical actors with a degree of agency denied them in many poststructural explanations.

Though the public education system was the chief conduit of the republican *morale* for Colette's generation, the school was embedded in a broader republican culture at the regional and town level, from popular lectures to local meetings of republican associations.[44] As a girl, Colette followed the entire cycle of secular primary education offered by the Third Republic's new system. For eleven years, she attended a gradually secularizing and republicanizing school. She witnessed the replacement of older textbooks with new, laic ones written especially for her school. She saw her old schoolhouse demolished and rebuilt. She watched as her teacher was replaced by an appropriately qualified woman from the newly created republican normal school. She lived through and benefited from her town council's energetic battle to establish superior primary education for girls, a fight in which her father took part. She campaigned with her father as he toured the countryside preaching the enlightened progress of the new laic schooling for girls. She played alongside the children of a national republican education minister, and when he died suddenly, she recited an ode to him at a public memorial. She accepted the fervent public accolades of her village when she passed her departmental exams and played a central part in the communal celebration that inaugurated her new school. The republican pedagogical revolution, then, was more than a backdrop to Colette's childhood; it was a social and intellectual reality that organized her daily life and marked her thought and action in the ensuing decades. Thus, moving back and forth between national ideology, local action, popular culture, and Colette's own biography allows one to plot the paths by which republican ideas were disseminated during this period. The cadre of secularizing elites who constructed the republican schools had their own notions of what pedagogical republicanism should achieve for France. Colette exemplifies the way in which students could and did formulate their own improvisations of this official ideology.

* * *

Such improvisation is the subject of the second half of this book. As the first generation of republican schoolgirls grew to adulthood, the values of *morale laïque* came to play a surprising role in the mass entertainment of the period, from popular fiction to vaudeville to physical culture. In 1893, when Colette married Henry Gauthier-Villars, a music critic and Parisian celebrity some twelve years her senior, and moved with him to the capital, she carried with her the lessons of the laic school. The provincial schoolgirl became a popular writer and vaudeville performer, and she developed a public persona that appealed to French audiences who, like her, had grown up in a culture saturated with republican ideology. As a rather infamous music-hall dancer and writer, Colette was far from the republican ideal envisioned by the pedagogues of the 1880s. Yet, in many respects, she epitomized some of the republican curriculum's fundamental goals.

My analysis of Colette and the popular culture in which she prospered is informed by a historiographical paradigm that asserts a dialogic relationship between turn-of-the-century artistic elites and the French state. Debora Silverman has demonstrated that French institutions evinced an adaptability that allowed a *rapprochement* of artists with the state—a striking contrast to the treatment of modernism in places such as Germany and Austria.[45] More recently, Jane Fulcher examines what she calls the "invasion" of French music by political culture in the fin de siècle.[46] Such studies build upon Jerrold Seigel's seminal argument that Bohemian artists, markedly ambivalent toward the moral structure and material comforts of middle-class life, nonetheless carried aspirations of reconciliation and synthesis with "respectable" French society. Like the artists of Seigel's study, Colette combined a radical celebration of personal freedom with an attraction for middle-class respectability and the values of the republican revolution.[47] Careful scrutiny of Colette's work and life illuminates the role of gender in such negotiations, an aspect that Seigel's study does not adequately problematize.

In her life, performance, and literary production, Colette reformulated the complex figurations of work and moral rectitude she had learned at school. Beginning with the publication of her first novel in 1900 and ending with the close of her music-hall career in 1913, Colette's writing and performance found a model and a foil in the mental and physical gymnastics of the republican school. Her investment in a particularly republican moral structure aligned her with the emphases of modern popular entertainment, and with a generation of Frenchwomen establishing new creditable public identities that diverged sharply from those of the fin de siècle. The feminine ideal of the Angel in the House, a woman detached from the marketplace in her hermetic "walled garden," while never a practicable reality for most Frenchwomen, still held powerful sway at the turn of the century. This feminine model perpetuated a notion of respectable femininity as grounded in moral purity and domesticity.[48] Intersecting and opposing this model was the reality of women's increasing public presence in higher education and commercial life. As Colette struggled to establish a degree of professional and personal autonomy still rare for most middle-class women, the bounds of socially acceptable femininity were being expanded on all sides by a surprising newcomer to the European social scene: the sometimes anxiety-provoking *femme nouvelle*.[49] As the century turned, such women began to seek out higher education, challenge traditional patterns of courtship and marriage, enter professions historically closed to women, and join increasingly vocal movements for women's political emancipation. Though generations of pioneering women and gradual reform stood behind them, the New Women of the fin de siècle witnessed a remarkable acceleration of changes in feminine roles, from fashion to educational opportunities to notions of sexual pleasure.

By the belle époque, the New Woman had become a common type in European popular culture in novels such as George Gissing's *The Odd Women* (1893), Marcelle Tinayre's *La Rebelle* (1905), and H. G. Wells's *Ann Veronica* (1909), and European women were experiencing significant changes in their legal status and educational and professional options. In 1907, the same year that Colette's husband sold all rights to the *Claudine* novels without her consent, a law was passed in France giving married women control of their earnings.[50] The following year, while Colette managed her separation from her husband, another legislative reform facilitated the divorce process for separated couples.[51] While some particularly visible New Women appealed for women's suffrage, political campaigns were not the only means by which women reinvented norms of feminine behavior at the turn of the twentieth century.[52] If some saw a flamboyant writer/actress as incompatible with her bluestocking sisters,[53] Colette's life and work in this period nonetheless made claims for sexual, financial, and social autonomy that harmonized with the demands of the New Woman.

In contextualizing such claims, I find instructive models in scholarly attempts by purveyors of the New Biography to map the geography of French femininity at the fin de siècle through exceptional New Women who helped reveal, in Jo Burr Margadant's words, the "constructed nature" of feminine identity and "fissures" in the dominant gender system.[54] In her study of cultural figures such as Marguerite Durand and Sarah Bernhardt, Mary Louise Roberts uncovers the means by which women began "to imagine themselves as worthy of more than a domestic destiny" in the "new, promising conditions of the Third Republic."[55] Roberts insists that "the subversive nature" of such women's public image derived not from "a new script" of femininity but rather from "the strategic reenactment of a conventional script," which became a "language of resistance."[56] I propose that the Third Republic's *morale laïque* was one important if unintentional source of just such a "language of resistance," and I ground my analysis of Colette in the methodological assumption that, as Roberts puts it, "in any given era, womanhood is learned within a fixed horizon that limits how the female self can be imagined."[57] My study not only distinguishes the possibilities for female identity at the turn of the century but also examines some of the historically specific cultural sources of these possibilities.

One of the most important and most hotly contested sites of "new" womanhood in France at the turn of the century was the girls' public school. Chapter 3 thus interrogates the historically specific cultural appeal of a new literary genre— the fictionalized girls' public school memoir—in the first decade of the twentieth century. Such novels, written by former secular teachers such as Gabrielle Reval and former students such as Colette, commemorated and challenged the Third Republic's Gospel of Work, a social philosophy that presented a deeply problematic definition of respectable femininity. In Colette's first novel, *Claudine à l'école* (Claudine at School; 1900), the wildly popular Claudine was seen by many contemporaries as exemplary of the new young French woman. This serial heroine's ambivalent relationship with the laic school demands a scrutiny that has been neglected by most studies of the *Claudine* novels. In addition, the contrast between Colette's fictional account of the laic school and the lesser-known fictionalized memoir of Lucie Rondeau-Luzeau, a working-class graduate of the same school system, helps expose the significant part played by class in the intellectual legacy of the "egalitarian" republican school.

Though the *Claudine* novels made her famous, much of Colette's belle époque fiction and celebrity developed out of her work as a vaudeville performer. She began performing in plays and pantomimes around 1905, as her first marriage disintegrated. Separated from her husband, living openly with a woman, and having authored several controversial novels, she compounded her growing notoriety by headlining pantomimes in which she often appeared almost nude. Her grueling tour schedule had her publicly disrobing in lowbrow music halls across France for weeks at a time, all the time recording the dim world of the *coulisses* in stories and novels. Historians of turn-of-the-century France have stressed the importance of commercialized pleasure realms such as the music hall as arenas in which bourgeois identity was continually reworked and tested.[58] But such studies have seen the music hall as a space of social liberation in which republican order was challenged and mocked.[59] A closer analysis of the popular fiction, reviews, and performances of Colette's music hall reveal a more complicated engagement with republican values in these mass cultural spaces.

By taking as its subjects figures who straddled artistic worlds of various classes and genders, this study seeks to integrate the history of belle époque French Bohemia with the period's popular theater culture.[60] In a period during which, as Edward Berenson puts it, actresses "were not real women" according to the standard of the *vraie femme*,[61] Colette skillfully fashioned an image of the female performer that merged the values of the working-class artisan, the belle époque artist, and the republican *femme au foyer*. Her version of the music hall countered the middle-class ideal of feminine domestic isolation with a new model of republican virtue: the once ill-reputed vaudeville performer. In Colette's fiction, physically fit performers devoted to a life of artistic expression outside of the bounds of middle-class respectability embodied values of domestic order, thrift, and moral sanctity. Contemporaries (and historians) might identify the music hall as a refuge from the world of regimented modern industrial work and middle-class strictures.[62] But Colette portrayed a realm that, while allowing unparalleled freedom from bourgeois sexual morality, in many ways replicated the order and discipline of the ideal republican home and workplace. Unlike the model bourgeois Frenchwoman, who was judged according to her sexual purity and maternal devotion, a new popular style of female performer emerged in this period who defined honorable conduct around work, artisanal pride, and physical salubrity. Chapter 4 explores this radical reconceptualization of feminine honor in the belle époque music hall and popular fiction.

Chapter 5 traces the music hall's presentation of a new kind of republican body in plays, vaudeville revues, and even female boxing matches—a body whose popularity was at least partially grounded in the republican curriculum's new attention to physical fortification. One of the most influential lessons of the laic school for this generation of French men and women was the union of the body and the soul. While historical studies of French physical culture at the turn of the century are inevitably drawn back to debates about national strength and natalism, an interrogation of popular entertainment reveals that physical culture was also an aesthetic concern.[63] Beyond the gymnasium, belle époque music halls were a crucial cultural site in which a modern aesthetic of the body could be worked through and take root. André Rauch suggests that during the belle époque the music hall "transformed Parisian entertainment" through the presentation of "corps fabuleux [fabulous bodies]" such as contortionists, gymnasts, clowns, and boxers.[64] I contend that the appeal of such "fabulous bodies" in part derived from a secular ethos that welded a certain notion of physical fitness with a certain notion of secular morality. This transformation of popular entertainment had at its base a heightened appreciation for the links between the moral and physical inherited from the republican ideology of the 1870s and 1880s, an appreciation not limited to concerns of national preparedness or pronatalist fervor. What is more, a new kind of female performer participated in and drove forward this aesthetic shift, both onstage and off. Colette was one such performer. While the peculiarly corporeal nature of her writing has been noted by some literary scholars—Jacques Dupont refers to a "Colettian body"[65]—her distinctive attention to the physical in her life and performance has too often been taken as idiosyncratic, rather than embedded within a rich and meaning-laden cultural context.

Belle époque popular culture was marked, then, by a profound valorization of physical fitness and wage-paying craft labor that pushed uncomfortably against cultural dicta encouraging women to find moral contentment within the confines of a respectable marriage and home. An even tenser confrontation between republican rhetoric and norms of gender and class erupted over the Republic's ambivalent treatment of art and the imagination. Chapter 6 explores the republican treatment of the *vie intérieure* (life of the mind) in the context of a spirited public debate about pantomime during the years leading up to World War I. This debate provoked impassioned responses from performers, novelists, art critics, and even politicians, and it exemplified the belle époque's effort to find a just accord between artistic expression, honest labor, and social order. Music-hall pantomime was one surprisingly vital realm in which popular definitions of modern art engaged the reality of mass commercial spectacle and democratized leisure. Indeed, later debates about modern aesthetics and cinema were preceded by a notable shift in the entertainment offered in the music hall from 1900 to 1914.

For Colette and for many proponents of the music hall, the working performer offered both an exemplary critique of the ills of the modernized Republic and, on some level, a cure to those ills.[66] Yet the praise of the working artist and the workingwoman that characterized her oeuvre was grounded in an impracticable (bourgeois) republican vision in which all social inequities could be resolved through a rather romantic cross-class ideology of work and art. Colette's fiction and performance, as well the French public's response to them, exposed the ultimately unsatisfactory nature of the *morale laïque*'s efforts to shepherd women and labor into the republican fold. This study therefore ends with a consideration of a workingwomen's popular conservatory founded in the belle époque, the Oeuvre de Mimi Pinson—an initiative that elicited contradictory responses from many of the same culture makers who had weighed in on the debate about modern pantomime. The manifest discomfort that Colette and many other cultural critics evinced in the face of this social program reveals the circumscribed scope of the *école laïque*'s promise.

* * *

Throughout her copious belle époque fiction, lectures, reportage, and interviews, Colette often slipped between identifying herself as a decent bourgeois, a *bas-bleu,* a manual worker, and a *caf'conc.* I suggest that this fluidity stemmed from the moment of significant cultural transition in which she lived and wrote. The explosion of the mass press, the birth of "democratized" luxury in the consumer sphere, and, most important, the construction of a centralized national primary education system meant that previously "classed" values were transmitted to men and women of all levels of society. There are ways in which the republican ideal of the laic school was indeed "bourgeois." Yet thrift and craft were not exclusively bourgeois values. (Indeed, the bourgeois women and men of Colette's novels are most often lazy, extravagant, and futile.) Miriam Levin has pointed out that the Third Republican hierarchy borrowed liberally from the language of working-class artisanal craft culture in creating their laic social philosophy, as this language was "a logical form for expressing the basic sentiments and social ideals cherished by both groups."[67] At the same time, republican officialdom found it necessary to transform traditional corporate language and values for the needs of laissez-faire capitalism. Nicholas Green contends that republican discourse combined "the stress on discipline, efficiency and corporate identity" with "a repertoire of individualisms, which both dove-tailed and, at times, cut against, the collective nationalism."[68] The curious educational brew that resulted had a significant impact on the popular culture of the belle époque—on the aesthetic demands of a generation of men and women who, while perhaps not devoted republicans, nonetheless produced and purchased art that had the paradoxical republican value system at its foundation.

The slippery employment of class in Colette's work and in the milieus in which she prospered also sheds light on the dark side of the republican ideal. The *solidaristes* of the late nineteenth century hoped above all to bridge the gap between labor and capital in France. Often, however, the practical effect of such efforts was less a bridge between classes than a rhetorical effacement of class inequity. Colette was sincere in her articulation of the honor of her craft, yet such an articulation covered over the very real differences between her life of celebrity performance and the crushing labor of the Parisian workingwoman to whom she compared herself. This covering over was a sign not simply of Colette's internalization of republican values but also of the unsatisfactory solution to class division and poverty offered by those very values. The complexity of class identities in belle époque France is threaded throughout the chapters that follow—from the way in which class informed the school memoirs of a working-class author such as Rondeau-Luzeau to Colette and her contemporaries' ambivalence about programs to bring art to the working classes.

To embed Colette in her social context as this study does is not merely to understand Colette better (though the details of her life are captivating), but to better understand the French at the dawn of the twentieth century. When Colette published a novel describing her childhood in the village public school, her readers understood that she was not merely recounting a rural idyll but commemorating and critiquing a sea change in French society. Critics who praised Colette's lucrative nude pantomimes as moral and healthful were articulating new aesthetic emphases deemed crucial to modern art and popular entertainment. Colette's readers intuitively agreed with her fictional celebrations of exhausted music-hall showgirls as the moral superiors of bourgeois housewives because they too were immersed in a moral structure that associated honor with manual labor. Colette's efforts at professional respectability and her reception by audiences had in common a moral and intellectual structure particular to this period in French history, a structure that helped the first generation of twentieth-century French men and women define concepts such as moral decency, physical health, honor, and art. This, then, is a study of how and with what cultural ingredients modern French values were formed, disseminated, and, in many cases, transformed in ways not envisioned by the architects of the Third Republic.

Notes

1. See Maurice Agulhon, *Marianne into Battle: Republican Imagery and Symbolism in France, 1789–1880*, trans. Janet Lloyd (London, 1981).

2. Two important studies that are attentive to the cultural impact of republican ideology and politics are Philip Nord's *The Republican Moment: Struggles for Democracy in 19th-century France* (Cambridge, MA, 1995) and Miriam Levin's *Republican Art and Ideology in Late Nineteenth-Century France* (Ann Arbor, MI, 1986). Nord examines the republicanism of the painters of the 1870s, while Levin studies the links between art and politics in the work of prominent men such as Victor Hugo and Jules Ferry.

3. Michèle Sarde, *Colette: Free and Fettered*, trans. Richard Miller (New York, 1980), 34; Judith Thurman, *Secrets of the Flesh: A Life of Colette* (New York, 1999), 83–84.

4. Elisabeth Charleux-Leroux and Marguerite Boivin, *Avec Colette, de Saint-Sauveur à Montigny* (Saint-Sauveur-en-Puisaye, 1995).

5. Julia Kristeva, *Colette*, trans. Jane Marie Todd (New York, 2004), 21.

6. On the periodization of the belle époque, see Diana Holmes and Carrie Tarr, eds., *A 'Belle Epoque'? Women in French Society and Culture, 1890–1914* (Oxford, 2007), 1–2. Michel Winock chastises previous studies for oversimplifying this complex period in *La Belle Époque: La France de 1900 à 1914* (Paris, 2002).

7. Holmes and Tarr, *A 'Belle Epoque'?* 3.

8. Musidora, "Conférence de Musidora," in *Cahiers Colette* 14 (1992): 33–34.

9. Jean Larnac published one of the first full-length biographies of Colette: *Colette, sa vie, son oeuvre* (Paris, 1927). See also Michèle Sarde, *Colette: libre et entravée* (Paris, 1978); Jean-Claude Charlet, *Colette, La Vagabonde* (Précy-sous-Thil, 1994); Jean Chalon, *Colette, l'éternelle apprentie* (Paris, 1998); and especially, Claude Pichois and Alain Brunet, *Colette* (Paris, 1999). Some of the many English biographies are Margaret Crosland's *Madame Colette* (London, 1953); Yvonne Mitchell's *Colette: A Taste for Life* (New York, 1975); and Joanna Richardson's *Colette* (London, 1983). Two nuanced biographies that treat political and social context are Claude Francis and Fernande

Gontier's *Creating Colette: From Ingenue to Libertine, 1873–1913* (South Royalton, VT, 1998), originally published in French as *Colette* in 1997; and Judith Thurman's *Secrets of the Flesh*.

10. Elaine Marks indicated this difficulty for studies of the author as early as 1960 in *Colette* (New Brunswick, NJ, 1960). For critical work on the subject of autobiographical novels, see Sidonie Smith, *The Poetics of Women's Autobiography: Marginality and the Fictions of Self-Representation* (Bloomington, IN, 1987); Jerry Aline Flieger, *Colette and the Fantom Subject of Autobiography* (Ithaca, NY, 1992); and Cheryl Walker, "Persona Criticism and the Death of the Author," in *Contesting the Subject: Essays in Postmodern Theory and Practice of Biography and Biographical Criticism* (West Lafayette, IN, 1991), 109–21.

11. Joan Hinde Stewart, *Colette* (New York, 1996), ix.

12. Pichois and Brunet, *Colette*, 10. For a detailed study of the development of Colette's literary reputation, see Marine Rambach, *Colette, pure et impure: Bataille pour la postérité d'un écrivain* (Paris, 2004).

13. Mona Ozouf, *Women's Words: Essays on French Singularity*, trans. Jane Marie Todd (Chicago, 1997), 159.

14. For the critical history of Colette, see Dana Strand, *Colette: A Study of the Short Fiction* (New York, 1995), and Lynne Huffer, *Another Colette: The Question of Gendered Writing* (Ann Arbor, MI, 1992).

15. Anne Poskin, "'Colette et 'l'Argus de la presse,'" *Études Françaises* 36, no. 3 (2000): 121.

16. Jennifer Waelti-Walters, *Feminist Novelists of the Belle Époque: Love as Lifestyle* (Bloomington, IN, 1990), 13, 18.

17. For a discussion of Colette's ambivalence toward militant feminism, see Mélanie E. Collado, *Colette, Lucie Delarue-Mardrus, Marcelle Tinayre: Émancipation et résignation* (Paris, 2003).

18. See, for example, Yannick Resch, *Corps féminin, corps textuel: Essai sur le personnage féminin dans l'oeuvre de Colette* (Paris, 1973); Huffer, *Another Colette*; Nancy K. Miller, *Subject to Change: Reading Feminist Writing* (New York, 1988), 205–29; R. S. E. Pickering's "Colette's Two Claudines: Problems in Writing the Divided Self," *Romance Quarterly* (1995); Carmen Boustani, *L'Écriture-corps chez Colette* (Bordeaux, 1993). Also see the *Women's Studies* special forum on Colette, vol. 8 (1981). For studies of Colette alongside other canonical French women writers, see Martha Noel Evans, *Masks of Tradition: Women and the Politics of Writing in Twentieth-Century France* (Ithaca, NY, 1987); Bethany Ladimer, *Colette, Beauvoir, Duras: Age and Women Writers* (Gainesville, FL, 1999); Catherine M. Peebles, *The Psyche of Feminism: Sand, Colette, Sarraute* (West Lafayette, IN, 2004); and Rachel Mesch, *The Hysteric's Revenge: French Women Writers at the Fin de Siècle* (Nashville, TN, 2006).

19. *Colette: The Woman, the Writer*, edited by Erica Mendelson Eisinger and Mari Ward McCarty (University Park, PA, 1981), is exemplary of this kind of analysis, with many keen studies of Colette's work, but limited to issues of gender and literature.

20. Diana Holmes, *Colette* (New York, 1991).

21. Michèle Hecquet, "Colette: Femmes au Travail," *Cahiers Colette* (1993): 40–41.

22. Bertrand Taithe, "Should the Third Republic Divide Us Least?" *French History* 18, no. 2 (2004): 223.

23. See Nord, *Republican Moment*.

24. See Raymond Grew and Patrick J. Harrigan, *School, State, and Society: The Growth of Elementary Schooling in Nineteenth-Century France—A Quantitative Analysis* (Ann Arbor, MI, 1991), 263. They list the number of boys enrolled in public primary schools in 1881–82 as 2,442,581; in 1886, 2,462,422. In 1881–82 there were 1,916,675 girls enrolled in public primary schools; in 1886, 1,982,146. They indicate that a significant percentage of these "public" schools could be considered Catholic schools, muddying the calculation of how many boys and girls received a laic public education. Table C.1 suggests that in 1886, some 3,819,109 students were enrolled in lay primary schools, although this number could include private lay schools (279).

25. Gordon Wright, *France in Modern Times* (New York, 1995), 230.

26. Ibid., 229.

27. On the construction of the secular school system, see Jean Cornec and Michel Bouchareissas, *L'heure laïque* (Paris, 1982).

28. Linda Clark, *Schooling the Daughters of Marianne: Textbooks and the Socialization of Girls in Modern French Primary Schools* (Albany, NY, 1984), 81.

29. Important works on the subject include Antoine Prost, *Histoire de l'enseignement en France, 1800–1967* (Paris, 1968); François Furet and Jacques Ozouf, *Lire et écrire* (Paris, 1977); Pierre Giolitto, *Histoire de l'enseignement primaire au XIXe siècle* (Paris, 1983); Robert Gildea, *Education in Provincial France, 1800–1914: A Study of Three Departments* (Oxford, 1983); Pierre Ognier, *L'École républicaine française et ses miroirs: L'idéologie scolaire française et sa vision de l'école en Suisse et en Belgique à travers la Revue Pédagogique, 1878–1900* (New York, 1988). For a comparative perspective, see Andy Green, *Education and State Formation: The Rise of Education Systems in England, France and the USA* (London, 1990), and Mary Jo Maynes, *Schooling in Western Europe* (Albany, NY, 1985).

30. Laura Strumingher's *What Were Little Boys and Girls Made Of? Primary Education in Rural France, 1830–1880* (Albany, NY, 1983) and Linda Clark's *Schooling the Daughters of Marianne* examine the gendered nature of the republican curriculum. See also Rebecca Rogers's study of girls' secondary education, *From the Salon to the Schoolroom: Educating Bourgeois Girls in Nineteenth-Century France* (University Park, PA, 2005).

31. Gildea, *Education in Provincial France*, 264. See also Christian Nique and Claude Lelièvre, *La République n'éduquera plus: La fin du mythe Ferry* (Paris, 1993).

32. James Lehning, *To Be a Citizen: The Political Culture of the Early French Republic* (Ithaca, NY, 2001), 5.

33. See, for example, Clark, *Schooling the Daughters of Marianne*.

34. Françoise Mayeur, "La femme dans la société selon Jules Ferry," in *Jules Ferry, fondateur de la République*, colloquium organized by l'École des Hautes Études en Sciences Sociales (Paris, 1985), 79–87.

35. Phyllis Stock-Morton cautions that even if the "moral" ends of the republican reforms were similar to the Church, there were important "differences in philosophical means employed by the two sides" (*Moral Education for a Secular Society: The Development of Morale Laïque in Nineteenth-Century France* [Albany, NY, 1988], 4–5). Rebecca Rogers states that the "conflicting messages of French schoolgirl culture did not produce rebels," though girls' schooling "generated . . . ways of thinking that did not directly conform to the dictates of domestic ideology" (*From the Salon to the Schoolroom*, 185, 195).

36. Joan Wallach Scott argues that French liberalism was constructed in opposition to women, and hence feminist action was, in essence, trapped by a liberal discourse which designated Woman as Other. See *Only Paradoxes to Offer: French Feminists and the Rights of Man* (Cambridge, MA, 1996). Joan Landes and Lynn Hunt hold that this exclusion carried within it the potential of feminist revolt. See Lynn Hunt, *The Family Romance of the French Revolution* (Berkeley, CA, 1993); Joan Landes, *Women and the Public Sphere in the Age of the French Revolution* (Ithaca, NY, 1988).

37. Nord, *Republican Moment*, 243.

38. Katherine Auspitz, *The Radical Bourgeoisie: The Ligue de l'Enseignement and the Origins of the Third Republic, 1866–1885* (Cambridge, 1982), 44–45.

39. Ibid., 10.

40. Michael Baxandall, *Painting and Experience in Fifteenth-Century Italy* (London, 1972); Carlo Ginzburg, *The Cheese and the Worms: The Cosmos of a Sixteenth-Century Miller*, trans. John and Anne Tedeschi (Baltimore, 1980). This is a tradition in cultural history that goes back to Lucien Febvre, *Le Problème de l'incroyance au XVIe siècle: La religion de Rabelais* (Paris, 1947).

41. Carl Schorske, *Fin-de-Siècle Vienna: Politics and Culture* (New York, 1981); Debora Silverman, *Art Nouveau in Fin-de-Siècle France: Politics, Psychology and Style* (Los Angeles, 1989).

42. Debora Silverman, *Van Gogh and Gauguin: The Search for Sacred Art* (New York, 2000).

43. Ginzburg, *The Cheese and the Worms*, 33.

44. Stock-Morton studies the evolution of *morale laïque* in the work of university theorists, politicians, and educators. See *Moral Education*.

45. Silverman, *Art Nouveau*; Schorske, *Fin-de-Siècle Vienna*; Peter Paret, *The Berlin Secession: Modernism and Its Enemies in Imperial Germany* (Cambridge, MA, 1980).

46. Jane Fulcher, *French Cultural Politics and Music: From the Dreyfus Affair to the First World War* (New York, 1999).

47. Jerrold Seigel, *Bohemian Paris: Culture, Politics, and the Boundaries of Bourgeois Life, 1830–1930* (New York, 1985). Colette also moved in a powerfully gynocentric bohemian circle of women writers and artists such as Natalie Barney. See Shari Benstock's comprehensive *Women of the Left Bank: Paris, 1900–1940* (Austin, 1986).

48. See Bonnie Smith, *Ladies of the Leisure Class: The Bourgeoises of Northern France in the Nineteenth Century* (Princeton, NJ, 1981), and Anne Martin-Fugier, *La Bourgeoise: Femme au temps de Paul Bourget* (Paris, 1983).

49. See Debora Silverman, "The 'New Woman,' Feminism, and the Decorative Arts in Fin-de-Siècle France," in *Eroticism and the Body Politic*, ed. Lynn Hunt (Baltimore, 1991), 144–63; Holmes and Tarr, *A 'Belle Epoque'?* especially the editors' chapter, "New Republic, New Women? Feminism and Modernity at the Belle Epoque."

50. James F. McMillan, *France and Women, 1789–1914* (New York, 2000), 152.

51. See Jean Pedersen, *Legislating the French Family: Feminism, Theater, and Republican Politics, 1870–1920* (New Brunswick, NJ, 2003), 7. Divorce had only been legal since 1884.

52. On the varieties of French feminism in the belle époque, see Jennifer Waelti-Walters and Steven C. Hause, *Feminisms of the Belle Époque: A Historical and Literary Anthology* (Lincoln, NE, 1994); Máire Cross, "1890–1914: A 'Belle Epoque' for Feminism?" in Carr and Holmes, *A 'Belle Epoque'?*

53. Patricia O'Hara points out the lack of affinity between female music-hall performers and "New Women" in Victorian England. "'The Woman of To-Day': The *Fin de Siècle* Women of *The Music Hall and Theatre Review*," *Victorian Periodicals Review* 30, no. 2 (1997): 141–56.

54. Jo Burr Margadant, *The New Biography: Performing Femininity in Nineteenth-Century France* (Berkeley, 2000), 9, 3.

55. Mary Louise Roberts, *Disruptive Acts: The New Woman in Fin-de-Siècle France* (Chicago, 2002), 8.

56. Mary Louise Roberts, "Acting Up: The Feminist Theatrics of Marguerite Durand," *French Historical Studies* (Fall 1996): 1103–38. See also *Disruptive Acts*.

57. Roberts, *Disruptive Acts*, 8.

58. T. J. Clark, *The Painting of Modern Life: Paris in the Art of Manet and His Followers* (Princeton, NJ, 1984).

59. John Kim Munholland, "Republican Order and Republican Tolerance in Fin-de-Siècle France: Montmartre as a Delinquent Community," in *Montmartre and the Making of Mass Culture*, ed. Gabriel P. Weisberg (New Brunswick, NJ, 2001), 15–36.

60. For studies of French society and theater in this period, see Pedersen, *Legislating the French Family*; Cecilia Beach, *Staging Politics and Gender: French Women's Drama, 1880–1923* (New York, 2005); and Sally Debra Charnow, *Theatre, Politics, and Markets in Fin-de-Siècle Paris* (New York, 2005).

61. Edward Berenson, *The Trial of Madame Caillaux* (Los Angeles, 1992), 92.

62. See Charles Rearick, *Pleasures of the Belle Epoque: Entertainment and Festivity in Turn-of-the-Century France* (New Haven, CT, 1985), 149–54; Munholland, "Republican Order."

63. See Marie-Christine Périllon, *Vies de femmes: Les travaux et les jours de la femme à la Belle Époque* (Roanne, 1981), 83; Mary Lynn Stewart, *For Health and Beauty: Physical Culture for French-women, 1880s–1930s* (Baltimore, 2001).

64. André Rauch, "Mises en scène du corps à la belle époque," *Vingtième siècle* 40 (1993): 33–44.

65. Jacques Dupont, *Physique de Colette* (Toulouse, 2003), 25.

66. Charles Rearick makes a similar argument, but for him, the music hall offered an escape for bourgeois bohemians from the Gospel of Work. See *Pleasures of the Belle Époque*.

67. Levin, *Republican Art and Ideology*, 73.

68. Nicholas Green, "'All the Flowers of the Field': The State, Liberalism, and Art in France under the Early Third Republic," *Oxford Art Journal* 10, no. 1 (1987): 79. Green dismisses the possibility that this "repertoire of individualisms" held much promise for women and workers.

I

"THERE ARE NO FOOLISH MÉTIERS"
Work, Class, and Secular Girls' Education

On September 28, 1890, capping more than a decade of renovations, the citizens of the quiet Burgundian village of Saint-Sauveur-en-Puisaye inaugurated their primary schools in an elaborate day-long fête. Local papers had trumpeted the upcoming celebration for weeks, particularly as the festival was to involve the visit of the French minister of agriculture and some two hundred other distinguished guests. In preparation for the occasion, the town's medieval streets had been transfigured by paper roses, wreaths, and tricolored banners acclaiming the Republic. Several of the public school's female students were chosen to represent their classmates in the ceremony, and among this privileged delegation was seventeen-year-old Gabrielle Colette. That morning, she joined the jubilant crowd that welcomed the minister at the train station and marched with him to the center of town to the sound of rifle shots. Gabrielle wore a fine dress, and her unusually long blond hair was freed from its typical plaits and hung loose, reaching almost to her heels. As the crowd cheered, she mounted the platform where the dignitaries stood, presented the minister with a bouquet of flowers, and recited ceremonial words of welcome. The festivities continued with a tour of the schools and a lengthy banquet at which Gabrielle's father, a municipal councilman, made a toast. A rowdy celebration followed, including a dance, a carnival, and a fantastic light display that transfigured the village streets throughout the night.[1] This choreographed festival, like many of its kind that took place around France in the later decades of the nineteenth century, performed a particular version of the Third Republic—a unified community devoted to secular progress and modernization. This performance publicized the ideals of laic education while simultaneously muting the fierce political opposition such ideals provoked. What is more, it provided young women with a visible role, both practical and symbolic, within the complex of republican cultural and political activities.

As the festival in Saint-Sauveur makes evident, the architects of the Third Republic venerated the cross-class public school and staked much of their political capital on its ability to reshape French society. Their optimistic notion of education as a social panacea sought to resolve the delicate problem of class difference by promoting a fictive "Gospel of Work" that praised professional craft. But they overlooked the gender implications of such praise. Republican ideology, with the laic school as its most visible avatar, proclaimed a unified *Patrie* in which worker and bourgeois, man and woman, were *concitoyens*, at once brave partners in the future of the French nation and yet still cozily nestled within traditional hierarchies of class and gender. Borrowing liberally from the language of the French artisan to articulate middle-class values,[2] republican pedagogues spoke in glowing terms of Woman as beatific laic mother and, at the same time, taught little girls the importance of wage-earning labor. Villages across France built secular public schools for their daughters as a means of forming sensible and obedient helpmeets, but officials also insisted that such schools provide girls with a practical professional training that threatened to upset traditional notions of women's social role.

Such a paradox, threaded throughout the republican curriculum of the 1870s and 1880s, offered children raised under its auspices an uncommon intellectual formation. The secular educational initiative reflected the Third Republic's internal contradictions and provided a generation of students, particularly girls, with a set of mental tools that bore the imprint and possibility of these contradictions. Although lessons about the honor of manual labor and the importance of *métier* (professional craft) were by no means new in the 1870s, the peculiar chemistry of the republican moment brought novelty and tension to social values that now dominated a nationwide secular school system. It is the contention of this study that the particular definition of work promoted by the instructional culture of the 1870s and 1880s had significant aesthetic and cultural consequences. This definition, which could be found throughout girls' and boys' textbooks, official directives, and cultural expressions, insisted upon the importance of wage-earning, manual labor, particularly that conducted as a métier. When applied to a mass population of schoolchildren of both sexes and across the social spectrum, this call to honorable, manual craft would be extremely influential and, in some cases, subvert the very social order it sought to bolster.

With the construction of a nationwide network of secular schoolhouses and teachers in the 1870s, many French girls were exposed for the first time to an education without explicit religious doctrine. And yet many of the historians who have analyzed the Third Republican school from the perspective of gender often gloomily conclude that little changed for girls in this transition from clerical to laic education, especially as Catholic instruction continued to dominate even some secular schools in these early years. Scholars contend that the new republican curriculum was deeply conservative in its treatment of women and thus differed little in the essentials from Catholic girls' education.[3] Though some historians concede that girls, particularly in rural areas, were provided a degree of ambiguity in their educational experience through exposure to both the ideal of the domestic *femme au foyer* and the call to commercially profitable labor, this ambiguity has been credited with little long-term effect on gender roles. Linda Clark has emphasized that both republican and Catholic authors enlisted women's domestic talents to help preserve political and social stability. Clark admits that a curriculum that emphasized the importance of work, wage-earning, and financial solvency, as well as intellectual achievement, "did carry the potential for diverting some women from the foyer," but that it was "unlikely that many would doubt that familial obligations ranked first among women's priorities, for the school, like other major institutions, did not endow alternatives with comparable value."[4]

The analysis of Third Republican educational culture that follows challenges this historiographical conclusion. Unlike comparable national educational reforms for girls in Western Europe in the late nineteenth century, the French *école laïque* was the result of an unusually politicized, highly centralized, and widespread pedagogical revolution.[5] While many of the laic curriculum's feminine images indeed differed little from those in Catholic textbooks, traditional feminine ideals of domestic virtue and maternal care were now accompanied by a host of images that elevated the importance of financial solvency, achievement, and work for girls and boys. In addition, the middle-class ideology perpetuated by the republican curriculum was not necessarily accepted passively by boys and girls. Rather, as historian Laura Strumingher notes, some children "worked out their own compromises, evasions, and selections from the portrait of the good life presented to them by middle-class representations."[6] Rebecca Rogers similarly argues that girls' educational practices in the nineteenth century, both lay and Catholic, "forged ways of thinking and behaving with wide-ranging consequences for the gendered organization of middle-class society" and "produced not one, but a variety of models of womanhood."[7] Thus, when evaluating the impact of the Third Republic's laic curriculum on girls, it is important to analyze overt references to women's social role alongside other prominent curricular and pedagogical maxims.

Curricular directives were executed (or not) within distinct local and regional contexts. To this end, this chapter not only reappraises the Third Republic's primary school system in the 1870s and 1880s but also scrutinizes one particular educational experience—that of young Gabrielle Colette. Born in 1873 to a proud bourgeois family, it was not a foregone conclusion that Colette would spend her formative years as a poster child for the secular pedagogical revolution. Her mother Sido had had two children—Achille and Juliette—by her first husband, Jules Robineau-Duclos, a wealthy and, by some accounts, mentally unstable landowner. After his death in 1865, Sido, now a well-heeled widow, promptly married the debonair local tax collector, Captain Colette. Sido and the captain had a son, Léo, in 1868 and a daughter, Gabrielle, in 1873. From Gabrielle's birth to approximately 1880, the Colettes lived the life of the provincial upper middle class, enjoying luxuries such as a private carriage, a piano, and several full-time servants. Both sons, Léo and Achille, were sent to boarding school, and Juliette to an expensive girls' *pension*. In 1879, however, for reasons not entirely transparent in the historical record, Gabrielle began her education at Saint-Sauveur's public girls' school—sharing her classroom bench with, among others, the daughters of a gendarme, a spice merchant, an innkeeper, a shoemaker, a councilman, and several farmers.[8] Around this time, Jules Colette's poor management of his wife's fortune began to compromise the family's economic position, though they continued to live in fine style in a spacious townhouse in the village center for the decade that followed. By 1890, however, matters had worsened, and the contents of the Colette home were sold at public auction. The family was obliged to move in with Achille, now a doctor in the nearby village of Châtillon-Coligny.

Gabrielle Colette attended Saint-Sauveur's girls' public school for eleven years, passing the required oral and written exams for both the *certificat d'études primaires* and the *brevet élémentaire*. After earning these diplomas, notable scholastic accomplishments for girls in this period, she remained informally in the *cours supérieur* (higher primary education) until her family moved from Saint-Sauveur in 1890. While Colette's childhood is not the principal subject of the curricular analysis that follows, the accents and emphases of her primary education are described herein, as I rely almost exclusively on pedagogical materials used in the department of the Yonne during the years of her schooling (1879–91). These instructional manuals and pedagogical works were used in primary schools throughout France, and their authors played key roles in the centralized national pedagogical push of the 1880s. The same themes and tensions present in these books can be found in any number of instructional works employed across the Republic. Focusing on those texts used in Yonne, however, strengthens the links between this republican *mentalité* and Colette, and demonstrates the important local component of the republican revolution. Not all departments took to the republican program as eagerly as the Yonne—indeed, Raymond Grew and Patrick Harrigan rank the Yonne as one of the most "anticlerical" and "de-Christianized" departments in France in 1886 and place it among the top ten departments with the lowest Catholic school enrollments in this same period.[9] Likewise, not all villages pursued girls' secular education as zealously as Saint-Sauveur-en-Puisaye. Thus, this study fuses a discursive analysis of a national instructional initiative with a microhistorical study of one village's active engagement with that initiative.

The standardization of republican education meant that often in the 1870s and 1880s, girls and boys learned from the same textbooks. Even textbooks written expressly for female students sometimes used primarily male examples, such as Madame Gréville's *Instruction morale et civique des jeunes filles* (1882).[10] A re-view of the *Listes des ouvrages scolaires* for Colette's department of the Yonne re-veals the dominating presence of coeducational or male-specific textbooks during the early 1880s. Such lists were drawn up during cantonal conferences of public school teachers, at which instructors chose books for their schools from the national curriculum. These cantonal conferences, though all working from the national list, could reject or add some books at their discretion (though rejections seem to have been infrequent in the Yonne). The Yonne list for the school year 1880–81, which included more than eighty books in civics and literature alone, contained only five books written specifically for girls or dealing with feminine topics such as domestic economy.[11] In these early years of the republican school, pedagogues raced to fill the instruction lists for civics and *morale laïque*, subjects that replaced religious moral instruction and in many cases needed to be written from scratch for the new political order. This meant that, especially in the field of moral and civic instruction, teachers in girls' schools had little option but to employ coeducational texts at times. Out of the Yonne list from 1880–81, not one of the chosen fourteen civic and moral instruction books was written specifically for girls.[12] Instead, the *morale* curriculum in the Yonne favored textbooks written by ardent local republicans such as Paul Bert.

Instead of learning from girls' textbooks, then, most female students in this first period of republican educational reform were exposed to books that combined some mention of men's and women's respective moral duties with more gender-neutral dicta. In her study of Third Republican *colonie des vacances*, Laura Lee Downs has hinted at the analytical complexity inherent in such a combination of gender-neutral discourse and heavily "gendered social practice."[13] I propose that in the realm of secular primary education, this uneasy mixture resulted in a language of republican labor that would leave its mark on belle époque popular culture in the generation that followed and permit some to redraw the lines of French femininity from within the republican ideal.

* * *

Work was omnipresent in the textbooks of the Third Republic, and children were taught to view hard work as an endeavor infused with duty, joy, and love. Charles Delon's *Lectures expliquées* (1875) cautioned students: "if each one only worked for himself, we would work much less and with much less courage. We would not have the heart for the task. When we had finished all that which was necessary to meet the needs of the day, we would throw down our tool, and we would say, 'That's enough.' But we work for that which we love. We work by *love*. . . . And so with ardor, with courage."[14] The young protagonists of Zulma Carraud's widely used textbooks, Jeanne and Maurice, were deemed exemplary by the author because of the enjoyment they found in honest labor. Carraud's books also featured misguided counterparts to Jeanne and Maurice, Marguerite and Frisé, who were decried for their laziness and their discontent with their rural work.[15] Clarisse Juranville's 1880 primary textbook for girls insisted that "man was born to work like the bird was born to fly. . . . The lazy child is a burden to others and to himself; he does nothing from morning to night: he kills time, watches flies, yawns, and is bored."[16] Gabriel Compayré's *Éléments d'instruction morale et civique* (1882) asked students to imagine the horrors of a world in which each person refused to do his chosen job, whether baker, merchant, or farm laborer. Compayré, who helped found the first national women's normal school in Fontenay-aux-Roses, warned his young readers of both sexes that in such a world it "would no longer be possible for you even to live."[17]

Auguste Burdeau, author of a moral instruction textbook used in Saint-Sauveur-en-Puisaye, linked work to the evolution of man from savagery to enlightened progress, telling his students: "Work is a necessity. If no one worked, no one could live. . . . Houses were not placed completed on earth; masons and carpenters were necessary. . . . *All useful things in life are the product of work*."[18] To underscore his point, Burdeau described an Oceanic tribe on the isle of Céram whose inhabitants seldom worked due to the benefits of a certain tree that filled all of their needs with minimal labor. Rather than ensuring happiness, however, this lack of work kept the inhabitants of Céram in a perpetual state of savagery:

> As they have never dreamed of having more to do than knock down a tree from time to time, *they have remained brutes*; they have neither clothes, nor dinghies, nor weapons. . . . In short, of all the savages in these waters, they are the most foolish and the most miserable. . . . *Without work, there would never have been progress*; the earth would only be peopled with savages, and we would know neither well-being, nor civilization.[19] (emphasis in original)

Like many Third Republic pedagogues, Burdeau considered hard work a fundamental ingredient of civilization. An existence of ease and inactivity at best resulted in misery; at worst, civilization was destroyed. These themes surrounding work were encapsulated in a poem by Victor de Laprade called "Let's work" ("Travaillons"), which appeared often in Third Republican textbooks.[20] De Laprade began by exhorting his readers, "My children, it is necessary to work; / It is necessary that all of us . . . have a trade [*métier*]" De Laprade underscored the reward that came through hard work and concluded, like Compayré, by equating lack of employment and death: "So, work, and without weakness: / To no longer work, that is to die."[21]

As De Laprade's poem illustrates, the republican ideal of work most specifically involved engaging in a métier, a trade or profession normally requiring some training and skill.[22] In her study of Third Republican ideology, Miriam Levin suggests that, in addition to serving bourgeois economic interest, a republican rhetoric of work was "a way of thinking which was natural to [Republicans]," as a result of social, family, and cultural roots that tied them to a language "traditionally used by the artisans and tradesmen working in the commercial world."[23] Bourgeois republicans did modify this language in one significant way; they expanded the definition of craft so that one's profession became part of "a larger system composed of many groups," which helped members "contribute to the welfare of society through their labor."[24] Thus, the values of craft *compagnonnage* were adapted to support a liberal democratic economy and political system. In addition, the decline in French craft exports after 1873 led, in the 1880s, to heightened anxieties about the nation's once undisputed craft supremacy in Europe[25]—anxieties that bled over into the republican curriculum's insistence upon the benefits of craft labor.

It is with this rhetorical and class complexity in mind that one must apprehend the insistent refrains about craft labor in the Third Republic curriculum. Most textbooks, in all subject areas, dedicated some space to describing children's possible future professions. Charles Defodon's 1880 book of *dictées* for primary schools told students:

> A person's profession is nothing other than the work to which one dedicates oneself in order to earn one's living. . . . We call this a métier. There are no foolish métiers, there are only foolish people. All honest professions are honorable. Laziness alone merits contempt. The bread that one eats by the sweat of his brow is worth a hundred times that which comes from alms. When one has two robust arms and good health, it is shameful to give oneself up to lazing about. . . . [Idleness] leads sometimes to prison, and surely to the hospital.[26]

This reading urged more than merely struggling against idleness; it defined work as a profession that enabled one to "earn one's living" and safeguarded one from all sorts of ills. The reference to robust arms and good health reinforced that, though all "honest" métiers were honorable, those that required physical fortitude were more so. Another textbook, designed explicitly for coeducational teaching, lectured students that "every creature is on the earth to work. You must habituate yourself . . . to being laborious, to doing your duty, and to displaying . . . your gratitude to your father by performing with zeal your métier as a student."[27] Boys and girls were encouraged to begin thinking of themselves as practitioners of a craft early, by identifying their own position as students as a profession.

The curriculum of the *école laïque* also placed a great emphasis on the proper use of money. Jules Payot compared those who made poor use of their money to savages and entreated his countrymen, "Let us be thrifty!" ("Soyons économes!").[28] Clarisse Juranville's *Premier livre des petites filles* employed a like tone in the lesson "Éléonore does not know how to count," a cautionary tale describing a young girl's mortifying trip to a candy store during which she incorrectly counts the coins for her purchase in front of the merchant.[29] The consequence of poor economizing was graver than simple humiliation. Compayré's *Éléments d'instruction morale et civique* directed students to heed Benjamin Franklin's fiery advice on personal economy: "The loaner and the debtor are two slaves. . . . Despise this double chain; conserve your liberty and your independence. . . . If someone tells you that you can grow rich through anything but work and economy, do not listen to him, he is a poisoner!"[30] Such lessons neatly allied thrift and freedom, and reflected a curriculum-wide acclaim of financial saving.

Although the republican curriculum deemed all types of work socially and morally beneficial, manual work elicited special praise. Bourgeois pedagogues were anxious to convince working-class students that the laboring rungs of French society were an estimable position on the social ladder. While all men were equal in theory, in practice the strength of French society would come from the specialization of each individual's function. As a tool of social control, this solidarist philosophy enabled bourgeois leaders to herald French social unity and to encourage the labor of the lower classes, all while maintaining their own ascendancy.[31] To this end, Third Republic textbooks directed a great deal of attention toward manual occupations, commonly devoting considerable portions of reading primers to this topic. Defodon's *dictée* defining métier was followed by another that gave detailed descriptions of possible professions, all manual in nature, for men and women, including carpenter, cobbler, joiner, milliner, tailor, and locksmith.[32] Caumont's *Lectures courantes des écoliers français* (1884) included four chapters on the building of a house, through which students read about every phase of the construction process and learned how to produce an architectural floor plan.[33] These chapters were accompanied by pages of extensively detailed illustrations and charts describing the various kinds of workers who constructed the house, which tools they used, and how they carried out their work. This list focused almost exclusively on manual laborers such as carpenters and masons, though mention was also made of the intellectual laborers who assisted in the process such as the architect and the entrepreneur who funded the construction.[34] In this way, schoolchildren were presented with an image of an ideal French society, in which each citizen fulfilled his or her specific function to create a harmonious whole. This social vision was rooted in the practice of manual labor. Textbooks even exhorted students to view their scholastic endeavors as worthy manual labor. An essay in Pellissier's *Gymnastique de l'esprit* equated the student and the agricultural laborer:

> Both work; both need diligence, patience, and attention; both repose at the end of their day, both are rewarded for their efforts by success. . . . The pupil *cultivates* his mind like the plowman *cultivates* his field; one says of the science acquired by the pupil, that he *reaps* that which he has *sowed*. . . . The instruments of the plowman are the plow and the harrow; the instruments of the pupil are the pen, the pencil, the ruler, and the compass.[35] (emphasis in original)

In this way, Pellissier transformed young students' stationary, intellectual work into a lively manual craft with its own specialized tools.

Beyond the textbooks, officials hoped to provide schoolchildren with practical experiences of manual work, whatever their career goals. During the 1880s instructional officials initiated a series of manual craft classes within the primary school system. Dr. Riant, a speaker in the lecture series given by the Ministry of Public Instruction at the Exposition Universelle of 1878, had expounded on the necessity of such manual courses in primary schools: "One does not go to school to become a scholar. . . . The majority go there to find the preparation essential to the practice of a trade and to progressing in the well-chosen profession that they will exercise in the future."[36] In such courses, working-class students would learn a métier that would serve them in later life; bourgeois students not destined for a manual occupation would learn to recognize the skill of manual artisans. Gambettist minister of public instruction (and close friend of Captain Colette) Paul Bert insisted that bourgeois students who handled the same tools and resolved the same artisanal problems as their working-class schoolmates would never disdain the simple, able worker because they would "know the difficulties of his workmanship" and "appreciate his value." Manual work classes would thus help achieve "social peace" and be "something truly great and useful."[37] Work would serve as the unifying force behind a dynamic new French society. Jost and Braeunig's *Lectures pratiques* (1881) was equally enthusiastic about the social solidarity that would result from children of all classes learning side by side in the new communal schools: "the son of the bourgeois comes to sit on the same bench as the son of the day worker and they are good friends. The esteem that they have for one another is not measured by the name or fortune of their fathers, but by work, by knowledge, by the accuracy of each."[38] Work would thereby supplant age-old social categories of wealth and lineage in the new, democratized educational sphere, a sphere that would serve as a model for society as a whole.

Curricular directives about manual work were enmeshed in a larger republican culture, so that a student such as Gabrielle Colette heard odes to a certain kind of labor from numerous sources in the 1870s and 1880s. Her father, Jules Colette, a civil servant whose regional political ambitions led him to run as a republican education candidate for the Conseil général de l'Yonne in 1880, penned several poems during Gabrielle's youth, poems that echoed the industrious patriotism of the textbooks. In one poem he compared military battles fought for France with the manual work of peasant life, calling upon his fellow citizens to "take your battle position! Whether one is fighting or working . . ."[39] He imagined an ideal society composed of "Rough artisans of the plow, / Workers with the arms of athletes, / Sculptors, painters, or poets, / Tool in hand or laurels around their head." He praised those who were "working without striking," thus distinguishing this heroic working-class figure from his more radical socialist brother.[40] This same theme appeared in another of the captain's poems, in which he exclaimed,

"Work! Labor lights the dark hour" in the "fields, in the workshops, in the count-less schools" of France. "Work!" he demanded of his *concitoyens*, "And without seeking sad reprisals, / Prepare your children for all battles!"[41] With implicit refer-ences to the defeat to Prussia, Captain Colette once again lauded manual work as a patriotic tool, here with the power to alleviate the national dejection that followed the war in 1870.

The social harmony invoked by such republican rhetoric in the schools and in popular culture, however, was often elusive. Pedagogues themselves had difficulty deciding what should be done about the thorny question of class in their new secular school system. In Léopold Mabilleau's *Cours d'instruction civique* (1883), a primer in civic rights and duties, a middle-class student watches with surprise as his father's male servant votes. The father explains: "There are times when the workers are not inferior to bosses, nor the farmers to the lords of the manor." However, he continues, this did not prevent the "most intelligent and the most active from having over the people a greater influence than the ignorant and the lazy."[42] Education and work were the keys to social superiority, in theory, but a clear class structure was foundational in these texts. The vision of the republican schoolroom as a space for class *rapprochement* was plainly more of an aspiration in 1880 than a social reality. Many bourgeois families still chose to have their chil-dren educated in private schools even at the primary level. However, as Colette's experience demonstrates, social mixing did occur in the public *école primaire*, particularly in villages where intense republican fervor made secular school at-tendance a charged political act. This social interaction was promoted by the schools as a significant component of the republican *morale laïque*, whatever the actual class composition of the average classroom, and as such held meaning for the generation of French children educated under its precepts.

* * *

Despite the ubiquity of often gender-neutral lessons about the importance of la-bor, the Third Republic's educational system was, to be sure, highly gendered; curricular directives about work did at times emphasize different social roles for male and female students. Laura Strumingher asserts that while the curriculum categorized men's work as public, as serving the family, and as a source of personal fulfillment, women's work was often defined only as a natural duty, an extension of her nurturing character best confined to the private sphere.[43] Rebecca Rog-ers concurs that while girls' schooling often promoted a healthy work ethic, "in the end the model of feminine identity that it presented is one that sacrifices personal desires and ambitions for the collective, or more frequently, the familial good."[44] Indeed, the Republic, like the Church, hoped to produce devoted, ef-ficient wives and mothers, and discouraged students from moving beyond their station, whether social or sexual. Yet the laic curriculum also contained an ideal-ization of craft labor that clouded an otherwise tidy republican vision of women's intellectual formation. The republican critique of idleness went beyond an exhortation to keep busy, extending to a veritable culture of work, in which one was defined through one's occupation and the successful earning of one's living—a dictum that equated a wage-earning profession with life itself.

Such an emphasis set the public *école primaire* apart from other options for girls' schooling in this period. At least during the first generation of the republican schools, the daughters of affluent families most often attended annexes of private secondary schools or were sent to convent schools. These institutions stressed the teaching of "feminine" skills that prepared young women for their future roles as *femmes de foyer*, not wage laborers.[45] The communal primary school, by contrast, was concerned with preparing the working-class population for their adult lives as productive laborers.[46] Ferdinand Buisson's republican tour de force, the *Dictionnaire de pédagogie* (1882), defended instructing girls in basic economics so that they would "know what is meant by *work, property, capital, salary, exchange, currency, tax.* . . . Employed by the thousands in commerce and industry, do women have less of an investment than us in knowing the laws of production, the relations between labor and capital?"[47] Though taught the same values of domestic orderliness and feminine virtue as upper-class girls, female students in the communal school were called upon to occupy themselves with useful (paid) manual labor, much like male students. Manual work was emphasized in the girls' primary curriculum, though it was given a feminine slant by way of a focus on needlework and other "ouvrages de femmes." Clarisse Juranville's *Le savoir-faire et le savoir-vivre* (1879) expressed concern that young girls were being sent out into the world without any understanding of their practical duties. Though most of her book covered a kind of home economics, Juranville also told her young female readers that if their revenue was not sufficient to meet the needs of the household budget they had organized, they should compensate with work outside the home.[48] Rather than resorting to loans, girls were instructed to economize money given to them by husbands or fathers, and even to earn money themselves.

Since many of the girls in Saint-Sauveur and the Yonne came from farming families, the cantonal book lists of the 1880s contained a good number of agricultural textbooks emphasizing the importance of diligent rural labor. One such manual, Louis-Eugène Bérillon's *La Bonne ménagère agricole, ou simples notions d'économie rurale et d'économie domestique* (1874), was written expressly for the primary girls' schools of the Yonne.[49] This book, which would make a cameo appearance in Colette's second novel, offers an effective example of the way in which republican notions of work could act in tension with approved gender norms. Bérillon, who attended the normal school in Auxerre and was a teacher in the Yonne, presented an ideal country girl who remained in the countryside, rather than being corrupted by the temptations of the city. Since Bérillon recognized that many such girls would also need to seek work outside of the home, he encouraged them to seek employment with a reputable farmwoman: "if you know how to act well, you will even be treated with consideration, treated by your masters like you were part of the family. Farm girls today earn good wages. By placing yours in a savings account, within several years, you will have made yourself a small dowry; you could then become the spouse of an honest plowman, thrifty and industrious like you."[50] Bérillon thus attempted to reconcile feminine work outside the home with the ideal of the *femme au foyer*. By seeking employment on a farm, these girls would be reintegrated into a family unit. At the same time, Bérillon emphasized the importance of earning competitive wages, economizing, and maintaining a savings account. He cloaked this economic agility in the language of domesticity, since his exemplary young woman saved money only for the eventual prize of a respectable marriage. Nonetheless, the outcome was female wage labor.

Jost and Braeunig's *Lectures pratiques* explored women's professional, wage-earning options in detail—devoting more than twenty lessons to occupations open to women, including seamstress, domestic servant, milliner, laundress, teacher, and nurse. Expressing some of the same concerns as Bérillon's *Bonne ménagère*, Jost and Braeunig wrote that when a woman was forced to work outside the home, her jobs should "all relate to the maintenance of the household." Leaving her parents' home would be emotionally trying for the young girl, but she would be consoled by "the thought that in a few months she will bring the fruit of her savings back to the house."[51] Later in the same book, Jost and Braeunig repeated this lesson about the consoling power of wages, telling girls who took on the isolating challenge of city work that they could comfort themselves with the higher wages paid to urban domestic servants. Earning "elevated" wages enabled the country girl to not only relieve some of her parents' debts but also save for her own future.[52] As in Bérillon's descriptions of female work, this displaced country girl would best be integrated into her employer's family and his children soon like her own. When obliged to work in the city, the rural girl was advised to keep her simple clothes, resisting the temptations of urban luxury consumerism. In addition, the rural girl was cautioned not to lose her native dialect or to attempt to set herself above her old friends on visits back to her *pays*.

Such lessons frequently reproached the moral failings of the young bourgeois lady who was attached to luxury and leisure, contrasting her with the hardworking lower-class girl. Clarisse Juranville's *Premier livre des petites filles* took aim at the temptations of vanity by instructing readers to associate beauty with labor rather than display. Juranville declared that a girl should not be complimented for the beauty of her charming silk dress. Rather, the insect who made the silk and the factory worker who manufactured the cloth should be honored, as pride lay in the product of hard work, not in the vain and idle enjoyment of these products.[53] Bérillon told his ideal working country girl that "more than one fine lady, overwhelmed under the weight of her leisure, consumed by her boredom, in her palace of gilded paneling, will be less happy than you, in your modest household."[54]

Work was thus presented to girls as not only a moral good but also a source of pride and a means of achieving merit-based success and prosperity. Jost and Humbert's *Lectures pratiques* (1881), for example, included the story of a country girl named Lisette, "a little girl, quite well-behaved and quite industrious," who made butter and sold it at market. Because of her diligent and capable work, Lisette's butter was the "most esteemed" at the market in Bayeux.[55] More than a hard worker, Lisette was a commercial agent who produced and sold a marketable good. A poem printed in Juranville's *Le Premier livre des petites filles* hailed diligent labor as man's "duty" and "consoler," and also as a source of worldly success and reward: "Work alone leads to prosperity. / Do not go along, stroking yourself with a vain hope, / Awaiting success without work and without difficulty. / One never obtains anything without having merited it."[56] In this way, traditional notions of work were combined with a new, achievement-oriented language that stressed meriting, succeeding, obtaining, and prospering. Another of Juranville's textbooks offered children lessons in letter writing, including sample letters from working women to employers who owed them money. Students were taught that some forms of address and tone would be more likely to ensure not only the receipt of the promised wages but also future work. Such lessons treated female students as future productive workers who would need to direct their own economic lives.[57]

Despite the many contradictions present in the curriculum's portrayal of female labor, no student could have missed the constant glorification of work and the abhorrence of idleness that filled these textbooks. The weight given to wage-earning manual labor as well as the importance of one's métier in the curriculum created a definition of work that had very specific accents. Whatever the gender of the examples used, the overwhelming prominence of this particular definition of work would have consequences for the next generation of republican women.

The Village

We now turn by way of a case study to an analysis of how the intersection of girls' education and work played out in practice as towns all over France negotiated the republican sea change. Indeed, in some regions it was only through the cooperation and engaged support of local republican culture that many of the national secularization initiative's goals were able to take root.[58] During the 1870s and 1880s, informal social gatherings were crucial arenas in which the hazy contours of the new Republic were defined.[59] These republican social circles included a wide range of activities defined by Maurice Agulhon as *périscolaire*: choral groups, gymnastic and shooting societies, brass orchestras—all associations that radiated out from the new laic schools created by the Ferry Laws, and which were often deliberately politicized.[60] Particularly in campaigns for the spread of popular education, local republican societies were a starting point, initiating campaigns for evening classes, lectures, free schooling and equipment for poorer students, and youth organizations.[61] Such initiatives, what Robert Gildea calls "struggle and compromise" at the local level, were as essential to the success and implementation of the new system as undertakings in Paris.[62]

Throughout the contentious first decade of the Republic, Colette's home province of Burgundy was a uniquely consistent source of republican support, what Odile Rudelle calls a kind of "political observatory" for the evolution of republicanism in the years 1877 to 1885.[63] As early as 1871, three out of the four departments that made up Burgundy showed strong electoral support for republican candidates. In these three departments, which included the Yonne, twenty-one out of twenty-six representatives in 1871 were already republican.[64] As early as 1875, 82 percent of the Yonne's primary schools were secular.[65] Saint-Sauveur-en-Puisaye particularly had long been a site of republican support.[66] Indeed, administrative reports from the Yonne are filled with references to the left-leaning disorder in Saint-Sauveur throughout the Second Republic and Second Empire.[67] In 1865 a police report indicated that the underground republican party in Saint-Sauveur, already entrenched in the 1850s, was now showing itself stronger than ever.[68]

Therefore, while republican educational initiatives often met with strong resistance in the early years of the Third Republic, in Saint-Sauveur-en-Puisaye the secularization and modernization of the local school system was pursued with zeal. This secularization could be traced back to 1848, when the inhabitants of Saint-Sauveur established a Protestant school, even though not a single Protestant lived in the village. Suspecting that the school was the townspeople's cover for creating a freethinking, anticlerical educational institution, a state official wrote to the prefect in 1852: "It is easy to recognize that these establishments have been formed with a political aim. It is to this school that all the great democrats of the commune sent and continue to send their children today. It is thus a schism, a flag of public opinion much more than of religious opinions."[69] Thus, already in 1852, Saint-Sauveur's schools were politicized institutions that focused republican action.

The townspeople of Saint-Sauveur were eager about the possibilities of the secular pedagogical revolution that came with the Third Republic. Throughout the 1870s and 1880s, they dedicated their time and resources to making the public schools in Saint-Sauveur centers of reason, patriotism, hygiene, and practical training. As early as 1874, new classrooms and a gymnasium were added to the existing school complex.[70] In 1882 the town embarked on a massive reconstruction of the boys' and girls' schools, a project that would not be entirely completed until 1889. Almost all of Gabrielle Colette's schooling took place during this period of rebuilding and modernization. In fact, this construction project later served as the model for the detailed fictional reconstruction and modernization project of the communal school in her novel *Claudine à l'école*.

Saint-Sauveur's system of secular girls' education was one of the town fathers' principal areas of concern in the 1870s and 1880s, particularly the creation of a *cours complémentaire*, or girls' superior primary education. Many townspeople deemed the creation of such a program a crucial step in modernizing secular female instruction in Saint-Sauveur. Girls' higher primary education was still somewhat rare in this period, particularly in rural villages. In 1881 only about eleven thousand girls in France attended some form of postprimary education. A little more than two thousand of these girls were in *cours complémentaires*, one- or two-year programs generally used in small rural villages because they were taught within an existing primary school building by the school's principal.[71] Even though such superior primary education programs were a rarity for girls, the town council of Saint-Sauveur, of which Jules Colette was a member, appealed to departmental officials for the addition of a *cours complémentaire* in their town by invoking the new ideals of girls' secular education and the necessity of practical training for the town's female children. Departmental officials, however, countered that a *cours complémentaire* for girls would be wasted in Saint-Sauveur, where, they contended, few girls required an educational formation more advanced than that already offered.

In a report to the government in December 1885, the municipal council vigorously contested the findings of the inspector from the Academy of the Yonne, asserting that, for one thing, the secular nature of the proposed program was an important motivation for its creation. The council was concerned that the establishment of a *cours primaire supérieur* at a rival confessional girls' school in Saint-Sauveur would soon mean the loss of students seeking a more competitive program of study to Christian instruction.[72] Alongside this secularizing motivation, however, were several issues of greater concern to the municipal council—namely, female professional training. Work, consequently, was central to debates about girls' superior primary education that took place in the 1880s in Saint-Sauveur. The population of Saint-Sauveur, while dedicated to expanding their children's knowledge, had narrow economic means, making a local *cours complémentaire* for girls preferable, they argued in the municipal council's report, to a *lycée* in a city:

> Haven't we the right to act on the fervor and the inescapable enthusiasm that pushes for the creation of a School responding so well to the needs and aspirations of the region? The Canton of St-Sauveur is, indeed, a village of small farming where the land is quite split up, the fortunes limited, and the love of instruction very developed. The farmer and the small property holder . . . who cannot use the services of their daughters before the age of 17 or 18 years old, and who are not wealthy enough, moreover, to send them to a boarding school in Auxerre . . . would be happy to have

them instructed for one or two years in an establishment within reach, in a town center where their business and trade constantly call them, and where they could surround [their daughters] with their most attentive solicitude and care.[73]

People of "limited" fortunes nonetheless endowed with a great love of learning, the councilmen accepted the inevitability of their daughters' need to work, most likely in the family enterprise. But during the years before they could become useful workers, these girls would be best served, the council insisted, by an advanced primary instruction in an institution that was both economically accessible and close to parental control.

Professional training was clearly a compelling motivation for the creation of the girls' superior primary program. The *cours complémentaire* was designed specifically for those girls who, having already obtained the *certificat d'études primaires*, wished to prepare for the *brevet* exams and entrance exams to the normal school in Auxerre. When referring to the new superior education program, the mayor of Saint-Sauveur and the local press often used the term "écoles agricoles et professionelles."[74] The council unequivocally described the higher education they sought for their daughters as one that would differ sharply from that of bourgeois girls in middle-class *lycées*:

> How [the farmer and the small property holder] would prefer their daughters have a practical instruction linked to their future situation, a kind of apprenticeship for the life on the farm, rather than the somewhat refined education of our bourgeois boarding schools! . . . The contact of the child of the bourgeoisie with the peasant girl risks developing in the latter a love of luxury, a repugnance for manual work, a disgust for the life of the fields; and [risks] making her dream of a milieu that is not made for her. The superior primary school would put girls of nearly identical position, from analogous social situations, face to face, and would give rise to and develop in them . . . a spirit of solidarity, a love of order and work, qualities that unfortunately have tended to disappear in our countryside.[75]

This passage demonstrates a strong local suspicion of the deleterious influence of feminine bourgeois luxury and idleness. The townspeople of Saint-Sauveur envisioned a school that would repudiate the urban, bourgeois values threatening the fabric of rural life. This school, far from egalitarian, would be explicitly designed for girls of the same "social situations"—here, farmers' daughters. Like many of the textbooks from the same period, the council of Saint-Sauveur articulated a dual mission: to provide their daughters with a practical and competitive professional education that enhanced their love of manual work, while at the same time dissuading them from abandoning rural life for the city.

Jules Colette was particularly invested in the deliberations regarding the *cours complémentaire* in which he took part as a council member. In 1885 his daughter

Gabrielle was twelve years old and rapidly nearing the end of the program of primary instruction offered in Saint-Sauveur. She was plainly not the kind of child the council was discussing. The daughter of relatively well-to-do parents, she was not expected to work someday as a farmwife or agricultural laborer. Indeed, her older siblings had attended the very bourgeois boarding schools of Auxerre so maligned in the council's report. Though not part of the social strata most targeted by the new curriculum, she was nonetheless a product of it, not simply by dint of her schooling but also through her family's strong support of girls' secular education in Saint-Sauveur. In addition, Jules Colette's financial woes had made a dowry for Gabrielle less feasible, and he may have believed that some advanced primary education would help prepare his possibly unmarriageable daughter for a moderately respectable career. Some scholars have claimed that the captain indeed encouraged Gabrielle to become a teacher during these years.[76]

In 1886 Saint-Sauveur's persistent municipal council was victorious. In a letter to the prefect of the Yonne written several months after the deliberations in Saint-Sauveur, the inspector from the Academy of the Yonne admitted that his earlier decision, denying the town's need for a girls' *cours complémentaire*, had been incorrect. Based on the documents submitted to him by the municipal council, he modified his previous ruling and now affirmed that "there are good grounds for the creation" of a girls' superior primary education program in Saint-Sauveur.[77]

The successful establishment of the girls' *cours complémentaire* in Saint-Sauveur depended on the recruitment of a teacher who could direct such an advanced level of instruction. Colette's first teacher, Fanny Desleau, had been encouraged to retire in 1879 when school inspectors noticed her indifference to new pedagogical methods.[78] Mlle. Desleau was succeeded as principal of the secular girls' school by Camille Viellard, a well-liked teacher who possessed the *brevet simple*.[79] Though such a level of study was satisfactory when Viellard was hired in 1879, by 1887 even many of her assistant teachers had obtained at least the *brevet supérieur*. Though a competent elementary school teacher, Viellard was incapable of taking charge of the superior curriculum that the townspeople now expected for their daughters.[80] In her eight years in Saint-Sauveur, none of Viellard's students obtained the *brevet élémentaire* or won admission to the normal school. The villagers of Saint-Sauveur found this record unacceptable. As a result, Mme. Viellard was replaced in 1887 by a twenty-four-year-old *normalienne* named Olympe Terrain.

A native of the Yonne, Terrain earned her *brevet supérieur* from the École normale d'institutrices in Auxerre in 1882.[81] After graduating, she taught for several years in public schools around the Yonne before winning an appointment as the *directrice* of the girls' school in Saint-Sauveur-en-Puisaye in October 1887. Upon her arrival, Terrain was entrusted with the direction of the five girls' primary classes, as well as the *cours complémentaire*. She had proven herself more than capable of such a responsibility-laden position in her five years as a public school teacher in villages where she had waged successful battles against well-entrenched confessional schools.[82] Terrain exemplified this period's advance guard of republican women pedagogues, whose entire higher education was conducted in the revolutionizing period after 1879.[83]

The Colette family was initially hostile to Terrain because she had been the appointee of the captain's republican political rival, Dr. Merlou. The first day that Gabrielle attended class with her new teacher, she arrived late and ostentatiously began to read the newspaper. Terrain, presumably noticing the difference between Gabrielle's social status and that of her classmates, calmly told the bourgeois girl: "My child, it must be completely disagreeable for you to attend the communal school where the rule of not reading the newspaper in class must be respected by all students."[84] From that moment, Terrain later recalled, Gabrielle was a well-behaved student. Within a year, Captain Colette penned a poem in honor of Terrain's twenty-fifth birthday, which was read aloud at a celebration in August 1888 by Gabrielle.[85] Biographers Claude Pichois and Alain Brunet note that the first known letter written by Gabrielle Colette was an order to a shop in Auxerre for a gift for her teacher, Mlle. Terrain.[86]

Within a short time of her arrival in Saint-Sauveur, Terrain fulfilled the town council's expectations for the new superior primary instruction program. In August 1889, impressed by local girls' success on the *brevet* exams, the council offered congratulations and "profound gratitude" to the woman who had, in just a year, "placed [their] school at the top row of *écoles supérieures* in the department."[87] Many of Colette's classmates from the 1880s went on to attend the women's normal school in Auxerre and later became teachers. Colette herself took the oral and written exams for the *certificat d'études primaires* (or *c.e.p.*) and the *brevet élémentaire*, diplomas that during this period represented a certain distinction.[88] Rebecca Rogers notes the significant "esteem attached to examinations and prizes" in this period, and the way in which exams "brought girls into a more public realm" in both laic and Catholic girls' schools in the second half of the nineteenth century.[89] Indeed, in Colette's later fictional re-creation of her childhood education, she described the immense importance of the exams, which involved a trip to the regional capital Auxerre, for the girls of a village public school.

Olympe Terrain remained a passionate advocate for the girls' school in Saint-Sauveur until the end of her career. In 1917, just a year before her retirement, she was still writing determined letters to the administration pleading for more state funding for her *cours complémentaire*, specifically asking for a grant for a student who hoped to pursue a career in teaching.[90] Terrain and her career in Saint-Sauveur exemplified the way in which this new generation of secular female teachers could give the ideals of the republican hierarchy concrete form in the quotidian push and pull of provincial life. The newly minted secular teachers of the 1880s were not simply bland bureaucratic parrots of the new pedagogy but, as Sharif Gemie puts it, "politicized" young professional women who "stood apart, in the full glare of the public sphere."[91] One should not underrate the impact such women could have in animating republican moral philosophy, while at the same time providing a radical new model of public womanhood. At the very least, Olympe Terrain provided her female students with a living object lesson that highlighted the possibilities and pitfalls of female métier.

* * *

While the Third Republic's praise of work was hardly a radical innovation, the particular definition of work articulated by the republican curriculum, and the particular prominence given this notion of work throughout republican culture in general, was novel. Just as education, and the School more specifically, bore tremendous cultural meaning in this period, so too did this republican Gospel of Work. By way of its very broadness, its ability to include manual laborers, scientists, farmwives, and even primary school students in the same universe of work, the republican rhetoric of *métier* served as an effective means of marrying otherwise contradictory maxims. It provided a fictive but puissant vision of a harmonious Republic of Work, in which all men and women could aspire to honorability by way of their labor. In trumpeting this vision, the men and women of the republican hierarchy presumed that every student would recognize and respect his or her place in that Republic of Work—a presumption that would be disproved by the rowdy social and cultural scene of the belle époque.

Notes

All translations are the author's unless otherwise noted.

1. See Elisabeth Charleux-Leroux, "Réalité et Fiction dans *Claudine à l'école*," *Bulletin de la Société des Sciences Historiques et Naturelles de l'Yonne*. 113 (1981):, vol. 113; 121–164.

2. See Levin, *Republican Art and Ideology*.

3. See Patrick J. Harrigan, "Church, State, and Education in France from the Falloux to the Ferry Laws: A Reassessment," *Canadian Journal of History* (April 2001): 51–83. He notes that recent studies challenge the notion that Catholic girls' education was completely negative. See also Nique and Lelièvre, *La République*.

4. Clark, *Schooling the Daughters of Marianne*, 55.

5. German primary schools underwent major changes under Bismarck's *Kulturkampf*, but these changes never, according to Marjorie Lamberti, extended to a "movement to abolish the instruction of religion in the schools." See *State, Society, and the Elementary School in Imperial Germany* (Oxford, 1989), 217. Some parts of Germany saw hostility to political Catholicism, but the result was not secular schooling. Instead, religious instruction was taken over by the state. These decades of political conflict over education "ended with a law that made confessional schooling the rule" (211). See also George and Lottelore Bernstein, "The Curriculum for German Girls' Schools, 1870–1914," *Paedogogica Historica* 18, no. 2 (1978): 275–95.

6. Struminger, *Little Girls and Boys*, 2.

7. Rebecca Rogers, *From the Salon to the Schoolroom*, 9, 7. Rogers's study brings together religious and lay, public and private schooling for girls in the nineteenth century.

8. Charleux-Leroux and Boivin, *Avec Colette*.

9. Raymond Grew and Patrick Harrigan, "The Catholic Contribution to Universal Schooling in France, 1850–1906," *Journal of Modern History* 57 (June 1985): 238.

10. See Clark, *Schooling the Daughters of Marianne*.

11. *Listes des ouvrages scolaires admis par les Conférences cantonales d'instituteurs et d'institutrices du département de l'Yonne, pendant l'année scolaire 1880–1881*, Archives Départementales de l'Yonne (hereafter ADY), 37 T 1.

12. Ibid.

13. Laura Lee Downs, *Childhood in the Promised Land: Working-Class Movements and the Colonies de Vacances in France, 1880–1960* (Durham, NC, 2002), 10.

14. Charles Delon, *Lectures expliquées: Tableaux et récits, accompagnés de nombreuses vignettes* (Paris, 1875), 133. This book was on the Yonne's *Listes des ouvrages scolaires* as of 1882, ADY 37 T 1.

15. Zulma Carraud, *Maurice ou le travail* (Paris, 1853) and *La Petite Jeanne ou le devoir* (Paris, 1853). See Strumingher, *Little Boys and Girls*, 157. These books were on the Yonne's *Listes des ouvrages scolaires* in 1880–81, ADY 37 T 1. On the curricular discourse regarding laziness, see Dominique Maingueneau, *Les Livres d'école de la République, 1870–1914: Discours et idéologie* (Paris, 1979).

16. Clarisse Juranville, *Le Premier livre des petites filles: Nouvelles lectures graduées* (Paris, 1880), 74. This book appeared on the Yonne's *Listes des ouvrages scolaires* as early as 1880. See ADY 37 T 1.

17. Gabriel Compayré, *Éléments d'instruction morale et civique* (Paris, 1882), 47. This book was on the Yonne's *Listes des ouvrages scolaires* as early as 1880. See ADY 37 T 1. Compayré (1843–1913) was a key figure in the republican pedagogical revolution. He was a professor in Toulouse, specializing in Darwinism, child psychology, and the history of pedagogy. In 1881 he served as a deputy from Tarn and as inspector general for secondary instruction.

18. Auguste Burdeau, *Instruction morale à l'école: Devoir et la Patrie* (Paris, 1884), 88–89. Emphasis in original.

19. Ibid., 89.

20. Victor de Laprade, "Travaillons," in Guillaume Jost and Frédéric Braeunig's *Lectures pratiques, (éducation et enseignement, instruction morale et civique), destinées aux élèves des cours moyen et supérieur* (Paris, 1881), 13–14.

21. Ibid. .

22. In exploring the language of métier, I am indebted to Debora Silverman, particularly "Pilgrim's Progress and Vincent van Gogh's *Métier*" (London, 1992), as well as *Van Gogh and Gauguin*.

23. Levin, *Republican Art and Ideology*, 68.

24. Ibid., 71.

25. See Silverman, *Art Nouveau*, 54.

26. Charles Defodon and J. Vallée, *Petites dictées pour les écoles rurales: Textes et explications* (Paris, 1880), 28. Defodon was editor-in-chief of the *Manuel générale de l'instruction primaire* and a normal school teacher. Vallée was a teacher and an inspector for the Ministry of Primary Instruction.

27. Caumont, *Lectures courantes des écoliers français* (Paris, 1884), 12–13. The earliest version of this book seems to have been published in 1877. Caumont was the pen name of Mme. Alfred Mézières (Anne-Marie-Louise Lardenois de Caumont). This book was used in Saint-Sauveur in the 1880s. See ADY 37 T 1.

28. Payot, quoted in Maingueneau, *Les livres d'école*, 202.

29. Juranville, *Premier livre des petite filles*, 97–99.

30. Compayré, *Éléments d'instruction morale et civique*, 198.

31. On *solidarisme* see Sanford Elwitt, *The Third Republic Defended: Bourgeois Reform in France, 1880–1914* (Baton Rouge, 1986); and Debora Silverman's "Aristocratic Ralliement and Social Solidarité," in *Art Nouveau*.

32. Defodon and Vallée, *Petites dictées pour les écoles rurales*, 28.

33. Caumont, *Lectures courantes des écoliers français* (Paris, 1884).

34. Ibid.

35. Pellissier, *La Gymnastique de l'esprit, 2e partie* (1874; Paris, 1893), 87. It appears on the lists in the Yonne as early as 1875. See ADY 37 T 1.

36. Dr. Riant, quoted in Guillaume Bès, *Souvenir de ma visite à L'Exposition Universelle de 1878: Mémoire adressée à mes collègues du canton.* AN F/17/9388. Bès was a teacher-delegate from the canton of Mur-de-Barrez (Aveyron).

37. Paul Bert, "L'Instruction dans une démocratie," Conférence faite au Havre (Cercle Franklin), 21 March 1880, in *Leçons, discours, et conférences* (Paris, 1881), 402–3. Bert (1833–86) was a politician from the Yonne.

38. Jost and Braeunig, *Lectures pratiques*, 262. Though this edition is from 1881, an earlier edition appeared on curricular lists in the Yonne as of 1880. See ADY 37 T 1, *Listes des ouvrages scolaires admis par les conférences cantonales d'instituteurs et d'institutrices du département de l'Yonne, pendant l'année scolaire 1880–1881.*

39. Jules Colette, "Gratitude," in André Fildier, ed., *Colette: Sa famille, ses amis à Châtillon-Coligny—des documents inédits* (Paris, 1992), 18. He wrote these poems under the auspices of the Vétérans des Armées de Terre et de Mer.

40. Ibid.

41. Jules Colette, "À la France," in Fildier, *Colette*, 23.

42. Léopold Mabilleau, *Cours d'instruction civique: Cours élémentaire et moyen* (Paris, 1883), 55. In 1883 this book was added to Saint-Sauveur's curriculum on the recommendations of a cantonal conference, one of only four books that the committee felt important enough to add to Moral and Civic Instruction. See Conférence pédagogique du 21 juillet 1883, Canton de Saint-Sauveur, *Révision de la Liste des ouvrages scolaires admis . . . dans les écoles primaires de l'Yonne*, ADY 37 T 1.

43. Strumingher, *Little Girls and Boys*, 3–4. Clark emphasizes that work, for both sexes, was linked to familial needs, not ambition, in an effort to lower the social mobility of the working class (*Schooling the Daughters of Marianne*, 104). Domestic lessons were common in other national education programs during this period. See Katharine Kennedy, "Domesticity (Hauswirtschaft) in the *Volksschule*: Textbooks and Lessons for Girls, 1890–1914," *Internationale Schulbuchforschung* (1991): 5–21.

44. Rebecca Rogers, *From the Salon to the Schoolroom*, 38. Rogers notes that girls' educational culture expanded work-based honor for women, though she indicates that such work was still best "nonremunerative" (255).

45. See Thérèse Bentzon and A. Chevalier, *Causeries de morale pratique* (Paris, 1899), a text for upper-class girls' schools, as well as Clark's discussion of this issue in *Schooling the Daughters of Marianne*.

46. See Prost's seminal study *Histoire de l'enseignement*.

47. Frédéric Passy, quoted in "Filles," *Dictionnaire de pédagogie et d'instruction primaire*, part 1, ed. Ferdinand Buisson (Paris, 1882), 1:1020. Emphasis in original. Buisson created the *Dictionnaire* as an "interested party in this great battle for the establishment of the laic school." See Pierre Hayat, *La passion laïque de Ferdinand Buisson* (Paris, 1999), 22.

48. Clarisse Juranville, *Le Savoir-faire et le savoir-vivre dans les diverses circonstances de la vie: Guide pratique de la vie usuelle à l'usage des jeunes filles* (Paris, 1879), 50–60. This book appears on departmental lists in the Yonne as of 1880–81. See *Liste des ouvrages scolaires admis par les conférences cantonales d'instituteurs et d'institutrices du département de l'Yonne*, 1880–81, 1882–83, ADY 37 T 1.

49. Louis-Eugène Bérillon, *La Bonne ménagère agricole, ou simples notions d'économie rurale et d'économie domestique: Livre de lecture à l'usage des jeunes filles des écoles primaires* (Auxerre, 1874). Bérillon's book appears on Yonne curricular lists as early as 1875. See *Liste générale des livres classiques en usage dans les écoles publiques, 1875* (Yonne), ADY 37 T 1.

50. Bérillon, *La Bonne ménagère agricole*, 20.

51. Jost and Braeunig, *Lectures pratiques*, 185, 187.

52. Ibid., 191–92.

53. Juranville, *Premier livre des petite filles*, 70.

54. Bérillon, *La Bonne ménagère agricole*, 20.

55. Guillaume Jost and V. Humbert, *Lectures pratiques: Destinées aux élèves du cours élémentaire* (Paris, 1881), 65. This book appears on the Yonne curricular list as early as 1880. See ADY 37 T 1.

56. Juranville, *Le Premier livre des petite filles*, 101.

57. Clarisse Juranville, *Premiers sujets de style avec sommaires raisonés: Méthode intuitive, mise à la portée des plus jeunes enfants* (Paris, 1869), 26–28.

58. As Patrick Harrigan writes, nineteenth-century changes in girls' education "came not primarily from the state but from society. Parents were willing to exert effort and to spend money for the elementary schooling of their daughters" ("Women Teachers and the Schooling of Girls in France: Recent Historiographical Trends," *French Historical Studies* 21, no. 4 [Autumn 1998]: 599). Also see Vivien Schmidt, *Democratizing France: The political and administrative history of decentralization.* (Cambridge, MA, 1990), 42.

59. Maurice Agulhon's discussion of the Opportunist period (1879–99) highlights the importance of social gatherings in consolidating a rather "nebulous" republicanism. See "Le parti républicain," in *Les Opportunistes: Les débuts de la République aux républicains,* ed. Léo Hamon (Paris, 1986), 1–14. Also see Katherine Auspitz, *Radical Bourgeoisie.*

60. Agulhon, "Le parti républicain," 5.

61. Gildea makes this point in *Education in Provincial France*, 280–81.

62. Ibid., 366.

63. Odile Rudelle, "Les élections en Bourgogne, 1877–1885" in Hamon, *Les Opportunistes,* 59.

64. Ibid., 59–77.

65. *Inspection générale de l'enseignement primaire,* Yonne, 1877, Archives nationales de France (hereafter AN) F/17/9277.

66. In the mid-nineteenth century, much of the village turned republican and ceased construction on the church they had been building for three centuries. See Francis and Gontier, *Creating Colette,* 1:21. In 1851, during a regional insurrection, secret republican societies led by insurgents from Saint-Sauveur marched on Auxerre. See Préfet à l'Intérieur, dispatch concerning the events of December 1851, 16 November 1868, in *L'Yonne au XIX siècle, 3e partie (1848–1870), Archives du département de l'Yonne, documents et inventaires complémentaires,* ed. Henri Forestier (Auxerre, 1967), 157–67. See also Jean-Pierre Rocher, "Auxerre pendant la première moitié du XIXe siècle," *Histoire d'Auxerre des origines à nos jours, education* (Le Coteau-Roanne, 1984), 338–39.

67. One 1850 report on socialist organizations in the Yonne refers to a subversive group in the village that was so successful in recruitment that "All of Saint-Sauveur's municipal council is red." Anonymous report, 30 September 1850, Auxerre. In Forestier, *L'Yonne au XIXe siècle,* 131–32.

68. Report of the *Commissaire de police,* 30 August 1865. In Forestier, *L'Yonne au XIXe siècle,* 440.

69. Hantule, *juge de paix* in Saint-Sauveur, to the prefect, 9 April 1852. In Forestier, *L'Yonne au XIXe siècle,* 265–66.

70. *Enquête sur la situation matérielle des écoles primaires en 1884 (Yonne),* ADY *F/17/3145.

71. See Clark, *Schooling the Daughters of Marianne,* 120–21.

72. Mairie de Saint-Sauveur-en-Puisaye, *Extrait du registre des délibérations du Conseil Municipal,* 10 December 1885, ADY 46 T 13.

73. *Extrait du registre des délibérations du Conseil Municipal,* 10 December 1885, ADY 46 T 13.

74. Charleux-Leroux, "Réalité et fiction," 128.

75. *Extrait du registre des délibérations du Conseil Municipal,* 10 December 1885, ADY 46 T 13.

76. Hecquet, "Colette: Femmes au travail," 43.

77. L'Inspecteur d'Académie à Monsieur le Prefet de l'Yonne, *Saint-Sauveur: Création d'un cours complémentaire annexé à l'école publique des filles*. Auxerre, 16 February 1886, ADY 46 T 13.

78. Elisabeth Charleux-Leroux, "Gabrielle Colette à l'école élémentaire," *Cahiers Colette* 12 (1990) : 146.

79. Clark notes that some anticlerical towns staffed their schools with secular teachers even before it was required; in other areas, decades would elapse before "the *congréganiste* became as much of a rarity in girls' schools as in boys' schools" (*Schooling the Daughters of Marianne*, 14).

80. See Boivin and Charleux-Leroux's discussion of this topic in *Avec Colette*, 201–2.

81. Born in 1863 in Pourrain, Yonne, Terrain attended the normal school in Auxerre from 1879 to 1882. Ibid., 181.

82. Ibid., 132–33.

83. Margadant discusses this generation in *Madame le Professeur*. Also see Anne T. Quartararo, *Women Teachers and Popular Education in Nineteenth-Century France* (Newark, DE, 1995), and Sharif Gemie, *Women and Schooling in France, 1815–1914* (Keele, 1995).

84. Terrain, quoted in Larnac, *Colette*, 41.

85. Quoted in ibid., 48–49.

86. Pichois and Brunet, *Colette*, 38. Colette ordered a mirror framed with sculpted black wood.

87. From the *Registre des déliberations du Conseil Municipal de St.-Sauveur*, 6 August 1889. Quoted in Charleux-Leroux, "Réalité et Fiction," 132–33.

88. Linda Clark notes that in 1882, 38,000 girls received the *c.e.p.* Within twenty years this number doubled. The *c.e.p.* was "especially prized in rural areas," as "a vehicle of limited social mobility." See *Schooling the Daughters of Marianne*, 109.

89. Rebecca Rogers, *From the Salon to the Schoolroom*, 184.

90. Letter from Olympe Terrain to Monsieur le Député, 30 November 1917, ADY 46 T 13.

91. Sharif Gemie, "Institutional History, Social History, Women's History: A Comment on Patrick Harrigan's 'Women Teachers and the Schooling of Girls in France," *French Historical Studies* 22, no. 4 (Autumn 1999): 619.

2

"A Healthy Soul in a Healthy Body"

Physical and Moral Education in the Third Republic

In 1882 the renowned educational reformer Félix Pécaut, who went on to found the secular teacher's training college for women at Fontenay-aux-Roses, re-marked that France was "becoming addicted to pedagogy."[1] Gabriel Compayré, a teacher who soon entered the national political arena, agreed that pedagogy, "long neglected" in France, suddenly had become "the fashion" in the giddy early days of the Third Republic.[2] Such breathless accounts of pedagogy's thrall over the French public might easily be mistaken as merely the hyperbole of two career pedagogues. But in fact, in the 1870s and 1880s, as the question of secular public schooling became a flashpoint for divisive cultural battles, pedagogy came to bear tremendous cultural weight in France.

When the French government began secularizing its schools in the last de-cades of the nineteenth century, republican officials and pedagogues were presented with the formidable challenge of creating a curriculum of moral in-struction that could replace the Catholic curriculum previously used in French schools. Many believed that clarified pedagogical strategies would constitute an invaluable weapon in the battle with their enemies on the right and a vital means of regenerating the nation's children after the crippling loss to Prussia in 1870. In addition to traditional values of hard work, public masculinity, and domestic femininity, this new *morale laïque* exhorted schoolchildren to cultivate the active life of the mind and of the body. While other European countries simi-larly modernized primary education at the turn of the century, France's national pedagogical push was organized by a dynamic faith in laicity that transformed both the content and practice of public education.[3]

In his assessment of the history of France between 1870 and 1914, Rob-ert Gildea once reflected that "the Third Republic has never had a very good press."[4] This statement appears particularly true of scholarship on this period's educational reforms. Historians acknowledge that the Third Republic expanded the sheer number of schools in France, particularly those for girls, and assured that all French children had access to primary schooling.[5] As to the content of the new schooling, scholars chronicle the maxims of patriotism, hard work, and clearly defined gender roles within the republican curriculum of the 1880s and probe the way in which this curriculum replicated middle-class officialdom's anxieties about the working classes, women, and the Church. In such formulations, however, the republican educational initiative appears as a somewhat lackluster and conservative, if anticlerical, tool of social control and citizen building. When the Third Republican school is credited with any lasting significance, it is as a conduit of some limited social mobility and a nesting ground for the militaristic anti-German jingoism that led a generation of Frenchmen to embrace war in 1914.

The following assessment of Third Republican pedagogy suggests that while socially conservative in many ways, the *morale laïque* of the 1870s and 1880s opened up some unintended spaces for gender subversion and cultural production. It did so by intensifying the links between the physical body and the soul, by elevating students' powers of sensory observation, and by generating novel intellectual techniques to guide and liberate the imagination. As with lessons about manual work and financial acumen, girls in the *école laïque* were confronted with an educational program that naturalized and confirmed gender difference while at the same time proclaiming new gender-neutral values of physical strength and imaginative vibrancy. The result was the construction of a secular selfhood that tested social norms as it reaffirmed them.

'Une âme saine dans un corps sain.'

While numerous countries in Europe and North America evinced an increased interest in physical culture throughout the nineteenth century, in early Third Republic France debates about national fitness were given a particular inflection by the pressing specter of depopulation and military defeat after the *année terrible* of 1870–71.[6] For the designers of the laic school, students' physical fitness not only guaranteed a vigorous new generation of soldiers and soldiers' mothers but also came to be closely associated with the overall mission of the Republic itself. This pedagogical commitment to physical culture was also part and parcel of a long-term historical process relating to the rise of the French middle classes. Particularly from the 1840s, bourgeois interest in physical health and fitness as a means of conserving and expanding family resources had grown steadily. As Gilbert Andrieu puts it, the bourgeoisie, "far from aping the aristocracy, and mindful of the strength of the People or workers, felt the need to associate reason and muscles, and to develop them jointly to generate a new kind of power."[7] Even though in the last decades of the nineteenth century the actual numbers of those engaging in daily physical sport or gymnastic exercise rose only modestly, we can ascertain a change in what Georges Vigarello refers to as the "cultural sensibility" about physical fitness. Vigarello suggests that "the originality" of this turn-of-the-century moment was "not passing from nonhealth to health, but rather deepening health itself, imagining its indefinite growth. . . . Never before had normal health seemed so modifiable, so perfectible, so inclined toward the future and toward progress."[8] The Third Republic's educational system was the perfect blank field upon which this ethos could take form and be institutionalized, even if (and perhaps because) the majority of students in the new schools hailed from the working classes.

French republicans endowed their new national public school system with this same spirit and forged important links between a certain kind of physical fitness and liberal democracy and secularization.[9] Some Catholic pedagogues, once similarly approving of physical exercise, began to decry *gymnastique* as the French state increasingly challenged the role of the Church in education from the late 1860s.[10] This did not mean, as Jacques Defrance notes, that religious instruction and physical fitness were fundamentally incompatible in this period.[11] Such polemic, however, did help solidify the connections between physical culture and *laïcité* in the early years of the Third Republic and set the French example apart from similar pedagogical movements in other European countries.[12]

Historians of the body and sport have supplied valuable studies tracing the history and evolution of physical education in France.[13] The analysis that follows seeks to complicate these histories by scrutinizing the novel notions of the physical self that came to be embedded in the Republic's new moral philosophy, girding not only all republican educational efforts but republican culture in general. This secular moral philosophy posited a healthful and beneficial union of the physical and the moral, a union that contrasted starkly with Catholic instructional calls to escape the confines of one's sinful corporeality in order to achieve the everlasting life of the soul. (Indeed, the *morale laïque* textbooks of influential pedagogues such as Henri Marion, Paul Bert, and Jules Steeg were so alarming to the Catholic Church that they were placed on the Index of banned books in 1882.)[14] Such a shift meant that the fortification and maintenance of the human body became a crucial pedagogical concern, and schoolchildren learned that physical salubrity was as important as that of their souls.

On the practical level, the new focus on healthy bodies led to the implementation of gym and hygiene classes throughout the normal and primary schools of France. Indeed, in the final decades of the nineteenth century, the public school was, in the words of Vigarello, "at the center of the campaign being waged against degenerative maladies."[15] Hygiene classes were founded upon the close connection that educators drew between moral soundness and the cleanliness and domestic orderliness of the poor who frequented the public schools.[16] Textbooks and teacher training stressed bodily hygiene as one of children's principal duties and related cleanliness to regular work habits and honorable conduct. Charles Schuwer's civics textbook from 1879 told students: "The child who washes well is the happiest and the best prepared for work. Hardworking students are always the cleanest." By keeping themselves and their clothing in a pristine state, Schuwer assured children, "you will honor your parents and yourself."[17] According to pedagogue and physician Elie Pécaut, teachers should accustom their students to tidy habits by way of discipline, but also should try to "awaken in the child a love, we might gladly say even a cult" of cleanliness.[18]

Physical exercise was an equally important tool of the new pedagogy in boys' and girls' education. During the 1880s primary school inspectors not only reported back to state authorities on the hygienic attributes of schoolhouses, including light, air, and washroom facilities, but also noted what kind of spaces, such as gymnasiums, were available for physical activity. As early as 1878, conferences by high-ranking pedagogical officials linked moral and physical hygiene, referring to gym in the schools as a "won cause."[19] In the 1880s the military exercises of earlier physical education gave way to less regimented games and sports that targeted the vigor of the corporeal whole.[20] When the Ministry of Public Instruction assembled an exhibit representing French education for the 1884 Universal Exposition in New Orleans, it included pieces of gymnastic equipment and photographs of boys and girls engaged in gymnastic exercises.[21]

In the first decade or so of the republican school system, the girls' physical education curriculum was, in principle, the same as that of boys (with the important exception that girls did not take part in the drills associated with *bataillons scolaires*).[22] Ferdinand Buisson's *Dictionnaire de pédagogie* insisted, "The rationale that advocates gymnastic exercise for boys' schools holds just as true for girls' schools. The maxim *Mens sana in corpore sano* is applicable to the two sexes."[23] In 1879 Paul Rousselot averred that in terms of physical education, girls were "not constituted any differently than boys"—making all the more unacceptable, he continued, that girls' physical education was shamefully neglected in French schools.[24] Rousselot, who authored a number of school primers used in Saint-Sauveur, counseled female teachers to join in their students' physical activities at recess and encouraged them not to fear games that were loud or that resulted in some disordering of their students' *toilette*: "The little girl who tears her dress while jumping about will learn to mend it herself, and the game will have had a double profit."[25] In 1881 a government commission released a program of gymnastic activity expressly for girls that provided detailed instructions on a wide range of exercises such as parallel bars, weights, swimming, balance beams, and numerous stretches and jumps focused on various body parts.[26] By the 1880s some women's normal schools set aside as much as six hours a week for physical education.[27] Such courses were increasingly taught by specialized professors of *gymnastique*.[28] In Colette's department of the Yonne, one such instructor gave several hours of gymnastic training every week to both the men's and women's normal schools in Auxerre.[29] One girl who attended Olympe Terrain's *école laïque* in Saint-Sauveur later fondly recalled the gymnastic fortification of her primary school days: "I knew classmates drunk with fresh air and knocking each other out to win the competition on the bars."[30]

Admittedly, every French schoolhouse did not have a gymnasium, and many teachers throughout this period were incapable of providing physical education classes that would produce the ideals postulated in normal school curricula and textbooks. Mary Lynn Stewart notes that some local school systems put off constructing much-needed gymnasiums for decades or neglected to offer physical education in any substantial way, particularly for girls.[31] But such limitations were not present in all schools. More important, practical physical education initiatives were only one part of a well-developed theoretical and pedagogical *programme* pervading the learning experience of even those students who never attended a gym class. Young secular teachers such as Olympe Terrain received a rigorous education at the nation's laic normal schools, which stressed the crucial union of mind and body. During the first year of the secular normal school program, students learned notions of psychology and moral theory that devoted sections to physical activity. Henri Marion's *Leçons de psychologie* (1882), a manual widely used in the secular schools, was emphatic that students and teachers had "an important reason not to disdain the science of the body and its functions. . . . The body is something of us, its perfection is included in our goals."[32] Marion, an influential professor and theoretician of the *morale laïque*, contrasted the Middle Ages, when the body was an object of contempt and only the spiritual life was esteemed, to the enlightened modern period, when thinkers had achieved a harmonious balance of mind and body. In this way, republican officials and pedagogues often associated physical education with modern liberal politics and secularization. Elie Pécaut, who authored a hygiene manual for laic schools, made this connection explicit: "the *culture physique* of children has always been very closely linked with the philosophical or religious ideas of the moment. It was neglected or artificial whenever an ethos of authority and asceticism prevailed; it has reemerged each time that liberty has gained the upper hand."[33] Georges Dumesnil echoed this polemical distinction in an 1882 article on moral instruction printed in the quasi-official organ of the secular educational corps, the *Revue Pédagogique:* "Between the ancient Greeks, so enamored with good health, and our fathers from the Middle Ages who martyrized their flesh until they resembled their emaciated and bloodless statues, it is clear that common sense, and even morality, are on the side of the Greeks." Dumesnil then quoted a phrase by English social philosopher Herbert Spencer, which appeared often in French discussions of physical education: "One must before all things be a good animal." Dumesnil added that "a good animal effortlessly carries within it the understudy of a good man and a free thinker."[34]

In the secular Republic, then, the physical and moral were mutually dependent and mutually sustaining. According to Henri Marion, the workings of the human body were the earthly accompaniments of one's moral life in this world. Consequently, he asked, "If our primary concern should be to watch over all the conditions of our moral life, would it not be imprudent and absurd to neglect the care of our body? . . . Breathing clean air and getting moderate exercise in a healthy atmosphere freshen the mind and bring harmony to our feelings." This was a reciprocal relationship in that "all that which the soul experiences has an effect on the organism, and, for example, is reflected in the face; the face is the mirror of our emotions."[35] Exercise became a crucial node of the laic moral revolution. In his *Leçons de morale*, Marion insisted: "it is absolutely necessary that we be scrupulous in developing . . . our physical aptitudes. Each of us is obliged to keep our body intact and healthy, to fortify it, to make of it a docile and vigorous instrument for the moral life. . . . Is not an unhealthy and deficient body a less powerful and sometimes even rebellious instrument in the service of the will?"[36]

This new attention to physical and moral harmony was echoed in the republican curriculum's ubiquitous glorification of manual labor. The crucial links between body and mind underlined the moral consequences of physical work. An 1880 conference on hygiene claimed that work was morally and physically useful: "Physically, [idleness] brings trouble to the organism and becomes a fertile source of illnesses. . . . [It] weakens the best feelings, develops bad habits, causes a deadly boredom, and sometimes is the cause of reprehensible acts."[37] While the industrious man could look forward to a healthy body and respectable career, the idle man would find himself not only unhappy but also sickly. Paul Bert argued that manual labor should be a significant part of republican pedagogy, not simply so that students could leave primary school with a trade, but also because "according to the ancient adage, 'in a healthy body lodges a healthy soul,' and because bodily exercises and gymnastics are one of the conditions of health." By combining the practical use of tools with a study of the history of craft, artisanal classes would link "a veritable intellectual gymnastics" with the "physical gymnastics" of work.[38] "Workers of the mind," such as lawyers and scientists, were encouraged to engage in some form of daily exercise, as simple as walking or gardening.

Henri Marion and Paul Bert were not only textbook authors and government officials but also key architects of the secular teacher training program for women. In 1881 Marion took charge of the *morale* classes at the first national women's normal school, an institution charged with training the teaching staff of the provincial normal schools.[39] Bert was the founder of the women's laic normal school in Auxerre (Yonne). Historian Jo Burr Margadant has examined the difficulties facing this generation of teachers (particularly women) formed in these normal schools, who often found themselves far from home in remote provincial towns facing hostile local populations who resented the new secular Republic.[40] In this context, the well-defined social philosophy and pedagogical strategies learned at the normal schools could be invaluable weapons in daily instructional battles. In envisioning their future roles as teachers in 1878, two students at the École normale d'institutrices d'Auxerre (the school that Olympe Terrain would attend just a year later) underscored the importance of strengthening their students' bodies as well as their minds. In answering a question for her pedagogy course on the role of the teacher in the village, student teacher Félice Ramon wrote that the fortification and cleanliness of her students' bodies would be her first priority in her future school.[41] Noémi Rossignol, another third-year student answering the same question, maintained that physical education would greatly benefit the intellectual and moral work of the school. Rossignol was confident that exercise and physical labor during school hours would ensure the success of the admirable republican program of "Making healthy souls in healthy bodies." Charged with, as she saw it, the intellectual, physical, and moral development of her students, Rossignol envisioned that her students' bodies would be "fortified from a young age, made more supple through exercise," and that "the energy of their character will grow through bodily labor." She concluded that her future school would have "gymnastic exercises of the mind quite as methodical as those of the body."[42]

Novice teachers such as Ramon and Rossignol brought the moral philosophy of the normal school curriculum with them to the towns, cities, and villages where they took up their first positions. As village teachers, they were given a pivotal role in designing their new schools' curricula by way of cantonal pedagogical conferences. In the Yonne, at least, teachers showed a predilection for adding texts by those who had designed the normal school *programme*, such as Henri Marion and Paul Bert. In July 1883 a pedagogical committee in Saint-Sauveur added Marion's *Leçons de psychologie* and *Leçons de morale* to their revised list of texts for use in their primary schools—two of only four books deemed exceptional enough to add to the list under the heading of "Moral and Civic Instruction."[43] (And this just a year after *Leçons de morale* was censured by the Catholic Church.) In 1885 Jules Ferry ordered that all books on the national *morale laïque* lists be provided to regional pedagogical libraries and that copies of these books be circulated amongst all primary school teachers so that they could familiarize themselves with their contents.[44]

The theoretical union of body and soul acclaimed throughout teacher's training colleges and pedagogical conferences in the 1870s and 1880s took hold in France's primary schools through not only gym and *morale* classes but also numerous other aspects of the curriculum. Hygiene lessons, like those outlined by Dr. Constant Saucerotte in his *Petite hygiène des écoles* (1876), taught students to be assiduous in their physical maintenance, giving them chapters on exercise and nutrition, as well as chapters exploring elementary notions of biology and anatomy.[45] As Cherilyn Lacy has demonstrated, the Third Republican curriculum was especially keen to provide rudimentary medical knowledge to female students, as women were expected to assume a "para-medical" role within the family as wives and mothers.[46] In advertising his hygiene textbook, Dr. Saucerotte wrote that teachers "will not have completely accomplished their task if, in caring for the health of the soul, they utterly neglect that of the body, because the two hold one another: both are necessary for attaining our goals in this world, both are inseparable conditions of our happiness. . . . The health of a child, lest we forget, lies in a vigorous body, in robust arms, and the bread necessary to one's existence."[47]

Such a glorified view of the body and physical strength contrasted sharply with that of a hygiene manual soon dropped from republican curriculum lists: Dr. Descieux's *Leçons élémentaires d'hygiène*. Descieux linked the needs of physical hygiene to humanity's innate sinfulness, originating in Adam's fall: "Because of the disobedience of our first father . . . the human race was given over to concupiscence, to sickness and to death. Since that is the origin of all misfortunes, of all the evils that afflict humanity, hygiene must take this into account."[48] Good physical hygiene was linked inextricably to good moral standing, a relationship that hygiene books such as those of Saucerotte also promoted, but without the same obsessive attention to man's wickedness. Descieux's hygiene manual focused on sinfulness as an unavoidable and ultimately unmanageable drain on the human body. Descieux continued:

> When life is prolonged, one sees fall all around him the majority of those that one loves . . . relatives, father, mother. . . . It would be even too painful and too long to list all of the miseries that come, each moment, to disturb our lives. . . . We are born to suffer. . . . The hygienist has advice to give, but that advice can only agree with and be contained by that which does not harm the soul's faculties. This advice is linked, as always, with the true morality: that is, to be resigned.[49]

Unlike later hygiene manuals, Descieux's book portrayed humans as doomed to inhabit weak, sin-provoking bodies until death, when they would be freed into a blissful and disembodied existence in heaven. He also warned students that, for the sake of their health, they should avoid poisonous doctrines such as atheism and materialism; the only medical science necessary for one's bodily health was that which developed naturally from "divine revelation" and the Ten Commandments.[50] Not surprisingly, Descieux's hygiene book was replaced in reading lists in the years after 1878 by hygiene manuals that depicted human bodies working with, not against, the soul.

Apart from hygiene and gym classes, more general textbooks and primers also increasingly included readings that depicted girls and boys engaged in physical exercise and play. Clarisse Juranville's textbooks excerpted the journal of a female student who played so energetically at recess with another girl that she tore her dress. Another reading from the same book described girls at recess jumping rope and playing a game with a racquet.[51] Reading books now incorporated essays on cleanliness and bodily attention, as well as examinations of the human body.

Caumont's collection of stories for schoolchildren placed chapters on respiration, circulation, and digestion alongside traditional tales of work, family, and rural life. Her descriptions of the human body and its functions posited an endless cycle of rejuvenation and fortification.[52] Jost and Braeunig's *Lectures pratiques* (1881) illustrated their discussions of bodily processes with detailed diagrams of lungs, a heart, an eye, and a throat.[53] A lesson explaining the circulation of the blood included a directive that students put their fingers on their wrists to feel the pulsing of their arteries.[54]

One civic instruction book from 1879 by Charles Schuwer, designed to teach young French citizens their duties and rights, included extensive discussion of children's duties to their bodies, alongside those to God, country, and family. Schuwer told his young readers: "Your primary practical duties . . . are those which you fulfill toward yourselves . . . the first, toward your body; the second, toward your soul . . . in a word, to have *a healthy soul in a healthy body*."[55] Though nominally a book of civic instruction, focusing on the political and social duties of France's citizenry, Schuwer's manual went into some detail about the importance of physical exercise, both in work and in play. Like so many other authors used in the *école laïque*, Schuwer linked the gymnastics of the mind with those of the body, noting that physical *gymnastiques* "benefit not only your body but also your intelligence, which works better with supple organs."[56] Paul Rousselot's *L'École primaire* (1880) declared that gym classes formed more nimble students and redirected energies once expended in destructive wandering and marauding by feckless youth.[57] Augustin Pellissier's *Gymnastique de l'esprit*, a five-volume manual first published in 1875 that taught students all aspects of intellectual and moral development, consistently compared the mental work of the student's mind with physical gymnastics.[58] In one exercise, Pellissier used a kind of secular catechism to demonstrate the point:

> **Teacher:** How do you explain the skill of a gymnast?
> **Student:** The skill, the agility, and the strength that a gymnast demonstrates in bodily exercises are also the result of attention, of application, and of daily exercise.
> **Teacher:** Why is it that a good student does his lessons better and faster than others?
> **Student:** A good student does his lessons better and faster than others because he applies himself more seriously and gives more attention to his work.[59]

In this way, students learned that daily mental "gymnastics" fostered an intellectual agility akin to the physical training received by gymnasts.

The human body and its importance were concerns that had recently been added to the curriculum—a shift evident in examining two versions of Charles Defodon's book of *dictées* for French primary schools from 1867 and 1880. The 1880 version of Defodon's text contained several excerpts on manual professions, as well as lengthy discussions of the human body, its parts, and its functions. A dictation titled "Les Jambes" stated that a child's legs, while initially weak, gradually "acquire the firmness and strength necessary to permit him to walk[,] . . . run, and finally jump and dance. All our organs are involved. Exercise alone develops power, flexibility, elasticity, and energy."⁶⁰ This 1880 collection also included dictations depicting male and female schoolchildren engaged in various physical activities to enhance strength and agility, including running and gymnastic exercises on bars. By contrast, Defodon's 1867 collection contained no references to physical exercise, and not one dictation on the human body or its functions. Only one lesson, titled "Jeannette's Stomach," even remotely touched on such topics, though in this case, Jeannette was a goat.⁶¹

Admittedly, the implementation of republican gymnastic and hygienic ideals for boys and especially for girls varied drastically according to the teachers, administrators, and local resources of the school in question. Nonetheless, this novel approach to the physical body confronted male and female students in the Republic's primary schools across the curriculum, from gym and hygiene courses to those lessons dealing with civic instruction and reading. The new curricular emphasis helps at least partially explain the dramatic shift in French ideas about the body, gender, and work at the turn of the twentieth century, as this generation of students grew to become adult workers, cultural producers, and spectators. At the very least, female students formed by the *école laïque* were exposed to a language and social philosophy that took the body seriously as a tool of moral improvement.

La Méthode Intuitive

When the founders of the Third Republic secularized and modernized the primary school system in the 1870s and 1880s, they were driven by a conviction that the survival of their newborn secular state depended on not merely what the nation's children learned but also *how* they learned. Laic pedagogues and officials understood that in order to transform French society, changes in the curriculum had to be accompanied by an effective pedagogical method.⁶² Like some other less wholesale nineteenth-century European efforts to replace rote memorization with more animated teaching methods,⁶³ republicans provided a new approach to the educational process that cultivated children's imagination and judgment in novel and sometimes even subversive ways. The republican revolution in education thus did not stop at the exterior, physical health of French schoolchildren. Rather, through the promotion of new pedagogical techniques, often called the *méthode intuitive*, national officials and provincial teachers alike sought to give French children new secular interior lives.

Jan Goldstein's work on the "post-revolutionary self" in France demonstrates that the development and eventual dominance of Cousinian philosophy in the early decades of the nineteenth century posited a secular selfhood that offered an influential alternative to that of Catholic philosophy. While access to the Catholic self was only possible through the mediation of God, Victor Cousin's unitary secular self employed methods of introspection unbound by religious authority or inspiration. Cousinian psychology, in Goldstein's words, "opened up an inner space without" God, an interiority "as fully free, active, and even as awe-inspiring as its divine equivalent."[64] As Goldstein points out, this Cousinian self, institutionalized in the late nineteenth century in the French *lycée* system, was carefully marked off as the privilege of bourgeois men only. My study, however, indicates that even the Third Republic's predominantly working-class primary school system bore the imprint of this secular conception of selfhood. Despite the extensive historiography devoted to the Third Republic's educational reforms, few scholars have analyzed the way in which the interior lives of French schoolchildren were targeted by the secular instructional revolution. Yet primary school students were taught to seek a profound knowledge of their psychological workings and to cultivate a vibrant secular *vie intérieure* that both mimicked and challenged organized religion's role as moral compass.

The *méthode intuitive*, an educational approach that stressed the cultivation in schoolchildren of an inventive but ordered mental world, was the driving force of the Third Republican pedagogical revolution.[65] This method originated in the eighteenth century in Germany with influential pedagogical thinkers such as Basedow, Campe, and Pestalozzi. While the tenets of the *méthode intuitive* had been popularized in France by thinkers as far back as Rousseau, it only came to be used in a systematic way on a mass population of schoolchildren during the Third Republic. The radicalism of this method lay not in the approach itself but rather in its widespread use on a heavily working-class population and its explicitly secular conception of the interior life.[66] While many of the men and women who made up the advance guard of the Third Republic's secularization effort were themselves privately religious, discussion of religion was generally removed from the curriculum since it was believed that any mention of religion would help buttress the political and cultural power of the Catholic Church in France.[67]

Though the *méthode intuitive* was a subject of discussion and limited practice before 1870, it burst onto the educational scene after the fall of the Second Empire. A provincial teacher from the Aveyron named Galtiers who visited Paris's Exposition Universelle in 1878 remarked that, while there had been virtually no discussion of the *méthode intuitive* at the exposition in 1867, by 1878 examples and discussions of this method everywhere "imposed themselves on the eyes and the attention of visitors." Indeed, the method had become so popular that it necessitated its own conference at the Exposition scolaire.[68] Gabriel Compayré's *History of Pedagogy* (1879) provided the new Republic with an instructional pedigree by gathering writings on pedagogy dating back to antiquity, including Hindu, Confucian, and Buddhist teaching practices. Given the wide scope of his project, his decision to devote several large chapters to Pestalozzi and his successors Froebel and Pape-Carpentier, early purveyors of the *méthode intuitive*, attests to the immense popularity of the *méthode intuitive* in the 1870s and 1880s.[69]

The new pedagogy was first introduced to the teachers-in-training at the newly created secular normal schools, regional centers from which the ideas and practices of girls' secular education radiated out into the surrounding villages. Founded in 1872 as the first secular normal school for women in the Yonne, the École normale d'institutrices in Auxerre stood at the vanguard of new republican pedagogical ideas.[70] Students took up to eight hours a week of courses in pedagogy and *morale laïque*. (The neighboring men's *école normale* only spent six hours a week on these subjects.)[71] The normal school in Auxerre had so successfully instituted its new pedagogical curriculum that it was praised at the Exposition Universelle in 1878, and Paul Bert and other teachers from the school were awarded medals for their work.[72] According to a regional report on the instruction of *morale laïque* in the Yonne, the *normaliennes* of Auxerre learned a "méthode inductive" that would help them transform the mental worlds of their future students. Young teachers were told to free learning from "the tyrannical influence of routine" and instead rely on "the knowledge of the child's nature, the laws of his intellectual and moral evolution." Using this method, daily tasks in the communal school would "become less heavy" and would be "filled with a sort of joy."[73]

In practice, the new method replaced the system of rote memorization with *leçons de choses* (object lessons) in which students learned through contact with objects that they could smell, touch, see, and feel.[74] Instructors were encouraged to use educational walks (*promenades scolaires*) around the village and surrounding countryside as dynamic lessons to teach natural history, chemistry, physics, geography, and French.[75] Galtiers, the teacher from the Aveyron, wrote that, with the new method, an "instruction by words gives way to instruction by the eyes" because with it "the senses are called upon to receive the exterior impressions to transmit to the mind."[76] As part of a lengthy entry on *leçons de choses*, the *Dictionnaire de pédagogie* proclaimed that such exercises, which "habituate children to availing themselves of their senses and to observing," should form "the foundation and the soul of all elementary instruction."[77]

To this end, Third Republican primary schools were equipped with more visual materials, such as maps and artwork. As of 1878, instruction in drawing was made mandatory in some fashion for both primary and secondary instruction.[78] The government commission charged with improving the visual aspects of primary education in 1880 declared that "it is not enough to teach drawing in the schools; we must make of the school a museum in and of itself, a sort of sanctuary where beauty reigns as much as science and virtue."[79] This attention to students' aesthetic sensibility was an integral part of a pedagogical strategy that prioritized visual acuity. Miriam Levin notes that republican art education sought to discipline the relationship between students' senses and the outside world, helping them "cultivate the perceptual and organizational faculties of French citizens and provid[ing] them with a common, preverbal system for perceiving, communicating, and satisfying their needs."[80] The 1880 commission on *imagerie scolaire* gave this aspect of the curriculum a nationalist dimension, insisting that "our race is more apt than any other perhaps . . . to receive this education of art by the eyes and to profit from it."[81] In 1883 the Ministry of Public Instruction proposed that "the intelligence of the child can be aroused and expanded by the beauty of images that we put before their eyes. . . . The schoolhouse, instead of being gloomy like a prison, can be modestly decorated; it is easy to give the child, by way of rewards, images that will speak to his mind."[82] Levin notes that republican pedagogues in this period hoped that art education in their schools would teach children "to perceive a subjective, internal ordering of sensory experience and its equivalent in the external world of matter."[83]

Yet this effort to order the *vie intérieure* by way of meticulous attention to the *vie extérieure* was echoed not only in art education but throughout the republican curriculum, in exercises that sharpened children's faculty of observation with an instruction "by the eyes." A manual designed to teach judgment and reasoning to children between the ages of nine and thirteen suggested that the student append a sketch to every assignment, rendering "all that he sees, all that he remembers, all that he imagines, making drawing a constant auxiliary of thought, making it as familiar as writing."[84] The *méthode intuitive* also recommended the use of daily observation journals for students, and many primary schools instituted this practice. In one of her textbooks, Clarisse Juranville provided excerpts of her young students' daily journals to demonstrate how this exercise could be both highly individual and pedagogically fertile. One boy, finding nothing to write about, described his observations of a fly climbing a wall, and from this simple observation he proceeded to reflect on the nature of human work.[85] Such techniques, from art to nature walks, were meant to strengthen schoolchildren's faculty of observation, a skill deemed invaluable by the practitioners of the *méthode intuitive*. In her 1878 essay, teacher-in-training Félice Ramon addressed this objective in an imagined lesson to her future students:

> Close those well-worn books upon which your gaze sleeps; it looks as if they have extinguished the fire of your eyes! . . . I want to teach you to see nature . . . to observe [all things] from every side . . . to judge them so that you can conceive their *raison d'être*, or utility. . . . Geography will soon enough unfurl before your delighted eyes the magical picture of the earth's uneven surface, animated by industrious cities. . . . I want to make you know through observation, to understand through judgment and to love through the heart.[86]

The goal of such an education was not merely the acquisition of knowledge but the cultivation of students' ability to observe the sensory world.

In a speech to like-minded pedagogues in 1880, Paul Bert argued that this process, by which students learned habits of naturalist observation, would keep young men and women tied to their *pays natal* in a dynamic way (thereby somewhat assuaging concerns about urban migration). The new pedagogy taught rural children "to take a keen interest in the things around them," to "recognize all that is appealing in the study of the life of plants and animals," to "understand the story that the plants and the earth herself are telling them." Boys and girls would learn to find the sacred in a new secular context: "With science, no more superstitions will be possible, no more foolish hopes, no more of that simple-minded gullibility, of that belief in daily miracles and in the anarchy of nature." He encouraged his listeners to contemplate the sky at night: "you will gaze up at those stars flying in their regular orbiting paths, and you will think about all that astronomy has revealed to us about their distance and their speed. All this order in such an immensity—isn't that the permanent miracle!" He also described the marvel of the human body itself: "this miniscule aggregation of molecules of nitrogen, carbon, hydrogen, oxygen . . . in a corner of this incommensurable Universe . . . who thinks, who reflects, who compares, who measures the course of those great stars, whose imagination penetrates the outer limits of this vastness with its audacious calculations . . ."[87] In Bert's pedagogical program, then, Christian miracles would pale alongside those of the secular, observed universe. By learning to record and study the natural world, students would tap a wellspring of laic wonder.

In freeing the lower classes from the moral shackles of the Church, republican pedagogues understood that a vibrant *morale laïque* was required to replace Christianity's moral imperatives and to regenerate the nation.[88] New pedagogical methods, it was believed, could enact just such a transfiguration by exhorting teachers and students alike to turn their newly honed skills of observation inward to make an intensive, sensory study of their inner workings. Self-evaluation and introspection were not tools exclusive to the *méthode intuitive*. Catholic pedagogues such as Bishop Félix Dupanloup utilized introspective methods with their students well before the Third Republic. Republican educational institutions, however, distanced these methods from devotional exercises and instead concentrated on connecting the interior, moral world with the exterior, physical world. No longer obliged to invoke supernatural aid in the teaching of morality, teachers needed only to turn their students' attentive skills of observation inward. Théodore Barrau's *Morale pratique* encouraged the primary school student to spend time each day engaging in a self-examination, "going over in his mind that which he did, said, heard, observed in the preceding day . . . to descend into the soul, to meditate, to recall all that one has seen, noticed, learned . . . to the profit or disadvantage of the body, of the mind, of the soul." The student was told to pose the following question to each day: "In what way have you benefited my physical, moral, and intellectual perfection, my happiness?"[89] Through this daily process of reflection and introspection, a method that republican pedagogues conceded they had inherited from religious *examens de conscience*,[90] students could perfect their spiritual, intellectual, and, significantly, physical selves.

Unlike comparable Catholic exercises, which directed children's thoughts away from their bodies and the material world, republican textbooks taught students that by combining observations of the sensory world with an inward examination, they could control their own development. Third-year *normalienne* Noémi Rossignol wrote that the fledgling teacher could best conduct the "gymnastics of the mind" in her classrooms by beginning with a sensory study of her own interior life: "she begins by studying herself in the present and in the past, she seeks to recall the first sensations of her childhood, the causes and the consequences of her impressions. . . . [Then] she brings this investigation to bear on that of her students."[91] By systematically recalling the physical and emotional sensations of her childhood, this teacher would be better equipped to guide her students' physical and emotional development. Charles Delon, a pedagogue who published texts on the *méthode intuitive*, created a primer used in the Yonne and around France that expressed this same process of moral and physical self-perfection, telling students: "You can perfect yourself in everything. You can exercise your organs, widen your intelligence, and, most important, become better each day. . . . You can do this, you must. It is only a matter of wanting [it]."[92] This secular self-exploration, then, differed from its Catholic predecessor in that inward reflection here was connected to a contemporary attention to sensory surroundings as well as attention to the sensations and state of the physical body.

Yet keen observation alone was insufficient. Many pedagogues agreed with the warning of the *Dictionnaire de pédagogie* (1887) that the student should not be "reduced to a passive and purely receptive role as observer."[93] Thus, the secular soul would ally this sharpened faculty of observation with free judgment and independent thought. In contrast to its Catholic counterpart, republican moral instruction, wrote one pedagogue, "will no longer be a formulary recited as lip service but an inner and profound acquisition of the soul . . . in which thought and free reflection will no longer be distrusted."[94] One provincial teacher praised the new *méthode intuitive* because it "speeds up the faculty of reflection by forcing the child to compare, to examine, to judge." He approved of this new "rational and fecund" method that encouraged children to learn based on their own judgments rather than on the lifeless words they read in textbooks.[95] According to the *Dictionnaire de pédagogie* (1887), a child's mental faculties should be allowed, like their physical body, "to run free, to frolic according to his/her liking."[96] In a speech given in 1880, Paul Bert pointed out that, through the use of object lessons, a young student would become "used to observing, not just taking people at their word, examining the facts . . . comparing, analyzing."[97] Thus *leçons de choses*, more than simply improving skills of observation, were to be the basis for refined, fortified individual judgment and will.

In an essay on female education for the *Revue Pédagogique* in 1880, Paul Rousselot specifically urged training girls to exercise free will and self-reflection.[98] He described, for instance, how such sharpened faculties would be useful when a girl on the cusp of adulthood was faced with the difficult decision of choosing a profession. She would consult her friends and family about the various "open paths" available to her and then begin a process of self-questioning. "At last," Rousselot writes, "she chooses, rightly or wrongly; she says: 'I want.' This is an appropriate action of the will, and consists of reflective and free determination. Reflective, for she has only made this decision after an examination of the question from all sides. Free, because the will is a force that evades all constraint."[99] This glorification of will and individual judgment manifests itself here in a startling form—an educated young woman weighing her professional options and acting according to the simple formula, "I want." Rousselot hastened to add that, of course, children needed to be taught that free will was limited by exterior factors and authorities. Nevertheless, he called upon educators to reinforce such qualities in their female students—and did so against a backdrop of presumed female professionalism that contrasted sharply with other compelling republican feminine models of motherhood and self-sacrifice.

Along with free judgment and fine-tuned skills of observation, an active and rich imagination was seen as a crucial acquisition of the new secular soul. Buisson's *Dictionnaire de pédagogie* demanded that children's imaginations be given wide berth, because the "pedagogy of a free country" should provide each student with "a constant prodding toward activity by way of exercises open to his particular ingenuity; to his spirit of resourcefulness, discovery and invention; to his artistic faculties of composition."[100] Republican textbooks focused a great deal of attention on the imagination, sometimes devoting entire manuals to its cultivation.[101] In 1887 a schoolteacher in the Yonne assessed the use of imagination in his region's primary schools and concluded that the imagination was "the creative power *par excellence*. Not only does it evoke memories, but it combines them in such a way that it makes of them new creations whose artificial reality provides us with the picture of an imaginary world, an absolute domain of fantasy and ideal. Without it, human intelligence would remain sterile."[102]

One textbook from the 1880s told students that they had a duty to cultivate their imagination "by personal reflection, by the advice of men of taste, by the examples of poets and artists; it is a duty to learn to grasp the beauty of things, to appreciate them, to savor them."[103] When used properly, one teacher wrote, imagination could be a "powerful auxiliary" for a wide range of academic subjects because it allowed students to see the places and people they studied "with the eyes of the mind."[104] In his instructions to primary school teachers using his textbooks, pedagogue Augustin Pellissier insisted that student imagination be granted substantial latitude, since it was a priceless learning tool. "Individual inventions," Pellissier wrote, "are aids that we must not neglect." Children's mental inventions naturally adapted themselves to the particular aptitude of the child and were, Pellissier contended, often far more effective than other learning tools.[105]

Henri Marion's psychology manual for new teachers declared that, when ordered and reasonable, the imagination could "render us inventive and ingenious . . . make us see very sharply and feel very strongly, [and] increase our energy for action." Because a healthy imagination was the natural accompaniment of a strong mind, Marion continued, the imagination should not be extinguished in the child but allowed to grow to its full strength. Children whose imaginative capabilities were feeble were often "more dull, more mediocre, less capable of . . . understanding quickly and of feeling sharply." Teachers were urged to excite the imagination of the lazy student, "by making the child see diverse and grandiose spectacles, by making him travel, by having him read good pieces of brilliant prose or poetry." Marion insisted that the imagination should be fostered, treated not as an enemy but as "the driving force of all our intellectual life."[106]

Reflecting the heightened interest in the imagination, textbooks from this period often incorporated exercises and readings to enhance children's imaginative capabilities. Charles Delon's primer recommended that children perform a mental exercise in which they visualized a perfect adult being, gifted with a healthy body, a strong will, and a rich imagination. The child then was instructed to go a step further: "Search, in your reverie, to visualize a child like you. Imagine him as intelligent, as reasonable, and as educated as is suitable to his age. Give him, in your mind, all the talents, all the qualities that a child can have. Imagine him so sweet, so gracious, and so kind that if he existed, you would want to be his friend. This will be your ideal, and you will tell yourself, 'That is what I want to be.'"[107] Through a careful, imaginative conjuring of their ideal being in the mental realm, children thus could organize their success in the material world. Even in more scientific lessons about natural phenomena, Delon suggested students combine physical observation with imaginative exercises. In order to learn about the sun and the solar system, the imagination could be as useful as a telescope: "Imagine," one exercise instructed readers, "a globe of immense fire, completely enveloped by flames. This globe, blazing like a cannonball that one has drawn out of the forge completely red, radiates heat and light all around it. It warms like a hearth, it lights like a torch."[108] Another textbook suggested developing a student's imagination by putting him in the "presence of one of the great spectacles of nature," exposing him to a flurry of primal emotions, and then leading him "to read and grasp within himself the natural seeds of those emotions, to know them, to understand them."[109] Such exercises, appearing throughout the textbooks of the period, called on children to conceive of the unfathomable using sensory memories from their own everyday world.

Republican pedagogues explicitly linked the enrichment of the mental life and the joys of hard work. "Work," declared an instructional manual for teachers, "gives ideas a rapid and lively flow. . . . It expands intelligence, enriches elevated, poetic feelings, and multiplies the sources of happiness."[110] The *Dictionnaire de pédagogie* explained that those in society who "work ardently to attain the object of their exertions" were those who could "imagine it with vivacity."[111] Thus, honest labor and the imaginative workings of the mind were complementary functions of a healthy student, male or female. Marion indicated that those with a "sickly" imagination should devote themselves to a regular task of some sort, as "work thus calms the soul."[112] Again and again instructional texts from this period used images of manual labor to describe the interior life. The process of self-perfection seemed to lend itself easily to such analogies. In one tale, a father suggests that his son think of interior self-improvement as a large field covered in thorns that must be cleared: if taken all at once, the task is disheartening; when taken patch by patch, the field can be cleared. Another lesson quoted Benjamin Franklin envisioning the process of self-improvement as the weeding of a garden.[113]

Though exhorting the cultivation of a rich imagination and mental life, republican officials, teachers, and pedagogues were concerned, like their predecessors, with the dangers inherent in an immoderate imagination—a weakness that they closely associated with Catholic superstition and irrational femininity. Ruth Harris postulates that Third Republicans' potent anticlericalism "in fact structured the very conception of the 'unconscious'" employed by the fiercely secular world of French psychiatry at the fin de siècle. If, as Harris contends, "French attitudes to mind-body relations . . . were pervaded by Catholic ideas and practices,"[114] the result in the field of education was both a guardedness about the interior life and a recognition of its extreme importance in the anticlerical renovation under way in French society. From the pedagogical perspective, fostering ordered and reasoned student imaginations that could resist the ecstatic excesses of Catholic piety became a paramount concern.

To this end, young women at the secular normal school in Auxerre were called upon to replace "the instinctive life with the reasonable life . . . to create in themselves first, and then in their students, an interior life which must manifest itself by just thoughts, a right conscience, by good habits."[115] Jules Payot's primary school textbook urged young readers to discipline their imaginations: "Your freedom begins when you intervene and *oblige* your ideas and your feelings to participate not as they want, *but as you want them to*."[116] Imagination could only have a positive transfiguring power when disciplined. Some textbooks proposed the mythological Antiope as a model of feminine behavior, a girl whose imagination was nicely ordered: "Antiope is a treasure worthy of being sought in the farthest lands. Her mind, no more than her body, was not adorned with vain ornaments; her imagination, while lively, was restrained by her discretion."[117] While the *Dictionnaire de pédagogie* defined the imagination in ecstatic terms, calling it "the most respectable, the highest, and the most precious of human faculties," it also noted that one needed "to rule it with reason in order to preserve it from lunacies."[118]

Imaginative exercises, then, often had a dual goal: to enrich the imaginative scope of France's schoolchildren but also to restrain and direct the development of children's imagination. One teacher from the Yonne counseled his colleagues that given the enormous influence of the imagination, it was crucial as an educator "to master it and regulate it, to direct it, to provide it with wholesome foods, to open pathways toward uprightness and decency." The teacher should "ensure that the first impressions of [his students'] imaginations are healthy and moral."[119] Because the imagination could lead to either "the greatest good or the greatest evil," Henri Marion wrote that it needed to be regulated by reason and "supervised with infinite care."[120] Augustin Pellissier defended the extensive treatment of the imagination in his manuals by exclaiming: "To what deplorable distractions has the Public Imagination abandoned itself, and what unbridled taste of the majority for dull, coarse, inane, and obscene works! From the beginning of life, one must cultivate the Imagination by casting there the seeds of a purer, more enlightened taste."[121]

Pedagogues soothed such concerns about excessive imagination by binding all imaginative flights firmly to the sensory, natural world with observation skills honed on the *leçons des choses*. In addition, republican instructional texts were sometimes constructed in such a way as to discipline their young readers' imaginative faculties. Pellissier's textbook insisted that "The Imagination is not, as we too commonly think, a totally spontaneous faculty, having no other law than caprice: it has laws just like reasoning does."[122] To this end, Pellissier's instructional volume on the imagination was organized like a dialogue akin to a Catholic catechism. Though the subjects were secular, the question-and-answer format was a means by which teachers could train this faculty in a sound direction. Pellissier included questions and instructions for teachers to accompany each reading, to remind them "of the logical order to follow in the examination of an object, from the point of view of the Imagination."[123] After every reading, the child was asked to give his general impression of the piece, to describe its principal qualities, and then to offer physical and moral analogies and contrasts. With such exercises, the teacher would "be sure his lesson has been understood" and would drill students' imaginations toward an effective ordering of sensory material.[124] Though rote memorization was repeatedly lambasted by Pellissier, he nonetheless avowed that the goal of his textbook was to "habituate our children to observing well in order to see well, by making them learn by heart these models of imaginative analysis."[125] Ferdinand Buisson agreed, claiming that the new methods would train children's minds with "a sort of intellectual gymnastics" that would dictate "the form and order of questions to ask themselves" when faced with any object.[126] Thus, the new secular primary schools offered, in both their content and practice, a novel interior life—at once liberated from religious strictures and also bound to empirical observation of the natural world and to regular labor.

Such an attention to the control of the imagination suggests a recognition on the part of republican pedagogues that the moral and intellectual renovation they were attempting might have destructive effects if not handled properly. More than simply recloaking Catholic instructional precepts in secular language, the *méthode intuitive* offered students interior lives characterized by individuality, inventiveness, and independent thought. Pedagogues hoped that this bolstered sense of individual judgment and intellectual training would help separate students, particularly girls, from the superstition and parochialism of the Church and encourage them not to rebel against the sanctioned authorities of the Republic. In its very ambiguity, however, this pedagogy opened up a unique space for critical thought and challenge in the minds of the very schoolchildren it sought to train in obedience and patriotic duty.

* * *

National and departmental officials had a keen interest in evaluating how widely the new pedagogy and its emphases were being employed at the local level. In the 1877 inspection of primary public education in the Yonne, the inspector expressed dissatisfaction that several teachers were still using rote memorization.[127] By 1889, however, use of the *méthode intuitive* and *leçons de choses* was noted throughout the Yonne by the inspector. Students were observed in *morale* classes using daily journals to describe a gradual process of moral improvement. Teachers were noted using excerpts from pedagogical journals in their classrooms. In Toucy, a town near Saint-Sauveur, the inspector remarked approvingly that the "instruction is directly from teacher to child. It is by such an analysis of moral facts, by the call to feeling, to observation, to reflection, that one attempts to pull from the child himself the principles that we wish to teach him."[128] Teachers in this school used examples from students' everyday life to develop more abstract ideas. Primary school teachers in Auxerre used "small stories" from children's everyday lives to "move them, to touch their hearts and to have born in their souls a feeling for the just and the good."[129]

Despite their sometimes isolated existence in rural village schools, young teachers remained linked to the republican educational community through professional associations, school alumni organizations, pedagogical and professional journals, republican festivals, and departmental conferences. Olympe Terrain offers a useful illustration of the way in which republican pedagogical culture could take root in even the smallest provincial village. A graduate of Paul Bert's normal school in Auxerre, Terrain was a woman devoted to the vocation of girls' secular instruction and particularly well versed in the new pedagogy. In October 1887, while teaching, Terrain obtained the *certificat d'aptitude pédagogique*, a degree only created in 1884. By 1887, only 17 out of the Yonne's 213 public women teachers could boast this specialized degree in pedagogy.[130] Teachers such as Terrain were kept abreast of developments in instruction through the creation, in the 1870s, of a *bulletin scolaire*, which the department sent to all primary public school teachers.[131] She could also take advantage of the two regional pedagogical libraries constructed in Sens and Auxerre in the 1870s for use by primary school teachers. In addition, secular teachers were offered half-price rail tickets to facilitate their attendance at national events such as the Exposition Universelle.[132] As a result of bulletins, conferences, and expositions of this kind, Olympe Terrain was kept firmly linked to the departmental and national pedagogical community and was able to follow trends in educational reform even in retirement in the late 1930s.[133]

But the corps of secularly trained teachers were not the only champions of the new pedagogy. Students such as Colette were part of a culture of instruction that stretched far beyond the schoolroom walls. Colette's father exemplifies the way in which Third Republican educational reforms, and specifically innovative pedagogy, helped define political and cultural activity in this period.[134] The captain was a literate, cosmopolitan, and colorful figure in the small provincial town, as well as an engaged if moderate republican who took to the barricades as a student in 1848, and in his early years as tax collector he came under criticism from his superiors in the government for his very public support of republican opposition to Napoleon III.[135] In 1880 Captain Colette retired from his position as tax collector, in part to pursue a run as a republican education candidate for the Conseil général de l'Yonne. He had been inspired by the educational demonstrations at the Exposition Universelle of 1878, especially the *méthode intuitive* presented by Caroline Kleinhan (which taught geography through extensive map drawing).[136] Gabrielle accompanied her father to the exposition and witnessed firsthand this showcase of the Third Republic's wonders, pedagogical and otherwise. (This was, remember, the same exposition at which the schoolteacher Galtiers noted that discussions of the new method everywhere "imposed themselves on the eyes.")[137]

New pedagogical methods were the centerpiece of Captain Colette's campaign for the Conseil général two years later, a political strategy that might seem unusual if not understood in the context of the wide cultural significance of educational questions in 1880s France. Gabrielle assisted in her father's presentations at country schools, during which he demonstrated new instructional methods and proudly presented his daughter, according to one biographer, as "the model of what a good lay education could do for women."[138] Colette later recalled the "delight" and self-importance she experienced when campaigning with her father, and decades later she could still remember her father's "propaganda": "I shall conquer the people by educating them; I shall instruct young people and children in the sacred names of natural history, physics and elementary chemistry. I shall go forth brandishing the magic lantern and the microscope."[139] Thus, the Captain founded his political platform on the practice of the new pedagogy and its potential as a panacea for social discontent.

Though his political campaign was unsuccessful, Jules Colette continued to take an interest in education from his position as a municipal councilman in Saint-Sauveur from 1881 until he and his family moved from the town in 1891. His name appears on many of the communal registers of council debates and meetings, particularly those initiating the wide-ranging renovation of Saint-Sauveur's schools in the 1880s, in an effort to make the commune's schools resemble more closely the national models set forth by the republican administration. He counted among his friends the Gambettist politician and Minister of Public Instruction Paul Bert, who lived in nearby Auxerre with his wife and daughters. Young Gabrielle was the Bert daughters' occasional playmate, and many years later she fondly remembered her time with these shining examples of girls' secular schooling.[140] When a statue of Bert was erected in Auxerre in 1888 following the local hero's untimely death, Jules Colette composed an *Ode à Paul Bert*, delivered at the ceremony by Gabrielle.[141]

As the captain's quixotic political career demonstrates, laic pedagogy was being applied throughout French society, not only in the schoolhouse but also in expositions, public libraries, regional literary journals, and adult education programs. More than simply an exciting trend in primary education, pedagogical innovations were a fundamental part of the republican cultural offensive that bled over into multiple aspects of public life. Republican festivals that centered around the school calendar—such as that inaugurating Saint-Sauveur's schools in 1890—also made republican pedagogy more than a mere educational issue. Such events indicate the way in which pedagogical culture had become in the 1870s and 1880s the cornerstone of an associative life that linked state, department, village, family, and child.

* * *

Though organized as a coherent curriculum, the educational maxims of the Third Republican pedagogical revolution presented some sharp contradictions for the millions of students it sought to mold into right-thinking citizens. Educational officials themselves became uneasy with the radical nature of their own reforms after this first phase of pedagogical innovation. Félix Pécaut later reflected (using an appropriately corporeal turn of phrase) that the pedagogical revolution had taught France's children "many new but imperfectly digested things."[142] One pedagogical conference in 1878 foretold the risk that the government took by exposing the working classes to such an elevated instruction: "We have understood that the more [the popular classes] were enlightened, the more they would have a consciousness of their duties, but at the risk of becoming at the same time more demanding regarding their rights. Let us not forget . . . that an educated people can govern itself."[143] The Republic was constructed on ideals of liberty, equality, and fraternity, but the ruling bourgeoisie was less than comfortable with the idea of handing the reins of power over to any of the marginal groups they claimed to be liberating from the Church, such as workers and women. Republican ideology, and as a result, republican pedagogy, had this contradiction at its core. Indeed, many of the same pedagogues and officials who worked tirelessly to establish girls' *écoles laïques* and women's normal schools with innovative and secular curricula saw nothing hypocritical about combining such efforts with an aggressive defense of traditional gender roles and, in some cases, deeply antifeminist assessments of women's intellectual capacities.[144]

The preceding analysis has attempted to penetrate not merely the discourse of early Third Republican pedagogy but also the way in which this discourse pervaded the concrete learning experience of schoolchildren during this period. The republican curriculum offered a very particular set of mental tools to this generation. Both the intentions of the republican instructional hierarchy and the unforeseen tensions created by these intentions need to be taken into account when examining the way in which graduates of this school system envisioned their intellectual and physical lives. Republican educational maxims presented a number of intellectual inconsistencies for Gabrielle Colette. As the bourgeois daughter of a dedicated republican family educated amongst the petit bourgeois and peasant children of her village, Colette was caught between the ideals of an elite bourgeois society attempting to foster its own hegemony and a rural working-class society experiencing the growing pains of industrial modernization and the pedagogical indoctrination of their bourgeois *concitoyens*. Colette was exhorted to work hard and save money, while at the same time to distance herself from the realm of commercial work as a *femme au foyer*. She was told to eschew immobility and to fortify her body through constant physical activity, even as popular culture and science pathologized the female body. She was encouraged to use honed skills of exterior observation to cultivate her imagination and enrich her intellect, even though, as a woman, her most valuable creation was expected to be healthy offspring and a blissful and efficient household. Though the changes wrought by this educational system would not be fully felt until well into the twentieth century, the boundaries of respectable femininity had already been redrawn and broadened by an ideological movement that challenged (if unwittingly) traditional assumptions about the relationship between the physical and moral, individual expression and judgment, and the rigidity of class difference.

Notes

The author thanks the Western Society for French History for allowing the reprinting of portions of an article that appeared as "Wholesome Imaginations: Pedagogy in the Early Third Republic," in the *Proceedings of the Western Society for French History* 29 (2003).

1. Quoted in Gabriel Compayré, *The History of Pedagogy*, trans. W. H. Payne (1879; London, 1888), xx. Translated by W.H. Payne (London, 1888) Originally *Histoire critique des doctrines de*

l'éducation en France depuis le seizième Siècle (1879). Pécaut's quote was from the *Revue Pédagogique* 2 (1882).

2. Compayré, *History of Pedagogy*, xx.

3. On similar efforts in Germany, the United States, and Great Britain, see Andy Green, *Education and State Formation*; Lamberti, *Elementary School in Imperial Germany*; Derek S. Linton, "Reforming the Urban Primary School in Wilhelmine Germany," *History of Education* 13, no. 3 (1984): 207–19; James Albisetti, *Schooling German Girls and Women: Secondary and Higher Education in the Nineteenth Century* (Princeton, NJ, 1988).

4. Robert Gildea, *France, 1870–1914* (New York, 1996), 80.

5. See Furet and Ozouf, *Lire et écrire, Tome 2*, 175. They assert that the educational conflicts between the Church and the State such as those in the Third Republic had little effect on broader trends in the expansion of literacy (350).

6. See Robert Nye, *Crime, Madness, and Politics in Modern France: The Medical Concept of National Decline* (Princeton, NJ, 1984); and Ruth Harris, *Murder and Madness: Medicine, Law, and Society in the Fin de Siècle* (New York, 1989). For a review of studies of French physical education, see Marcel Spivak, "Quelques aperçues de la recherche en histoire de l'éducation physique et des sports en France," *Histoire de l'Éducation* 10 (1981): 1–19.

7. Gilbert Andrieu, "La gymnastique de plancher: Une pratique pour une bourgeoisie se preparant à prendre pouvoir?" *Stadion* 11, no. 1 (1985): 56. Also see Gilbert Andrieu, *L'homme et la force* (Joinville-le-Pont, 1988).

8. Georges Vigarello, *Le Sain et le Malsain: Santé et mieux-être depuis le Moyen Âge* (Paris, 1993), 241, 277.

9. For a general discussion of the rise of sport and physical fitness in nineteenth-century Europe, see Georges Vigarello, "Hygiène du corps et travail d'apparences," and Georges Vigarello and Richard Holt, "Le corps travaillé: Gymnastes et sportifs au XIXe siècle," in *Histoire du corps: Tome 2, De la Révolution à la Grande Guerre*, ed. Alain Corbin, Jean-Jacques Courtine, and Georges Vigarello (Paris, 2005).

10. Jacques Defrance, *L'excellence corporelle: La formation des activités physiques et sportives modernes, 1770–1914* (Rennes, 1987), 166–67. Defrance holds that this was only a temporary difference.

11. Ibid.

12. Derek Linton demonstrates that pedagogical reform in German schools took place around this time, but piecemeal, not as part of a national initiative, and fitness became a concern only in the 1890s. See "Reforming the Urban Primary School."

13. See André Rauch, *Le Souci du Corps: Histoire de l'hygiène en éducation physique* (Paris, 1983); Pierre Arnaud, ed., *Les Athlètes de la République: Gymnastique, sport, et idéologie républicaine, 1870/1914* (Paris, 1997); and Mary Lynn Stewart, *For Health and Beauty*.

14. See Stock-Morton, *Moral Education*, 105. She writes that some teachers continued to use the texts, and some "even met to condemn the condemnations" (105).

15. Vigarello, *Le Sain et le Malsain*, 232. Also see Mary Lynn Stewart, *For Health and Beauty*, and Georges Vigarello, *Le corps redressé: Histoire d'un pouvoir pédagogique* (Paris, 2001).

16. See Georges Vigarello, *Concepts of Cleanliness: Changing Attitudes in France Since the Middle Ages*, trans. Jean Birrell (New York, 1988).

17. Charles Schuwer, *L'École civique: Les droits & les devoirs de l'enfant, de l'homme, du citoyen* (Orange, Vaucluse, 1879), 17. This text was on the *Listes des ouvrages scolaires admis par les Conférences Cantonales d'Instituteurs et d'Institutrices du Département de l'Yonne, 1880–1881*, ADY 37 T 1.

18. Dr. E. Pécaut, "Hygiène scolaire," in Buisson, *Dictionnaire de pédagogie*, part 1, 1:1307.

19. Dr. Riant, "Conférence sur l'hygiène de l'école," in Bès, *L'Exposition universelle*, AN F/17/9388.

20. Gilbert Andrieu, "L'influence de la gymnastique suédoise sur l'éducation physique en France," *Stadion* 14, no. 2 (1988): 168.

21. AN F/17/9389, *New Orleans 1884–1885*.

22. Stewart, *For Health and Beauty*, 159.

23. Buisson, "Filles," in Buisson, *Dictionnaire de pédagogie*, part 1, 1:1020.

24. Paul Rousselot, "La Pédagogie dans les écoles de filles, à propos du concours d'admission aux fonctions de directrice d'école normale," *Revue Pédagogique* (July-December 1879): 562. Rousselot (1833–1914) was a philosophy professor and inspector for the Academy of Nancy and Amiens.

25. Ibid., 563–64.

26. Ministère de l'Instruction Publique, *Manuel de gymnastique à l'usage des écoles primaires et secondaires de filles et des écoles normales primaires d'institutrices* (Paris, 1881). Another gymnastics manual especially for girls was Antonin Louis, *Chants et exercices de gymnastiques pour les jeunes filles, suivis de la chanson des jeux, avec paroles* (Paris, 1885).

27. *Écoles normales: Programmes*, November 1884, AN F/17/9680.

28. Defrance, *L'excellence corporelle*, 146–58.

29. *Écoles normales: Programmes*, November 1884, AN F/17/9680.

30. Marise Querlin, "L'École de Claudine," *Marianne*, 19 January 1938.

31. Stewart, *For Health and Beauty*, 159.

32. Henri Marion, *Leçons de psychologie: Appliquées à l'éducation* (Paris, 1882), 24.

33. Dr. E. Pécaut, "Hygiène scolaire," 1302.

34. Georges Dumesnil, "Cours d'instruction morale et civique, (suite)," *Revue Pédagogique* 2 (February 1882): 146–47. Dumesnil was a philosophy teacher in Valenciennes. See Rousselot, "La Pédagogie"; Paul Soquet, "De l'Éducation intellectuelle, morale et physique," *Revue Pédagogique* (July-December 1880): 327–50. For more on the *Revue Pédagogique*, see Ognier, *L'École républicaine*.

35. Marion, *Leçons de psychologie*, 26–28.

36. Henri Marion, *Leçons de morale* (Paris, 1884), 198. An earlier edition appeared in 1882. *Révision de la liste des ouvrages scolaires de l'Yonne, Saint-Sauveur-en-Puisaye, 1882–1883*, 21 July 1883, ADY 37 T 1.

37. *Onzième Conférence*, "Le Travail," AN F/17/11782.

38. Paul Bert, "L'Instruction dans une démocratie," lecture given at Le Havre (Cercle Franklin), 21 March 1880, in *Leçons, discours, et conférences*, 402–3.

39. Stock-Morton refers to teachers complaining in 1882 that Marion's *morale* program was too sophisticated for some normal school students. See *Moral Education*, 103.

40. See Margadant, *Madame le Professeur*; Gemie, *Women and Schooling*.

41. "Du rôle de l'Institutrice dans sa commune," Félice Ramon, eighteen years old, third-year student. *Conseil général de l'Yonne, deuxième session de 1878, Rapport sur le service de l'Instruction Primaire dans le département*, ADY 31 T 2. Terrain attended this school from 1879 to 1882.

42. "Du rôle de l'institutrice dans sa commune. Des moyens qu'elle doit employer pour y augmenter discrètement son influence. Du bien qu'elle peut en doit y faire." Noémi Rossignol, third-year student, École normale d'institutrices in Auxerre, 12 April 1878, AN F/17/9277.

43. *Révision de la Liste des ouvrages scolaires admis . . . dans les écoles primaires publiques de l'Yonne, Saint-Sauveur-en-Puisaye, 1882–1883*, Conférence pédagogique, 21 July 1883, ADY 37 T 1.

44. Jules Ferry, *Circulaire relative à l'enseignement morale dans les écoles primaires*, 17 November 1885, AN F/17/11630.

45. Constant Saucerotte, *Petite hygiène des écoles: Simples notions sur les soins que réclame la conservation de la santé* (Paris, 1876).

46. Cherilyn Lacy, "Science or Savoir-Faire? Domestic Hygiene and Medicine in Girls' Public Education," *Proceedings of the Annual Meeting of the Western Society for French History* 24 (1997): 28.

47. Saucerotte, *Petite hygiène des écoles*, 6–7. Earlier editions of Saucerotte's manual were published before the Third Republic, and it was reprinted throughout the 1890s.

48. Dr. Descieux, *Leçons élémentaires d'hygiène* (Paris, 1875), 139.

49. Ibid., 169–70.

50. Ibid., 141.

51. Juranville, *Premiers sujets*, 13, 2–3.

52. Caumont, *Lectures courantes des écoliers francais* (Paris, 1884). Caumont was the pen name of Mme. Alfred Mézières (Anne-Marie-Louise Lardenois de Caumont).

53. Jost and Braeunig, *Lectures pratiques*, 11, 12, 20, 34, 39. Earlier editions appeared on curricular lists in the Yonne as of 1880. *Listes des ouvrages scolaires . . . département de l'Yonne, pendant l'année scolaire 1880–1881*, ADY 37 T 1.

54. Jost and Braeunig, *Lectures pratiques*, 15.

55. Schuwer, *L'École civique*, 15–16.

56. Ibid., 20–21.

57. Paul Rousselot, *L'École primaire: Essai de pédagogie élémentaire* (Paris, 1880), 63.

58. Augustin Pellissier, *La Gymnastique de l'esprit (méthode maternelle), 3e partie: Directions pour la mémoire et l'imagination* (Paris, 1887), 9. The book began appearing in the Yonne curriculum the year it was first published, 1875. See *Liste générale des livres classiques en usage dans les écoles publiques, 1875* (Yonne); *Liste des livres proposés pour être mis en usage dans les écoles primaires publiques du département de l'Yonne*, 10 August 1880, ADY 37 T 1.

59. Pellissier, *Gymnastique de l'esprit, 3e partie*, 9.

60. Defodon and Vallée, *Petites dictées*, 111–12.

61. Charles Defodon, *Cours de dictées: Adaptés à la grammaire des écoles primaires* (Paris, 1867), 90.

62. Stock-Morton discusses this issue in *Moral Education*, 155–65.

63. On broader pedagogical change in modern Europe, see Maynes, *Schooling in Western Europe*. Linton notes some of the same pedagogical interests in primary schools in Germany, but such reforms stayed at the level of local experiments. See "Reforming the Urban Primary School."

64. Jan Goldstein, *The Post-Revolutionary Self: Politics and Psyche in France, 1750–1850* (Cambridge, MA, 2005), 245.

65. For a comprehensive definition see "Intuition et méthode intuitive," in Buisson, *Dictionnaire de pédagogie*, part 1, 2:1374–77.

66. See Pierre Giolitto's discussion of the intuitive method in *Histoire de l'enseignement primaire*, 1: 259–61. The Third Republic both owed a debt to reforms under Guizot and diverged from them. See Pierre Rosanvallon, *Le Moment Guizot* (Paris, 1985), and Douglas Johnson, *Guizot: Aspects of French History, 1787–1874* (Toronto, 1963).

67. Many of the Third Republic's leading pedagogues were themselves liberal Protestants. See Stock-Morton, *Moral Education*, 91.

68. "Gymnastique des sens—méthode intuitive," *Rapport sur l'Exposition scolaire de 1878, par Galtiers, instituteur à Couoiac, Aveyron*, AN F/17/9388.

69. Compayré, *The History of Pedagogy*, 1888. Originally *Histoire critique des doctrines de l'éducation en France depuis le seizième siècle* (1879).

70. Secular women's normal schools were also founded during the years 1872–76 in Paris, Moulins, Chartres, Montpellier, St.-Egrève, Maçon, Amiens, and even in Algeria. See Strumingher, *Little Girls and Boys*.

71. *Écoles normales: programmes*, November 1884, AN F/17/9680.

72. *Récompenses supplémentaires accordés par le Ministère de l'Instruction publique à ses exposants*, 1878, AN F/17/9388.

73. *Rapport du département de l'Yonne sur l'Enseignement de la morale*, Auxerre, 19 March 1889, AN AJ/71/19.

74. Gildea discusses the emphases of the new pedagogy in *Education in Provincial France*, 262–63.

75. Paul Berton, "L'Enseignement par l'aspect, à l'école primaire: musées technologiques et promenades scolaires" in the *Revue Pédagogique* (July-December 1879) 580–596.

76. Galtiers, "Gymnastique des Sens—Méthode Intuitive." *Rapport sur L'Exposition scolaire de 1878. Par Galtiers, instituteur à Couoiac, Aveyron*. AN F/17/9388.

77. Platrier, "Leçons de choses," in Buisson, *Dictionnaire de pédagogie*, part 1, 2:1528–34.

78. On art education in France, see Marie-Claude Genet-Delacroix, "L'Enseignement artistique au XIXe siècle," *Historiens et Géographes* 83, no. 338 (1992): 213–26; Daniel Sherman, "Art Museums, Inspections, and the Limits to Cultural Policy in the Early Third Republic," *Historical Reflections/Réflexions Historiques* 15, no. 2 (1988): 338; Gonzalo J. Sánchez, "Hephaistos in the New Athens: Design-Art Industries in Republican France, Between Politics and the Museum, 1871–1894," *Nineteenth Century Studies* 11 (1997): 56. On the administrative history of the Republic's engagement with art, see Genet-Delacroix, "L'Enseignement artistique" and "Esthétique officielle et art national sous la Troisième République," *Le Mouvement social* 131 (Apr.-June 1985): 105–20.

79. Report by Charles Bigot from the Commission de la décoration des écoles et de l'imagerie scolaire, 11 April 1881, quoted in "Imagerie scolaire," in Buisson, *Dictionnaire de pédagogie*, 2:1321.

80. Levin, *Republican Art and Ideology*, 78.

81. Report by Charles Bigot, quoted in "Imagerie scolaire," in Buisson, *Dictionnaire de pédagogie*, part 1, 2:1321.

82. *Rapport de la Commission des musées scolaires d'art*, December 1883, AN F/17/1478.

83. Levin, *Republican Art and Ideology*, 82.

84. Pellissier, *La Gymnastique de l'esprit, 2e partie*, 2.

85. Juranville, *Premiers sujets*, 11.

86. "Du rôle de l'Institutrice dans sa commune," Félice Ramon, ADY 31 T 2.

87. Bert, "L'Instruction dans une démocratie," in *Leçons, discours, et conférences*, 400–401.

88. M. Martin Guiney argues that republican pedagogy involved a "dual strategy" vis-à-vis the Church: "it presented a secular ('lay') alternative to the sectarian values that had dominated education for centuries. . . . In tandem with this manifest strategy was an occult one, in which Christianity was not the enemy to be assimilated, but rather the model to be imitated" (*Teaching the Cult of Literature in the French Third Republic* [New York, 2004], 70).

89. Théodore Barrau. *Livre de Morale pratique, ou choix de préceptes et de beaux exemples destinés à la lecture courante dans les écoles et dans la famille* (Paris, 1857), 42. This book appears on Yonne curricular lists in 1880. *Listes des ouvrages scolaires admis par les conférences cantonales d'instituteurs et d'institutrices du département de l'Yonne, 1880–1881*, ADY 37 T 1.

90. Paul Janet, "Nouveaux programmes d'études dans les écoles normales primaires: Plan d'un cours de psychologie," *Revue Pédagogique* 7 (July 1881): 1–24.

91. " Du rôle de l'Institutrice dans sa commune," Noémi Rossignol, 12 April 1878, AN F/17/9277.

92. Delon, *Lectures expliquées*, 186–87. This book appeared on the Yonne's *Listes des ouvrages scolaires* as early as 1882. ADY 37 T 1. Delon collaborated with Mme. Pape-Charpentier on some texts, and he authored a book of children's exercises based on the methods of Pestalozzi and Froebel that was also used in the Yonne.

93. Georges Dumesnil, "Imagination," in Buisson, *Dictionnaire de pédagogie*, part 1, 2:1323.

94. Compayré, *History of Pedagogy*, 567–68.

95. "Gymnastique des sens—méthode intuitive," *Rapport sur l'Exposition scolaire de 1878, par Galtiers, instituteur à Couoiac, Aveyron*, AN F/17/9388.

96. Buisson, "Intuition," in Buisson, *Dictionnaire de pédagogie*, part 1, 2:1377.

97. Bert, "L'Instruction dans une démocratie," in *Leçons, discours, et conférences*, 397–98.

98. Paul Rousselot, "La Pédagogie dans les Écoles de Filles, à propos de l'examen d'admission aux fonctions de directrice d'école normale, (suite)" *Revue pédagogique*," (July-December 1880) 14–32.

99. Ibid., 28–29.

100. Dumesnil, "Imagination," in Buisson, *Dictionnaire de pédagogie*, part 1, 2:1323.

101. Pellissier, *Gymnastique de l'esprit, 3e partie*.

102. Emile-Albert Legrand, "Étude de pédagogie théorique: L'Imagination.—Son rôle à l'école primaire," *L'Alouette: Revue de l'Yonne et du Centre de la France, Littéraire, Artistique, Pédagogique* 6 (April 1887): 90–91. Legrand was a teacher and a member of the Académie de l'Yonne et du Centre de la France.

103. Pellissier, *Gymnastique de l'esprit, 3e partie*, 68.

104. Legrand, "Étude de pédagogie théorique."

105. Pellissier, *Gymnastique de l'esprit, 3e partie*, 6.

106. Marion, *Leçons de psychologie*, 392–93.

107. Delon, *Lectures expliquées*, 187.

108. Ibid., 20–21.

109. Pellissier, *Gymnastique de l'esprit, 3e partie*.

110. Payot, *Aux Instituteurs at aux institutrices: Conseils et directions pratiques* (Paris, 1897), 167.

111. Gabriel Compayré, "Imagination," in *Dictionnaire de pédagogie et d'instruction primaire*, part 2, ed. Ferdinand Buisson (Paris, 1887), 1: 1006.

112. Marion, *Leçons de morale*, 201.

113. Barrau, *Livre de morale pratique*, 43–44.

114. Ruth Harris, "The 'Unconscious' and Catholicism in France," *Historical Journal* 47, no. 2 (2004): 333, 353.

115. *Rapport du département de l'Yonne sur l'enseignement de la morale*, from the Inspecteur de l'Académie de l'Yonne, Auxerre, 19 March 1889, AN AJ/71/19.

116. Jules Payot, *Cours de morale* (1904; Paris, 1930), 49. Emphasis in original.

117. François Fénelon, quoted in Jules Messin, *Les Lectures quotidiennes de l'école et de la famille: Recueil de morceaux choisis à l'usage des cours moyens et supérieurs* (Paris, 1877), 148–49.

118. Dumesnil, "Imagination," in Buisson, *Dictionnaire de pédagogie*, part 1, 2:1323.

119. Legrand, "Étude de pédagogie théorique."

120. Marion, *Leçons de psychologie*, 392–93.

121. Pellissier, *Gymnastique de l'esprit, 3e partie*, 33.

122. Ibid., 33–34.

123. Ibid., 34.

124. Ibid., 34.

125. Ibid., 33–34.

126. Buisson, "Intuition," in Buisson, *Dictionnaire de pédagogie*, part 1, 2:1377.

127. *Inspection générale de l'Enseignement primaire, Yonne*, 1877, AN F/17/9277.

128. *Rapport du département de l'Yonne sur l'enseignement de la morale*, from Inspecteur de l'Académie de l'Yonne, Auxerre, 19 March 1889, AN AJ/71/19.

129. *Enseignement de la morale dans les écoles primaires, Inspecteur primaire d'Auxerre*, 6 March 1889, AN AJ/17/19.

130. Charleux-Leroux, "Réalité et fiction," 132–33.

131. *Rapport sur la situation de l'Instruction primaire dans le département de l'Yonne pendant l'année 1876*, 16 July 1877, ADY 37 T 1.

132. *Participation de la Ministre d'Instruction Publique à l'Exposition Universelle*, 1878, AN F/17/9388.

133. Querlin, "L'École de Claudine."

134. Jules Colette graduated from Saint-Cyr in 1850 and fought in the Crimean War. He was then sent to Italy, where Napoleon III was assisting the Italians in their battle with the Austrians. At Melegnano, Colette's leg was crushed by a cannonball and later amputated.

135. Francis and Gontier, *Creating Colette*, 1:32.

136. Ibid., 1:47.

137. "Gymnastique des sens—méthode intuitive," AN F/17/9388.

138. Francis and Gontier, *Creating Colette*, 1:47.

139. Colette, *My Mother's House*, trans. Roger Senhouse (London, 1953), 40. Originally *La Maison de Claudine* (1922) and *Sido* (1929).

140. Colette, letter to Éliane Carco, 1942, in *Lettres à ses pairs* (Paris, 1973), 244.

141. Paul Bert died in 1886, and in 1889 his statue was unveiled in Auxerre. According to Francis and Gontier (*Creating Colette*, 1:82), Colette recited the *Ode à Paul Bert* at the ceremony. Pichois and Brunet suggest the poem may not have been read (*Colette*, 32).

142. Quoted in Giolitto, *Histoire de l'enseignement primaire*, 1:265–66.

143. "Enseignement des sciences physique et naturelle par M. Maurice Girard, professeur au Collège Rollin," April 1878, in Bès, *L'Exposition Universelle,* AN F/17/9388.

144. Holmes and Tarr note that Marion later devoted a series of lectures and a book to arguing that women were "ill-adapted to rational thought" and that civilization meant "the maintenance of firm gender boundaries." See "New Republic, New Women? Feminism and Modernity at the Belle Epoque," in A *'Belle Epoque'?* 14.

3

CLAUDINE IN PARIS

The Republican School in Memory and Fiction

Reminiscing in a lecture later in life, French actress and film director Musidora recalled her youthful reading habits, and those of her fellow schoolgirls, at the dawn of the twentieth century:

> It was in 1906 that the young girls of the era lent each other *Claudine at School*, slipped it open under the pages of [a textbook] . . . in case the teacher questioned them. . . . At recess, we were not commenting on the classics but underlining our favorite passages in *Claudine at School*. The young language was so new, the characters so lively, so like us, that we were all left delirious with enthusiasm.[1]

Claudine, the heroine of Colette's 1900 novel and of the series that would follow, was the quintessential belle époque gamine—frank and mischievous, fearless and ironic, sexually knowledgeable but chaste. Colette, having married at the age of twenty and moved to Paris, had written this fictional account of her secular education in Saint-Sauveur for her new husband.[2] Henry Gauthier-Villars was a writer and music critic known to tout Paris as Willy, a man who employed a team of ghostwriters to produce marketable novels of scant literary merit.[3] Around 1896, Colette (as her husband took to calling her) became one of these ghostwriters, when she produced a hefty manuscript recounting her school days. The manuscript lay in Willy's desk for two years until he rediscovered it and, so the story goes, for the first time recognized its commercial value. In 1900 *Claudine at School* was published under Willy's name.[4]

Forty thousand copies of the novel sold in just two months, inspiring Colette to recycle her popular heroine in a series of Claudine novels between 1900 and 1907.[5] In these years, Claudine's name and likeness were used to hawk any number of consumer products: Claudine perfume, ice cream, cigarettes, and even toothpicks.[6] The series spawned a stage show produced by Willy, as well as other original shows loosely inspired by the fictional heroine: *Claudine aux deux écoles* (1902), *Claudine en vadrouille* (1902), *Claudine s'amuse* (1902), *Claudine et Claudin* (1903), and *Claudine à l'école de commerce* (1903).[7] In 1909 Colette toured thirty-two provincial towns in a theatrical adaptation of the novels in which she starred as Claudine. After performing in her native Yonne before a packed audience, she was lauded by local papers for "the creation of the typical woman of the century . . . the ultimate modern character."[8]

In *Claudine at School* a bright, irreverent provincial teenager recounts her final year of primary education and details the amorous entanglements and scrapes of her public school. Many reviewers on the left and the right were scandalized by the novel's portrayal of precocious adolescent girls, debauched school administrators, and Sapphic eroticism.[9] But for many, Claudine was the emblem of a new French girl, an appealing type for the modern era.[10] In studying *Claudine at School*, scholars have concentrated on the circumstances of the novel's production, or have attempted to assess the book within the broader scope of Colette's later oeuvre and life.[11] *Claudine at School* was, on one level, a frothy and titillating mockery of rural life designed for the entertainment of worldly Parisians. But, though it has been neglected as such, the novel was also a startling "thick description" of the republican school of the 1880s and a forceful illustration of the concerns of laic culture in this period.

* * *

The Claudine novels and their unprecedented popularity can best be understood within the context of a new interest in the category of adolescence at the turn of the century in France. As Kathleen Alaimo has demonstrated, young people, particularly young women, became "increasingly visible in public policy, age-graded institutions, popular culture, art and literature, and social commentary" in France in this period.[12] Indeed, recent historical studies of girlhood have posited the female adolescent as one of the "bearers of emergent European modernity."[13] Rebecca Rogers brings pointed attention to the importance of "schoolgirl culture" in nineteenth-century France, arguing that "schools and a certain type of woman professional deserve attention within the landscape of modernity alongside such objects as the new apartment houses, the department store, the wax museum, women shoppers, and women actresses."[14] Female adolescence was, according to David Pomfret, a "life stage with a relative iconic vacuity compared with that of adult womanhood," making teenage girls a useful field upon which pleasing images of the nation could be projected at the turn of the century.[15] Taken together, such studies suggest that the adolescent French girl was saddled with conflicting and powerful cultural functions at the turn of the century.

Colette's first novel capitalized on the contemporary fascination with the adolescent girl, but also helped define this evolving social category by making the secular school an essential component of modern French girlhood. Indeed, Claudine's status as the prototypical modern girl relied on her location within the secular school—an institutional setting that, given the peculiar prominence of girls' education in political debates in the Third Republic, conveyed a wealth of cultural meaning to readers. The ubiquity of Claudine and other female students in belle époque popular fiction confirms that, indeed, the schoolgirl had become, by 1900, one of the legible types of modern French society. This interest in teenage girlhood and education spurred the creation of a genre of girls' school novels at the turn of the century, often written by former republican teachers such as Gabrielle Reval (1870–1938).[16] Reval's many novels, including *Les Sévriennes* (1900), *Un lycée de jeunes filles* (1901), and *Les Lycéennes* (1902), set out to expose, in Jo Burr Margadant's words, the "daily ordeal of injustice visited on young women teachers."[17] Juliette Rogers suggests that many of these sorts of French education novels by women in this period offered "a critique of the national education system for girls" along with "a more idealized vision of what the national education system could and should provide for girls."[18]

At first blush, *Claudine at School* seems to fit uneasily within the new genre of schoolgirl novels. Claudine is not a steely and principled heroine who rises courageously by way of (or in spite of) her school experience, but rather a blasé teenaged cynic who stands apart from the republican earnestness that characterizes other schoolgirl novels. And yet Colette's oddly precise retelling of her childhood education in *Claudine at School* and its sequel, *Claudine in Paris*, suggest that the author was deeply and actively engaged with the republican pedagogical culture of her youth, a decade after she had left the school. The *école laïque* became, for Colette, a kind of shorthand for feminine success, as well as a distinctive means of visualizing and disciplining her mental life.

In identifying the specific pedagogical investment of the *Claudines*, I assess the series alongside other lesser-known fictionalized accounts of the laic school, particularly those that were written by and take the perspective of the female student, rather than the courageous and harried secular teacher. One fictionalized memoir in particular, that of the scientist and poet Lucie Rondeau-Luzeau, dramatically underscores the difference between Colette's school experience in the Yonne and the experience of that same school system by a working-class woman. Their respective fictional versions of the *école laïque* exposed the sharp social paradox of the "egalitarian" republican school and shared sense by these very different women of the girls' school as a powerfully modern and powerfully female public space.

* * *

Before assaying the close connections between the girls' school novel and republican pedagogy, we begin with the making of Claudine, the most popular and iconic teenager of the belle époque. By the time Colette began writing *Claudine*

at School, she had become, with her husband, an offbeat Parisian celebrity, min-
gling in social circles with cultural luminaries such as Marcel Proust, Anatole
France, Catulle Mendès, and Rachilde. In gathering material for the novel, this
newly minted Parisian salonnière returned to Saint-Sauveur several times in
order to revisit her childhood haunts. In May 1896 she and Willy lunched with
the teaching staff at her old school, which included Olympe Terrain as well as
some of Colette's former classmates.[19] At the time of the visit, Gabrielle Colette's name was still affixed to the schoolhouse wall on the list of prizewinners, according to two women who attended the school in this period.[20] The
Gauthier-Villars returned to the village again that July to attend the school's
graduation ceremonies, this time staying overnight in the dormitory.[21] Stimu-
lated by these trips and beginning to work on the novel, Colette wrote to Terrain (with whom she had been corresponding since leaving Saint-Sauveur in
1891): "I have discovered an astonishing young girl. Do you know who she is?
She's exactly me before my marriage."[22]

By the time *Claudine at School* went to press, Colette had been living in Paris
for seven years and was nearing thirty. Yet her public image was still the playfully
erotic, too-wise country girl, with her long braid, Burgundian dialect, and coarse
rural frankness. Once the novel was published in 1900, the publicity-savvy Willy
set about accentuating the similarity between the young provincial heroine and
her real-life creator. Colette cut off her own braids in 1902, a year after Claudine
appeared in print sporting a short bob in the second novel of the series. Colette
posed for publicity postcards as Claudine, in which her youthfulness was emphasized with a schoolgirl-like dress, collar with necktie, and textbook (see figure 1).
In order to promote the stage version of the novel, Willy had Colette and Polaire
(the actress who played Claudine on stage) dress as girlish twins in matching tail-
leurs and showed them off around Paris, in Polaire's words, "like one would walk
a couple of greyhounds."[23] Such outings played up the erotic ambiguity of the
women's relationship with the portly and middle-aged Willy.[24] Polaire later wrote
in her memoir that she was able to play the adolescent Claudine due to a "late
development that had not yet permitted me to develop very much—I still looked
like a kid [gamine], especially with my short hair."[25] (This late onset of puberty
would have been tardy indeed—though Polaire claimed in her memoir to have
just turned eighteen when she played Claudine, she was actually closer to thirty.)
Soon after Polaire began performing the role, she learned that dissolute imitation
Claudines were popping up as a fad in the Parisian sex trade: "every nightclub,
pickup joint, and even the most miserable dives had their 'Claudine,' in her black
smock, large white collar, red necktie, and, of course, the short hair."[26]

Such risqué uses of the teenage heroine were inspired in part by the novel
itself. The first novel played up the erotic appeal of schoolgirl sexuality; Claudine and her classmates are sexually precocious and understand themselves as
nubile objects of lust for older men, their teachers, and each other. Educational

COLETTE WILLY

Ch. Gerschel, phot. — Paris

Figure 1 Colette posing as Claudine. Fonds Centre d'études Colette.

officials appear as lecherous cads who prey on the girls of the laic school. The schoolmistress Mademoiselle Sergent, a rather cruel caricature of Olympe Terrain, has an affair with the district superintendent Duterte (a veiled portrait of Captain Colette's political rival Pierre Merlou), as well as a charged relationship with one of her teaching assistants.[27] Because of the thin disguise Colette gave real figures from her childhood, the publication of the novel led to outrage back in the Yonne, engendering local hostility toward Colette that would endure well after her death in 1954.[28] Decades after the publication of the novel, Olympe Terrain expressed her keen disappointment in the clever former student who had provided ammunition for the "enemies of the école laïque who used and misused Claudine à l'école against us."[29] Biographers Claude Pichois and Alain Brunet write that because the novel "appeared at a particularly febrile moment in the struggle between the partisans of the public school and those of the confessional school," it could be "considered as a pamphlet against 'the laic school' and was used as such."[30]

Yet, however acidic her rendering of Saint-Sauveur and the école laïque, Colette also produced a novel that replicated with painstaking, almost loving detail the secular school and the republican culture that surrounded it.[31] Elisabeth Charleux-Leroux's meticulous examination of the relationship between fiction and reality in Claudine at School points out a noteworthy excision in the novel: Colette never mentions Saint-Sauveur's rival école libre (confessional school) in her fictional account.[32] Rather, she depicts a rural village united in communal republican fervor centered on the laic school. In fact, nearly all of the novel's action takes place in the secular schoolhouse or at school-sponsored events—creating a hermetic universe in which the girls' laic school is the village's principal social institution, embraced enthusiastically by the community and unchallenged in its pedagogical supremacy. Despite and perhaps because secular schooling was still a divisive social issue by 1900, Colette created a fictional world in which only the republican school exists and in which female students reign supreme.

What is more, though she attended the communal school for more than a decade (1879–91), Colette chose to memorialize an exceptionally radical moment in her education in the first Claudine novel—the period that she spent preparing for the brevet exam and attending the newly created cours complémentaire (superior primary education) under the direction of a schoolmistress fresh from the republican normal school. While the creation of the girls' cours complémentaire and the rebuilding of the schools were only part of the years of renovation and educational reform in Saint-Sauveur, the novel compresses this decade of change into one academic year.

Claudine at School was more than a succès de scandale. Despite its tone of youthful irreverence and derision, the novel reproduces the themes and pedagogical concerns of the republican culture of Colette's youth with unusual precision. Claudine's ruminations about the sexual adventures of her teachers and fellow students are framed by exercises, lessons, and narrative devices drawn from the *méthode intuitive*. Throughout the novel, Claudine draws maps, sketches still lifes, and completes writing assignments that call upon the imagination, all examples of what the fictional village priest refers to indirectly as the "scandalous *leçons de choses* heaped on the youth in your Godless Schools."[33] As the book opens, Claudine quotes from her *Manual of Departmental Geography* and then offers her own textured description of the landscape's topography and botany.[34]

The curriculum of Claudine's school also mirrors Third Republican pedagogy's attention to the functions of the human body and the importance of physical fitness. Claudine and her classmates are drilled on the role of "gastric juices in the process of digestion" and on the distinct parts of the ear.[35] Throughout the school day, the girls run and play with great physical exertion. In one scene, Claudine gathers her long hair into a ponytail as to be less restricted in her physical game playing.[36] As in the morality texts of the republican school, physical and moral fitness are intimately allied in Claudine's curriculum and daily activities. One arithmetic exercise quoted at length depicts the good worker as one with "solid" muscles, while the languid idler is sickly. After a disturbing day, Claudine finds mental release in a physical task: she sweeps until her arms are sore, reflecting, "It was a relief to tire myself out like that."[37] She organizes a lively game with her classmates in order to, as she puts it, "shake up my thoughts" ["me dégourdir les idées"] and, another day, exorcizes an upsetting encounter in class with the physical activity of recess: "I made myself breathless and galloped about . . . re-straining myself from thinking as best I could." The girls return to class, "still out of breath."[38] In this way, Claudine repeatedly connects physical exertion with an effort to sharpen her mental faculties.

Claudine's primary education is also infused with the *morale laïque*'s idealization of manual work. In the great community festival celebrating the inauguration of Montigny's new schools, Claudine and the other girls sing a hymn for the visiting minister that includes an elegy to work: "Haste, arise! . . . Honest toil demands our sweat!"[39] The girls are exposed to an object lesson in manual labor through the massive rebuilding and modernization of Montigny's secular schoolhouses. After playing gleefully in the scaffolding while the builders eat lunch, Claudine returns to class dusted with mortar and plaster, covered in the signs of manual labor.[40] When she and the other older girls of the *cours complémentaire* are enlisted several times to help move furniture, books, and lumber, Claudine affirms the "unadulterated joy" of such activities.[41] The female students also perform demanding manual chores as part of their school day, including chopping and hauling logs for the fire, a process that, Claudine notes, serves to "ruin one's hands."[42]

The novel's careful transcription of school exercises involving manual labor hints at the ubiquity of idealized manual work in the republican curriculum, and at the way students may have responded to such lessons. Early in the novel,

Colette quotes a lengthy arithmetic problem involving a worker constructing a fence, including precise information on the parameters of the project, the minutes of rest required, and the costs of materials and labor. Students are asked to calculate the area of the property and the total cost of the fencing operation.[43] Though only a math problem, the exercise embraces the assumptions of the republican *morale* during this period; it presents the model citizen as the manual worker and connects useful, manual labor to the protection of property and the calculations of wages. The extensive transcription of this arithmetic problem is followed by Claudine's ironic musings on the ideal manual workers who populate her lessons: "Oh! in what unhealthy imagination, in what perverted brain do these revolting problems with which they torture us germinate? And the workers who join forces to complicate the amount of work of which they are capable . . . And the number of needles a dressmaker goes through in twenty-five years . . ."[44] Through her heroine, Colette here wryly acknowledges the repetitive attention to manual labor that typified the laic curriculum of the 1880s.

Later in the novel, Colette offers another comment on the transparent intentions of the republican Gospel of Work by detailing an assignment asking students to comment on Benjamin Franklin's aphorism "Idleness is like rust, it wears one out more than work." Claudine's response demonstrates a firm grasp of the answer that will ensure academic success:

> Here we go! Let us differentiate the shiny key and its rounded contours, polished and turned in the lock twenty times a day by hand, from the key eaten away by reddish rust. The good worker, who labors joyfully, risen since dawn, whose solid muscles, etc., etc. . . . Let us juxtapose him to the idler, who, lying listlessly on oriental divans, watches come and go at his sumptuous table . . . etc., etc. . . . unusual dishes . . . etc. . . . which fail to reawaken his appetite . . . etc., etc. . . . Oh! This can be thrown together soon enough![45]

Colette's heroine here summarizes republican maxims about the delight and physical strength of useful work and the moral benefit of labor. By contrast, idleness is associated with wasteful luxury and degenerating health, symbolized none too subtly by the rusty key and the meager appetite. Claudine offers a frank evaluation of the lesson's inherent contradictions: "As if workers who labor all their lives don't die young and worn out! But come on, mustn't say so. In the Exam Curriculum things don't happen as they do in life."[46] Literary critic Juliette Rogers has argued that such moments in the novel in which Claudine contends with the national curriculum are evidence of the "action of a 'counter-public sphere,'" where women and girls work together in opposition to rules established in mainstream society."[47] As this all-female "counter-public sphere" was a creation of the French state, Claudine's character gives voice to the internal contradictions of the state's initiative regarding girls' education. Such passages also show Claudine oscillating between disdain for the school's naïve lessons and a candid desire for scholastic success. She restrains herself from "writing pure spoof or highly subversive opinions" when assigned particularly loathsome composition subjects, but she adds that she is an "outstanding student" who excels at these exercises.[48]

Colette's consistent depiction of Claudine's success in the academic realm, as well as the accurate detailing of school exercises, seems to qualify the fictional heroine's ridicule of her lessons.[49] Though mocking the textbook lessons and keenly aware of the problematic social vision they promote, Claudine nevertheless appears to live by many of their dicta throughout the novel and its sequel, whether connecting the physical and moral in her daily activities or eschewing idleness with the fervor of a republican official. Claudine's ostensible scorn for the curriculum is particularly complicated by the last third of the novel, which recounts the two climactic moments of Claudine's girlhood: the regional exams and the community festival that inaugurates the new schools. Both events position Colette's fictional doppelganger at the center of a rich local republican culture and indicate that the école laïque represented quite a bit more to the exiled Burgundian than critics have generally argued.

Colette used the final portion of her first novel to give a meticulous chronicle of her own departmental exams in 1889, down to the structure and subject matter of exam questions.[50] As Claudine and her classmates throw themselves into preparation for the brevet exam, they are motivated by aspirations of professional success as well as by a sense of civic pride, "the honor that our possible success would reflect on this fine new school."[51] The exam days provoke anxiety because, as Claudine notes, most of her classmates "had their futures on the line."[52] Comfortably bourgeois, Claudine does not intend to pursue further education but instead takes the exams "'for the honor of the School,' to win one more brevet for it, one more glory for this unique, remarkable, and enchanting School."[53] Arriving back in Montigny after the exams, Claudine describes the entry of the students into the village as a "triumphal return."[54] The townspeople gather in their doorways to salute the returning heroines, Mlle. Sergent having already telegraphed the results.[55]

The novel's other climactic event is the inauguration of Montigny's recently renovated secular schools, renovations that serve as a backdrop for the entire novel. Claudine refers several times to the contrast between the new buildings and the old school, which was "crumbling and insalubrious," filled with "rickety" furniture.[56] The new school, by contrast, is "perfect to the last detail, white and spotless," with a spacious playground, "gleaming" modern desks with hinges, "well-kept" water closets, and attractive dormitories.[57] Part of the Third Republic's revolution in education involved the construction of new, modern, hygienic schoolhouses, and it was a commonplace of textbooks from this period to include readings that contrasted "the school of olden days" ["l'école d'autrefois"] and the modern republican School, in much the same way that Claudine does in this passage.

A fictional retelling of the 1890 schoolhouse dedication in Saint-Sauveur takes up the last quarter of *Claudine at School* and adheres closely to the original event.[58] In the novel, preparations begin weeks before the day itself. The boys' and girls' schools practice songs for the celebration and create handicrafts to be exhibited at the inauguration, when all the village would "admire the display of our work."[59] In these animated days leading to the festival, the students "live in a state of pure joy."[60] Indeed, the entire village is soon swept up in the preparations for the school ceremony. Neighborhoods "battled among themselves" to create the most fantastic street decorations for the school festival—archways across roads, sidewalks dug up and planted with trees, and even a greenery display made to resemble a medieval castle.[61] The female students fashion thousands of tissue-paper roses to decorate the schools and the town. The flowers, pine boughs, Venetian lanterns, banners, and flags result in streets that are "hardly recognizable, transfigured as woodland footpaths and picturesque parks."[62] Amongst all the festive décor, Claudine remarks, "the masterpiece, the gem, was our School."[63]

Claudine is chosen as one of the trio of garlanded, white-robed maidens who leads the student procession and presents the visiting minister with red, white, and blue bouquets representing the Republic. With a white flower wreath in her hair and holding a bouquet of white camellias, Claudine finds herself at the emotional center of the day's events as part of "the living tricolor flag":[64] "A rapturous crowd in its Sunday best . . . let out a great 'Ah!' when we appeared, as if we were fireworks. We processed slowly, with downcast eyes, proud as little peacocks, and inwardly bursting with vanity. . . . Positively beaming, we exchanged sidelong glances and delighted smiles with each other."[65] Claudine and the other flower girls lead the rest of the school's students, who carry pennants with inscriptions acclaiming the Republic and liberty. The girls form an appealing patriotic battalion, a young "army of female Gauls," as they lean "warlike on the poles of their pennants" in their "bouffant dresses and puffed-up hair."[66] Colette repeatedly describes the girls taking part in the festival as elevated and delighted by their role: "inflated with joy," "flushed crimson with pride," "eyes . . . [shining] with pride," "radiant with vanity."[67] The older girls have helped set the younger girls' hair in curlers, because, Claudine informs the reader, "in Montigny a student could not attend a prize-giving ceremony, or any such solemn event, without having her hair duly curled or waved."[68] The flower girls welcome the minister on behalf of the schoolchildren of Montigny, with Claudine declaring their "unwavering fidelity to Republican institutions."[69] As Claudine and the other two flower girls lead the procession toward the school and the crowd continues its frenzied cheers, Claudine imagines that "it was the three of us that they were applauding, as much as the minister."[70] Not merely a spectator, Claudine has become the focal point of the celebration's praise and acclamation. "You would think the celebration was for us!" she exclaims elsewhere.[71]

French politicians at the turn of the century sought, as David Pomfret puts it, to "transcend damaging class divisions" by "elevat[ing] young females to new roles in civic ritual."[72] Colette's fictionalized memoir makes evident the way that girls indeed could feel meaningfully implicated in a wider adult community of patriotic enthusiasm and republican ideals. Whether excelling on departmental exams or singing for a visiting minister, girls were given a civic role as important as that of their male counterparts, if not more so. Indeed, like Claudine, French schoolgirls could easily confuse the town's celebration of secular civic pride with a celebration of the students themselves.

Such festivals, often held in conjunction with the annual distribution of school prizes, lauded female educational accomplishment in a new political environment, with girls from the working and middle classes as the center of attention. Prize-giving ceremonies at girls' schools were not entirely new, as they had been common in some early nineteenth-century elite institutions for young women.[73] But under the Third Republic, female students took on a novel public position as the representatives of a sea change in French politics. The heady experience of such a position marks the writing of a number of female graduates of the secular educational system. Yvette Prost (1874–1949) depicted a school festival very similar to that in *Claudine at School* in her 1905 novel *Salutaire orgueil* (The Saving Pride).[74] The novel's heroine, an impoverished orphan named Marie Höel, describes the transformation of her town center and the heady excitement surrounding the laic school's annual distribution of prizes: "There was the lofty platform built upon barrels, sumptuously veiled with turkey-red; there were glorious flag-trophies, green wreaths with a pungent odor; and there were the imposing rows of fine gentlemen, crowded and perspiring, whose shiny shirt fronts and light gloves deeply impressed us." Marie is elated when chosen as one of the students to read some lines by Victor Hugo at the ceremony: "When a girl was selected to recite a piece, it was, for her and her relatives, a glory without equal."[75]

Lucie Rondeau-Luzeau, a writer who grew up in the village of Moutiers, not far from Saint-Sauveur, evoked her own childhood delight in early Third Republic festivals in her poetry and prose. In her 1914 novel *Le Livre d'une étudiante*, Rondeau-Luzeau referred to the giddy village dance that followed the annual distribution of prizes.[76] She recalled another such festival in a 1939 poem, this time a celebration of the planting of a liberty tree next to her village school. Along with a classmate in red and a classmate in blue, the young Rondeau-Luzeau, like Claudine, donned a white dress to represent the tricolor flag during the planting; she fondly remembered the "three little girls wearing the colors of the flag," smiling and emotional, making a living "tricolor garland" for the tree.[77]

More than merely attractive symbols of republican patriotism, the schoolgirls evoked in these women's writing are also, like Claudine, driven by a desire for scholastic success. The heroine of Rondeau-Luzeau's *Le Livre d'une étudiante* is a gifted young student named Marthe Dormoy, a girl from a humble farming family whose coveted position as "first" in her class at her village primary school defines her childhood and even her adult life. For Marthe the primary school is a source of delight very much tied to educational achievement: "What a joy to find once again the classroom with the large windows, the courtyard lined with lime trees, the murmur of the young girls bent over their books, the familiar sound of the desks opening and closing, rustling paper, sabots knocking, and her place, the first, next to the chair of the teacher."[78]

The position of "first place" is a scholastic honor that Marthe cherishes and one that wins her the respect and occasional "ill will and jealousy" of her class-mates. When she is honored at the distribution of prizes, an envious classmate cries out, "Again the prize of excellence to Marthe Dormoy. It is an injustice." One student's mother bursts into the classroom to accuse Marthe of "scheming to steal the place of her little girl."[79] Marthe does have some supporters—chiefly those classmates who owe their own positions and good grades to her tutelage. When a rival for the first position spreads lies about Marthe, the other girls enact a kind of rough justice. At recess Marthe slaps the "cursed gossip" and then holds her while the other girls line up to strike her as well. Those loyal to Marthe, are, according to the narrator, "attracted by the prestige of her rank."[80] The fierce pride in scholastic success, a pride defended in this case with physical violence, offers a glimpse of how the experience and memory of late nineteenth-century girls' schooling could expand and push against contemporary ideals of respect-able girlhood.

That women such as Prost, Rondeau-Luzeau, and Colette used their first for-ays into the literary world to memorialize moments from their primary school days indicates the unusual sway such scholastic pride could have over graduates, sometimes for decades afterward. In the last pages of her last work, *Le Fanal bleu* (1949), Colette reflected on a reading contest she had won at the age of twelve, a contest developed by a departmental official in the Yonne to encourage literacy amongst the region's children. Almost sixty-five years later, Colette claimed to remember the exact verse by Madame de Sévigné whose recitation won her a red and gold book and a certificate. She explained: "A line of poetry does not always have to be beautiful to adhere to the deepest recesses of our memory and slyly occupy the same space that certain loathsome but indelible melodies have already invaded."[81] A year before her death in 1954, Colette approvingly told Louise Faure-Favier, the first woman to fly across the English Channel, "One must always be first, as one is at school."[82]

Unlike Colette, however, Lucie Rondeau-Luzeau and Yvette Prost remem-bered the "school of the People" as an arena in which such scholastic success came only by way of painful class confrontations. Marie Höel, the heroine of Prost's *Salutaire orgueil*, is denied the honor of public recitation at her school's prize ceremony because she lacks the sartorial resources of her more affluent classmates. Marie's classmates wear fine white muslin dresses, and one student even acquires luxurious white shoes made of "unborn calf skin" for the ceremony. When Marie arrives in a threadbare dress of old yellowed silk, she is eyed disapprovingly: "My companions, all in white dresses trimmed with ribbons and all excessively frizzled, looked at me in silence with big eyes, but I did my best not to notice them."[83]

While shot through with social tensions, the secular school is still, in Prost's novel, a site that rewards merit. While Marie is deemed too unsightly by the teaching assistants to recite Hugo's verses on stage, she nevertheless wins the school's prize of honor, a recognition that not even her poor dress can prevent. Though the teaching assistants try to lead only those prizewinners with "the handsomest dresses and the most pleasing frills" toward the visiting *député* [member of Parliament] for the presentation, the *député* insists on handing Marie her prize personally. The egalitarian ethos of the school is preserved by this upright politician who is oblivious to class distinctions.[84] In a similar act of republican benevolence, Marie's teacher recognizes the unfortunate girl's potential and helps her compete for a scholarship from the state to pursue her studies beyond primary school.

In Rondeau-Luzeau's *Livre d'une étudiante*, the protagonist Marthe is also hampered from fully realizing her scholastic aspirations by material constraints. She is forced to leave her "beloved school" because her parents require her to work and do not see the value in her continuing her studies, as teaching is the "*métier* of the idle." Marthe's younger sister Antoinette later leaves a newly created superior primary program for girls in the neighboring town, because she wants to "earn some money right away." But Antoinette is also driven from her studies because of the "simpering" and "stuck-up" young ladies ["demoiselles à simagrées" and "pimbêches"] who torment her in class.[85] As in Prost's *Salutaire orgueil*, the girls' public school in *Livre d'une étudiante* is the scene of sharp social tension, a far cry from the solidarist dream of the Third Republic's pedagogues and politicians. For these women writers, the schoolhouse is remembered as a formative intellectual experience, but one whose rewards and pleasures are enjoyed only fleetingly or at great cost for working-class girls.

At least some of the disruptive social divisions described in these novels echoed real-life encounters. Lucie Rondeau-Luzeau was born in 1870 to a farming family not far from Saint-Sauveur-en-Puisaye. In fact, her younger sister Pauline Luzeau, the model for *Livre d'une étudiante*'s Antoinette, attended school with Colette in Olympe Terrain's *cours complémentaire*. Pauline, called Line, died at a young age, after purportedly being driven from the *cours complémentaire* because of Colette's relentless teasing. Rondeau-Luzeau's biographer Pierre Grosclaude wrote that Gabrielle Colette "never ceased launching mocking jibes" at Line, the sweet, young peasant girl.[86] Colette remembered this teasing affectionately in a letter to Rondeau-Luzeau in the 1930s: "When I was at school, I knew the little Luzeau and all the Luzeaus were lovely. Of course, we called them 'Luzottes' like we called the Bruneaus the Brunottes."[87] Lucie Rondeau-Luzeau also remembered this habit of name changing, but less fondly than Colette. According to Grosclaude, Rondeau-Luzeau recalled that this kind of diminutive "almost always had, in the Puisaye, a pejorative meaning: it expressed a certain disdain. One did not use it so familiarly with people . . . belonging to the socially superior classes." Thus, it demonstrated that "the adolescent Colette wanted to mark the difference that existed between her, the daughter of the town tax collector, and the young Line . . . who was only the daughter of a farmer."[88] While for Colette such primary school *taquinerie* was a lighthearted memory, Rondeau-Luzeau remembered a distinctly class-colored encounter, in which her sister was deprived of an educational opportunity by the snobbish ribbing of her social superior.

Indeed, Rondeau-Luzeau's novel, as well as her own lived experience of the Third Republic *école laïque*, offer a fascinating pendant piece to Colette's middle-class remembrances in *Claudine at School*. *Le Livre d'une étudiante* often mirrors the themes of a Third Republican textbook. Marthe and her sisters are dutiful and active participants in the operation of the farm: "No one is inactive."[89] The women of the family spend their evenings sewing and reviewing the farm budget. In their spare time, they discuss the glories and tragedies of the Republic's history. In the novel's first chapter, young Marthe dutifully reminds her family of Gambetta's important role in the construction of the Third Republic.[90]

Like Claudine, Rondeau-Luzeau's Marthe is a girl from rural Burgundy who excels in her local primary school and finds immense personal satisfaction in academic performance. But unlike Claudine, Marthe's scholastic aspirations are hindered by the jealousy of her classmates, the resistance of her family, and the financial constraints of her social position. Rondeau-Luzeau's story follows Marthe beyond the schoolhouse, as she begins a long journey to construct an intellectually enriching life in the face of significant financial and social obstacles. Unlike Claudine, whose only practical implementation of her education following graduation is some occasional embroidery, Marthe is thrown into a world of labor where school lessons of thrift, economic acumen, and hard work have daily significance. Working at her aunt's newsstand in Paris, she evinces impressive commercial ability, skillfully managing the business's accounts and increasing her aunt's profits. Despite her small salary, her own savings grow, as she has "a passion for saving. She mended her dresses and did up her own hats and her lingerie, with an eye to banking more money."[91]

If the textbooks of the laic primary school idealized such labor, Marthe finds little fulfillment in her long workdays because her mind is left unchallenged. She sells newspapers to the students in the neighborhood and follows "them with a look of envy while they [move] off toward the university."[92] She tries to forget her scholarly ambitions after taking a well-paying job at a department store, but, as Rondeau-Luzeau writes, "Marthe was born for the *vie intérieure* [the interior

intellectual life]. The efforts she made to drag herself away from her true nature . . . had become a daily torment." Marthe asks herself: "Tomorrow and the
days after, would she have to begin again this unskilled manual labor, stifling
the aspirations of her avid brain, and all this just to earn two francs a day?"[93]
Though Marthe does not, like Claudine, overtly critique the republican curriculum's idealization of hard work, even so she embodies the contradictions of an
educational system that encouraged girls to achieve in the academic realm but
consigned many of them to adult lives of grueling manual labor.

After much hardship, Marthe can no longer deny her intellectual desires, and
she takes the unusual step of returning to school in her twenties. She pays for her
schooling through her savings and by giving private lessons. For a time she works
as a teacher and ultimately attends university in Paris. She sacrifices everything
for her studies, knowing that "later she would have her reward," when "mighty
with acquired knowledge" she would "dominate this life that had humiliated and
bruised her."[94] In the chapters that follow, as Marthe takes up university studies, she ruminates on cellular evolution, space, and society, often echoing the
notions of a strong will and body that defined republican lessons in the period
of Rondeau-Luzeau's youth. "We are the masters of our own perfectionning,"
Marthe resolves one day, as she thinks over a reading on Lamarck:

> "We evolve ceaselessly. . . . Gymnastic exercise develops the activity of our muscles;
> immobility atrophies them. Excessive food makes the body heavy. Exercising our
> intellectual faculties develops thought. Aren't I free to do gymnastic exercise, to be
> sober and studious? If my will is too weak, I can condition my will to obey me." And
> she repeated to herself: "We are indeed the masters of our own perfectionning."[95]

Training the will, the body, and the mind, Marthe here repeats some of the fundamental dictates of the republican *morale laïque*, and she does so in the form of
an introspective self-examination in which she imagines her own perfection.

Le Livre d'une étudiante closely followed the author's own experience. In 1892,
at the age of twenty-two, Rondeau-Luzeau returned to a *cours complémentaire* at
the secondary school in Auxerre founded by Paul Bert. (She even took classes
with one of Bert's daughters.) She paid her way at school by working as a student
teacher for the younger classes.[96] Eventually earning her doctorate in natural science in 1902 (the first woman in France to do so), she became a successful scientist, as well as a poet and fiction writer.[97]

Rondeau-Luzeau kept in close contact with the school in Auxerre where she
had continued her studies in the 1890s. By way of a newsletter, the school tracked
former students' marriages, career moves, and honors years after the students
had graduated. Lucie Luzeau's university exam results, detailed conclusions from
her thesis at the Sorbonne, and her marriage to the architect George Rondeau
were all reported in the pages of the school's newsletter.[98] Bulletins and alumni

associations of this sort helped keep students connected to republican school culture and its lessons well after they had left school. Indeed, Rondeau-Luzeau maintained a close interest in the fate of students from her old school in Auxerre, and in 1905 she helped form a "Home" in Paris for former students of girls' *collèges* and *lycées*. Offering graduates recently arrived from the provinces a place of support and encouragement, the association was, according to Rondeau-Luzeau, "a work of feminine *mutualité*," to which she eventually devoted some forty-five years as secretary general.[99]

Le Livre d'une étudiante offers an often pitiable account of a working-class girl's experience of the republican school system, through the university level. Its proud and often resentful tone says much about the challenges and disappointments sowed in a school system that preached social solidarity but not social mobility. As one of the few women of her generation to successfully complete a university education, Lucie Rondeau-Luzeau was, like Colette, less than typical of the girls who attended the *école laïques* in the 1880s, even if both women's fictionalized memoirs helped expose the contradictions and possibilities of the Third Republic's educational system.

The working-class girls with whom Colette and Rondeau-Luzeau attended primary school were far more representative of the republican curriculum's goals in the 1880s. The Marchant sisters, who attended school with Colette and were immortalized in her first novel, both became primary school teachers. Odile Henrion, a classmate who was caricatured as Anaïs in the *Claudines*, also became a primary school teacher and later principal in the Yonne and married a future senator. Marie Gentilhomme (Marie Belhomme in the *Claudines*) failed the *brevet* exam in 1890 and became a salesgirl in Auxerre. Claudine's beloved Aimée was based on Marie-Hyacinthe Duchemin, a student teacher in Saint-Sauveur during Colette's youth who left teaching in 1892 to marry. Her sister, Jane Duchemin, another of Colette's classmates and the model for the fictional Luce, attended normal school in Auxerre and later taught in Saint-Sauveur with Olympe Terrain. She left the village in 1902, perhaps in part due to the publication of the *Claudines*.[100]

The Third Republican educational system provided its female students with few practical options for social mobility other than teaching. Colette's *Claudine* novels attest to the thankless and grueling nature of the teaching profession, one of the only viable alternatives to marriage and manual labor offered to girls in the laic curriculum. During her exams, Claudine imagines the life of the schoolmistress awaiting many of her classmates: "they would struggle from seven in the morning until five in the evening . . . all to earn seventy-five francs per month! . . . To avoid working the land or in textiles, they preferred yellowing their skin, sinking their chests, and deforming their right shoulder. . . . But at least, they will wear hats, they won't sew someone else's clothes, they won't tend to livestock, they won't draw buckets out of a well."[101] With such a passage, Colette repudiated the Third Republic's glorification of manual labor and took her educational system to task for providing narrow options for its female students.

* * *

Colette's second novel, *Claudine in Paris* (1901), similarly challenged the republican virtues so tirelessly exhorted by the school lessons of her childhood. *Claudine in Paris* finds the teenage heroine, now finished with school, relocated with her father from the rural paradise of Montigny to the capital. Here, she explores the city streets, spends time with her gay cousin Marcel, and falls violently in love with Marcel's father, Renaud. In this new seductive urban environment, the pedagogical structure of the laic school's textbooks continues to discipline Claudine's daily life. When she writes to a friend back in Montigny, for example, she describes the letter as a "French composition: Letter from a young girl to her friend to announce her arrival in Paris."[102] In the first novel, Claudine quotes a textbook exercise asking students to consider objects from both the moral and physical perspective, a common strategy in the 1880s curriculum. She uses this very method to describe her friend Luce to Marcel in the sequel: "From the moral point of view, Luce does not exist. I therefore consider her only from the physical point of view and I tell you she has green eyes and soft skin."[103] Following a walk around Paris, Claudine mimics the promenades scolaires of her childhood curriculum by listing her observations: "(1) it is much warmer than in Montigny; (2) one's nose is blackened somewhat on the inside on returning from a walk; (3) one draws attention to oneself when stopped alone in front of a newspaper kiosk; (4) one also draws attention by not allowing oneself to be disrespected on the sidewalk."[104] Colette here chooses the form and content of the daily observation journals commonly used in republican schools to structure Claudine's approach to challenging new urban surroundings—here the leering regard of strangers on the street. Claudine later summarizes her first months in Paris using a scholastic metaphor: "My 'fair-copy book', as we used to say at school, is up to date. . . . I'm making some charming little chemises for my always-needy wardrobe, and some little knickers (closed ones)."[105] Though this passage plays with the erotic possibility of a teenage girl's lingerie, it also has the heroine structuring her day around the upstanding routine of the primary school—speaking of her life as a "fair-copy" book and filling idle hours with diligent sewing.

On moving to Paris, Claudine "piously" brings her old textbooks and places them on her bedroom desk, including Bérillon's *La Bonne ménagère agricole* (The Good Country Housewife).[106] Claudine fondly recalls memorizing and mocking a lesson in Bérillon that decried the dangers of urban temptations for rural girls, a passage that now has new resonance: "Wretched child! How great is your error! . . . Dismiss as detestable the thought of thus moving far from your parents and far from the simple house where you were born! If you knew at what price those ladies whose luxury you envy purchased the silks and jewels with which they adorn themselves!"[107] This passage is an exact quotation from *La Bonne mé-nagère*, a textbook written specifically for the girls' primary schools in the Yonne and used in Saint-Sauveur in the 1870s and 1880s.[108] While writing the novel, Colette most probably either had her old textbooks on hand or actually had memorized the passages. Merely an abstract lesson when Claudine mocked Béril-lon at school, the implied sexual fall of the bejeweled city woman carries a new urgency for Claudine as she wanders Paris.

In revisiting a number of the students from the first novel, *Claudine in Paris* provides a pointed critique of an educational system that lionized hard work and yet released its students into a society that offered few honorable options for women living on their own. Anaïs, a student first introduced in *Claudine at School*, reappears in the sequel, training to be a teacher (and engaging in affairs with women). Another of Claudine's fellow classmates, Luce, turns up in Paris as the mistress of a wealthy Parisian uncle after she fails the entrance exam for the laic teacher's college. The *morale* of the laic school is given its ultimate perversion when Luce's uncle forces her to dress as a schoolgirl and to work on lessons at a small desk to heighten his sexual excitement. When he scolds her for mistaking some dates in English history, Luce revolts: "I yelled at him, 'English history! That's material for the *brevet supérieur*, I've had it!'"[109] Appalled by the luxurious trappings of Luce's room and the sexual arrangement they represent, Claudine employs the language of their old school: "Luce, are these the fruits of dishonor? You know, 'the deceptive fruits that leave a taste of ash in the mouth', if we are meant to believe our old *Morale en exemples*."[110]

Despite the glee Colette seems to take in dismantling the republican feminine ideal throughout the novel, she does so by way of a heroine who abides by and even relishes many aspects of that ideal. Though she pretends to be clever and world-weary, Claudine admits that she has become somewhat "prudish . . . virtuous even," and that she flees "vice with a noble gesture." She tells herself, "Deep down, Claudine, you are nothing but an ordinary, honest girl."[111] Later in the novel, she links her distance from the School with a slackening moral code, declaring that she has "fallen" since her move to Paris. She has "lost the innocent happiness of moving, climbing, bounding about," and she feels her inactivity keenly: "I have no more schoolwork to do. And if I no longer explain in essay form at least twice a year why 'Idleness is the mother of all vice,' I better understand how it engenders some."[112] In the same way that she uses references to their old *morale* lessons to chastise Luce, Claudine finds fresh meaning in school assignments and curricular themes in this new realm of urban independence. When she is busy and energetic in Paris, she remarks that she is "gay as I used to be at the School, active and bustling."[113]

An idle bourgeois girl, Claudine falls back on the gymnastic training of the republican curriculum to battle her moral degeneration in the city. Every day, she engages in stretching exercises and refers to such exercises throughout the novel as a curative to the moral ills of urban life. She notes that though she is "in an awfully bad state of mind . . . , [her] body is doing well." She explains that her daily stretches are designed to maintain her agility, "even though I've no longer a tree to climb." After falling in the tub during one such balancing attempt, she assures the reader, "I excel at other exercises: touching my feet behind my head or a reversed arc with the head at the level of my calves." Her maid Mélie admires Claudine's suppleness but warns against "an excess of *gymnastique*."[114] Like much of the novel, this description of Claudine's body doubtlessly was intended to excite some readers with the image of an eroticized teenage girl. Yet it is significant that the author employed a discussion of moralizing gymnastic exercise to do so. In this way, Colette connected moral rectitude with new republican standards of fitness and feminine beauty. Similarly, when Claudine returns from an overstimulating afternoon in the city, her mind "on fire," she calls to her pregnant dog: "Come on, Fanchette! A little gym! Come and give your future children a bit of exercise!"[115] Years later, writer Jean Larnac would insist that *Claudine at School* was "for us, like a portrait of the young girl of the beginning of the century, loving freedom, fresh air, movement, and laughing at danger—the prototype of our *sportives* and our *garçonnes*."[116] Though Larnac does not make the connection, Claudine's attention to bodily health was tied to a specific pedagogical context.

Although the *Claudines* included many accurate depictions of Colette's experiences in Saint-Sauveur's secular school, the novels were designed primarily as droll, marketable tales. Willy and his wife understood the commercial value of racy anecdotes that played to the belle époque's fascination with "aberrant" sexuality. By creating a fictional laic primary school in which a female teacher seduces her female teaching assistant and young girls engage in "unnatural" adolescent sexual explorations, Colette was in some ways taking sides with fierce contemporary critiques of secular schools by those who opposed the Third Republic's educational reforms. Yet the character of Claudine remains fairly virtuous throughout the series (she ends as a relatively happy married wife), and more than once she relies on the lessons of the *école laïque* to guide her adult actions. Some contemporary critics even defended the *Claudine* novels as moral and natural. In 1905 Jean de la Hire asked, "who would dare maintain that Claudine is not an honest woman? . . . Her husband had her as a virgin, she loved him as deeply as is possible, and very exclusively. . . . How many haughty and prudish spouses who purse their lips in horror at merely the name of Claudine have rolled in the sheets with countless lovers!"[117] André du Fresnois noted in 1909 that "despite her daring gestures, Claudine is the wife of a single love. She remains attached to her roots by memory."[118] Jean Larnac wrote in 1927 that while some "severe moralists" had been outraged by the "perverted mind" of Claudine, others found that Colette's first novel "in fact brought to literature a breath of fresh air from the country and the rustic echoes of a completely new flavor."[119] Like Musidora's statement that the characters of *Claudine at School* were "so like" her as a girl, Larnac attested to the startling and appealing contemporaneity of the *Claudines*, their author having captured the new French woman in all of her paradoxical glory.[120]

* * *

Just as Claudine acclimated herself to Parisian life using the structure of her schooldays, Colette found the School a powerful metaphor and a source of persistent inspiration throughout the belle époque. She wrote the original manuscript for *Claudine at School* on a set of school exercise books she discovered in a stationer's shop, later recalling that the sight of the books motivated her writing. Recovering from a long illness that had left her "sluggish in mind and body," Colette remembered coming across the exercise books "similar to those I used at school" in the shop. The sight of them, she remembered, "re-awakened the urge, a sort of itch in my fingers to do an 'imposition', to fulfill a prescribed task. A well-remembered watermark in the thick, laid paper, took me back six years. Diligently, with complete indifference, perched at the corner of the desk, the window behind me, one shoulder hunched and my knees crossed, I wrote."[121] Thus, particularly during her early years as a writer, Colette associated the School and its accessories with the act of work itself.

Colette continued to use the School as a structuring device throughout her belle époque fiction. Renée Néré, the heroine of her 1911 novel *The Vagabond*, describes her moral lapses and interior reflections several times with school metaphors.[122] That same year, Colette's story "Littérature" featured her goddaughter comparing the writer's craft to homework assignments: "It's like a composition: are you forced to hand in your homework on the day they tell you to? . . . What would they say if you handed in your notebook with nothing in it?"[123] In January 1912 this girl returned in the story "Ma Filleule" to expound on the importance of the School as a child's place of business: "do you tell Papa what he should do at his office? Me, at school, that's the same thing. . . . School is like a different world."[124] This ten-year-old girl reflected Colette's own experience of the laic school and echoed a Third Republican pedagogical theme that taught students to think of themselves as practitioners of an honorable profession.

In the 1920s Colette participated in several celebrity surveys on the subject of schooling and wrote short essays on subjects such as pedagogy. In one *enquête* she recalled "having endured, during summer vacation, the nostalgia for school . . . this vague thirst that can only be the pain of idleness. . . . Yes, summer vacation is too long. To what child over the age of seven can three months of idleness profit?"[125] By the 1940s the School had become an established site of mythic significance in Colette's memory: "Must I call my school a school? No, but a sort of rude paradise where ruffled angels broke wood in the morning to light the stove."[126] In an ode to autumn, she evoked the long boredom of her childhood summers, "sated with idleness, listless from missing school. . . . As I write, there once again returns the season celebrated by a former schoolgirl because, precociously, she loved it."[127] As in *Claudine at School* written some forty years before, Colette's school is a site of activity and a curative to idleness.

* * *

On closer examination, Colette's earliest literary work serves not only as a compelling primary source articulating one extraordinary graduate's engagement with the rich republican culture of the 1880s but also as an instructive illustration of the way in which the laic school and its moral dicta could persist as an intellectual structure in the early decades of the twentieth century. Colette's use of the schoolgirl as a literary device reflected a broader interest in the essential modernity of a new kind of French femininity—a femininity that could be both deeply troubling and appealing. For a middle-class woman such as Colette, the school was an institution where bourgeois idleness was purged by physical activity and where feminine obedience and submission were bested by a powerful notion of academic success. The lessons of the school served to order the author's controversial rejection of bourgeois norms in her adult life. A working-class woman such as Lucie Rondeau-Luzeau could employ the modern schoolgirl to launch a searing critique of the Third Republic's unrealized promise. For her, the schoolhouse and its lessons opened the door to a public feminine identity founded on scholastic achievement and intellectual reflection, but did little to mitigate the sharp class inequities that awaited girls like her outside of the classroom. In both cases, the secular school served as a rich cultural field in which the class and gender contradictions of the republican instructional revolution could be tested.

Notes

1. Musidora, "Conférence de Musidora," 33–34. Musidora, born Jeanne Roques (1889–1957), was an early silent film actress, screenwriter, and director.
2. Colette's schooling ended in fall 1891. See Sarde, *Colette: Free and Fettered*, 82. She earned her *brevet élémentaire* in 1889 and then continued in the *cours complémentaire*.
3. Gauthier-Villars, born in 1859, was fourteen years Gabrielle's senior. They met in Paris during Captain Colette's visits to the Gauthier-Villars' publishing house.
4. In the book's preface, Willy wrote that he was sent the manuscript by an anonymous girl.
5. This figure is cited in Sarde's *Colette: Free and Fettered* (146) and in Richardson, *Colette*, 15. The entire series is composed of *Claudine à l'école* (1900), *Claudine à Paris* (1901), *Claudine en ménage* (1902), *Claudine s'en va* (1903), and *La Retraite sentimentale* (1907). The first four were originally published under Willy's name, while the last was published under the name of Colette Willy.
6. Claude and Vincenette Pichois list Claudine products in *Album Colette* (Paris, 1984), 61–62, as does Larnac in *Colette*, 84–85.
7. Pichois and Pichois, *Album Colette*, 68.
8. April 1909, quoted in Francis and Gontier, *Creating Colette*, 1:283.
9. Ibid., 1:166.

10. Juliette M. Rogers argues that the popularity of the Claudines can in part be explained by audience expectations: "the government's new definitions of the typical schoolgirl" and the "cultural way of life of the adolescent 'bourgeoise' from the turn-of-the-century era." See "Claudine's Peers: Social and Historical Expectations for Colette's First Heroine," *Symposium* 50, no. 4 (Winter 1997): 225, 228.

11. Many critics have taken the line of Elaine Marks, who claims the novel's scandal-provoking passages indicate that Colette's mask as a ghostwriter allowed her to write with "no moral or aesthetic obligation" (*Colette*, 71).

12. Kathleen Alaimo, "The Authority of Experts: The Crisis of Female Adolescence in France and England, 1880–1920," in *Secret Gardens, Satanic Mills: Placing Girls in European History, 1750–1960*, eds. Mary Jo Maynes, Birgitte Søland, and Christina Benninghaus (Bloomington, IN, 2005), 151, 150.

13. Mary Jo Maynes, Birgitte Søland, and Christina Benninghaus, "Introduction," in Maynes et al., *Secret Gardens, Satanic Mills*, 2.

14. Rebecca Rogers, *From the Salon to the Schoolroom*, 11.

15. David M. Pomfret, "'A Muse for the Masses': Gender, Age, and Nation in France, Fin de Siècle," *American Historical Review* 109, no. 5 (December 2004): 1451.

16. Also see Marguerite Bodin's *Les Surprises de l'école mixte* (Paris, 1905). On Reval, see Juliette M. Rogers, "Educating the Heroine: Turn-of-the-Century Feminism and French Education Novels," *Women's Studies* 23, no. 4 (1994): 321–34, and *Career Stories: Belle Epoque Novels of Professional Development* (University Park, PA, 2007); Gretchen Van Slyke, "Monsters, New Women and Lady Professors: A Centenary Look Back at Gabrielle Reval," *Nineteenth-Century French Studies* 30, nos. 3 and 4 (2002): 347–62. On studies of education novels about the New Woman in other national contexts, see Patricia M. Mazón, *Gender and the Modern Research University: The Admission of Women to German Higher Education, 1865–1914* (Stanford, CA, 2003).

17. Margadant, *Madame le Professeur*, 169.

18. Juliette Rogers, "Educating the Heroine," 323.

19. This according to Larnac, *Colette*, 55.

20. "Souvenirs inédits de deux condisciples de Claudine," *La Grive*, July-September 1960. Colette exchanged affectionate notes with these women as late as 1953.

21. Terrain later told Larnac that Colette "insisted I put her up, saying that she would be, among us, a role model of all one shouldn't do." Quoted in Thurman, *Secrets of the Flesh*, 94. Colette describes this visit in *Claudine en ménage* (1902), and two students later recalled it as well. "Souvenirs inédits de deux condisciples de Claudine," *La Grive*, July-September 1960. Plans for a third visit were cancelled, in part due to the disapproval that some in Saint-Sauveur expressed regarding the couple's behavior at the school. See Thurman, *Secrets of the Flesh*, 94–95.

22. Larnac, *Colette*, 57. Quoted and translated in Thurman, *Secrets of the Flesh*, 97.

23. Polaire, *Polaire par elle-même* (Paris, 1933), 119.

24. Ibid., 119–20.

25. Ibid., 116.

26. Ibid., 129.

27. Rumors of this sort were spread about Olympe Terrain and Pierre Merlou. See Charleux-Leroux, "Réalité et fiction," 134.

28. An archivist in the Yonne still referred to local bitterness toward Colette in a conversation with the author in 1998.

29. See a letter from Olympe Terrain to Mme. Van Glytenbeck (Marie-Louise Quinlin, a former student, who wrote under the pseudonym Marise Querlin), 2 February 1929, St-Sauveur, Yonne, Bibliothèque Nationale de France (BNF) NAF 18708, #270. According to Charleux-Leroux and Boivin, Terrain considered leaving her position after the book's publication. See *Avec Colette*, 182.

30. Pichois and Brunet, *Colette*, 88.

31. In his study of images of school life in French novels, Claude Pujade-Renaud argues that fiction delivers a truth "which sometimes eludes historical research." See *L'école dans la littérature* (Paris, 1986), 11.

32. Charleux-Leroux and Boivin remark that the *école libre* did not provide much competition in Saint-Sauveur, "the école laïque triumphing easily in 'this free-thinking region." See *Avec Colette*, 154.

33. *Claudine à Paris*, in *Oeuvres complètes de Colette* (Paris, 1973), 1:339. All subsequent references to the French edition will be to this publication. The priest refers here obliquely to scandals at the school, but it is interesting that Colette uses *leçons des choses* and godlessness as polemical shorthand for the secular school system.

34. Colette, *Claudine at School*, trans. Antonia White in *The Claudine Novels* (New York, 1987), 11. All subsequent references to the English translation will be to this edition. Joan Hinde Stewart describes the novel's opening as a challenge to "the practice of traditional autobiography, standard geography, conventional sight and discernment, schoolbooks, and, by extension, education" (*Colette*, 17).

35. *Claudine at School*, 106.

36. Ibid., 41.

37. Ibid., 58–59.

38. *Claudine à l'école*, 70, 46, 47.

39. *Claudine at School*, 178.

40. Ibid., 66.

41. *Claudine à l'école*, 26.

42. Ibid., 41.

43. *Claudine at School*, 31.

44. *Claudine à l'école*, 42.

45. Ibid., 117.

46. Ibid.

47. Juliette M. Rogers, "The "Counter-Public Sphere": Colette's Gendered Collective," *MLN* 111, no. 4 (1996): 739.

48. *Claudine at School*, 24.

49. Diana Holmes mentions the "creative contradiction" of Colette's education: "On the one hand, the extension of State education created effective channels for the transmission of a repressive ideology," but it also gave girls "legal right to an existence and an identity outside the home" (*Colette*, 15–16). Joan Hinde Stewart sees the novels as a critique of the "system of formal education" in general (*Colette*, 19).

50. Charleux-Leroux compares Claudine's and Colette's respective exam experiences, down to the exam questions, in "Réalité et," 148. Also see Léon Dubreuil, "Le Brevet de Colette," *Le Cerf volant* 18 (July 1957).

51. *Claudine at School*, 107.

52. *Claudine à l'école*, 143.

53. Ibid., 144.

54. Ibid., 176.

55. *Claudine at School*, 143.

56. *Claudine à l'école*, 19, 99.

57. *Claudine at School*, 13; *Claudine à l'école*, 99, 107. Charleux-Leroux gives an excellent summary of Saint-Sauveur's school construction in "Réalité et fiction."

58. Charleux-Leroux (in "Réalité et fiction") exhaustively records the ways in which Colette's fictional recreation of these events mirrored accounts of the fête in Saint-Sauveur.

59. *Claudine at School*, 146.

60. *Claudine à l'école*, 190.

61. Ibid., 196–97.

62. Ibid., 200.

63. Ibid., 197.

64. *Claudine at School*, 168.

65. *Claudine à l'école*, 208.

66. Ibid., 209.

67. Ibid., 206, 207, 208, 209.

68. Ibid., 194.

69. Ibid., 211. Newspaper accounts seem to confirm that Colette more than likely served in this function in 1890. See Charleux-Leroux's "Réalité et fiction," 151–52.

70. *Claudine à l'école*, 212.

71. Ibid., 208.

72. Pomfret, "A Muse," 1441.

73. Rebecca Rogers examines prize-giving ceremonies in upper-class secondary schools in the early nineteenth century in *From the Salon to the Schoolroom*, 69. In *Madame la Professeur*, Jo Burr Margadant writes of the "resplendent pride" associated with the publicity surrounding exams in this period for young women (216).

74. Yvette Prost, *Salutaire orgueil* (Paris, 1905). Born in 1874 and the author of two novels about the *école laïque*, Prost was likely a graduate of the system. She wrote another fictional memoir of the *école laïque* titled *Catherine Aubier* (Paris, 1912), discussed by Waelti-Walters in *Feminist Novelists of the Belle Époque*.

75. Yvette Prost, *The Saving Pride*, trans. Frank Alvah Dearborn (New York, 1912), 25. Marie states in the novel that she was born in 1876.

76. Lucie Rondeau-Luzeau, "Le Livre d'une étudiante, deuxième partie," *Le Temps*, 27 May 1914. This novel was serialized in *Le Temps* between 20 May 1914 and 17 June 1914. Lucie Luzeau was born in 1870 in Moutiers.

77. Lucie Rondeau-Luzeau, "L'arbre de la Liberté," in *La Porte du Rêve, poèmes* (Paris, 1946). Pierre Grosclaude refers to the real-life source of this poem in his biography of Rondeau-Luzeau, *Une Femme de science et poète* (Paris, 1958), 40.

78. *Le Livre d'une étudiante*, 23 May 1914.

79. Ibid., 22 May 1914.

80. Ibid., 23 May 1914. According to Grosclaude, this scene was based on real events in Rondeau-Luzeau's childhood.

81. Colette, *Le Fanal bleu*, 240. According to Pichois and Brunet, Colette misremembers the event, as records show that she recited words by Voltaire and Béranger, not Sévigné (*Colette*, 39).

82. From Louise Faure-Favier, "La Muse aux violettes," *Mercure de France*, 1 December 1953. Quoted in Richardson, *Colette*, 5.

83. Prost, *The Saving Pride*, 32–33.

84. Ibid., 33–34.

85. *Le Livre d'une étudiante*, 27 and 28 May 1914.

86. Grosclaude, *Une Femme*, 28.

87. Quoted in ibid., 47. Colette wrote to Rondeau-Luzeau after the publication of the latter's book, *Chants de la nature*, in 1938.

88. Grosclaude, *Une Femme*, 47–48.

89. *Le Livre d'une étudiante*, 21 May 1914.

90. Ibid., 20 May 1914.

91. Ibid., 28 May 1914.

92. Ibid.

93. Ibid., 29 May 1914.

94. Ibid., 31 May 1914.

95. Ibid., 4 June 1914.

96. Grosclaude, *Une Femme*, 23–24.

97. Rondeau-Luzeau's 1902 thesis, directed by Alfred Girard, was titled "Action des chlorures en dissolution sur le développement des oeufs de Batraciens."

98. See issues of *L'Echo du Lycée: Bulletin de l'Association amicale des ancienne élèves du collège et lycée de jeunes filles d'Auxerre*, 1895–1906.

99. Grosclaude, *Une Femme*, 35.

100. Information on Colette's classmates can be found in Charleux-Leroux and Boivin's *Avec Colette*.

101. *Claudine à l'école*, 143–44.

102. *Claudine à Paris*, in *Oeuvres complètes de Colette*, 1:249–50. All subsequent references to the French edition will be to this version.

103. Ibid., 265.

104. Ibid., 262.

105. *Claudine in Paris*, trans. Antonia White, in *The Claudine Novels*, 206. All subsequent references to the English translation will be to this edition.

106. *Claudine à Paris*, 279.

107. Ibid., 280. Bérillon's quote is from *La Bonne Ménagère agricole, ou simples notions d'économie rurale et d'économie domestique* (Auxerre, 1874).

108. *Claudine in Paris*, 228. Bérillon appears on curricular lists in the Yonne as early as 1875. *Liste générale des livres classiques en usage dans les écoles publiques, 1875* (Yonne), ADY 37 T 1.

109. *Claudine à Paris*, 343.

110. Ibid., 329.

111. Ibid., 345–46.

112. Ibid., 349.

113. *Claudine in Paris*, 321.

114. *Claudine à Paris*, 296.

115. *Claudine in Paris*, 227.

116. Larnac, *Colette*, 68.

117. Jean de la Hire, *Willy et Colette* (Paris, 1905), 50.

118. André du Fresnois, "Colette Willy," *Akadémos*, 15 February 1909, 178–84.

119. Larnac, *Colette*, 68.

120. Claudine made appearances in Colette's oeuvre in the decades that followed. Colette titled her 1922 memoir about her childhood *La Maison de Claudine*, and she coauthored some songs in the film version of *Claudine à l'école* in 1938. In 1941 Claudine made her last appearance in print in a sketch Colette published. See Pichois and Brunet, *Colette*, 91.

121. Colette, *My Apprenticeships*, trans. Helen Beauclerk (London, 1957), 19. Originally published as *Mes Apprentissages* (Paris, 1936).

122. Colette, *La Vagabonde*, in *Oeuvres complètes de Colette*, 3:360, 392.

123. Colette, "Littérature," *Le Matin*, 7 December 1911.

124. Colette, "Ma Filleule," *Le Matin*, 18 January 1912.

125. Colette, "Enquête sur les devoirs de vacances," *Nos Loisirs*, 1 August 1923, in *Cahiers Colette* 12 (1990).

126. Colette, *Looking Backwards*, trans. David Le Vay (London, 1975), 17. Originally published as *Journal à rebours* (1941) and *De ma fenêtre* (1942).

127. Colette, *Looking Backwards*, 25.

4

EARNING HER BREAD

Métier, Performance, and Female Honor, 1906–1913

In February 1913 the well-heeled citizens of Nice gathered in a fashionable theater to hear the *femme de lettres* Colette Willy lecture on her years as a music-hall performer. The author, who had made her stage debut in 1906, disappointed her audience. While her listeners had come to hear Colette divulge "sensational details" about music-hall life, a journalist noted that "Mme Colette Willy revealed nothing at all, or rather, she tried to demonstrate that the music hall was quite simply a place whose atmosphere was moral and hygienic and where one could live tranquilly. She even insisted that young girls were more secure there than on the promenade of the Champs-Elysées; that the men [of the music hall] are all honorable, the women never wicked."[1]

The Niçois' surprise was perhaps reasonable. After all, the divorced Mme. Willy had launched her stage career by publicly kissing her female lover, had toured three countries with a pantomime in which she appeared nude, and was the author of numerous novels that dealt gleefully with adultery, homosexuality, and even incest. By all appearances, she was a sexually liberated Bohemian *artiste* and a seemingly poor exemplar of respectable French womanhood. Nonetheless, throughout her years as a music-hall performer, Colette drew on the potent cultural resources of her republican girlhood to offer a new model of French femininity, one that found honor not in sexual virtue, piety, or motherhood but in paid manual labor. As a product of the new republican school, Colette spent her formative years immersed in a *morale laïque* that both presented manual craft and financial solvency as the path to moral perfection and shored up traditional feminine domesticity. Music-hall work provided a unique opportunity to reconcile these taut republican values.

Colette scandalized family and friends when she made her stage debut in 1906 at the Théâtre de Mathurins, playing a faun in the pantomime *L'Amour, le désir, la chimère.* This new stage career was a necessity of sorts, as Colette had received virtually none of the profits from the novels she had written under Willy's name when the couple separated in 1906.[2] Left without substantial financial resources, Colette, while continuing to work as a novelist and journalist, sought to capitalize on her substantial notoriety by embarking on a lucrative career as a headlining vaudeville performer. She would do so for more than six years, only leaving the stage in 1913 after becoming pregnant with her first and only child. During this period, while Colette toured music halls and theaters across France, Belgium, and Switzerland with her stage partner Georges Wague,[3] she also published a corpus of novels, stories, and vignettes exposing the backstage life of the theatrical world.

Colette's exceedingly popular version of the belle époque music hall can only fully be appreciated when viewed against the backdrop of her highly publicized personal and professional life in this period. By the time the Willys began the long process of separating in 1905, their unconventional domestic arrangements had already become the stuff of Parisian legend. With the third installment of the *Claudines, Claudine en ménage* (1902), the Willys pitilessly fictionalized their own turbulent threesome the previous year with an American socialite named Georgie Raoul-Duval. So thinly veiled were the characters in the book that Raoul-Duval bought up the entire first print run of the novel and had it destroyed.[4] Though the novel ends with Claudine happily recommitted to Renaud and their marriage, the frank sexuality of the book and the titillating autobiographical nature of the story added a new piquancy to Colette's public image. Colette soon was a regular fixture in the artistic and social circles of Paris Lesbos, performing in amateur theatrical productions in the gardens and salons of women such as Natalie Barney. She had also begun a six-year relationship with the former Marquise de Belbeuf, Mathilde de Morny, a wealthy aristocrat, lesbian, and transvestite known to her near and dear as Missy.[5] In 1906 Colette moved from the apartment she shared with Willy to 44 rue Villejust, close to Missy's home. At the same time, she embarked on a theatrical and music-hall career that had her performing in scanty costumes, publicly kissing men and women, and even appearing nude on stage. Colette and her estranged husband were now sensational international celebrities—Willy's remarriage in 1911 to the actress Meg Villars was even covered by the *New York Times*, which made a point of noting the unusual state of Willy's relations with his now ex-wife Colette.[6]

It was out of and against this public reputation that in the years following her stage debut, Colette fashioned her own version of her music-hall career by way of fiction, press interviews, and letters. She embraced an uncommon notion of the female performer: a woman who, while living outside the bounds of middle-class respectability, found moral contentment in honest, wage-paying manual labor and domestic order. By melding such representations in her literature and public image, Colette managed to forge a feminine identity that obeyed many of the dicta of the republican ideal while also allowing an essential transgression of those dicta.

She did so as the mounting visibility of the New Woman coincided with an increasing presence and scrutiny of women in the urban workforce. As Judith Coffin skillfully demonstrates, debates about workingwomen intensified in the latter part of the nineteenth century.[7] In 1906, the year that Colette took the stage, women made up some 37 percent of the industrial workforce in France; by 1911, 41 percent of the banking and commercial workforce was female.[8] These growing numbers of workingwomen did not go unnoticed by anxious social observers, already apprehensive about the creeping emancipation of middle-class women. Colette also celebrated the female music-hall performer as the exemplary republican worker at a time when France was being shaken by strikes and working-class protest. In 1906 France was experiencing one of the worst years of labor unrest in its history. In May of that year, two hundred thousand workers responded to a call for a general strike, and the minister of the interior was forced to announce a state of siege in Paris and to use troops to restore order. A wave of strikes continued over the next two years, seemingly threatening the stability of the Republic itself.[9] Nevertheless, while the government oscillated between ameliorating the workers' plight and controlling the "dangerous" classes, Colette chose to lionize the working-class *artiste* as an exemplar of moral rectitude, industriousness, and physical health. She did so at a time when the music hall was regarded as a "delinquent" and suspect retreat from the Third Republic's Gospel of Work.[10]

The turn of the twentieth century also saw a profound shift in the perceptions of and possibilities for public women in France, what Lenard Berlanstein refers to as "liberating changes in gender understandings" that were embodied by "republican actresses."[11] Once pariahs, theater women could now in some cases be offered as models of bourgeois behavior.[12] Colette, though radical in her celebration of sexual freedom in her literature, life, and performance, also consistently recognized the attractions of middle-class respectability.[13] Mary Louise Roberts details an analogous struggle in this period by the feminist Marguerite Durand to "reconcile her own lifelong need for both personal freedom and social probity" by cultivating a theatrical public image that combined "conventional" feminine allure with feminist action and personal liberation.[14] Roberts's study focuses on Durand's feminist "aesthetics" and "theatrics" as a deliberative act. Durand, she writes, "deployed conventional feminine wiles as tactics" to render her deviation from feminine norms "more appealing to her male contemporaries . . . making the New Woman culturally palatable."[15] I propose that, while Colette's use of certain republican language and mental techniques accomplished similar ends, it was also the reflection of a powerful if conflicted cultural framework. For Colette, the labor of the music-hall profession was far more meaningful than its performative elements, a distinction that has been lost in evocations of Colette as an offbeat belle époque entertainer. Her sustained attention to labor, thrift, and domestic orderliness throughout her life and work demonstrates both her discomfort with the transgression of social norms she was attempting and the forceful mental framework that organized this discomfort.

The Women of the Music Hall

Colette's formulation of the music hall as a realm of dignified labor and chaste propriety contrasted starkly with the contemporary image of the female performer. Throughout the nineteenth century, actors and street performers had been regarded as social pariahs, and this attitude endured well into the twentieth century. A commentator on theater in 1908 wrote that some small French towns still refused to rent hotel rooms to actors. In one village, inhabitants crossed themselves when theater professionals passed by on the road.[16] Female entertainers were especially suspect, given the already precarious state of working-class feminine virtue in the eyes of bourgeois observers. Women who took the stage were regularly conflated with prostitutes.[17] Émile Zola's Nana was the fin-de-siècle archetype of the promiscuous actress—a careless and degenerate woman whose stage performances were advertisements for her sexual availability to wealthy admirers. According to Anne Martin-Fugier, by the first decade of the twentieth century, these ready associations between actresses and immorality had begun to be challenged somewhat.[18] But the earlier lewd type was still common in the popular literature of the belle époque, in which female performers often appeared as the licentious mistresses of the debauched upper-class men who ogled them from the audience.

Popular fiction relished the image of the music hall as a sphere of moral and physical laxity and sensual excess, the opposite of the neat and ordered hearth tended by the middle-class housewife. *Dans la peau*, a 1907 pulp novel by René Schwaeblé, epitomized this kind of representation. The novel describes a group of dancers and their coterie of lovers, investors, and hangers-on. The vain, manipulative star of the troupe announces her desire for limitless sexual encounters with her male audience: "She would have liked all of her admirers to sleep together in her bed, and to possess her all at once."[19] She and her fellow dancers confess that they perform onstage not out of financial need but out of boredom and exhibitionism.[20] This, then, was the prevailing image of the belle époque music-hall dancer—attractive, amoral, and sexually voracious. The belle époque dancer's amorality spread out from her too-carnal body to contaminate her male conquests and French society in general. Such a woman inevitably brought about the moral and physical degeneration of her numerous lovers, as well as the ruin of their fortunes and families. In 1909 an anecdote in the droll magazine *Fin de siècle* told of a music-hall director who sent his virgin son backstage to lose his "flower of innocence." In a short time, the boy was indeed deflowered, but much to his father's displeasure, "it is in the dressing room of a performer of the masculine sex that one can find him regularly every night." Quite unimaginably, "not one sweet lady from the establishment" would "sell him her favors."[21] The humor of the episode only works if one assumes that the music hall was a place of sordid sexual commerce.

Middle-class wives in popular literature of the era seemed doomed by their virtue to lose their husbands to the tawdry allure of the prostitute/actress. *Dans la peau*'s Madame Bonay is a reserved bourgeois housewife who attempts to reclaim her adulterous husband's affection by becoming a music-hall demimondaine like his mistress. She perfumes her body, applies makeup, and dons the scanty apparel of a dancer. When none of these efforts bears fruit, in desperation Madame Bonay joins the same music-hall troupe as her husband's lover and ends as a pitiable figure, begging dancers for advice on winning him back.[22] The entertainment value of the sketch relied on the evident comic implications of a bourgeois woman debasing herself on a music-hall stage. Jules Leroy's 1909 vignette "Les Planches" employs this assumption to similar comic effect. A drama critic protests to a friend when his wife expresses a desire to take the stage: "my wife is honest! She was raised in the bourgeois fashion by decent *rentiers*. . . . She is mad." The critic's friend, however, defends the logic of her proposition, insisting that his wife knows well that he has developed a "very particular idea of Woman" from his time spent backstage: "you need the leotards, the costumes, the makeup, the wigs, the low-cut necklines . . . the filth of the corridors, the submission to the stage manager and director, the display and offering of the secrets of the flesh. You need all of this . . . and well, all of this your wife does not give you!"[23] That the world of the theater is one of dissimulating sexuality and promiscuity is taken for granted by the two men and by the despondent wife.

It is not by accident that Leroy includes the "filth of the corridors" in his description of the moral disorder of the music hall. In both fictional and nonfictional representations of this milieu, indictments of the moral slackness of the music hall were often accompanied by concerns about material filth. Andrew Aisenberg has noted the cultural currency of ideas about contagion and filth in turn-of-the-century republican notions of social reform, in which the "insalubrious home" seemed to menace French society.[24] Broader republican concerns with the sanitation of French living spaces, particularly those of the working classes, carried over into the indictment of theater women, as public health officials regarded theaters and music halls as moral and physical cesspools.[25] In 1908, when new health ordinances were put in place for such venues, the municipal councilman charged with examining this issue commented gravely, "in too many theaters and music halls . . . the communal dressing rooms of the chorus, the dancers, or the extras were deficient from every point of view."[26]

Imagined as insensible to middle-class standards of order and hygiene, the actresses and dancers of popular fiction were invariably slovenly, frivolous, and thoroughly incapable of the domestic orderliness demanded of a respectable housewife. The heroine of Meg Villars's story "Chorus-Girl," published in *L'Indiscret* in 1912, exemplifies this kind of portrayal. Villars, a vaudeville actress and Willy's second wife, opened her story with a music-hall dancer named Doris awakening to find a man asleep next to her whom she hazily remembers meeting after her performance the previous night. As she rises from the bed and dresses, her unnamed companion awakens and silently observes her morning *toilette*. Wearing a grimy nightgown whose sleeves she has shortened with a less than skillful hem, Doris begins to clean herself with a "dirty handkerchief." She

squeezes a blackhead, and then uses the same cloth to clean the red grease left in her nostrils by the makeup of the night before. . . . She heads toward the washbasin, which is encumbered with empty bottles[,] . . . pours out the water, wets a tiny corner of the sole towel, and sits on the floor, if not to wash, at least to dust off her feet. . . . Then, returning to the washbasin, where the dirty water has already traced a gray circumference, she slips off her nightgown.[27]

The man in Doris's bed is aroused by her half nudity and seems willing to forget her unsanitary morning ablutions as she disrobes before the washbasin. Indeed, the narrator remarks, "all [Doris's] future depends on a gesture, and she makes exactly the one she shouldn't." Without washing, she shivers and puts her nightgown back on. By way of compensation, she brushes her teeth with the dirty water from the basin. Her disgusted lover slips away without a word while she is in the kitchen preparing coffee. All hopes of wrangling money or gifts from the nameless man dashed, Doris wonders why her men always leave so quickly in the morning.

Villars's showgirl is promiscuous, careless, and, worst of all, untidy. Her work in the music hall offers no professional fulfillment but rather serves as publicity for her more consuming career as a cocotte. Doris's slack moral code is reflected in the way she keeps her household and her body. Significantly, she is incapable of even the most basic feminine duty—sewing—as demonstrated by her sloppily hemmed nightgown. Though Villars's intention in this story was doubtless to provide an amusing look at the private life of the showgirl, her depiction provides important clues about the common perception of music-hall professionals during the belle époque. As "Chorus-Girl" makes evident, the music hall was regarded as a raucous public spectacle that mixed sex and entertainment in a morally suspect fashion, not a site of hard work or professional satisfaction. Vaudeville performers were men and women deemed incapable of even the most rudimentary prerequisites of middle-class respectability: hygiene, thrift, and domestic order. Moreover, such images of female performers were understood within and intensified broader cultural anxieties regarding women and work.[28]

Colette's Music Hall

By all accounts, Colette should have been an effective example of the dissolute dancer, given her unconventional lifestyle during the belle époque. When she began her lessons with the celebrated mime Georges Wague in 1905, she was the author of numerous racy works of fiction, her marriage was collapsing, and she was unabashedly pursuing new extramarital and bisexual pleasures. Her first public shows called for her to don revealing and provocative costumes as, in turn, a bare-legged faun, a lothario (in drag), a lusty gypsy, and the mistress of a pagan god (clothed in nothing but a panther skin).[29] In addition, Colette broke new ground, theatrically speaking, by foregoing the flesh-colored leotard normally worn by performers under such costumes.

On January 3, 1907, Colette's already startling decision to take the stage became the focus of intense scandal when she opened at Paris's Moulin Rouge in *Le Rêve d'Egypte,* a pantomime in which she starred with her lover Missy.[30] Missy played a male archeologist bewitched by an Egyptian mummy who unravels herself before his eyes, revealing Colette in a skimpy jeweled breastplate and serpentine bracelets (see figures 2 and 3). When Colette and Missy shared an ardent kiss in the climactic scene of the show's premiere, the audience at the Moulin Rouge, primed by members of the de Morny and Belbeuf clans who were incensed by the use of their family names in such an enterprise, exploded.[31] Spectators hurled objects at the stage and shouted insults ("Down with the dykes!" among them, according to Judith Thurman).[32] Willy and Meg Villars, in attendance that night, were obliged to literally box their way out of the theater.[33] The prefect of police, Louis Lépine, ordered the production shut down unless Missy withdrew from the show.[34] *Le Figaro*'s editor, Gaston Calmette, spoke for many when he applauded the audience's violent response: "Did one suppose that Paris's morality had fallen so low that it would indefinitely endure shows like these that have tried its tolerance for too long? . . . Paris, indulgent to so much weakness, demands at least that such exhibitions be brief or discreet . . . If not, it decides one fine night to police its own reputation, and it is entirely correct."[35]

The indignation elicited by *Rêve d'Egypte* was a significant backdrop to Colette's career as a pantomime performer. From the outset, her performances were discussed in the press with varying degrees of approval, shock, and cynical amusement. One journalist summed up the reaction of some when he expressed heavy-hearted compassion for this "charming, literary, ever so delicate, little *bourgeoise*" who had "fallen as far as the *caf'conc'*."[36] When Stéphane Lauzanne, editor of *Le Matin*, was informed several years later that his coeditor intended to publish Colette's stories, Lauzanne reportedly threatened to quit if "that circus entertainer" ("cette saltimbanque")[37] became associated with the paper. While any bourgeois woman endangered her good standing by taking the stage, Colette's reputation was further jeopardized by her divorce, her nude performances, and her sexual

Figure 2   Colette in costume for *Le Rêve d'Egypte*, 1907. Fonds Centre d'études Colette.

Figure 3 Colette in costume for *Le Rêve d'Egypte*, 1907. Fonds Centre d'études Colette.

relationship with a woman. In fact, Emily Apter situates Colette's *Rêve d'Egypte* within a belle époque trope of "sapphic theatricality" by which women such as Colette reappropriated orientalized female stereotypes "as a means of partially or semi-covertly outing sapphic love."[38] And indeed, this transgressive outing signaled Colette's decisive turn from the rules of polite bourgeois society and from a certain construct of French femininity.

Following the violent premiere, Colette told a journalist that she was determined to continue with the show's run: "You can be certain that these demonstrations do not scare me, and that I will persevere, unless because of them, my engagement is broken tonight and I am forced to go abroad to try to earn my bread [gagner mon pain]."[39] This prioritizing of "earning her bread" was more than a defiant retort aimed at her attackers—it was also, I argue, the keystone of Colette's moral system in these years. For all her social and sexual transgression—indeed perhaps *because* of it—Colette set about establishing a literary and performative version of French vaudeville that was characterized by earnest labor, thrift, and modesty rather than lust and cupidity.

In 1910 Colette began serially publishing a semi-autobiographical novel, *La Vagabonde* (The Vagabond), which follows the vaudeville tour of a divorced writer turned dancer, Renée Néré.[40] She also regularly published short stories on the subject of the music hall for *Le Matin* beginning in 1910, and she issued a collection of stories titled *L'Envers du music-hall* in 1913, all featuring a narrator named Colette. Both Renée and the narrator-Colette of the short stories are bourgeois women who find themselves declassed by a divorce and obliged to work in the music hall. The rootless musicians and showgirls who populate these stories eschew middle-class respectability, yet they yearn for its comforts and identify with its moral code. In portraying her music-hall and literary career in this way, Colette, I argue, was attempting to square her unconventional lifestyle with her culturally shaded notions of work and moral soundness.

Throughout these years of literary and stage production, Colette would often insist that her Bohemia was a domain of domestic orderliness and fiscal responsibility, a Bohemia that, she held, differed fundamentally from that which she had frequented as Willy's wife in the 1890s. Willy's Bohemia, she later reflected, had "suited [her] as badly as a feathered hat or a pair of dangling earrings." Instead, Colette preferred a Bohemia of her own making, a realm organized around work, order, and a very different kind of femininity: "That Bohemia there, with its slightly maniacal attention to work and punctuality, could have met the standards of any bursar."[41] In letters that Colette wrote daily to friends and literary colleagues while on tour in these years, work (whether literary or theatrical) appeared not simply as a financial exigency but as a moral imperative. Again and again, Colette mentioned the details of her workday, frequently including how many hours she had worked and what she had accomplished, even during vacations. In 1908 she wrote to Georges Wague: "All I ask this winter is to work."[42]

On a break from newspaper assignments in 1913, she wrote that she planned "to relax for eight days, by working on my novel."[43] Renovating her beach house in Brittany in 1914, she barely had time to write a friend: "I'm dropping you a line, between urgent, manual tasks, and I am resorting to my métiers."[44] In her study of Colette's correspondence, Catherine Slawy-Sutton goes as far as to argue that the "real constant" in the author's letters over the course of her entire life was "the multiple repetitions" of the often painful burden of work.[45]

But if work was painful, it was also, throughout Colette's fiction and life, a fundamental and transformative human need. In *The Vagabond* she described Renée Néré and her partner Brague (a fictional portrait of Georges Wague) seeking out short-term jobs in the intervals between theatrical engagements to avoid "the idleness that demoralizes, enfeebles, and addles out-of-work actors."[46] Renée admits to being "joyously reconquered by an active passion, a need *to work*, a mysterious and undefined need."[47] In Colette's letters from this period, work was likewise connected with an intangible reward, or *récompense*. Writing to Léon Hamel in 1909 about some real estate negotiations, Colette insisted, "I really think . . . that Missy and I are going to get a reward [toucher une récompense] for our work these last few days."[48] In 1910 she wrote: "I have just finished an enormous tour, thirty cities in thirty days; it seems to me that I merit a magnificent reward [une récompense magnifique]."[49] In June 1912 she confided to Hamel: "I have worked well these days, against myself and toward my salvation."[50] Though Colette's understanding of *récompense* included financial compensation, it also involved a more penetrating moral reward.

Like Colette, *The Vagabond*'s Renée associates work with a kind of vague spiritual reward. During one performance she notes, "a mysterious discipline dominates and protects me. . . . All is well. . . . Our tough Saturday audience rewards us with a tumultuous jumble of bravos, whistles, shouts, and cordial obscenities."[51] For Renée, writing is like any other rewarding occupation: "the debauchery of invention from which one emerges aching and stiff, numbed, but already rewarded, the bearer of treasures which one unloads slowly onto the blank page."[52] Literary work is then, at once, heady liberation and a manual task to be recompensed. In fact, Colette often depicted her writing as patient, careful, even tedious work. Anne Poskin has observed that belle époque critics of Colette's literature placed her firmly within the category of "littérature féminine," which was "instinctive," "natural," and thus "incapable" of careful workmanship, calculation, and "cerebreality and construction."[53] Given the potent valorization of work in her childhood, Colette would have been particularly sensitive to such a classification.

Work, whether writing, performing, or laboring at any number of jobs, held a precise meaning for Colette and her literary alter egos; all tasks were framed in the language of craft labor, a trade or métier.[54] This tendency to view work in terms of a craft vocation reflected a republican culture that taught children to think of themselves as practitioners of a certain métier even as students. By consistently describing performance as a craft, then, Colette situated her music-hall career within a long, honorable tradition of artisanal pride. But in so doing, she was also appropriating a language usually coded male. In her study of working-class women in the Third Republic, Helen Harden Chenut writes that while "skill (*métier*) was an important component of worker identity," it was in this period "recognized almost exclusively as a male attribute or 'property.'" Yet increasingly at the turn of the twentieth century, there was a "striking discrepancy" between some women's "own conception of their métier, and the devalorized social image of the job."[55] Colette's insistence on the category of métier in explaining her work must be understood within this context.

Colette found an unusually receptive environment for such an understanding of work in belle époque pantomime. In marked contrast to the capricious entertainers of popular fiction, the pantomime artists who taught Colette consistently represented themselves as capable tradesmen who practiced a respected métier. Paul Franck, one of the most celebrated mimes of the era, who worked with Colette in one of her first shows, wrote in defense of his profession: "I don't know if pantomime is an art, but it is indeed the most fascinating métier there is."[56] At the close of a 1908 interview, Georges Wague excused his effusiveness in a lengthy discourse about pantomime by telling the journalist, "I adore my métier."[57] Wague saw his profession not as an escape from the rhythms of modern work in the music hall but as a way of abiding by the rules of regular labor. In another interview he described his annual holiday in Brittany as "the great rest of his work year," in which he permitted himself to temporarily "forget the métier."[58]

When Colette began her career as a mime, she made sure the press understood that her performances were not an opportunity for egotistical abandon but the exercise of an arduous craft. One journalist noted this peculiarity: "An authentic and well-known *femme de lettres* appearing on the music-hall stage is already singular enough, isn't it? . . . But a mime proud of her métier and speaking of raising it to the dignity of an art, there is something that is really surprising."[59] Willy explained the negative reaction of an upper-class audience to Colette's first public performance in 1906 by saying that they sought "to punish Colette for having definitely declared herself *for* professionalism, abandoning the Salons."[60] This formulation of vaudeville as a professional métier also pervades Colette's fiction from this period. Her performers are committed practitioners of an honorable craft with its own rigorous code of conduct and discipline: Renée Néré remarks in *The Vagabond*, "How ill-reputed, how misunderstood, and how denigrated are the *artistes* of the *cafés-concerts*. . . . Quixotic, proud, full of an absurd, old-fashioned faith in Art, they are the only people around who still dare to declare, with a reverential passion: 'An *artiste* must not . . . an *artiste* cannot accept . . . an *artiste* should not consent to . . . '"[61] As a bourgeois alien in this working-class milieu, Renée emulates her colleagues' professionalism and commitment to "craft," asserting that she has chosen music-hall work because it is "a métier that the most untalented woman can learn quickly, when her freedom and her life depend on it."[62] When her wealthy, upper-class lover Max questions her choice of profession, asking why she works in the *cafés-concerts*, Renée retorts: "Why don't you work as a cabinet maker? . . . What would you like me to do? Sew, type, or walk the street? The music hall, that is the métier for those who have never learned one."[63]

Viewing a métier as something more than a financial necessity, Renée takes fierce pride in her professional fitness. She is offended when Brague warns her to rest up for an upcoming show: "I don't deign to answer. Does he take me for a beginner?"[64] Renée resents that people refer to her as "a *femme de lettres* who has turned out badly," or say that she "does theater" but never call her an actress: "A subtle nuance, a polite refusal . . . to grant me any rank in this career that I have nevertheless chosen."[65] She refers to her stage makeup as "these tools of my métier" and ascribes the same professionalism to her dog, Fossette, who has "grown up in the métier."[66]

Throughout the novel, Renée refers to her colleagues in the music hall as her "comrades," her "brothers," and her "compagnons de route [fellow journeymen on the road]," thereby presenting herself as a hardworking member of a craft brotherhood. (Colette used similar terms when referring to Wague in her letters.[67]) In this music-hall guild, as described by Renée, performers lose their sex and exist only as professionals to one another: "Brague is a comrade; Bouty too. The svelte and muscled acrobats who reveal, under their pearly leotards, the most flattering features of their anatomy . . . well, they are only acrobats. . . . Have I ever considered that Brague, who grips me so tightly in *The Possession* that he bruises my ribs, and seems to crush my mouth with an ardent kiss, has a sex? No."[68] When invited to dinner by Brague one evening, Renée trusts the professional propriety of this meal: "We are two *comrades*, and the protocol—there is one!—of comradeship between artists banishes all ambiguity."[69]

The vaudeville of Colette's letters and interviews was characterized not by the caprice and chaos of popular fiction but by schedules, rehearsals, and professionalism. She and her fellow performers referred often to their disciplined training and grueling practices. Colette paid close attention to schedules, making sure to arrive on time for rehearsals and performances, and she had a habit of repeatedly asking her companions the time over the course of a day. Wague consequently nicknamed her "What-time-is-it."[70] A backstage dresser in Colette's story "Nostalgia" tells a performer: "The music hall, as I always say, is built on punctuality."[71] The narrator-Colette of another story asserts that music-hall performers strike less than other kinds of workers because "even at the word 'strike' these emotional little Parisians have vague images of people descending into the streets, riots, barricades . . . They aren't in the habit of striking. The simple, rigorous discipline that governs us abides no infractions."[72]

While popular fiction imagined actresses as indolent coquettes who would more likely be found lolling in perfumed dressing rooms than rehearsing, Colette's stories specified the discipline and physical exertion of music-hall rehearsals. In the last *Claudine* novel, 1907's *La Retraite sentimentale* (Retreat from Love), Claudine describes a rehearsal in which the mimes "expend fantastic amounts of energy, they make the same gesture fifteen times over, and gradually it becomes uncluttered and precise."[73] In the story "The Bad Morning," Colette depicts another such rehearsal led by Brague (Wague): "From his lips emanates the too familiar sound of rough instructions and necessary invective. What ugly words surrounding such beautiful gestures! Multiple attempts and failures appear on the faces of the three mimes, where effort applies a too easily broken mask."[74] By emphasizing the grueling effort of rehearsals, Colette sought to make a case for pantomime as a craft requiring skill and practice.

Not content with the prevailing notion of the music hall as a realm of moral and physical laxity, Colette elevated the theatrical profession to meet republican standards of honest labor—work that was manual. Her letters often called attention to the physical fatigue that accompanied her long days of rehearsal and performance. "I'm dog-tired," she wrote in the fall of 1908, and later, "Today we had a dress rehearsal for five and a half hours straight. . . . I'm covered with dust up to my nostrils."[75] "Wague and the ballet instructor are exhausting me!" she exclaimed to her friend Hamel in 1911. "I'm going to bed, I can't take any more."[76] Such descriptions of her music-hall tours as physical labor were a meaningful way for Colette to express the dignity of her new métier to friends and colleagues. When asked by a magazine to give a clever response to a question about Kant, Colette replied, "Sir, I am too fatigued by matinees to accord you the interview. . . . What's more, I would have nothing of genius to tell you."[77] In this way, Colette often played down the intellectual pretensions of her role as a *femme de lettres* and instead focused on the physical work of the music-hall trade. In 1909 she wrote an essay on the music hall for the magazine *Akadémos* in which she described the exhaustion of stage work and asked, "Is it much more fatiguing than a day in the life of a *femme du monde* who goes out, lunches, dresses, receives, dines, goes out again, and suppers? I doubt it."[78] In Colette's estimation, the fatigue of paid labor was preferable to that of leisured activity.

The physicality of music-hall work is also a constant refrain in Colette's fiction. Renée Néré declares that her need to work can be satisfied "just as well dancing as by writing, running, acting, or towing a handcart," thereby placing her professions alongside physical labor and exercise.[79] She and her fellow performers work their bodies mercilessly during rehearsals. In evident contrast to the leisured *femme au foyer*, Renée revels in the physical strength that such work brings and gives her body scrupulous attention, "with the somewhat obsessive rigor of an owner attached to his property."[80] She is gratified by her "pleasant and painful labor" that brings "weary and happy muscles."[81]

Colette accentuated the affinity of performance and honest labor in her fiction by constantly likening "the hardworking *caf' conc'*" to other so-called respectable professions. Her fictional music-hall *artistes* are compared to "government clerks" and employees "in the same factory."[82] The stage, "booming and vibrating beneath the feet of the dancers," is like the "the floor of a mill in action."[83] One dancer rests from her rehearsals, "like a saleswoman in a department store," and another bears her fatigue like "the washerwoman who has just let down her load of clean linen."[84] Part of the appeal of a vivacious ingénue named Jadin is her resemblance to an average manual laborer, with "her sloped shoulders that seemed still to haul a laundry basket."[85] In "La Fenice," narrator-Colette sees through the makeup of a flamboyant performer to the "red wrists under a layer of greasepaint, the hardened hands that cook, that wash, that sweep . . ."[86] The story "La Grève, bon dieu, la grève" ("The Strike, Good God, the Strike!") equates the work ethic of female performers with that of their laboring sisters in the urban workforce. In between rehearsals and shows, these women have "just enough time to stop by [their] place" to "make sure the kid hasn't fallen out the window and hasn't burned himself on the stove, and, off we go, back again. . . . We pile into the bus, the metro, the tram with all the other female workers—clerks, cashiers, milliners, dressmakers, typists—who have finished their workdays."[87] Thus, female music-hall performers are portrayed once again as diligent laborers, not pleasure-seeking slatterns. Colette's music hall was not a retreat from the world of reputable labor but rather an extreme version of that world.[88]

Unlike some formulations of artistic occupations that focused on their immaterial, creative vocation, Colette regularly avowed that, first and foremost, stage performance was a means of making a living, "gagner sa vie." Though she did not completely avoid references to the art involved in music-hall work, she was eager to underscore that her pantomimes and writing were profitable wage labor—just as she had after the riotous premiere of *Le Rêve d'Egypte* when she spoke of "earning her bread."[89] After only a few months on stage, Colette had adopted the professional ethic of a conscientious worker who was merely making a living. Years later, this would be the version of her music-hall career that commentators such as Jean Larnac would recall: "Disregarding the rumors that greeted her debut on the stage of the Moulin Rouge, Colette continued courageously earning her living as dancer and mime."[90] In 1907 Colette offered her skills as a mime to author Claude Farrère for a production of his latest work, and she excused her forwardness: "I am guided by the insane ambition to earn my living myself, as much in the theater as in literature."[91] Writing to Wague in 1912 during a break from touring, Colette insisted that she was content "to earn my living scribbling on paper."[92]

In Colette's estimation, the worthiness of music-hall performance was not diminished by this connection to monetary gain. On the contrary, *because* it allowed one to earn a living, music-hall work was honorable. This conviction came through most noticeably in her fiction from this period. *The Vagabond*'s Renée is driven by the pride of supporting herself: "On my good days, I joyfully say over and over to myself that I earn my living."[93] When a friend suggests that she accept the financial and social security offered by her moneyed lover, Renée replies incredulously: "You want to perturb my recaptured peace by advising me to take up a concern other than that rigorous, bracing, and natural concern of securing my own living?"[94] In a fascinating inversion of traditional gender norms, Colette here characterizes earning her own living as the natural state for a woman, rather than being cared for by a respectable suitor.

According to Colette's formulation of music-hall work, simply earning a living was inadequate unless accompanied by business acumen. "Earning one's living" demanded shrewd financial ability that countered the common notion of bourgeois women as blissfully isolated from the marketplace. Colette's letters to Wague reveal that she was intimately involved with the arrangements the two made with various theaters. She wrote of juggling engagements and seeking out the most lucrative offers, warning Wague in January 1907: "Keep me updated . . . and do not consider this a definitive acceptance. Because I am once again in talks with the Moulin."[95] Another of her letters sketched out a proposed budget for an upcoming show, confirming that Colette was aware of every financial detail of her productions, from the cost of stage sets to copyright fees.[96] She recognized that her celebrity was a valuable commercial asset and actively campaigned to maximize this value. In describing successful contract negotiations with a theater in 1909, she boasted to Wague, "I negotiated with Brussels (Alcazar), receiving excellent terms, the same as *Polaire*."[97] She described simultaneous negotiations between two rival theaters the same year: "If the Alhambra cannot pay me as much as the Gaîté-Rochechouart, so much for the Alhambra. It's an outfit that should be able to pay, at the least *reasonably*. And then, too, when I have a name with proven box-office value, why should I contract myself never to get more than five louis? When *shall* I raise my price . . . Two hundred francs outside Paris, one-fifty in Paris . . ."[98] Colette here evinces an astute awareness of herself as a commercial figure, both as a businesswoman and as a performer of marketable worth. She often managed her own publicity, sending her photograph to magazine editors with precise instructions for captions and placement.[99] She sometimes wrote such instructions on postcards bearing studio photographs of herself in various poses, part of a series titled "Beautés Parisiennes."[100] Colette was so pleased with the promotional posters for her show in Switzerland that she sent one back to Wague for use in future publicity campaigns.[101]

The characters of Colette's music-hall fiction are also virtuosos of business sense and thrift. In fact, the performers in her fictional troupes more closely resemble upright clerks than the wasteful Bohemians of popular imagination. A group of German acrobats even discuss stock investments during rehearsal breaks.[102] Colette portrays such fiscal prudence as an important precept of the

music-hall métier, not merely a financial necessity. In one story, the extravagant diva Roussalka is disdained by more seasoned music-hall performers because she "shone brightly among the mended leotards [and] home-laundered
dresses" of her colleagues.[103] One veteran performer is lauded because he can
set his own price with the theaters, does not drink, does not carouse, and wisely
invests his money.[104]

Having fled the bourgeois circles of her first marriage, Renée enthusiastically
pursues the satisfaction of paid labor and commercial ability in the music hall:

> Other undertakings and worries claim my attention at the moment, above all that
> of earning my living, of exchanging my gestures, my dances, and the sound of my
> voice for hard cash. . . . I have rapidly developed the habit and taste for this, with
> a rather feminine appetite for money. . . . In my good moments, I joyfully repeat
> to myself over and over that I earn my living! The music hall . . . has also made
> me into a tough but honest little businesswoman—much to my surprise when I see
> myself calculating, haggling, and negotiating.[105]

Like Colette, Renée recognizes the value of her labor, and she does not hesitate
to exploit the commercial possibilities of her body, a savvy she deems an inherently feminine trait. When negotiating an upcoming tour with a theatrical
agent, Renée, not her male partner Brague, takes the initiative in bargaining
over the contract.[106]

* * *

In paying tribute to the working-class women of the music hall, Colette was
contesting the middle-class woman's position as the moral paragon of French
society. The daily routine of the bourgeois wife is judged in Colette's fiction by
the standards of the music-hall code of conduct. Renée Néré mocks the bourgeois women who watch her from the audience, whose fashion makes them appear "convalescent and unwashed."[107] Renée's unconstrained, fit dancer's body is
enough "to insult those bodies, restricted by their long corsets and weakened by a
fashion that demands that they should be thin."[108] She later refers to the women
of the French suburbs as "*bourgeoises* in their camisoles who yawn and get up
late in order to shorten their empty days."[109] Such an idle, sleep-filled existence
offers a striking contrast to the vigorous activity of the music-hall performer.
Renée explicitly links her physical strength, her work, and her "weary and happy
muscles" with a "wild mistrust" and "disgust" for the bourgeois milieu where she
once "suffered."[110]

Colette's music-hall fiction also contested the proposition that marriage was
a woman's surest route to respectability. When a friend encourages Renée to accept Max's marriage proposal, she responds with a vicious portrait of middle-class
marriage: "To be married . . . is to tremble if Monsieur's cutlet is overcooked, his

Vittel water not cold enough, his shirt badly starched. . . . Marriage is 'Tie my tie!' 'Fire the maid!' 'Clip my toenails!' . . . [It is to be] steward, nurse, nanny—enough, enough, enough!" She insists that the role of a harem concubine would be preferable to such a condition.[111] Through her protagonist, Colette here turns on the republican call to virtuous wifehood and instead depicts marriage as a wearying endeavor that saps women of their natural vitality and reduces them to a moral level somewhere below sex slaves. Such denunciations of middle-class marriage appear in the works of other female novelists in the belle époque—writers such as Colette Yver, who depicted professional women rejecting traditional conjugality and choosing instead the rewards of their vocations.[112] But Colette grounds her heroine's rebellion on a precise understanding of the value of manual work, a language of honor through métier, which is a forceful presence throughout her oeuvre.

Renée estimates that her paid manual work also sets her above bourgeois men like her suitor Max. When he begs her to "abandon your métier" and "come back among your equals," Renée asserts that her rightful place is among her craft brethren of vaudeville: "I have no equals, I have only *compagnons de route*. . . ."[113] Max deplores Renée's music-hall work because of his conventional notion of middle-class female honor. When he hears Brague and Renée discussing plans to economize on an upcoming tour by sharing a suitcase, he is offended by the thought of Renée's undergarments mixed in with those of Brague. "It's monstrous!" he cries. "You have lost your mind! . . . What a mockery, what penury!"[114] Renée is bewildered by Max's affronted modesty, and she concludes that his inherited wealth is to blame: "Where would this spoiled child have learned that money, the money that one earns, is something respectable and serious, that one treats with care and speaks of with gravity?" In defending herself against his charge of the "promiscuité des coulisses," she maintains that she is simply a "very levelheaded *caf'conc'* who lives by her métier." Max angrily replies, "To hell with your métier!" and offers to shower her with luxuries if she quits her job and marries him.[115]

The heated exchange between Max and Renée is rooted in the couple's incongruent notions of respectable behavior. An affluent landowner, Max does not practice a trade. Renée finds this unproductive idleness indecent. The former *bourgeoise* recognizes the distinct contrast between her lover's values and those of her music-hall trade: "Disconcerted, I contemplate this man who has nothing to do, who finds money in his pocket just like that. . . . He has no métier: no sinecure disguises his idler's freedom. . . . He can give himself over completely to love, day and night, like . . . like a prostitute. . . . This baroque idea that, of the two of us, he is the courtesan, causes me an abrupt gaiety."[116] Popular formulations would most naturally compare Renée to a courtesan, given her seminude performances and upper-class lover. Colette gleefully twists this formulation in her novel—the respectable *rentier* becomes an indolent prostitute, and the music-hall dancer his industrious moral superior. The ethical yardstick of this contest is labor.

During a conversation later in the novel, Renée's partner, Brague, expresses similar shock when he discovers that Max practices no real profession:

> . . . Your friend has an office?
> —An office? No, he has no office.
> —Has he got . . . an auto factory? At least, he dabbles in something, right?
> —No.
> —He does nothing?
> —Nothing.
> Brague lets out a whistle that can be interpreted in at least two ways.
> —Nothing at all?
> —Nothing . . .

Brague finds it "amazing" that a person "could live like that. No office. No factory. No rehearsals . . ." He insists that he would die if forced to live without an occupation. Renée confesses that Max's "idleness," this "*flânerie* of a teenager on perpetual school holiday," scandalizes her as well.[117] She prefers the exhausting, wage-earning labor of her profession to her lover's comfortable inactivity, and she rejects Max's offer to join her on tour, saying: "Leave me alone with my métier that you dislike. . . . Let me finish my tour, attending to it with a military-like conscientiousness and the diligence of an honest workingwoman."[118]

Literary scholars interpret Renée's ultimate rejection of Max as, above all, a vaguely ahistorical assertion of feminine independence over masculine control (though some, like Diana Holmes, have pointed to single women's precarious socioeconomic position in the belle époque as an important context for the novel).[119] Most studies fail to recognize the historically specific significance of Renée's fictional decision.[120] I propose that, with the conflict between these two characters, Colette constructed a dialogue between two culturally constructed codes of honor. Superb scholarly work has explored the complexity of masculine codes of honor in the nineteenth century, codes that delineated an ideal egalitarian public sphere of rational male exchange and necessarily excluded women.[121] While such studies rightly historicize masculinity, they also inadvertently perpetuate the exclusion of both women and workers so scrupulously maintained by the nineteenth-century bourgeois. William Reddy indicates the "misconception" by contemporaries and historians alike that male honor was indeed rational, distinct from the (feminine) realm of feeling.[122] The "egalitarian male-only republicanism" of postrevolutionary France, Reddy writes, provided a "new configuration of gender identities" that held "ambiguities that allowed it to be challenged almost from its inception but also allowed the challenges to be reincorporated into its structure in unusual ways."[123] James Lehning also highlights the ambiguity of the Third Republic's "inherently democratic" code of honor as public virtue, which granted "participation and even leadership to anyone who fulfilled the requirement of being honorable and virtuous." Lehning alludes to the way in which such a democratized notion of honor could indeed work in tension with the republican hierarchy's efforts to "marginalize and, if possible, eliminate . . . broad claims to popular participation."[124] Andrea Mansker's study of the dueling belle époque feminist Arria Ly exposes one dramatic example of women's efforts in this period to dispute the notion "that public honor was exclusively attached to and embedded in male bodies and relationships."[125] Along these lines, I suggest that historians be more attentive to how belle époque women could adopt codes of honorable conduct not necessarily conforming to their social role as irrational vessels of sentiment.

In the traditional aristocratic sense, *The Vagabond*'s Max was honorable. A member of the haute bourgeoisie, he did not sully his hands with crass commercial work, and he judged women by their sexual purity and separation from the sphere of production. Renée and the performers she emulates regard this ethic with surprised disdain and appraise themselves on the basis of very different standards— artisanal skill, business acumen, and physical stamina. These conflicting notions of honorable conduct are apparent in a scene following Renée's seminude dance of the veils at an upper-class soirée. While her bourgeois clients are mortified when they must present the scantily clad woman with her payment, Renée is unabashed. She wonders, "What is embarrassing about that?" and leaves "joyfully clasping" the five hundred francs she has earned.[126] While the gentlemen find awkward any broaching of monetary issues with a half-naked formerly bourgeois woman, Renée feels no such discomfort because she is engaging in what she perceives to be honorable work. In describing Renée's performance in this way, Colette revealed her very personal understanding of music-hall work as honorable craft and her intense need to have her stage career understood as such by others.

Colette's valorization of métier was not simply a convenient language appropriated by the author to facilitate her fictional heroine's liberation or to justify her own unorthodox lifestyle to the public. Rather, this valorization reflected a deeply ingrained mental system inherited from the Third Republic's *morale laïque*, which saturated her notions of honorable conduct. A bourgeois woman molded by the "School of the People," Colette's formulations of work and craft offer historians a way of thinking about how men and women educated in the new schools of this period may have articulated their own code of public honor— a code that differed significantly from that of the quasi-aristocratic bourgeois duel. This alternative code of honor, I suggest, grew out of a tense reconciliation between traditional corporate identity, the reality of modernized labor, and the intellectual legacy of popular republicanism.

* * *

While Colette disparaged the constraints of bourgeois conjugality, she did value domestic order as an important component of honorable behavior, if allied with profitable work. As Renée Néré's diatribe against marriage suggests, Colette saw nothing redeeming in the middle-class housewife's daily routine of cooking and cleaning. Her fiction, however, described a music hall in which such domestic tasks could become morally sanctified activities if performed by productive female workers. Like popular literature that connected the physical and moral disorder of the music-hall dancer, Colette associated domestic and financial order with moral regeneration. To this end, her literary work and letters from this period posited a music hall of orderly domestic habits in which morals were laundered along with the dirty linen.[127]

When asked in 1913 why she worked in the music hall, Colette responded, "It's that . . . I love to live tranquilly."[128] Indeed, her fictional music hall invariably evokes the serenity of a well-ordered domestic hearth, as her fictional music-hall professionals struggle to provide a sense of domestic calm amid the disarray of life on the road. Her nomadic performers are more levelheaded homebodies than fun-loving Bohemians. In between acts, the dancer Bastienne sits like "a housewife keeping an eye on her kettle."[129] She breastfeeds her infant daughter backstage, is faithful to the merchant who keeps her, and "blossoms at home, at ease in a large apron like that worn by the women who deliver bread."[130] On tour, Renée Néré confesses to being "orderly to an obsessive degree."[131] Rather than a carefree transient, she is a remarkably domestic vagabond. Her newly acquired "taste for moving and travel" harmonizes with her "inborn and peaceful fatalism of a little *bourgeoise*." While she admits that she is now a "gypsy [bohème] . . . carried from town to town on tour," she is in fact "an orderly gypsy, who carefully patches up her well-brushed clothes herself; a gypsy who nearly always carries her slight fortune on her person; though, in her small buckskin bag, the *sous* are on one side, the silver on the other, and the gold hidden safely away in a secret pocket."[132] Despite ceaseless travel, Renée remains devoted to the ideal of feminine domestic orderliness by meticulously caring for her clothing and meager funds, referring to herself elsewhere in the novel as a "salaried gypsy."[133] Colette's use of the term "bohème" in the original French would have been a charged term in 1911, carrying with it all the connotations of the imagined criminal wandering of vagabonds and the unconventional lifestyles of Parisian Bohemia, a realm of perceived social transgression and perversion of bourgeois norms.[134] Colette, then, is suggesting an unusual definition of Bohemia, one compatible with, not opposed to, bourgeois maxims of domestic order.

Though the music halls themselves could often be, according to Colette, "sordid, airless compartments" with "foul latrines," the women of vaudeville diligently battle such disorder.[135] In stark contrast to Villars's chorus-girl Doris, Renée Néré washes assiduously following her performances: "I can't manage with any less than a good fifty minutes of bathing and grooming."[136] The "familiar odor" of the backstage area is a mélange of "soapy water, rice powder, and ammonia."[137] Ida, a vaudeville weightlifter who refers to herself as a "meticulous" and "cozy sort," preaches the importance of domestic routine for her and her performer husband:

> As for us, we have our work, which takes priority over everything. . . . Do you think it's easy to see to the upkeep of two people, underwear and all, not even counting the leotards and costumes? I can't bear to see a stain or a stitch coming undone. That's just how I am. Between Saint-Étienne and Tunis, I've made myself six chemises and six pairs of knickers, and I would have done twelve if Hector hadn't realized that he needed some flannel undershirts. . . . And then there's the dressing room to be kept clean, the hotel room to be tidied up, the bills to calculate, the money deposited at the bank.[138]

This performer embodies the republican feminine ideal—hardworking and scrupulous about the hygienic state of her family's garments as well as their living space. Ida is a sensible household manager, keeping careful accounts of expenditures and saving money. Still, this is a woman who lifts weights (and her husband) for a living, has no fixed address, and admittedly puts professional work before all other considerations. Ida's passion for her physically engaging and profitable métier obeys republican dicta on work and at the same time subverts republican norms of acceptable feminine behavior.

The dancer Bastienne is similarly attached to domestic order. Though an unwed mother, she epitomizes Colette's virtuous music-hall laborer, with her "peaceful, domestic, home-loving dancer's soul." When she window-shops, she ignores furs and velvets and instead covets "unbleached linens." While other chorus girls of popular fiction entertain themselves by seducing wealthy admirers from the audience, Bastienne finds pleasure in domestic tasks:

> Right now, she is smiling, with a wholesome sensual delight, over her favorite job: standing with her handsome arms covered in lukewarm froth, as beautiful as a queen in a washhouse, she is scrubbing her daughter's underwear in a basin with soap. . . . Why couldn't her life, her future, and even her duty be kept within these four walls of flowered wallpaper, in this dining room smelling of coffee, white soap, and iris root? Living . . . means first, dancing, and then working, in the humble and domestic sense given this word by an honest race of females.[139]

With such a description, Colette played off of and countered the popular image of the attractive if frivolous and slovenly music-hall dancer. The sensual vision of Bastienne, "her handsome arms covered in lukewarm froth," echoes the titillating portraits of the chorus girl found in popular literature. Yet in Colette's hands, the scene is suffused with probity and domestic calm. This honest, hardworking woman is nearly allegorical, "beautiful as a queen." Thus, Colette's rejection of middle-class marriage did not include a rejection of the equally traditional notion of woman as the bearer of household order. I suggest that this attention to domestic orderliness was, in part, one way for Colette to mitigate unease about female labor.

There is some evidence that this fresh image of the music-hall actress was increasingly popular by the outbreak of World War I. Cadum soap, for example, though most known for advertisements featuring a cherubic toddler, also employed music-hall actresses in its publicity campaign during this same period. Théâtre Michel's Lyse Berty posed angelically in one ad from 1914, wearing a pearl necklace and demure expression, with a caption in which the actress endorsed this "hygienic and absolutely pure" product. Berty insisted that while she had used many brands of soap, Cadum was the best. The music-hall sensation Mistinguett figured in a similar Cadum advertisement in 1912 in which she appeared, like Berty, in a rather formal headshot with pearls.[140] Such publicity campaigns associated these theater women with hygienic washing habits and fresh beauty, a far cry from the Nanas of the fin de siècle.

At the base of Colette's years of music-hall work and countless fictional depictions of this milieu was a firm conviction that labor and domestic order were inextricably linked with the health of the soul. During a vacation in 1902, Colette wrote to her friend Jeanne Muhlfeld: "My account book is like a well-tended flower bed. This is my annual debauchery of virtue . . . that restores me to the moral level of a laborer or animal keeper."[141] Because of its connections to métier, orderliness, and discipline, Colette found the theater an ideal site in which to achieve such moral regeneration. She once described her troupe's delight on arriving at a particularly well-kept music hall in Marseilles, where they were performing in a pantomime in which Colette appeared seminude: "A large music hall, all in white, varnished, polished, as clean as a well-kept bathroom . . . What a joy and what a surprise to find that in Marseilles! In our scrubbed cell, we dress gaily. . . . Once again, the atmosphere of the music hall has restored to me a light, docile, innocent soul, the peaceful soul of a novice, of a regimented female factory worker."[142] Again defying popular perceptions of vaudeville performers, particularly those that performed nude, Colette associates the music hall's bright cleanliness with a moral cleansing, leaving her with the tranquility and innocence of an "ouvrière enregimentée."

In Colette's fiction, the world of the theater, so often associated with dissolute living, is transformed by labor and order into a realm of moral rectitude. Her fictional performers in The Vagabond are noted for their "obstinate modesty," and the dancers spend their time backstage sewing, not engaging in wanton seductions.[143] In "The Sewing Room," five dancers in between acts similarly "give themselves over to the recreation of being, with all naivety, young cloistered women who sew . . . they have the chaste bent backs of diligent workingwomen." This chaste recreation quiets and soothes the women, "like a spell."[144] Though debased by her failed first marriage, Renée Néré finds moral rehabilitation and a "purified" heart in music-hall labor.[145] She has "become an old maid again with no temptations" and her dressing room a "cloister."[146] She likens her music-hall years to a "long moral convalescence" during which she has regained her strength and health.[147] Work is the agent of this cleansing revitalization.

Contemporaries took note of Colette's startling new view of the music hall. After hearing her speak at the Université Populaire in 1913, George Martin noted that in describing the music hall, "where others see a ridiculous pride, [the author of *The Vagabond*] perceives nobility." For Colette, Martin continued, "Only in the music hall has the sense of the intangible and the sacred been preserved. To believe Mme. Colette Willy, the artists of the music hall have a love of their work and give themselves to it entirely. They have healthy bodies and intact souls."[148]

And yet, while Colette offered up *The Vagabond* as an homage to the pride and dignity of music-hall labor, she was also at times clear-sighted about the brutal underside of the world of work. During one bout of fatigue on tour, Renée reconsiders her attitudes toward work:

> So must I . . . withstand this battle against fatigue . . . must I find and incessantly renew within myself this reserve of energy which is required by the life of wanderers and solitaries? . . . And to achieve what? What? What? . . . When I was little, they would tell me: "Effort brings its own reward," and indeed, whenever I made a special effort, I would wait for a mysterious, overwhelming reward, a kind of grace to which I would succumb. I am still waiting for it.[149]

This extraordinary passage is one of the rare moments in which Colette appears to question deeply held beliefs about the importance of work as a means of spiritual or moral reward. If the republican school provided her with a powerful rhetorical foundation to shore up her public identity, it also failed to provide a satisfying synthesis of its contradictory maxims and did little to mitigate the crushing exhaustion of a life entirely given over to labor. Colette was plainly struggling with this dissatisfaction in passages such as the one above. Throughout her music-hall fiction, the honorable work of the music hall is accompanied by isolation, fatigue, and alienation from general society. This was the dark corollary of the Third Republic's idealized call to manual labor.

Though Colette and her fictional alter egos (all bourgeois women in a working-class sphere) find moral regeneration in the music hall by releasing themselves from undignified bourgeois idleness, the working-class denizens of this milieu have a more ambiguous relationship with their labor. Throughout Colette's fiction, characters appear flattened and demoralized by the long hours of enervating toil. *The Vagabond's* singer Bouty is a pathetic figure whose "illness and difficult métier are killing him."[150] One comic is known for spending his time in between acts collapsed in a corner with his head in his hands. Renée Néré reflects that on tour, "We grow thin with fatigue, and no one complains, pride before everything else! We go from music hall to dressing room to hotel to room with the indifference of soldiers out on maneuvers."[151] The professional performers of Colette's fictional vaudeville find dignity and worth in their work only by sacrificing integration with the rest of society. In her stories, performers are set off from the middle classes by the "barrier" of the footlights, separate entrances, and incessant travel.[152] More than once Colette refers to music-hall performers as "exiles," solitary artists who have chosen a life of artistic expression and dignified labor, but at the price of tremendous isolation.[153]

It is worth noting the remarkable nature of Colette's formulation of her writing and performing as manual craft. A bourgeois woman who never seems to have completed a day of manual labor during her long life, she nonetheless repeatedly portrayed her professions in this way. At the height of her music-hall career, Colette could earn in a single performance what lesser stage players made in a month—and considerably more than what the average Parisian worker made in a month.[154] Her fiction does offer occasional indications of the great difference between her leisured lifestyle and the deadening labor of working-class women. But she also employed a language of honorable métier that allowed her to efface these very real differences. To a certain extent, Colette seems to have made use of the image of the working-class woman for her own psychological (and commercial) advantage, though this doubtlessly was not an entirely conscious effort. Yet it surely highlights one of the more troublesome aspects of the republican social program: that the architects of the Third Republic indeed sought this very effacement of class difference. The cross-class laic language of métier was an effective means of covering over the disquieting reality of class divisions and of rhetorically smoothing over the jagged effects of an industrial, capitalist economy that allowed the middle classes to prosper but crushed those below them on the social scale.

In 1910, the same year that chapters of The Vagabond began appearing in La Vie parisienne, a former dressmaker named Marguerite Audoux published her semi-autobiographical novel Marie-Claire. This best-seller, which went on to win the Prix Fémina that year and was tremendously popular with bourgeois readers, tempered the pathos of the working-class heroine's difficult life with her merry resignation to her lot. Angela Kershaw suggests that "proletarian literature" of this kind, which avoided didactic political arguments, "did not represent a threat to the bourgeois world view" and "could in fact confirm it" by offering "conservative messages about gender."[155] In a sense, Colette's music-hall fiction can be taken within this same school of belle époque literature—stories that used sensational, realistic details about workers' plight to elicit reader emotion as they simultaneously shored up socially conservative notions of the value and virtue of hard work. At the same time, by availing herself of the republican code of honor through métier to justify female autonomy, Colette did alter and even radicalize the dominant (secular) social values of her time.

The Shackle

Though the life of the music-hall performer provided Colette with considerable liberation and satisfaction, her metamorphosis from bourgeois hostess to craft comrade was not free from tensions. Powerful notions of middle-class respectability, marriage, and femininity made her foray into the working-class world of the music hall a complicated endeavor. On tour, yet continuing to write, Colette sometimes expressed concern that literary colleagues would disapprove of her career.[156] She often found it difficult to fix her class position verbally, referring to herself or one of her fictional alter egos in this period alternately as a "nice little bourgeoise," a "level-headed little caf'conc'," a "milliner," an "honest working-woman," or a "regimented factory worker."[157] Such oscillation exposed the author's liminal identification with middle-class society. When Renée Néré dances at an upper-class soirée in front of acquaintances from her days as a Parisian hostess, she is disconcerted by those bourgeois spectators who watch her with "that malevolent courteousness that a man of the world shows to a woman regarded as déclassée, to a woman whose fingertips he used to kiss in her salon and who now dances on a platform half-naked."[158]

While Colette's fiction often portrayed marriage as a dishonorable and ultimately unnecessary path to domestic order, she sometimes evinced a persistent attachment to the middle-class conjugality she so zestfully attacked. In *The Vagabond* Renée confesses that her "old *bourgeoisisme*, ever on guard, is secretly pleased" by Max's gentlemanly attentions.[159] At one point, she is briefly tempted by the prospect of wifely devotion: "If [Max] wants, I will tie his tie . . . and I will bring him his slippers . . . a female I found myself to be again, for better or for worse."[160] The domestic possibility provided by Max's courtship prompts Renée to distance their relationship from her work. The logistical details of her upcoming tour become "wretched little things, precise and commercial," that she attempts to conceal from Max, "my darling lazy friend."[161] The coexistence of these two realms, one domestic and feminine, the other public and commercial, is clearly problematic for Colette's vagabond. Unable to renounce the trappings of marriage unequivocally, Renée impels both realms into an uneasy, and ultimately temporary, accord. In the end, métier and autonomy triumph over the attractions of the comforting domestic hearth, and Renée leaves Max.

Soon after the publication of *The Vagabond,* Colette's own life turned from the path she had charted for her protagonist. In 1910 she met Henry de Jouvenel, editor of the newspaper *Le Matin,* scion of an aristocratic family, and a devoted republican partisan and later politician.[162] After a rather melodramatic courtship in 1911, Colette ended her relationship with Missy and took up residence in Jouvenel's house.[163] A little more than a year later, in December 1912, the two were married. Often away on business, Jouvenel left Colette to the interior decoration of their home and informed her that only some of her former friends would be permissible in their new life.[164] Months before her mother's death, Colette wrote merrily of Jouvenel "allowing" her a three-day visit to the ailing woman, "at the maximum."[165] Less than a year after her marriage to Jouvenel, she wrote to Hamel:

> Since you left, my life has been made up of hard work and facile vanities. The latter have been presidential and republican. Luncheon with the president and his wife at Brive (Madame Poincaré is charming and wants a blue cat). Culinary expositions, a dinner, with myself as hostess, for eighty-seven guests . . . and during all this time I have been trying to find a synonym for *avid*. Don't look, Hamel. There isn't one— or at least not the one I want. . . . At present I am sociable, attentive to conversation, very nice, and futile. Soon I am going to be able to crochet. . . . The day before I finished *L'Entrave* [The Shackle]. I worked six hours. The last day, eleven hours. As the end was no good, I had to begin all over.[166]

This letter is highly suggestive. Through her marriage to Jouvenel, Colette now epitomizes the model *bourgeoise* she had so carefully deconstructed in *The Vagabond*. Now occupied with "facile" vanities, Colette is a gracious hostess who discusses house pets with the president's wife. Her description of herself as "sociable, attentive to conversation, very nice, and futile" conforms to the feminine ideal of ornamental idleness the author normally disdained. Though still attentive to work, Colette is tellingly unable to find a particular word, as if her productivity has been stunted by her new conjugal role.

The novel Colette refers to in the letter above, *L'Entrave* (The Shackle), was a sequel to *The Vagabond* and, apparently, a fictionalized account of her relationship with Jouvenel. No longer financially obligated to work due to a bequest from a wealthy relative, Renée Néré has left the music hall and taken to aimless travel with dissipated friends in the south of France. This life of easy pleasure leaves her dissatisfied; she remarks, "I no longer have a métier."[167] Once an "honest wage-earner," Renée scorns her traveling companions' indolence, even though she is also now guilty of unprofitable idleness: "I am trailing about in old bedroom slippers and my dressing gown gapes open over a crumpled chemise, whose slotted insertion is empty of ribbon. . . . In the days when I earned my own living, humbler lingerie never lacked ribbons or buttons."[168] Renée's domestic disorder is directly connected to her separation from wage-earning labor. One evening, she visits her former partner, Brague, backstage and finds that he has little interest in her, "because I no longer work, because I am finished. . . . I no longer exist."[169] As she is ushered out a door for spectators only, her "heart [is] swollen with sorrow and jealousy."[170]

The entire novel is pervaded by this sense of melancholic exile from the music hall, a sadness, I argue, rooted in Renée's lack of occupation. When she eventually falls in love with a seductive womanizer named Jean, Renée frames their affair as a contest between professional satisfaction and feminine submission. However, unlike the denouement of *The Vagabond*, romantic surrender here triumphs over honorable work. With erotic resignation, Renée repeats her line from the beginning of the novel: "I no longer have a métier. . . . There is one objective before me: this man who does not want me and whom I love. . . . From now on, that is my métier."[171] The novel ends with Renée remaining in their vacation house while Jean returns to work: "It seems to me, as I watch him launch out enthusiastically into life, that he has changed places with me; that he is the eager vagabond and that I am the one who gazes after him, anchored forever."[172] The ambivalence of this passage is palpable. Jean seems to have taken on those characteristics with which Renée once joyfully distinguished herself from Max and from the other bourgeois women in *The Vagabond*: energetic physical activity and engagement with the world of work.

The novel's conclusion was one that Colette herself admittedly found unsatisfactory. Decades later, she reflected: "Consider, hypothetical readers . . . the scamped ending, the inadequate corridor through which I desired my diminished heroes to pass. Consider the fine but empty tone of an ending in which they do not believe."[173] The very difficulty Colette experienced in writing the sequel to *The Vagabond* points to the tensions inherent in the kind of reconciliation she was attempting. What is most important for the purposes of this study is not that Colette has her heroine choose marriage over métier but that the author posed this problem at all. While she and her fictional doppelgangers did sometimes opt for conjugal domesticity, Colette never truly relinquished a firm conviction that professional craft was the essential route to moral soundness. Some historians depict Colette as an ideal *vraie femme* who effortlessly accepted traditional femininity and the sexual division of labor. Anne Martin-Fugier uses Colette as an example of the turn-of-the-century Frenchwoman who recognized that "the happiness of a woman is to understand that which should be prioritized, the home. . . . That which gives rhythm to their existence is not their métier but the departure and return of their companion."[174] As the preceding analysis makes clear, Colette's approach to the problems of work, femininity, and respectability was decidedly more complex than such studies indicate. Colette continued to perform onstage after her marriage to Jouvenel, and even after she was several months pregnant with their daughter.[175] Throughout their marriage, she gave lectures on the music hall, embarked on reporting assignments all over France, and regularly published novels and stories. If she served as a hostess for a dinner party here and there, Colette never wholly embraced the role of the sequestered bourgeois wife. Indeed, the greater part of her literary career took place after she and Jouvenel divorced in 1925.

Colette's music-hall fiction can most usefully be read as an imaginative, often paradoxical attempt to reconcile the tangled threads of a powerful, if flawed, republican *morale*. I am most interested in the historical specificity of Colette's construction and reconstruction of female identity during this period. The creative labor that went into the writing of characters such as Renée Néré is emblematic of the kind of mental figurations many women worked through during this intense period of social transition in France. Even disregarding the flowering of French feminism during the period 1900–1914, many women of the belle époque were experiencing unprecedented new liberties in education, in the workplace, and in their private lives. Women such as Colette made sense of the evolution from Angel in the House to *femme nouvelle* using a new laic moral structure that elevated wage-paying labor and professional métier in a new context.

Colette once commented that the music hall was a "world where corporate solidarity is a magnificent thing, but where the fierceness of the individual is no less magnificent."[176] Thus, her music hall achieved the heartfelt dream of a generation of republican officials—the perpetuation of traditional, socially beneficial corporate values and the simultaneous triumph of the autonomous individual. William Sewell, who has examined the persistence of the language of corporate labor in the French revolutionary rhetoric of 1848, examines how the "meaning of corporate phrases or institutions was inevitably altered" by historical change.[177] Applying Sewell's study more broadly, I suggest that the way in which Third Republican institutions may have integrated the language and ideology of labor into their own tense handling of class and work offers a rewarding field of inquiry. Colette's own experience indicates that age-old craft ideals may have served a new function in the radically different work world of industrializing, early twentieth-century France.

Though her career as a performer was over by the outbreak of World War I, Colette returned to the music hall often by way of lectures and writing in the decades that followed. In 1922 she spoke of her nostalgia for the music hall: "It is a convent; it is silence . . . a life of regularity and strict training . . . the last temple of personal merit."[178] During a 1924 lecture on the music hall, Colette told the audience that while for them "these memories are nothing, a little image in passing," for her they "took on the force of an *état d'âme* [a state of soul]."[179] This *état d'âme*, which located rectitude in craft labor, commercial ability, and domestic order, marked Colette's literature and life until her death in 1954. However, any understanding of her later work must begin with this crucial early period, during which she first imaginatively reworked the definition of *une vraie femme*, selectively patching together deep-rooted republican ideals of work, honor, marriage, and domestic order.

Notes

The author acknowledges Duke University Press for allowing the reprinting of portions of this chapter that appeared as "Earning Her Bread: Métier, Order, and Female Honor in Colette's Music

Hall, 1906–1913," in *French Historical Studies* 28, no 3 (Summer 2005): 497–530; and Rowman and Littlefield for allowing the reprinting of portions of this chapter that appeared as "Colette: The New Woman Takes the Stage in Belle Époque France," in *The Human Tradition in Modern Europe*, ed. Cora Granata and Cheryl Koos (2007).

1. Henri Giraud, "Mme Colette Willy parle de l'Envers du Music-Hall," *Le Petit Niçois*, 10 February 1913.

2. Colette and Willy enacted a *separation de biens* in May 1905, though they lived under the same roof until November 1906. Their divorce was finalized on 21 June 1910.

3. Georges Wague (1874–1965) attended Catholic schools, including the Collège Stanislas. In his adult life, he often moved in left-leaning circles. See Tristan Rémy, *Georges Wague: Le Mime de la belle époque* (Paris, 1964).

4. Thurman, *Secrets of the Flesh*, 127.

5. Born in 1863, Mathilde de Morny, the niece of Napoleon III, divorced the Marquis de Belbeuf in 1903.

6. "Gauthier-Villars to Wed: French Writer, Known as 'Willy,' to Marry Mlle. Maniez," *New York Times*, 2 April 1911. Born Marguerite Maniez (1885–1958), Meg Villars married Willy in 1911 and was friends with Colette.

7. Judith G. Coffin, *The Politics of Women's Work: The Paris Garment Trades, 1750–1915* (Princeton, NJ, 1996).

8. Gildea, *France*, 27, 30.

9. Ibid., 65.

10. See Munholland, "Republican Order," 15–36; Rearick, *Pleasures of the Belle Époque*, 149–54.

11. Lenard R. Berlanstein, *Daughters of Eve: A Cultural History of French Theater Women from the Old Regime to the Fin de Siècle* (Cambridge, 2001), 180–181. Roberts offers a valuable examination of some of the same issues in *Disruptive Acts*.

12. Berlanstein, *Daughters of Eve*, 181.

13. On this dynamic in French Bohemia see Seigel, *Bohemian Paris*.

14. Roberts, "Acting Up."

15. Roberts, *Disruptive Acts*, 69–70.

16. See F. W. Hemmings, *The Theater Industry in Nineteenth-Century France* (New York, 1993), 145.

17. Alain Corbin points out that many women employed by the *cafés-concerts* engaged in prostitution in the belle époque. See *Women for Hire* (Cambridge, MA, 1990). Beginning in the 1890s, performers' trade unions waged campaigns against "the trade in artistes," gaining momentum around 1903 (173). Colette's fiction and letters refer to attempts by spectators to buy sex from her.

18. Anne Martin-Fugier, *Comédienne: De Mlle Mars à Sarah Bernhardt* (Paris, 2001), 351.

19. René Schwaeblé, *Dans la peau: Roman de moeurs de café-concert* (Paris, 1907), 101.

20. Ibid., 84–85.

21. *Le Fin de Siècle*, 7 March 1909.

22. Schwaeblé, *Dans la peau*, 120–21.

23. Jules Leroy, "Les Planches," *Fin de Siècle*, February 1909.

24. Andrew Aisenberg, *Contagion: Disease, Government, and the "Social Question" in Nineteenth-Century France* (Stanford, CA, 1999), 136.

25. See Alain Corbin's "Commercial Sexuality in Nineteenth-Century France: A System of Images and Regulations," in *The Making of the Modern Body*, ed. Thomas Laqueur and Catherine Gallagher (Berkeley, CA, 1987) 209–219.

26. Paul Delay, "La Nouvelle Ordonnance des Théâtres et Concerts," *Echo de Paris*, 27 March 1908.

27. Meg Villars, "Chorus-Girl," *L'Indiscret*, May 1912.

28. Joan Wallach Scott demonstrates the discursive links between working women and prostitutes in *Gender and the Politics of History* (New York, 1988), 142.

29. In February 1906 Colette premiered as a faun in *Le Désir, la chimère et l'amour*. That year she also appeared in Willy's play *Aux Innocents les mains pleines* as a gigolo, and in Paul Franck and Edouard Mathé's pantomime *La Romanichelle*. In November she joined Wague in *Pan* at l'Oeuvre, in a speaking role as Paniska.

30. The publicity for the pantomime never named Missy but referred instead to the mysterious "Yssim." The marquise was listed as the pantomime's author, though it may have been written by Willy, Georges Wague, and/or Émile Vuillermoz. Like Colette, Missy was taking mime lessons from Wague. For an analysis of this show and the public response, see Michael Lucey, *Never Say I: Sexuality and the First Person in Colette, Gide, and Proust* (Durham, NC, 2006).

31. Such onstage pairings (two women, one in drag, playing lovers) were not uncommon in the music hall. Christine Kerf, Wague's other stage partner, often played male parts in pantomimes, sometimes opposite Colette. Missy's transgression, then, lay in dressing as a man all the time. Also, much of the audience knew her to be Colette's lover.

32. Thurman, *Secrets of the Flesh*, 171.

33. See a letter from Meg Villars to Willy's son Jacques following the premiere, quoted in Pichois and Brunet, *Colette*, 141–42.

34. Henceforth, Wague replaced Missy as the archeologist in the renamed *Songe d'Egypte*.

35. Gaston Calmette, *Le Figaro*, January 1907. Quoted in *Le Matin*, 5 January 1907.

36. "Une Femme de lettres," *Les Guêpes*, 25 April 1912.

37. The coeditor was Henry de Jouvenel, later Colette's second husband. Quoted in Thurman, *Secrets of the Flesh*, 219. Lauzanne ultimately remained.

38. Emily Apter, "Acting Out Orientalism: Sapphic Theatricality in Turn-of-the-Century Paris," in *Performance and Cultural Politics*, ed. Elin Diamond (New York, 1996), 24. In *Sisters of Salome* (New Haven, CT, 2002), Toni Bentley calls Colette's performance career "the first time Salome had appeared overtly as both a femme fatale and a lesbian" (172).

39. Paul Lagardère, *Le Petit Parisien*, 5 January 1907.

40. On autobiographical fiction, see Flieger, *Colette and the Fantom Subject*.

41. Colette, *Mes Apprentissages*, in *Oeuvres complètes de Colette* (Paris, 1973), 8:196.

42. Letter to George Wague, 1 September 1908, in *Letters from Colette*, trans. Robert Phelps (New York, 1980), 12.

43. Letter to Georges Wague, January 1913, in *Lettres de la Vagabonde*, ed. Claude Pichois and Roberte Forbin (Paris, 1961), 87.

44. Letter to Léon Hamel, 15 July 1914, in ibid., 104.

45. Catherine Slawy-Sutton, "Colette's Correspondence, or 'Ceci n'est pas une lettre, c'est un petit bulletin sanitaire,'" *Pacific Coast Philology* 34, no. 1 (1999): 10.

46. Colette, *La Vagabonde*, in *Oeuvres complètes de Colette*, 3:298. All subsequent references to the French version will be to this edition. F. Dubief's *La Question du vagabondage* (Paris, 1911) linked periods of unemployment for seasonal workers with descent into vice, especially for women (see 173–74).

47. *La Vagabonde*, 289. Emphasis in original.

48. Letter to Léon Hamel, 1 June 1909, in *Lettres de la Vagabonde*, 35.

49. Unpublished letter from 1910, BNF NAF 18708, #256.

50. Letter to Léon Hamel, 26 June 1912, in *Lettres de la Vagabonde*, 68.

51. *La Vagabonde*, 222.

52. Ibid., 226.

53. Poskin, "Colette et 'l'Argus de la Presse,'" 118.

54. For an analysis of the use of métier in a different context, see Silverman, "Pilgrim's Progress" and *Van Gogh and Gauguin*. Janet Whatley mentions Colette's craft language in "Colette and

the Art of Survival," in *Colette: The Woman, The Writer*, ed. Erica Mendelson Eisinger and Mari Ward McCarty (University Park, PA, 1981), 32–39.

55. Helen Harden Chenut, *The Fabric of Gender: Working-Class Culture in Third Republic France* (University Park, PA, 2005), 171, 172. Also see Chenut's "The Gendering of Skill as Historical Process: The Case of French Knitters in Industrial Troyes, 1880–1939," in *Gender and Class in Modern Europe*, ed. Laura L. Frader and Sonya O. Rose (Ithaca, NY, 1996), 77–107.

56. Paul Franck, "Pour la Pantomime," *La Liberté*, 18 September 1910.

57. E. Rouzier-Dorcières, "La Pantomime à notre époque," January 1908, Bibliothèque de l'Opéra, D412 (3), 60–61.

58. Georges Maurevert, "Paris-Côte d'Azur, Rapide," *L'Eclaireur de Nice*, 11 March 1910.

59. Joseph Gravier, "Un Entretien avec Colette Willy: Académicienne sans fauteuil," *La Presse sportive et littéraire* (Lyon), 24 December 1910.

60. Letter from Willy to Curnonsky, quoted in Thurman, *Secrets of the Flesh*, 164.

61. *La Vagabonde*, 245. Emphasis in original.

62. Ibid., 238.

63. Ibid., 334.

64. Colette, *The Vagabond*, trans. Enid McLeod (London, 1954), 192. All subsequent references to the English translation will be to this edition.

65. *La Vagabonde*, 226.

66. Ibid., 350, 269.

67. Pichois and Brunet, *Colette*, 182.

68. *La Vagabonde*, 282.

69. Ibid., 287. Emphasis in original.

70. Letter to Georges Wague from Rozven, 10 April 1911, in *Lettres de la Vagabonde*, 51. Colette recalled this nickname in *L'Etoile Vesper* (Évreux, Eure: Fayard, 1986) 143.

71. Colette, "Nostalgie," *L'Envers du music-hall*, in *Oeuvres complètes de Colette*, 4:233. *L'Envers du music-hall* was originally published in 1913.

72. Colette, "La Grève, bon dieu, la grève!" in *L'Envers du music-hall*, 214.

73. Colette, *Retreat from Love*, trans. Margaret Crosland (New York, 1974), 115. Originally *La Retraite sentimentale* (Paris, 1907).

74. Colette, "Le mauvais matin," *L'Envers du music-hall*, 177.

75. Letters to Georges Wague, dated 1 September 1 and 14 November 1908, in *Letters from Colette*, 12.

76. Letter to Léon Hamel, 19 August 1911, BNF NAF 18712.

77. "Colette Willy," *Paris-Théâtre*, 25 April 1908.

78. Colette Willy, "Music-Hall," *Akadémos*, January 1909.

79. *La Vagabonde*, 289.

80. Ibid., 265.

81. Ibid., 241.

82. *The Vagabond*, 185; "La Travailleuse," *L'Envers du music-hall*, 197.

83. *The Vagabond*, 6.

84. Colette, "Après minuit," *L'Envers du music-hall*, 200; "La Travailleuse," 198.

85. *La Vagabonde*, 229.

86. Colette, "La Fenice," *L'Envers du music-hall*, 257.

87. Colette, "La Grève, ," 216.

88. Michèle Sarde discusses this theme in Colette's music-hall fiction, viewing the workmanlike approach to vaudeville as one that came "very naturally" to her given the social background of her music-hall comrades and her financial straits. See *Colette: Free and Fettered*, 258.

89. Paul Lagardère, *Le Petit Parisien*, 5 January 1907.

90. Larnac, *Colette*, 97.

91. Letter from Colette to a friend (presumably written to Farrère after Colette debuted in *La Chair* in 1907), in *Sido: Lettres à sa fille—précédé de lettres inédites de Colette*. (Artigues-près-Bordeaux, 1984), 25.

92. Letter to Wague, December 1912, BNF NAF 18708, vol. 3.

93. *The Vagabond*, 27–28.

94. *La Vagabonde*, 286.

95. Unpublished letter to Wague, January 1907, BNF 18708, vol. 3, #5–6.

96. Unpublished letter to Wague, 1908 or 1909, BNF NAF 18708, vol. 3, #36–37.

97. Letter to Georges Wague, Summer 1908, BNF NAF 18708, vol. 3, #15–16. Emphasis in original.

98. Letter to Georges Wague, 29 April 1909, in *Letters from Colette*, 15. Emphasis in original.

99. Unpublished letter, presumably to Gaston de Pawloski, January 1910, BNF NAF 18708, vol. 3.

100. See postcards sent around 1909, BNF NAF 18708, vol. 3, #261–62.

101. Letter to Georges Wague, 1 September 1908, in *Lettres de la Vagabonde*, 21–22.

102. *La Vagabonde*, 96.

103. "Le Laissé-pour-compte," *L'Envers du music-hall*, 246.

104. *La Vagabonde*, 368.

105. Ibid., 237–38.

106. *The Vagabond*, 96–98.

107. *La Vagabonde*, 253.

108. Ibid., 254.

109. Ibid., 359.

110. Ibid., 241.

111. Ibid., 337–38.

112. See Juliette Rogers, "Feminist Discourse in Women's Novels of Professional Development," in *A 'Belle Epoque'? Women and Feminism in French Society and Culture, 1890–1914*, ed. Holmes and Tarr. Also see Rogers's *Career Stories*.

113. *La Vagabonde*, 392.

114. Ibid., 354.

115. Ibid., 355.

116. Ibid., 332.

117. Ibid., 351–52.

118. Ibid., 373.

119. For Diana Holmes, the novel expressed women's desire for financial independence in a patriarchal society; these women "do not choose marriage or cohabitation out of mere inclination: it is also their principal means of economic survival" (*Colette*, 62).

120. For an overview of critical readings of *La Vagabonde*, see Collado, *Colette, Delarue-Mardrus, Tinayre*. In *Colette: A Study of the Short Fiction* (New York, 1995), Mari McCarty says the novel conveys an expression of Colette's choice of a "gynocentric" world (145). For Jennifer Waelti-Walters, the novel demonstrates Colette's "traditional attitude to women which makes her see emancipation in terms of sexual freedom only" (*Feminist Novelists of the Belle Époque*, 140). Renée leaves Max with "no sense of emancipation or delight in her own independence. Rather she sees herself as diminished" (154). Nancy Miller mentions that the novel does "pose the possibility of a female identity self-consciously constructed through work" (*Subject to Change*, 252).

121. Berenson writes that belle époque France "possessed a culture of honor . . . that counted the appearance of strength in men, and of sexual virtue in women, above else" (*Trial of Madame Caillaux*, 169).

122. William Reddy, *The Invisible Code: Honor and Sentiment in Postrevolutionary France, 1814–1848* (Los Angeles, 1997), 228.

123. Ibid., 230. According to Robert Nye, an unmarried woman's sexual purity was the primary component of her honor. See *Masculinity and Male Codes of Honor in Modern France* (Los Angeles, 1993), 29, 41.

124. Lehning, *To Be a Citizen*, 77.

125. Andrea Mansker, "'The Pistol Virgin': Feminism, Sexuality, and Honor in Belle Époque France," (Ph.D. dissertation, University of California at Los Angeles, 2003), 12. Also see "'Mademoiselle Arria Ly Wants Blood!' The Debate Over Female Honor in France," *French Historical Studies* 29, no. 4 (Fall 2006).

126. *La Vagabonde*, 255.

127. Patricia O'Hara notes the tendency by some critics of the 1890s British music hall to describe the real-life femininity of female performers to temper the discomfort provoked by their work. See "The Woman of To-Day," 146.

128. Georges Martin, "Une Interview de Colette Willy," *La Renaissance Contemporaine*, 10 January 1913.

129. Colette, "Le mauvais matin," 177.

130. Colette, "L'enfant de Bastienne," *L'Envers du music-hall*, 222.

131. *La Vagabonde*, 375.

132. Ibid., 276.

133. *The Vagabond*, 187.

134. Dubief's *La Question du vagabondage* exemplifies contemporary anxieties about the music hall as a haven for the idle and easily corrupted.

135. *La Vagabonde*, 122–23.

136. Ibid., 225.

137. Ibid., 269.

138. Colette, "Le Cheval de manège," *L'Envers du music-hall*, 180.

139. Colette, "L'enfant de Bastienne," 222.

140. See Michel Wlassikoff and Jean-Pierre Bodeux, *La fabuleuse et exemplaire histoire de bébé Cadum* (Paris, 1990). Mistinguett appeared in Cadum ads well into the 1920s.

141. Letter to Jeanne Muhlfeld, mid-July 1902, in *Lettres à ses pairs*, 54.

142. Colette Willy, "Marseille," *La Vie parisienne*, 10 July 1909.

143. *La Vagabonde*, 245.

144. Colette. "L'ouvroir," *L'Envers du music-hall*, 185.

145. *La Vagabonde*, 345.

146. Ibid., 282.

147. Ibid., 266.

148. Martin, "Interview de Colette Willy."

149. *La Vagabonde*, 315.

150. Ibid., 230.

151. Ibid., 384.

152. Ibid., 241, 251.

153. Ibid., 376.

154. Pichois and Brunet compare Colette's earnings to other professions (*Colette*, 159).

155. Angela Kershaw, "Proletarian Women, Proletarian Writing: The Case of Marguerite Audoux," in Holmes and Tarr, *A 'Belle Epoque'?* 264, 266.

156. See letter to Francis Jammes, April 1906, in *Letters from Colette*, 8; letter to Robert de Montesquiou, mid-January 1909, in *Lettres de la Vagabonde*, 28–29.

157. *La Vagabonde*, 334, 355, 373 ; "Marseille," *La Vie Parisienne*, 10 July 1909.

158. *La Vagabonde*, 253. The story also appears in "Le Cachet en Ville," *Paris-Journal*, 20 January 1910.

159. *La Vagabonde*, 261.

160. Ibid., 346.

161. Ibid., 353.

162. Born in 1876, Henry de Jouvenel was educated (like Willy and Wague) at the Collège Stanislas and the Sorbonne, worked in government ministries allied with the republican left between 1902 and 1906, and was an editor at *Le Matin*. In the 1920s he was elected as a senator, in the last years of his marriage to Colette. See Pichois and Brunet, *Colette*, 205; Thurman, *Secrets of the Flesh*, 224–26.

163. Jouvenel was wounded in a duel then rushed to Switzerland, where Colette was performing, and professed his love. When his mistress threatened to kill Colette, he had her sequestered in a house. Letter to Léon Hamel, 31 July 1911, in *Letters from Colette*, 23.

164. Letter to Léon Hamel, 17 August 1912, in *Letters from Colette*, 31.

165. Letters to Léon Hamel, 6 August 1912 and August 26, 1912, in *Letters from Colette*, 30–31.

166. Letter to Léon Hamel, 16 September 1913, in *Letters from Colette*, 37–38.

167. Colette, *L'Entrave* (Paris, 1913), 11. All subsequent references to the French version are to this edition.

168. Colette, *The Shackle*, trans. Antonia White (London, 1964), 33. All subsequent references to the English translation are to this edition.

169. *L'Entrave*, 100.

170. Ibid., 104–5.

171. Ibid., 301.

172. *The Shackle*, 224.

173. Colette, *The Evening Star (Recollections)*, trans. David Le Vay (London, 1973), 137. Originally published as *L'Étoile vesper (souvenirs)* (Paris, 1946). Colette gave birth while writing the novel.

174. Martin-Fugier, *La Bourgeoise*, 268–74. See also Mona Ozouf, *Women's Words*.

175. Colette performed in *L'Oiseau de nuit* in Geneva in March 1913, despite being visibly pregnant. Colette Renée de Jouvenel was born on 3 July 1913.

176. "Des Deux côtés de la rampe," 9 February 1924, BHVP: Bouglé, Série 30.

177. William H. Sewell, *Work and Revolution in France: The Language of Labor from the Old Regime to 1848* (New York, 1980).

178. Quoted in Alexandra Pecker, "Colette," *Excelsior*, 4 June 1922.

179. Colette, "Des Deux côtés de la rampe," 9 February 1924.

5

"THE TRIUMPH OF THE FLESH"

Women, Physical Culture, and the Nude in the French Music Hall, 1900–1914

In June 1907 the Parisian magazine *Fantasio* announced an upcoming stage show called *La Chair* (The Flesh), featuring Georges Wague and an actress known as "la Belle Impéria."[1] In this mimodrama, an unfaithful peasant named Yulka is nearly murdered by her smuggler lover when he discovers her in an amorous embrace with a young soldier. When Yulka's dress is torn in the struggle, the murderous cuckold is halted in his tracks by the startling power of his mistress's nude body. Instead of murdering his lover, he nails his hand to a table with a knife, while Yulka promptly goes mad. Impéria defended her decision to perform in this pantomime to *Fantasio*: "In a time when female nudity in the theater only offers spectators a rather deplorable exhibition . . . la Belle Impéria wanted, to the contrary, to give a truly artistic show, proclaiming without false shame the triumph of the shape of the female body, the proud poem of the flesh."[2] The show became a box-office hit later that year when Colette replaced Impéria in the role of Yulka (see figure 4). During the four years that Colette and Wague toured with *The Flesh* in France, Belgium, and Switzerland, Colette's justifications for her nude performance repeatedly echoed those of Impéria: that the nude female actress was not an object of salacious interest but a work of art. While some reviews of *The Flesh* played up the lascivious possibilities of the show's nudity and reproduced the contemporary conflation of music-hall dancers with moral license, other critics unexpectedly praised the sobriety and dignity of Colette's nude form. Such a reception of this performance was made possible by a new approach to the body shared by performers, reviewers, and audiences alike, an approach that found its most spectacular expression in the physical aesthetic of belle époque popular entertainment.

In the years leading up to the Great War, contemporary concerns about bodily fitness were informed by an expansive modern aesthetic connecting the moral

Figure 4   George Wague and Colette as they appeared in the last scene of *La Chair*, around 1907. Fonds Centre d'études Colette.

and the physical, which embraced but was not restricted to pronatalist fervor and found a rich field of expression in the music hall. As Rae Beth Gordon makes plain, the French music hall's passion for the physical—the "epileptic" dancer whose ugliness and convulsive movements were read as expressions of nervous pathology, primitivism, and supposed African savagery—broadcast the period's "fascination with the hysterical body" and close linkage of modernity and neurosis.[3] But if one music-hall physique traded on an erotic fixation with notions of the ugly, the savage, and the degenerate, another began to identify the movement of scantily clad bodies with moral salubrity. The staging of such a body attested, I argue, to the formidable cultural sway of the republican *morale laïque*, a political and cultural system of thought that transformed public iterations of the feminine at the turn of the twentieth century.[4] Through *morale laïque* schoolboys were drilled in *bataillons scolaires*, schoolgirls were taught to be fruitful and multiply, and both were trained to knit body and soul together as integral halves of a whole being.[5] Third Republican institutions, from the popular press to primary schools, affirmed the maintenance of the body as a moral imperative for all rational beings (not as a gender-specific duty) and plotted a path to moral perfection by way of the physical, rather than by a flight from corporeality. Fin-de-siècle health and physical education curricula presented French girls in particular with a persistent linking of physical beauty and moral goodness, as well as, in the words of Mary Lynn Stewart, "gendered appeals to women's duties toward their families and, more seductively, to their right to take care of their bodies."[6]

Historians have underestimated the cultural impact of such contradictory appeals, with women's physical culture too often serving either as a footnote to broader histories of anxious, masculine patriotism and elite recreation or as an exceptional prelude to the feminine style of the 1920s.[7] Yet by relocating analytical focus from organized and recreational sports (in which women may have been a minority) to the physical spectacles of the music hall (which involved women as much if not more than men), it becomes evident that new forms of active femininity did not simply parrot nationalist and natalist rhetoric. Rather, the women of French vaudeville and their staged bodily fitness coincided with and drove forward a significant shift in popular culture at the belle époque.

* * *

During the period of her music-hall career, Colette found fresh meaning in primary school lessons of moral regeneration through physical fitness. When she moved to Paris with Willy following their wedding in May 1893, she felt like a conspicuous outsider in her husband's social circle, in which Decadent and Symbolist artists tested their bodies with alcohol and opium and pursued the life of the dream through intoxication.[8] For these writers and poets, the human body was naturally perverse, and some cultivated a personal style that reflected this view. Willy, though only in his mid-thirties during the early years of his marriage to Colette, exaggerated his weight and sartorial style to appear more portly and considerably more aged than he was in actuality.

The life of a leisured Parisian hostess did not sit well with Colette, and she fell gravely ill in the winter of 1894—an illness she later portrayed as an emotional and physical deterioration brought on by the move to Paris and by her demoralizing marriage to Willy.[9] In the period that followed, she discovered a potent means of contending with her crumbling marriage and, later, with the disquieting independence that accompanied its end: the fortification of her body. Like many bourgeois women in the late 1890s, she began filling her time with activities such as tennis, swimming, and bicycling.[10] In time, Colette's interest in physical exercise became more systematic as she began participating in the belle époque's burgeoning *culture physique*.

As scholars such as Gilbert Andrieu have established, the fin de siècle brought a new generation of French men and woman enamored with the development of muscular strength through any number of fashionable activities: gymnastics, fencing, boxing, dance.[11] An early adept of this *culture physique*, Colette had her husband install a gym in their Parisian apartment, including parallel bars, rings, ladders, and a trapeze.[12] She brought this portable gym with her to the couple's country house during the summers, setting it up in the yard and waking early to exercise.[13] In 1904 Colette bragged to fellow writer Francis Jammes: "I can do cartwheels, tricks on the rings, and I can knock myself in the head with my feet from behind. Don't you like that?"[14] Two years later, after she had begun performing publicly, she offered Jammes: "If you like, I will send you a photograph of me dressed as a faun, apropos my nice muscles."[15] She also boasted of her "beautiful muscles" in a letter to Robert de Montesquiou around this time.[16] In a 1906 interview with *Gil Blas,* Colette connected her gymnastic proficiency to her schooldays, insisting to Michel Georges-Michel that in Saint-Sauveur she had been "brilliant in French composition and in gym. Oh! in gym even today. I can execute cartwheels that make Francis de Croisset blush, and I can perform exercises on the trapeze and the mat."[17]

During the final years of her cohabitation with Willy, Colette made use of gymnastic exercise as a moral and physical outlet. Describing her gym in a memoir years later, she distinguished herself from upper-class Parisians who furnished their attic studios "with garden benches, divan-beds, Japanese umbrellas, church vessels, and choir stalls." Unlike these illicit love nests and orientalist fantasies, Colette's studio "had no ornaments beyond the fittings of a gymnasium, the horizontal bar, trapeze, rings and knotted rope. I used to swing and turn over the bar, suppling my muscles . . . exercising my body much in the way prisoners, although they have no clear idea of flight, nevertheless tear up their sheets and plait the strands together."[18] A bourgeois woman with no reliable income, Colette was well aware of the dire financial straits that awaited her should her marriage end, and she took to the exercising of her body as a means of physically and morally steeling herself for the daunting liberation to come.

Gymnastics complemented Colette's wider participation in the belle époque's flourishing physical culture throughout her music-hall career. In these years she published her fiction in newspapers and magazines alongside articles chronicling cycling, soccer, rugby, and boxing. Her regular column for *Le Matin* included numerous pieces on sporting activities such as boxing, female *culture physique*, and the Tour de France.[19] She sometimes employed sport culture vocabulary to explain her activities, writing her friend Léon Hamel during one vacation, "you should know that I have worked patiently and have regained my former muscles, *culture physique*, raking, polishing the parquet floor, lugging the armoires . . . I feel incredibly in shape for a match of anything you like."[20] She added boxing to her exercise regime in these years (and around the same time had a brief relationship with the department store heir and amateur boxer Auguste Hériot).[21] While performing a series of shows at the Ba-ta-clan in 1911, Colette bemoaned a temporary lack of exercise in a letter to fellow *culture physique* devotee Christiane Mendelys. Colette predicted that Mendelys, who was a music-hall performer and Georges Wague's wife, would return from a trip to Switzerland "with bumps of muscles all over, athletic and rosy, in the hope . . . of arousing in me some base jealousy." She defended her own hiatus from methodic exercise by insisting that she was working constantly and that her new romance with Henry de Jouvenel ("Sidi") was offering superb physical activity: "who says that I'm neglecting *culture physique*? I have a new method, that's all. The Sidi Method. Excellent. No public classes. Private lessons . . ."[22]

In 1913, despite being several months pregnant, Colette performed the rather physical choreography of the pantomime *L'Oiseau de nuit* (The Night Bird). When *Le Matin's* Charles Sauerwein remarked that she was having a "man's pregnancy," she replied, "A man's pregnancy? A champion's pregnancy, even . . . and the flat, muscled belly of a gymnast," thereby transforming the most womanly of activities into an athletic feat.[23] Only a month after the birth of her daughter, she wrote exultantly to her friend, the actress Charlotte Lysès: "It is truly pleasing to feel oneself light, flat, fit for tennis . . . and to discover that one has not sustained even the smallest damage."[24]

Beyond taking pride in her athletic prowess and muscular physique, Colette consistently linked the physical exertion of exercise or manual work with moral and mental regeneration. On the road with *The Flesh* in 1909, she wrote to an ailing Léon Hamel: "the tour would have done you good! . . . We look superbly well. . . . Our feet are worn out but our bodies and minds are healthy and free. . . . It seems to me that the training has worked extremely well for us."[25] Visiting Tunisia in 1911, she again claimed to be "tired out but in a good physical and moral condition."[26] Similarly, demoralization could, for Colette, provoke physical ailments. When her mother died in September 1912, Colette did not attend the funeral, told almost no one, and continued to work, performing in *L'Oiseau de nuit*. Yet, in a letter to Hamel, written the day after her mother's death, Colette related the distinctive way in which her grief was manifested: "I continue . . . to live as usual, that goes without saying. But, like each time that a grief is worth it, I experience an attack of . . . internal inflammation that is very painful."[27] Though not

articulating grief in a conventional fashion, Colette observed that her body re-
acted physically to the emotional pain of her mother's death, her body expressing
the most profound convulsions of her soul. Literary scholars Julia Kristeva and
Jacques Dupont have referenced this peculiar habit, in which Colette's "states of
mind," as Kristeva puts it, "were incarnated, expressed in bodily terms."[28] But such
studies are most interested in the "corps colettien" as an intrinsic component of
Colette's writing, rather than as part of a historically contingent cultural shift
(though Dupont concedes that Colette's bodiliness was "not totally independent
of history").[29] In fact, Colette's seemingly eccentric attachment to the physical
tied her to a new brand of popular entertainment that embraced a secular approval of the natural, the earthbound, and the fit.

Physical Culture in the Music Hall

When Colette began taking pantomime lessons with Georges Wague in 1905,
she entered a milieu that was captivated by *culture physique*. The belle époque
music hall blended sports and the performing arts in highly physical spectacles
that celebrated bodily fitness as an essential accompaniment of the life of the
mind and of art. Pierre Arnaud and Thierry Terret observe that while most sports
in the first half of the twentieth century were practiced in urban and "nonspecial-
ized public places," historians have "rarely emphasized their localization and the
dynamics of their spatial diffusion."[30] Following Arnaud and Terret, I posit the
belle époque music hall as an especially inventive cultural site in which a modern aesthetic of the fit body was articulated and disseminated, perhaps even more
widely than in the gym or on the athletic field. Music-hall professionals prided
themselves on physical agility and exercised regularly as part of their training.
Trade magazines that catered to men and women working in the music hall, such
as *Artistique revue* and *Le 'Music-hall,'* invariably reported on sporting events and
advertised fitness equipment and athletic clubs for its readers. A 1909 benefit for
destitute performers hosted by the theater magazine *Comoedia* included sporting
competitions between various music-hall performers. (Colette's stage partners
Christine Kerf and Georges Wague competed in the bicycle and foot races.[31])
Magazines such as *Théâtre-Sports* (launched in 1909) and *La Presse sportive et
littéraire* (launched in 1903) exemplified a new hybrid genre of magazine that
reported athletics and theater side by side.[32]

In the first decade of the twentieth century, shows involving sport or gymnastic displays became increasingly common theatrical fare. Plays with titles such
as *Three Champions for a Miss* (1909) and *The Boxing Champion* (1912) appeared
in Parisian music halls, featuring athletic heroes as principal characters.[33] The
1912 play *A Sensational Match: A Sporty Story* included a hero crooning about
his cross punches and uppercut, a chorus of swimmers, and a climactic boxing

contest between the protagonists choreographed with detailed stage directions.[34] The 1902 stage version of *Claudine in Paris*, starring Polaire, began with an act in Montigny's school playground, prominently furnished with gymnastic equipment for Claudine and her classmates.[35] In Willy's later operetta based on the *Claudines*, which premiered at the Moulin Rouge in November 1910, schoolgirls amused themselves with athletic activities, chanting, "A game of badminton! To the jump rope! To gymnastics! To the trapeze! Yes, yes, to the trapeze!"[36] Even some literary lectures during this period integrated live demonstrations of boxing, fencing, and wrestling as examples of the topic at hand.[37]

In the same period, music halls began staging dazzling vaudeville revues that incorporated athletic events. In the spring of 1909, three Parisian magazines hosted a "grande fête sportive et mondaine" at the Casino de Paris called the "Aéro-Redoute," which incorporated an orchestra, music-hall dancers, and several boxing matches.[38] When Colette's *The Flesh* premiered at the elegant Parisian music hall the Apollo in 1907, every evening concluded with several bouts of the Great World Wrestling Championship (with competitors such as "Constant the Sailor" and "Rouen Raoul").[39] The program of Lyon's Casino-Kursaal where *The Flesh* played in October 1909 included a troupe of Japanese "sauteurs équilibristes" (aerialist tightrope walkers).[40] Reviewers noted that such "audacious" intermingling of sport and theater produced impressive box-office receipts.[41]

That same year, Max Viterbo parodied the pervasive integration of music hall and athletics in a one-act play, *Sports in the Theater in 1909*.[42] As the play opens, a theater director practices jujitsu, lifts weights, and discusses the need for sport-related additions to an upcoming romantic play. He insists on hiring famous athletes as stars, inserting sports jargon into the dialogue, and even adding an announcer with a megaphone to call out characters' names as they enter. The romance gradually is rewritten as a boxing match between the lovers Gisèle and Godefroy. The comic value of Viterbo's parody relied on the audience's familiarity with theatrical shows featuring sports.

Bodybuilding enthusiast George Rozet expounded on the new phenomenon of the sportive music hall in *Comoedia* in 1910. He wrote that, though it may seem "paradoxical," "the theater has a considerable interest in sports. . . . It is not a question of transforming our stages into a home for sporting events; it is unlikely that a cycling track will be installed on the stage of the Théâtre Michel nor a soccer field on that of the Capucines." It was, however, "reasonable" that theater become "more *mouvementé*."[43] The French theatergoers of 1910, the "sporty youth . . . accustomed to the sensations of effort and speed," were no longer satisfied with traditional performances, those immobile "dialogues between legless cripples." While such staging may have been appropriate in ancient Greece, nothing now justified such stilted performance. Grand revues and plays in particular should have more "muscular activity." Rozet maintained that "physical movement" was "indispensable to the fantasy of the stage" and gave theater its "gaiety and spirit."[44] The public demanded theater and performers that reflected its passion for a physically active lifestyle:

> In a society so keen on sport, if performers do not wish to look inferior in appearance, grace, and harmony, to the virtuosos of muscle . . . they must consider engaging in some other exercise than 5 o'clock bridge matches. . . . The public likes to find in their favorite actors qualities of *sveltesse* and agility that once upon a time they demanded only from acrobats. The pudgy comic . . . is no longer in style. . . . A new school of performing artists has appeared, who, practicing several sports . . . bring to the stage an almost clownlike vivacity and burn up the stage with the impact of their soles as much as by the fire of their lines.[45]

For Rozet, the music hall's *culture sportive* originated not in the isolated milieu of upper-class diversions or nationalistic preparedness but in an upsurge of public demand for an art or spectacle that corresponded with new active lifestyles. As is made evident by Rozet's promotion of muscles and trimness over "legless cripples" and "pudgy" comedians, this new music-hall aesthetic was located squarely on the body of the performer. Colette echoed Rozet in a column for *Le Matin* in 1914 in which she explained that Russian ballet dancers appealed to French audiences because "we have a passion especially for the extrahuman aspect of a choreography that is inaccessible to normal strength: the insectlike leaps, the momentum of a jet of water . . ."[46]

Women were prominently featured in the *culture physique* so captivating popular entertainment in this period. Willy proclaimed in his 1909 "Chronique sportive": "We sing of sport in verse as we celebrate it in prose. . . . The most extraordinary thing is that women are joining in on it."[47] Among a group of drawings representing the coming year 1910, the magazine *Fin de Siècle* began with one titled "Sportswoman!" that depicted a woman in an athletic *maillot* exercising with wall cords and dumbbells.[48] Magazines gave weekly attention to the exploits of famous "sportswomen" such as the *aviatrices* Hélène Dutrieu and Meryl Marvingt, "well known for her exploits as a pilot and as a skier," and also covered female sporting pastimes.[49] In 1908 *Echo de Paris* described elegant female skaters "swept away by the intoxication of balance, developing their torsos, bending their waists, inclining their heads . . . with a relaxation of all of their muscles."[50] The new fashion for ice-skating was proof, another writer maintained, of a harmonious alliance between "duty" and "pleasure" by *Parisiennes;* "it reconciles charm and hygiene. Its enthusiasts . . . return home with a healthy glow and brighter color in their cheeks."[51] Such commentary perceived a distinct correlation between hygiene, physical health, and feminine beauty.[52] To be sure, women's athletic activity could also excite concerns about degeneration, masculinization, and social disruption. Female bicyclists, for example, were particularly troubling to cultural observers in this regard.[53]

Yet despite (or perhaps because of) the worries associated with female physical culture, the belle époque music hall embraced the spectacular possibilities of women's involvement in athletics. Mary Lynn Stewart has suggested that women's theatrical gymnastic routines at times even met with a level of approval denied more systematic female sporting activities.[54] A perusal of some of the popular entertainment of the years 1907–14 reveals that female music-hall performers were at the forefront of French physical culture. Recasting traditional notions of respectable femininity, the physically fit women of the music hall were received by audiences not as masculinized amazons but as the epitome of modern grace and, most interestingly, moral rectitude. The 1909 comedy *Three Champions for a Miss*, for instance, followed the efforts of an American "sportswoman" named Miss Sparklett to choose a marriage partner.[55] Miss Sparklett interviews prospective fiancés while she exercises, battering a punching bag and surrounded by photographs of torsos and biceps. Sporty, independent, and desirable, she examines the physique of each suitor and makes her decision based on which man accomplishes the most original athletic feat. Far from emasculating her suitors with her physical mastery, Miss Sparklett inspires them to greater athletic ability and strength.

The music-hall craze for female boxing in the years just before World War I offers some of the most revealing commentary on female performers' feminine and, at times, moralizing *culture physique*. The main event of the Casino de Paris's 1909 theatrical extravaganza "Aéro-Redoute" was a series of boxing matches between female music-hall performers and famed (often African American) male boxers such as Sam Mac Vea. Though spectacular novelty and sexual titillation were doubtlessly interests of those promoting the show, the matches involved actual boxing and rigorous training by the *boxeuses* (female boxers).[56] Reviews of the Aéro-Redoute did not treat the *boxeuses* as fearsome anomalies of their sex but rather combined an appreciation for the women's athletic ability with admiration for their beauty and grace. Max Derive cheered the *boxeuse* Meg Villars, who "takes the punches marvelously" and "demonstrates a will, a tenacity, and an endurance that are extraordinary."[57] When Villars fought the well-known athlete Toto Jackson, Derive declared the show "aesthetic": "Meg, as pretty as she is lithe and elegant, has proved to us, once again, that boxing matches do not constitute brutal spectacles. . . . The feminine boxing contests are at once graceful and attractive." Derive noted that the immense popularity of women's boxing in the Aéro-Redoute had inspired many women to take up the sport: "we have been told that a boxing gym will soon be opening its doors which will be off limits to representatives of the nastier sex."[58]

In 1912 *Fantasio*'s Henry Dispan reported that a number of actresses and music-hall dancers were boxing as a means of physical training. Christiane Mendelys could be found every morning at the gym of the "pope of muscles," the boxing champion Émile Maitrot, where she "hits the punching ball, brutalizes the sack of sand, and

. . . nimbly jumps rope."[59] Colette was taking lessons from Maitrot as well and had shown "a most winning aptitude" for the new sport: "She is presently," Dispan reported, "a formidable boxer, who possesses the stealthiest punch one could hope for."[60] (Colette indeed referred to Maitrot's training in her letters, and she displayed a comfortable familiarity with boxing jargon.[61]) Dispan described these *boxeuses* as lissome, appealing performers whose musical or theatrical skills were enhanced by their athletic proficiency. Among the "graceful cohort of female pugilists" taking up the sport, Mendelys was "charming" and Reine Gabin, whose "hard biceps" could be admired at La Scala, was "as adroit a boxer as she is a pretty girl."[62] To emphasize the attractiveness of the new female boxers, Dispan's article was accompanied by a cartoon of a shapely woman in an exercise *maillot* and boxing gloves working a punching bag (see figure 5). The *boxeuse* wears delicate high-heeled shoes, and her hair is fashionably braided about the ears. The caption reads: "Ce n'est plus dans l'oeil qu'elles tapent" ("The ladies are no longer just striking our eyes").

While the fin-de-siècle French feminine ideal had been the virtuous and necessarily immobile bourgeois *femme au foyer*, Dispan imagined a process by which middle- and upper-class women now would imitate their socially marginal sisters in the music hall. Before too long, he wrote, one would overhear society ladies discussing their daughters thusly: "Mother Superior complains that Arlette has been neglecting her 'punching ball.' But I have to say, she did come in second in the quarterly interconvent championship.'" Dispan observed approvingly that "the noble art" of boxing already "reigns supreme over the century," so that even "the wives of magistrates and doctors are going to learn from the master the art of delivering a perfect 'hook' or 'swing' between visits to their dressmaker."[63] For Dispan, the popularity of boxing among middle-class women was an emblem of a new kind of belle époque woman:

> Spinning wheel and diligent needles of our grandmothers, you will disappear forever, because the most delicious half of the human species are reveling in other pastimes. . . . The time will soon arrive where, in the perfumed tepidness of the boudoir, the novels of Paul Bourget will give way to the memoirs of Sam Mac Vea. . . . One has to conclude from all this raising of adorable fists that we must behave nicely toward the once weak, now Herculean sex. From now on, the imprudent man who, on the bus, leaves a lovely lady standing, must beware: at the descent, a shattered jaw and several punches in the ribs will teach him to behave more gallantly in the future.[64]

With amusing hyperbole, Dispan underscored the stark contrast between the traditional bourgeois girl and the sporty *boxeuse*. While the fin-de-siècle woman sewed and read romantic novels in an overheated boudoir, the modern woman was a "Herculean" but lovely urban wanderer, no less worthy of masculine gallantry than her fin-de-siècle counterpart.

Ce n'est plus dans l'œil qu'elles tapent.

Figure 5 "Ce n'est plus dans l'oeil qu'elles tapent." Illustration in Henry Dispan, "Boxe féminine," *Fantasio*, 15 February 1912. Bibliothèque nationale de France.

A real-life version of such a scene played out on the streets of Nice in 1911 when the stage performer Mary Hette was accosted on the promenade and was able to box her way out of the compromising situation. Le 'Music-Hall' declared this incident "proof that it is good to know how to defend oneself in the street."[65] Thus, feminine physical strength could be used to enforce moral restraint in the metropolis. Mary Lynn Stewart notes that a feminine self-defense manual from 1913 mitigated fears about such activities by assuring readers that women would still remain "physiologically inferior" to men, so that "women's self-defense (like their physical training) would not threaten patriarchy."[66] Yet it seems clear that such representations of female physical fitness suggested a widened range of feminine activities, as well as a new female type that had destabilizing cultural power well before the upheaval of World War I.

A comic strip that appeared in Fin de Siècle in 1909 intimated just such an upheaval in its depiction of a boxing "sportswoman."[67] The woman is pictured in a form-fitting shirt, exercise shorts, gym shoes, and boxing gloves, awaiting her drunk and disorderly husband—an elegant if inebriated figure in top hat and tails stumbling through the doorway (see figure 6). In the panels that follow, the "sportswoman" pummels her immoderate spouse, at one point lifting him over her head and hurling him against the wall. The comic ends with the battered and bandaged husband snugly in bed while his wife, now in a stylish dress and flowered hat, prepares to go out. The accompanying captions—a perversely loving interpretation of the attack by the besieged husband—are expressed in the dulcet register of the ideal bourgeois marriage: "When by chance it happens that I arrive home a little, well, tipsy, she always awaits me with resignation. The moment that I return, she receives me effusively. With the most unequivocal gestures, she shows me again and again the joy that my return causes her."[68] The romantic conjugal hues of the captions are set against the hypermodern and fantastic marriage depicted in the panels. While some features of the comic indicate the potentially troubling gender inversion inherent in such a marriage (the sportswoman's gown is topped by a fitted jacket and cravat, which seems to mimic the evening wear in which her husband arrives), other details suggest that the sportswoman is quite conventionally feminine. Despite the violent action of the scene, she is portrayed as attractive, womanly, and relatively demure. Her body is curvaceous and feminine, if subtly muscled, and her long blond hair is tucked into a tasteful chignon. The bedroom into which she tucks her husband is neat and well appointed, with trim curtains, dust ruffle, and rug. Finally, she uses her physical strength to restore the moral order of her household, and her husband seems glad of it.

These representations of boxing women offered a novel variant of the femme nouvelle—another example of what Diana Holmes and Carrie Tarr label the "creatively hybrid mix of femininity and feminism" that was the New Woman in this period.[69] An appealing alternative to the menacing and unsightly viragos of the

... Et c'est seulement quand elle m'a douillettement couché dans mon petit lit, qu'elle se décide, la bonne âme, à aller à son tour prendre un peu de bon temps.

... Elle me balance ...

Figure 6 Detail from René Préjelan, "Sportswoman! (suite)" *Fin de siècle*, 7 November 1909. Caption: " ... Elle me balance ... Et c'est seulement quand elle m'a douillettement couché dans mon petit lit, qu'elle se décide, la bonne âme, à aller à son tour prendre un peu de bon temps." Bibliothèque nationale de France.

fin-de-siècle's popular imagination,[70] this updated Angel in the House enforced her moral standards through physical fitness and health rather than through isolation from the marketplace and spiritual devotion. As these reactions to music-hall *boxeuses* make clear, many commentators not only approved of female physical culture but also saw an essential identity between physical vigor and feminine moral rectitude.[71] As the actress Armande Cassive told *Fin de Siècle* in April 1909, sports provided "the flexibility without which there is no elegance" and were "the best conservator of physical and moral health."[72] While the sportswomen of such popular depictions did not pose political demands, they maintained and enlarged traditional gender norms by way of a physically liberated but sexually attractive female body.

* * *

The infusion of music-hall spectacles with *culture physique* was not simply a box-office stunt but a dynamic aesthetic investment in a new corporeal ideal. Roland Huesca argues that aspects of belle époque Parisian ballet demonstrated French culture shaking off "the ennui and lassitude" of fin-de-siècle performance. Huesca notes that many in 1909 situated the commanding appeal of Sergei Diaghilev's Ballets Russes in the physical virtuosity and strength of the dancers. He asserts that "this technology of the body" acquired "a political sense" in this period and that the ballet's virtuosic physicality "exalts the virtues of the Christian ideal" and "poses an abnegation of the body." Republican France still dwelled, he claims, in "a radically religious system of representation" that found comfort in "visions of a body in which animality was absent."[73] While Huesca's politicization of the performing body is suggestive, my analysis of belle époque music-hall entertainment indicates that this fascination with physical force and skill was not limited to the rarefied climes of the ballet, nor was it necessarily an expression of a "radically religious" worldview. Far from offering an "abnegation of the body," music halls quite literally placed the celebration of the earthbound physical body center stage. Physical fitness was also not inevitably allied with the politics of the extreme right—a point effectively made by Christopher Forth in his study of the cult of the male body at the turn of the century.[74] Indeed, the physical culture of the belle époque music hall was embraced by critics across the political spectrum as a thoroughly modern and thoroughly moral approach to the body.

The fin de siècle had seen a rich cross-fertilization between pantomime and theater, with innovators such as André Antoine and the Théâtre Libre borrowing in part from pantomime to articulate a new more physical style of stage acting.[75] Colette's coach Georges Wague gained prominence at the turn of the century as the master of a modern, more physical pantomime that broke from the stylized gestures of classical Pierrots. He sought the realistic expression of human emotions through the body, making the "literary oeuvre" a "living oeuvre" through the "elements of life, muscles, nerves, and blood."[76] While this style of pantomime, like early cinema, flew in the face of artistic sensibilities that denigrated mimetic art forms as low culture, it was embraced by others as a truly modern art.[77] Actresses such as Polaire, Caroline Otéro, and Odette Valéry took lessons from Wague and regarded his training in bodily expression an invaluable tool for the theatrical profession. His pantomime and its physicality even became the subject of heated debate in Parisian newspapers around 1910, with one critic calling it an art that was "unhealthy" (*malsain*) because it drew "excessive attention to clowneries that are solely physical."[78] Colette embraced Wague's more corporeal pantomime, finding in this highly physical craft an incomparable means of uniting body and soul. "Colette Willy," wrote critic Henri Gibet, "does not pantomime with the conventional, ordered gestures of mime artists. Rather, all that she wants to express she exteriorizes with her physiognomy."[79] Nudity was only a part of this larger aesthetic program—and one that was articulated through popular entertainment venues such as the music hall.

Popular fiction had long used nudity as a narrative tool for emphasizing the troubling carnality of women who took the stage (Zola's Nana again comes to mind). This trope of the amoral, lustful dancer/actress still held currency in the belle époque. For the promiscuous heroine of René Schwaeblé's pulp novel *Dans la peau* (1907), for example, performing nude in the music hall was an opportunity for sexual excitation: "She aroused herself. She would have stayed like that forever to give her nudity to everyone, to allow herself to be examined by connoisseurs. With her cynical desire to give herself to the greatest possible number of men, she loved to be nude on stage: all the theater possessed her at the same time."[80] This scene epitomizes one popular view of belle époque music-hall dancers and actresses: licentious women who displayed their bodies as a means of exciting lust, whether their own or that of their paying spectators. From the time that Colette first took the stage in 1906, displaying her body to a degree uncommon even for a music-hall performer, some critics evaluated her performances according to this dissolute type. Referring to her appearance in the 1906 mimodrama *Pan*, one journalist described Colette as "outrageously naked beneath some animal skins" and called the show "a veritable ignominy." A spectator was heard to cry out, "It is absolutely repugnant!"[81]

Yet this same period also witnessed an effort on the part of artists, writers, and physical culture enthusiasts to transform notions of the nude as immoral, unwittingly providing a language with which some critics could understand and defend Colette's performances.[82] A brief analysis of several pieces from the illustrated monthly *La Culture Physique,* an important bodybuilding magazine with some thirteen thousand readers in this period, gives a sense of the polemical tone this question could take during the belle époque, as well as the way in which such polemic could be linked to artistic change.[83] A 1905 article unambiguously titled "The Nude Is Not Immoral" repeatedly assured readers that a forthcoming album of "artistic" nude photographs would contain nothing of even "the least immoral character" and that "all license will be severely banished [from the photographs]."[84] Physical culture sought, as another contributor put it, beauty above all else, "the synthesis of all the physical faculties . . . whose deliberate acquisition is an assurance of true morality."[85] The insistent assurance of this link between nudity and morality suggests that the editors of *La Culture Physique* were not summarizing a hegemonic view of the nude body but rather defending a novel approach to physicality. Gilbert Andrieu suggests that the *culturistes'* "valorization of the beauty of forms" through the development of muscles was a sort of "republican humanism" that set this brand of French physical culture apart from its more military versions.[86] It also explicitly allied the fit body and modern art. In a 1904 essay, Dr. Stratz explicated the role of the nude in renovating the arts, declaring that after years of "overly tormented artistic attempts" during which "art's creators have become anemic through bizarre compositions," a time had arrived "when the cry for the return to nature emanates from every mouth."[87] Another article equated the sculptures of the Louvre, wondrous examples of "human genius," with bodies "manufactured by living nature."[88] Beyond a polemical defense of the nude as moral, adherents of *culture physique* insisted upon the fundamental role of, as the bodybuilding physician Georges Rouhet put it, the "cult of physical beauty" to teach humanity "the religion of art that leads to the True and the Good," and to raise society's "moral level."[89]

The cult of the nude body was not a phenomenon particular to France—other European countries, most notably Germany, had a burgeoning nudist culture in the years just before the Great War which involved artistic photography, gymnastics, and dance. Indeed, as Karl Toepfer illustrates in his study of German *Nacktkultur*, the early twentieth century saw an effort by many "to physicalize modernity within the body and to view the body itself as a manifestation of modernist desire."[90] In France, similar debates about the artistic nude invaded realms of modern mass entertainment such as the music hall in the first decades of the twentieth century. Increasingly, critics came to see such performances as evidence of the moral purity and beauty of a healthy body, and they deemed bodily movement the most perfect and most artistic expression of emotional states. When the French dancer Adorée Villany, known across Europe for her nude performances, was ordered by police in 1913 to cover up after a semiprivate show in Paris, she defended herself using the vocabulary of *culture physique*.[91] Her much-quoted manifesto on nude dance declared: "I dance with my entire body, and not only with my legs. My unveiled body bares my soul." Echoing Georges Wague's and Colette's defenses of their pantomime, Villany wrote that in her dances "the rhythm of the mind is passed to the body, which records its movements with such an exactitude that it seems we can read a graph of our passions on paper. There, the states of our souls are rendered visible, as if drawn."[92]

Many French critics applauded Villany's daring attempt to reform and revitalize modern art. Gabriel Mourey wrote in *Paris-Journal* that Villany's goal was "the expression of the total beauty of the human being—not only made up of the body, but of the body and the soul."[93] *Le Rappel* intoned against the authorities' prudery: "There is no connection between clothing and healthy morals. Our society, imprisoned in the prejudices of Christianity, is trying to break out of the carapace that suffocates it."[94] Villany insisted upon the "unobjectionable character" of her dance, and she admitted that though she expected such treatment from German authorities, she had believed Paris would "show a truer appreciation of pure art." She avowed that she would only accept judgments on her performance from a "tribunal of artists and sculptors, with M. Rodin as president," and she challenged the police to arrest her, declaring, "I will brave anything for art."[95]

This celebration of the power of physical beauty, especially the nude, intersected in the belle époque with a vision of Frenchwomen as the guardians of the abstract values of the Beautiful and the True. Françoise Labridy-Poncelet suggests that during this first decade of the twentieth century, "the moralizing principle of the beautiful" was pervasive and understood as "a feminine type of perfection" that would help society avoid barbarism. Feminine athletic activities evolved as one expression of this social mission during the belle époque.[96] Such ideas coincided with a pan-European and American modern dance movement pioneered by dancers such as Isadora Duncan and Ruth St. Denis, who, according to Sally Banes, celebrated the natural, human (but particularly female) form and posited "female sexuality as fresh and vital, and also graphically [joined] it to nature."[97]

Though Colette's shows, literal bodice-rippers, were quite different from the avant-garde dances of Duncan, St. Denis, and Villany, she and her supporters justified music-hall nudity in the same terms, employing a language that merged the values of *culture physique* and the moral power of female beauty.[98] In her earliest performances, Colette physically asserted the majesty of the body in its natural state by refusing to wear the *maillot* (a flesh-colored leotard worn under costumes).[99] She dispensed with the leotard first in 1906, in both *La Romanichelle* and *Pan,* in which she wore only a panther skin.[100] In foregoing the *maillot* Colette upheld the contention of Duncan and others that the nude human form was too beautiful to be distorted by a leotard. She did so even though (and perhaps because) the social setting of many of her performances differed dramatically from that of avant-garde dance. It was one thing to present a nude dancer in an abstract stage setting before a mostly elite audience of artists and intellectuals, as in the case of Adorée Villany. It was quite another to include nudity as part of a somewhat salacious popular melodrama on the stage of a music hall, as would be the case with many of Colette's performances.

Many critics nonetheless placed Colette's music-hall shows in the same lofty artistic pantheon as avant-garde dance. In his review of *La Romanichelle* at the Olympia, the music critic and writer Curnonsky defended Colette's seminude performance as art. He dismissed the evident shock on the part of the Olympia's audience when they realized that Colette was not wearing a leotard:

the abolition of the *maillot* has become one of the necessities of dance, and the bareness of two beautiful, lively legs where the muscles play beneath the splendor of the skin certainly seemed more chaste than the display of padded giblets that has for too long inflicted on us an obscene and adulterated sight. . . . Colette Willy is not the first to free herself from the convention and constraint of the maillot: Miss Ruth Rhada, Suzy Deguez, Isadora Duncan . . . and all dancers with pretty legs no longer wear it.[101]

Colette used comparable terms when justifying her nude performance to a Swiss journalist in 1911: "I want to dance naked if the *maillot* hampers me and humiliates my form. My contempt for conventions possibly provokes anger in people who violate them shamefully in the shadows."[102] That same summer, Colette was interviewed while changing out of her costume after a show in Geneva, and rather than covering herself, she ordered the journalist: "Look at my arms and legs of steel." Though the reporter noted Colette's "superb body," he assured his readers that this dishabille did not lead to the backstage promiscuity imagined by popular literature. Instead, despite the presence of a blushing young admirer from the audience, Colette departed with her "colleague" Wague to read the morning newspaper.[103]

The Flesh, written by Wague and Léon Lambert, more than any of Colette's previous shows, was conceived as an artistic allegory of the power of bodily beauty and placed the nude body at the center of the dramatic action.[104] Rather than an "abnegation of the body" in which the corporeal was lost in the extrahuman act of creative performance, descriptions of this show paid careful attention to Colette's body and her bodiliness; reviewers took time to describe and praise her thighs, hands, breasts, legs, and arms. *L'Illume* in Brussels reviewed the pantomime in 1911 and, before saluting Colette's "proud and charming independence," felt obliged to comment that "Colette Willy, going further than ever, shows us her thigh and her impeccable legs."[105] *Le Rire* reported that Colette "performed *The Flesh*, in the flesh, and her means permit her to do so. . . . Her legs, with their slender curve, were bare from the ankle to her hips, and her breasts, veritable goblets of alabaster, displayed themselves fraternally."[106] Several critics found Colette's nudity cause for titillation and sexual innuendo, with some magazines carrying cartoons of her baring her breasts, along with ribald poems.[107] Others made thinly veiled jokes connecting her onstage nudity to her offstage relationship with Mathilde de Morny.[108] In February 1908 an order by the prefect of the Alpes-Maritimes that Colette's left breast be veiled in performances of *The Flesh* in Monte Carlo generated considerable press attention, with several newspapers mocking the prefect for his prudery and defending Colette's maligned breasts.[109] In 1910 a critic in Marseilles complained that he had preferred *The Flesh* two years before, when Colette's dress fell off completely in the climactic scene, rather than only revealing her breasts. This reviewer found the original version more successful, "the nude being more artistic and more chaste than the semiclothed body."[110]

Indeed, a surprising number of commentators linked the naturalness, flexibility, and liveliness of Colette's physique with the essential morality of *The Flesh*. Indeed, in some ways, Colette's body was the only place where reviewers could situate the high art that they perceived in the show. For one thing, the moral lesson of the mimodrama was difficult to discern. One reviewer joked, "The moral of this story is that a husband . . . is very wrong to sleep with his wife without ever stripping her of her lingerie . . . [because if he did] he would not feel that overwhelming shock at seeing [her nakedness] suddenly unveiled, and nothing would thus prevent him from killing the harlot as he wishes."[111] And the private life of the show's star—Colette was separated from her libertine husband and in a semipublic relationship with a woman—provided further ammunition to those who disapproved of *The Flesh*.

So, if not in the pantomime's plot nor in the reputation of the star, where could reviewers ground their elevated moral descriptions of the show? Again and again, reviewers found such a grounding in the bodies of the performers. Many critics recognized that Colette's onstage nudity was intentional and meaningful. *Album comique* of 1908 devoted much of its portrait of Colette to a discussion of her "project" regarding nude performance, which began with her scanty costumes in *La Romanichelle* and *Pan* and now culminated in *The Flesh*. The *Album* explained that Colette had "very fixed, very personal ideas on the conventional nude of the *maillot* as opposed to the genuine nude of the skin."[112] After complimenting Colette on the "flexibility of her figure" and "the proud nobility of her poses," Fernand Brulin declared that the combination of Colette's show and the "muscled" wrestlers whose bouts preceded it in the revue had assured "the triumph of the flesh all night long."[113]

A number of reviews praised *The Flesh* with language that evoked the new *culture physique*. Marius Cevair lauded Colette's performance, insisting that "her gestures generated no indignation nor offensive remarks, thus proving eloquently, in spite of some falsely alarmed modesties . . . that the '*truly beautiful nude cannot be indecent*.'"[114] The *Lyon mondain* exclaimed that her show was "the glorification of that which is most beautiful, most pure, and most artistic in the Nude."[115] *La République* avowed that Colette had proven "by the force of art and of conviction" how "fragile and specious are the scruples of those who hold the nude in contempt."[116] Louis Delluc, referring to her nude performances in general, wrote of Colette's "perfect feet and legs" and her "harmonious nudity" in which there was "something inexplicable and very pure."[117]

Beyond touting Colette's nude performance as dignified and respectable, many reviewers went a step further and elevated her nudity to a work of art. The *Journal des théâtres et concerts* raved that *The Flesh* proved "what a grave error it is to pretend that artistic attempts in the Music Hall have no chance of success!"[118] When Christine Kerf, who normally played Yulka's young male lover, switched parts with Colette in a 1911 performance, a reviewer described her body in similar terms, praising her "supple body, undulating with harmonious lines," the "realism" of her "pearly bosom," and the "beauty of this living model" with its "touch of truly academic art."[119] Émile Vuillermoz (1878–1960), a friend and collaborator of both Colette and Wague, considered *The Flesh* exemplary of the music hall's capacity to educate the bourgeoisie, a class that normally disdained this milieu.[120] The music hall was a "marvelous aesthetic laboratory":

> Exalting the grace, strength, and nobility of the human race by offering the public the living lesson of the juggler and the athlete, the gymnast, the mime, the dancer and the model . . . clothing and unclothing the rarest Phrynés . . . Isn't this a lofty instruction for the bureaucrat and the bourgeois who walk through life with such a cramped body and soul? The music hall, in the hands of artists, should be as respectfully honored as a museum.[121]

As in belle époque descriptions of female boxers, Vuillermoz put forward a naked music-hall performer as the guardian of a cultural and even moral standard against which the bourgeoisie should measure itself.

The novelist, art critic, and leftist writer Léon Werth (1878–1955) evaluated Colette's appearance in *The Flesh* in 1911 as part of a longer review of nudes in the paintings of Jean Ingres and Albert Marquet, placing her onstage nudity alongside that displayed in these museum exhibits. For Ingres, Werth wrote, the act of painting was "an act of possession"; his nudes had "flesh . . . molded out of his desire." Marquet was "a cruel painter" who abused the women he saw on the street by painting them. Colette, however, "achieved on the stage of a low-class neighborhood music hall the dream of artists who would like to paint landscapes inhabited by beautiful nudes who are not mythological." Colette's body communicated the health of the nude in nature, a nude separated from debasing lust. Her body evoked wholesomeness not by breaking free from earthly associations but indeed *because* of its links to the natural world. In watching her, Werth mused, "It seemed that we were outstretched in the shade of a tree. Between the swaying shrubbery, a woman was running and playing. . . . She is as lithe as that young gray cat leaping on the rocks down by the ocean. . . . We are without sadness." This is nudity separated from possessive desire or licentiousness. Colette's body contained "that aptitude which never leaves plants, animals, children, and women who have not curbed their instinct."[122]

What made Colette's body praiseworthy was its lively, active, and natural qualities. Her arms, observed Werth, were not "attached with strings like those of Javanese dolls" but were "attached to her instinct." He referred to their "strength" and "subtlety," a striking contrast to the "lifeless roundness" of most women's limbs: "The arms of other women seem to be made out of a fleshy fabric that is crudely stitched at the springs of the wrist and the elbow." Colette's arms were "alive," "like the palpitation of a wing before flight." He also contrasted Colette's body to those of the *café-concert* singers who followed her in the music-hall revue, who moved with robotic boredom: "Their bodies sleep." Upper-class ladies also suffered by comparison to Colette: "Even the breasts of ladies *en soi-rée*, visible in their bodices, lack the habit of exposure. The oscillation [of such breasts] is anxious. They have the appearance of poultry who have been plucked alive. . . . When [such women] have taken off their clothes, [they] display their bodies with the embarrassment of a child who hides his eyes behind his arm and dares not look." Werth thereby condemned the modesty of respectable bourgeois ladies while elevating the onstage nudity of a divorced *artiste*. He explained this startling inversion by emphasizing the moral dimension of Colette's vigorous, natural physique. While she displayed her body with no sense of traditional modesty, Colette was not sexually available: "[Her] body contains a will and it is not an object that one needs merely reach out one's hand to possess. If all [bodies] were like this, there would be no girls in the street. Men take irresponsible bodies that do not know themselves."[123] The degradation of prostitution would not exist, Werth suggested, if all women's bodies contained the physical strength, naturalness, and will of Colette's nude form. This review of *The Flesh* proposed the same view of the corporeal self that, I argue, Colette and her comrades in the music hall were promoting. The ideal body, for Colette as for Werth, was active, natural, and liberated from the strictures of shame. A new Third Republican ideal of the body echoed these same values: a fit body viewed by its possessor not as a repugnant, sin-producing vessel but as an instrument for the dictates of one's will.

Unlike other artistic media, pantomime performances allowed Colette an artistic expression that used only her body. Though she appeared in several speaking plays during this period, she wrote to Wague in 1908: "It is rather curious, in a play where I am having success, I am seized all at once by a need to no longer speak, to express in gestures, in physiognomy, in the rhythm of dance that which I am in the process of saying! Funny, isn't it?"[124] Placing even her writing below pantomime, Colette told a journalist in 1912 that "the most moving pages cannot equal 'the beauty of a successful gesture'" and that she preferred "that one compliment her on the curve of her legs or the precise grace of a body exhausted by dance positions."[125]

In the music hall Colette found a cultural space that echoed and amplified her own deeply held conviction about bodily vigor and moral wholeness. In offering theatrical fare that was noticeably more *sportive*, music-hall performers were responding to both cultural imperatives and audience demand, but they also sought an aesthetic based upon the harmonious union of the thinking soul and the active body. For female performers in particular, such an aesthetic offered an expansive definition of feminine norms, as well as persistently rigorous bodily regimes.[126] For onstage nudity did not mean liberation from all moral standards but rather attention to a novel but equally exacting moral code regulating the relationship between body and soul.

Writing the Body

Colette's public took notice of the unexpected healthfulness of her nude performances. Likewise, her literature was often perceived as fresh and wholesome, although it spoke of homosexual and premarital sex, and the turbulent life of the imagination, just like the Decadents. What was the difference? Quite simply, Colette's treatment of the body and of sexuality enabled critics and readers alike to see in her fiction modest and even moral tales. From the beginning of her career, readers and critics alike saw in Colette a new kind of female writer, one who diverged from the style of the Decadent and Symbolist circles of her early married years. In 1909 André du Fresnois contended that most women writers tended too often toward the mistakes of fin-de-siècle literature: "They have confused feeling with a disorder of the senses. Now, we are weary of the hysterias maintained with care, of the pathology, of the sickly confessions." For this reason, he wrote, "Colette Willy's books seduce us with their air of health." Du Fresnois easily reconciled the nude music-hall dancer of *The Flesh* with this "daughter of the provinces and of the French bourgeoisie": "She says: 'I will dance nude if it pleases me.' But she does not . . . endeavor to found a moral system upon the caprice of the blood or the frenzy of the legs. . . . It is this intellectual equilibrium . . . that is the benefit of [her] style."[127] Despite the scandals and unconventionality of her life in this period, Colette was, for du Fresnois, the antidote for a generation of hysterical, ailing writers who indulged in vice and whose only relationship with their bodies was one that followed the "frenzy" of blood and limbs.

In reviewing her in this way, critics such as du Fresnois were responding to something beyond the subject matter of the novels. Most of Colette's characters from this period live on the boundaries of respectable society or break its dicta from within: divorced dancers, unwed mothers, adulterous wives, precocious children, artists, drug addicts, womanizers, and dandies. Still, as the belle époque crashed to an end in 1914, Colette found herself a well-respected *femme de lettres* who was lauded as the voice of a new generation. At least one source of this acceptance by a mass of the French public was the new, secular, and in many ways republican understanding of the body that her literature offered its readers.

References to and metaphors from the era's *culture physique* and bodily fitness pervade Colette's belle époque writing. Her music-hall stories are populated with men and women who fortify and proudly exhibit their muscles, rehearse until dripping with sweat, and perform estimable feats of strength.[128] Watching the rehearsal of some gymnasts on a trapeze, *The Vagabond*'s Renée Néré remarks that "all of this graceful and supple strength being expended all around me . . . stimulates and fires in me a contagious emulation." As she rehearses, she begins to feel "the beauty of [her] perfected movements," as if her body were "suddenly recloaked in finery."[129] The music hall becomes an ideal realm in which gender and sex difference are effaced, as men and women alike are judged by the same standard of fitness. Renée proudly asserts that she now belongs to a milieu "where masculine and feminine beauty ranked equal, where you used the same appreciative words for the marvelous legs and narrow hips of a handsome gymnast as for the shapeliness of a female acrobat or dancer."[130]

Beyond common references to sport and physical aptitude, Colette's treatment of the body in her belle époque fiction signaled the birth of a novel relationship between French women and their physical selves. A far cry from the ideal convent-educated girl discouraged from scrutinizing her body, Colette's heroines inspect their bodies and those around them carefully and admiringly. In *Claudine at School* the protagonist and her classmates in the primary school compare their developing breasts.[131] The *Claudine* series as a whole allowed readers to follow the bodily development of a fictional character from adolescence to mature womanhood. In *Claudine in Paris*, the teenage Claudine examines her body during baths and approvingly remarks on the muscular strength and flexibility she has retained through gymnastic exercise.[132] As a newlywed in *Claudine Married* (1902), she continues this physical self-assessment in front of a mirror and is "proud" of her robustness and "muscular tallness."[133] In the series' final installment, *Retreat from Love* (1907), though "no longer very young," Claudine takes satisfaction in her body: "I've kept my figure, my freedom of movement; I still have my tight covering of flesh, which fits me without a crease."[134] As Colette aged in the decades to come, she continued to detail the successive phases of bodily maturation in her fiction.

Colette's female characters from the belle époque also exhibited an understanding of the workings of internal human anatomy. Minne, the heroine of 1909's *L'Ingénue libertine*, thoroughly examines her body with a mirror in order to discern her skeleton through her skin.[135] Claudine studies anatomy as a young girl, and years later, she discusses hygienic remedies to increase circulation with her female friends.[136] Renée Néré is given detailed advice on her various organs by an older unmarried friend, Margot: "'Tongue? . . . whites of the eye? . . . pulse?' . . . She turned up my eyelids, applied pressure to my wrist with a sure, professional hand. . . . It's just that we know, Margot and I, the value of good health and the anguish of losing it."[137] As single women, Renée and Margot fear falling ill and possibly dying alone, "far from everyone, forgotten." Renée remarks, "I care for myself, I take an interest in my intestines, my throat, my stomach, my skin, with the somewhat obsessive rigor of an owner attached to his property."[138] Such passages demonstrate a glorification of bodily fitness, as well as an amateur knowledge and curiosity about human anatomy. This is noteworthy given the

Third Republic's addition of just such knowledge to its primary curriculum, especially for girls.

One corollary of Colette's celebration and investigation of the body and its workings was a forthright appraisal of sex throughout her fiction.[139] From her earliest novels, Colette offered frank descriptions of female sexual pleasure. While critics have remarked upon this aspect of Colette's literature, I position these images within a broader analysis of Colette's treatment of the body and corporeal health. Claudine and another of Colette's young female characters from this period, Minne, both candidly describe the act of lovemaking with their husbands as moments of intense sexual pleasure divested of the shame and horror that accompanied conjugal relations in many nineteenth-century references.[140] When Minne at last finds sexual fulfillment with her husband, Alain, this adulterous young wife is moralized by the orgasmic pleasure she has futilely sought outside of her marriage. Because Alain has at last "made this miracle," Minne's "happy body" rests against him, and she listens "deep inside herself to the tumult of joyous blood."[141] At times, Colette approached sex as merely another invigorating exercise. In *The Shackle* Renée boasts of an encounter with a lover as "a harmonious wrestling bout." She remarks the delight of "this intelligent pleasure of the flesh" and is pleased to have found "a splendid adversary well suited to [her]."[142] Colette's descriptions of sexual acts are often healthy and even chaste, and the partners are shown taking mutual pleasure in the assessment of the other's body. If such descriptions were absent from the republican pedagogical culture in which Colette was raised, this candid approach to sexuality is inseparable in Colette's writing from a broader conception of the body and bodily health.

Colette's belle époque fiction also attests to the early Third Republic's profound connection of the corporeal and emotional. Echoing her own letters from this period, Colette's fictional characters identify moments of moral unease or distress as physical discomfort. In *The Shackle* Renée describes the emotional distress of a love affair: "I knew that my pallor, my tiredness, my slight aberrations of taste and touch . . . had an obvious cause."[143] Claudine similarly explains her emotional extremes as physical occurrences in *Retreat from Love*: "'In love,' feeble words to express so much! Imbued, that's a better way putting it . . . imbued in body and soul, for unchanging love entered so deeply into the whole of my being that I almost expected to see my hair and skin change color."[144] When Claudine is painfully separated from Renaud, who is hospitalized in Switzerland, she remarks: "It's not grief that I'm enduring; something's lacking; it's like an amputation, a physical malaise so indefinable that I confuse it with hunger, thirst, migraine, or fatigue."[145] Colette here presages her description in a letter several years later of the physicality of her grief over her mother's death. This conviction about the important union between the body and soul meant that Colette often depicted moments in which mental stress is relieved through physical activity, particularly manual labor. Her formulations of music-hall performance as a manual métier, for example, also associated moral regeneration with physical exertion.

* * *

Colette's treatment of the body, particularly female bodies, throughout her fiction can be read on one hand as a rich primary source that attests to changing cultural attitudes toward physical health and mobility. On the other hand, in depicting bodies in this way, Colette was unconsciously harmonizing her own commanding desire for social autonomy and sexual liberation with powerful cultural imperatives that sought to control such impulses. She did so by formulating her sexual, financial, and professional independence as highly moral, highly salubrious acts of regeneration that accorded with the most stringent dictums of the republican morale laïque.

The poet Guillaume Apollinaire once wrote of Colette's fiction: "There one finds beauties of the first order that are nothing but *thrilling frissons of the flesh*."[146] But scholars have too hastily dismissed Colette's exceptional fleshiness as merely an element of her liberated eccentricity and thereby have missed the substantial cultural sources of her bodily *morale*. They have been similarly inattentive to the links between such an appreciation of physical fitness and a new popular culture of the body that characterized music-hall performance during the belle époque. The presentation and reception of certain female performing bodies in the belle époque, the enthusiasm with which these bodies were described, defended, and admired, indicate that these performances took place in a significant moment of transition regarding French attitudes toward the body.

Performers, cultural critics, and fitness enthusiasts who embraced a modern, physical aesthetic were all perhaps rather too insistent in their bold proclamations about the morality of nude forms and their painstaking attention to healthful bodiliness. More than outraged reviewers and blushing prefects, it is the defiant tone of this aesthetic's defenders that alerts us to the novelty of the bodily *morale* being presented onstage, in popular fiction, and in the mass press. I propose that this body did not signify a wholesale violation of cultural strictures but rather offered a means of satisfying an exacting moral code. Artistic choices such as those made by Colette and her colleagues were scripted in part by the rigorous binding of the moral and physical that characterized the secular moral system of this period. This earthbound delight in the physical was not only transgressive; it was also an oblique means of conforming to republican values. In this way Colette's chaste nude was more closely connected to the hysterical gyrations of the performers in Rae Beth Gordon's study than it might appear at first glance. Both styles of performance demonstrated an anxiety about the side effects of modern life. The Third Republic's *morale laïque* was a social philosophy born of such anxiety—anxiety about national health, the working classes, Catholic institutions. As such, its lessons were designed to provide an internalized physical and moral firmness that would prevent an insecure democratic liberal society from yielding to anarchy. The prospect of a heterogeneous mass culture muddling conventional gender roles was thus ordered by deep-seated secular moral constraints. Change was made tolerable by way of such constraints. And those that lived on the borderlands of middle-class respectability could reassure themselves that, as long as body and mind were sound and diligent, artistic and social transgression were defensible.

Notes

The author would like to acknowledge Duke University Press for allowing the reprinting of portions of this chapter that appeared as "The Triumph of the Flesh: Women, Physical Culture, and the Nude in the French Music Hall, 1904–1914" in *Radical History Review* 98 (Spring 2007): 63–80.

1. Wague wrote the show with Léon Lambert. Wague and Impéria performed *The Flesh* at the Casino de Paris on 16 June 1907. See Rémy, *Georges Wague*, 71.

2. "La Belle Impéria dans la Chair," *Fantasio*, 4 June 1907.

3. Rae Beth Gordon, "Natural Rhythm: La Parisienne Dances with Darwin: 1875–1910." *Modernism/modernity* 10, no. 4 (2003): 617–56. Also see Gordon's *Why the French Love Jerry Lewis: From Cabaret to Early Cinema* (Stanford, CA, 2001).

4. Heather Dawkins argues that the "conventions of displaying images of the nude in public . . . were profoundly affected by the republican reform of state institutions." See *The Nude in French Art and Culture, 1870–1910* (New York, 2002), 8.

5. On the general history of sports and physical education at the turn of the century, see Arnaud, *Athlètes de la République*. Eugen Weber traced two separate impetuses for physical culture—one coming from the patriotic push of post-1870, and another, "a means of freeing French youth from deadening disciplines" of the modern state. See "Gymnastics and Sports in Fin-de-Siècle France: Opium of the Classes?" *American Historical Review* 76 (February 1971): 70–98. Richard Holt roots modern sport in the *fête populaire* and street culture, insisting that gymnastic activity was "never simply a patriotic or pedagogical device. . . . Its true social role was as a source of good fun" linked to public entertainment. See *Sport and Society in Modern France* (London, 1981), 59–60. The resulting *mentalité* has been studied in terms of the men of the Generation of 1914, who sought to break from the pessimism of their fin-de-siècle predecessors by cultivating an active lifestyle. See Robert Wohl's *Generation of 1914* (London, 1980).

6. Stewart, *For Health and Beauty*, 14, 74.

7. Marie-Christine Périllon suggests that female sport in the period was part of a "veritable patriotic duty" (*Vies de femmes*, 83). See also Jacques Thibault, "Les origines du sport féminin," in Arnaud, *Athlètes de la République*, 331–40. Thibault sees a shift toward more widespread "pratiques sportives" by women between 1912 and 1920 (337).

8. Asti Hustvedt demonstrates that Decadents sought to empty the body of natural content. See "The Art of Death: French Fiction at the Fin de Siècle," in *The Decadent Reader: Fiction, Fantasy, and Perversion from Fin-de-Siècle France*, ed. Asti Hustvedt (New York, 1998), 10–29. Emily Apter explores a similar treatment of the female body in "Sexological Decadence: The Gynophobic Visions of Octave Mirbeau," in Hustvedt, *Decadent Reader*, 962–78. By contrast, *naturisme* depicted women as the emblem of organic harmony and the beauty of nature. See Debora Silverman's "The 'New Woman'."

9. Some biographers claim the illness was a nervous breakdown brought on by the discovery of Willy's infidelities, while others argue that Colette contracted a venereal disease from her husband.

10. On vacation in 1895, Colette would wake Willy at 4:00 A.M. to bike. See letter to Marcel Schwob, Summer 1895, in *Lettres de la vagabonde*, 27.

11. Andrieu, *L'homme et la force*, 222–23.

12. The gym was installed at least by 1901.

13. See Thurman, *Secrets of the Flesh*, 118.

14. Letter to Francis Jammes, May 1904, in *Lettres à ses pairs*, 113.

15. Letter to Francis Jammes, April 1906, in *Lettres à ses pairs*, 113.

16. Quoted in Thurman, *Secrets of the Flesh*, 209.

17. Michel Georges-Michel, "Chez Colette," *Gil Blas*, 1 February 1906.

18. Colette, *My Apprenticeships*, 118.

19. See "Impressions de Foule," 30 May 1912; "La Culture Physique et les femmes," *Le Matin*, 18 December 1913; "La Fin d'un Tour de France," 28 July 1912. In Colette, *Contes de mille et un matins* (Paris, 1970), 147, 61, 141.

20. Letter to Léon Hamel from Rozven, 1 August 1914, in *Lettres de la vagabonde*, 105.

21. Thurman refers to Hériot as an "amateur boxer" (*Secrets of the Flesh*, 196); Pichois and Brunet describe him as a "sportif bien musclé." (*Colette*, 196).

22. Letter to Christiane Mendelys, 29 August 1911, in *Lettres de la vagabonde*, 59–60. Mendelys (1873–1957) was born Clotilde Marigaux. She and Wague officially married in 1915.

23. Colette, *L'Étoile vesper (souvenirs)* (Paris, 1946), 201.

24. Letter to Charlotte Lysès, 4 August 1913, in *Sido: Lettres à sa fille*, 13. Lysès (1878–1957) was the first wife of Sacha Guitry.

25. Letter to Léon Hamel from Avignon, April 1909,. in *Lettres de la vagabonde*, 33.

26. Letter to Léon Hamel from Tunis, 21 March 1911, in *Lettres de la vagabonde*, 47.

27. Letter to Léon Hamel, 27 September 1912, in *Lettres de la vagabonde*, 80.

28. Kristeva, *Colette*, 50. Emphasis in the original. Also see Dupont, *Physique de Colette*.

29. Dupont, *Physique de Colette*, 217.

30. Pierre Arnaud and Thierry Terret, "Avant-propos: les sports à la conquête de l'espace," in *Les Sports et ses espaces, XIXe-XXe siècles*, ed. Arnaud and Terret (Paris, 1998), 8. Also see Vanessa Schwartz on turn-of-the-century mass culture in *Spectacular Realities: Early Mass Culture in Fin-de-Siècle Paris* (Los Angeles, 1998).

31. "La Fête de 'Comoedia' pour rapatrier les Artistes abandonnés," *Comeodia*, May 1909.

32. *Théâtre-Sports: Revue mensuelle littéraire, théâtrale et sportive* offered theater and book reviews, poetry, and reports on soccer, rugby, boxing, cycling, and tennis. *La Presse sportive et littéraire* (later *Lyon Mondain*) published reviews of Colette's music-hall work.

33. *Trois champions pour une miss*, in a summary in *Fin de Siècle* in 1909, was described as a "Pièce sportive destinée du Théâtre du Gymnase." *Champion de boxe*, written by Yves Mirande, played in February 1912 and starred Polaire as a woman whose flabby lover attempts to win her by hiring a boxer to allow him to knock him out, thus proving his strength. On the same bill, she was in a one-act play with Wague called *Zubiri*.

34. *Un Match sensationnel: Fantaisie sportive en un acte et deux tableaux* by A. Mirabaud was first performed in November 1912 at the Bobino Music Hall in Paris.

35. This according to Polaire in *Polaire par elle-même*, 123.

36. Willy, *Claudine: Operette en trois actes, d'après les romans de Willy et Colette Willy* (Paris, 1910).

37. See Marguerite Bistis, "Creating Cultural Space: Paris Lectures at the Turn of the Century," *Proceedings of the Annual Meeting of the Western Society for French History* 27 (1999): 114.

38. The Aéro-Redoute was promoted in the journals that sponsored it: *Comoedia*, *L'Auto*, and *Le Fin de Siècle*. *Comoedia* was a theatrical journal, *Le Fin de Siècle* a "Journal Littéraire, Théâtral et Mondain," and *L'Auto*, a sports daily. On *L'Auto*'s editor, see Christopher Thompson, "Controlling

the Working-Class Sports Hero in Order to Control the Masses? The Social Philosophy of Sport of Henry Desgrange," *Stadion* 27 (2001): 139–51. The show also included *clowns aéronautiques*, men who propelled themselves around the Casino in miniature hot air balloons.

39. *L'Éclair* gave a description of the wrestling matches in the review "Soirée Parisienne: à l'Apollo," 4 December 1907. When *La Chair* was reprised at the Apollo in 1908, it appeared on the same bill as the Amoros Sisters, acrobats, jugglers, and "comic skaters." See *Nouveau Journal*, 17 April 1908.

40. *Le Progrès*, 23 October 1909. "Le Grand Championnat du Monde de lutte" was often reviewed alongside *La Chair*. See *Echo de Paris*, *L'Éclair*, and *Gil Blas*, all in November 1907.

41. Several reviews referred to shows' high box-office receipts. See *Le Figaro*, 7 November 1907.

42. Max Viterbo, "Le Sport au Théâtre en 1909," *Le Fin de Siècle*, 21 March 1909.

43. Georges Rozet, "Les Artistes Sportifs," *Comoedia Illustré*, 1 August 1910. Christopher Forth notes that Rozet was a "regular contributor to *La Culture physique*," a magazine founded in 1904 as a venue for bodybuilding and "commercialized physical culture." See *The Dreyfus Affair and the Crisis of French Manhood* (Baltimore, 2004), 231, 217.

44. Rozet, "Les Artistes Sportifs."

45. Ibid.

46. Colette Willy, "École de danse," *Le Matin*, 28 May 1914, in *Contes des mille et un matins*, 98.

47. Willy, "Chronique sportive," *Fin de Siècle*, 16 May 1909.

48. *Fin de Siècle*, 7 November 1909. The English word "Sportswoman" is used.

49. *Excelsior*, 29 November 1910. Mary Lynn Stewart indicates that Marvingt "competed in skating and shooting events as well as in cycling, skiing and bobsled races" (*For Health and Beauty*, 168). Lenard Berlanstein notes a positive attention to female athletic activities in *Femina* in these years. See "Selling Modern Femininity: *Femina*, a Forgotten Feminist Publishing Success in Belle Epoque France," *French Historical Studies* 30, no. 4 (Fall 2007): 633.

50. "On Patine," *Echo de Paris*, 7 January 1908.

51. J. F., "Le Skating est un sport à la mode," *Excelsior*, 28 December 1910.

52. Gilbert Andrieu shows that Desbonnet's guide for feminine health connected the moral and the physical, and also asserted that engaging women in a vital *culture physique* could help France regenerate. See "A propos d'un livre: 'Pour devenir belle . . . et le rester', ou, La culture physique au féminin avant 1914," in *Histoire du sport féminin, Tome 2: Sport masculine—sport féminin: éducation et société*, ed. Pierre Arnaud and Thierry Terret (Paris, 1996), 27–39. Hélène Salomon's "Le corset: Entre la beauté et la santé (1880–1920)" maintains that women's fashion changed to fit a new ideal of the female body as muscled and supple (in Arnaud and Terret, *Histoire du sport féminin*, 2:11–26).

53. Christopher Thompson, "Un troisième sexe? Les bourgeoises et la bicyclette dans la France fin de siècle," *Le Mouvement Social* 192 (2000): 9–40.

54. Stewart, *For Health and Beauty*, 164–65.

55. Max Viterbo, "Trois champions pour une miss," *Fin de Siècle*, 20 June 1909. It was described here as a "Pièce sportive destinée du Théâtre du Gymnase."

56. Meg Villars, "Impressions de Boxe," *Fin de Siècle*, 2 May 1909.

57. Max Derive, "L'Aéro-Redoute," *Fin de Siècle*, 16 May 1909. As mentioned in note 38 above, *Fin de Siècle* was one of the magazines that sponsored the Aéro-Redoute.

58. Ibid.

59. Henry Dispan, "Boxe féminine," *Fantasio*, 15 February 1912. Mendelys had been taking lessons with Maitrot since at least the summer of 1911, as she mentions it in a letter from that August.

60. Ibid.

61. Colette joked to Wague that on returning from vacation, his wife "va me faire la pige, pour les biceps, le grand droit, le grand oblique et tout le reste." See letter to Georges Wague, May or June 1911, in *Lettres de la vagabonde*, 53–54. In another letter she complained that she had no time

to "maitropoliser, je travaille." See letter to Christiane Mendelys, 29 August 1911, in *Lettres de la vagabonde*, 59. Colette reported on a boxing match in "Façons de dire," *Le Matin*, 26 March 1914.

62. Dispan, "Boxe féminine."

63. Ibid.

64. Ibid.

65. "Petites nouvelles artistiques," *Le 'Music-hall'* (Marseilles), no. 3, 30 May 1911.

66. Stewart, *For Health and Beauty*, 172.

67. "Sportswoman! (suite)," *Fin de Siècle*, 7 November 1909.

68. Ibid.

69. Holmes and Tarr, "New Republic, New Women? Feminism and Modernity at the Belle Epoque," in Holmes and Tarr, *A 'Belle Epoque'?* 22.

70. Debora Silverman describes the "hommesse" who captivated the press in the 1890s as a woman who was "desiccated, rigid, [and] divested of all feminine 'coquettishness'" ("The 'New Woman,'" 150).

71. While Stewart's study notes changing attitudes toward athletic women that saw grace in female tennis players, golfers, and boxing actresses, she locates this shift in the 1920s and 1930s. See *For Health and Beauty*, 169–70.

72. Armande Cassive, "Mes sports favoris," *Fin de Siècle*, 4 April 1909. Cassive condemned women's sports such as fencing and gymnastics but saw pistol shooting as an acceptable feminine activity.

73. Roland Huesca, "Succès des ballets russes à Paris: 1900–1911—Renouveau technique et fusion des arts," in Arnaud and Terret, *Les Sports et ses espaces*, 358.

74. Christopher Forth, *Dreyfus Affair*, 213.

75. On Antoine and his interest in more physical shows, see Charnow, *Theatre, Politics, and Markets*, 93–94.

76. Francis Norgelet, "La Mimique," *La Société Nouvelle*, November 1911. Norgelet had known Wague since their youth in the Latin Quarter of the 1890s. See Rémy, *Georges Wague*, 65, 20–23, as well as Robert Storey, *Pierrots on the Stage of Desire: Nineteenth-Century French Literary Artists and the Comic Pantomime* (Princeton, NJ, 1985), 313.

77. See Natasha Staller, "Méliès' 'Fantastic' Cinema and the Origins of Cubism," *Art History* 12, no. 2 (June 1989): 202–32.

78. Gabriel Boissy, "Une Classe de Pantomime au Conservatoire: La Pantomime n'est qu'un art secondaire," *Excelsior*, November 1910.

79. Henri Gibet, "Colette Willy dans 'La Chair'; Edmée Favart dans 'Cabriolette,'" *Théâtra* (Marseilles), 11 October 1910.

80. Schwaeblé, *Dans la peau*, 28–29.

81. Albert de Moulin, *Paris-Lumière*, December 1906.

82. Dawkins notes that at the turn of the century, "the meaning of the nude at the site of its production was defined by an artistic discourse that could not hold as the nude acquired an audience beyond the studio and the art school" (*The Nude*, 172).

83. Statistic quoted in Defrance, *L'Excellence corporelle*, 135.

84. L. D., "Le Nu n'est pas immoral," *La Culture Physique: Revue mensuelle illustrée, Étude documentaire du développement musculaire rationnel par les Sports* 14 (April 1905): 40.

85. Albert Surier, "L'Amour," *La Culture Physique* 3 (April 1904): 41–42.

86. Gilbert Andrieu, "Les médecins culturistes à la fin du XIXème siècle en France," *Stadion* 12–13 (1986–1987): 313–14.

87. Docteur Stratz, "La Beauté Féminine," *La Culture Physique* 7 (September 1904): 151–53.

88. "La Culture physique développe le sentiment de Beau," *La Culture Physique* 8 (October 1904): 173.

89. Dr. Georges Rouhet, "De la necessité de la culture physique (suite)," *La Culture Physique* 8 (October 1904): 173. On Rouhet, see Andrieu, *L'homme et la force*, 208–9. For more discussion of the magazine *La Culture Physique*, see Forth, *Dreyfus Affair*, 218–31.

90. Karl Toepfer, *Empire of Ecstasy: Nudity and Movement in German Body Culture, 1910–1935* (Los Angeles, 1997), 7. England saw some debates about the indecency of music halls' *tableaux vivants* featuring nude women. See Barry J. Faulk, *Music Hall and Modernity: The Late Victorian Discovery of Popular Culture* (Athens, OH, 2004).

91. The order came from the prefect of police, Louis Lépine, the same man who had closed Colette's *Rêve d'Egypte* in 1907. Villany came to the public's attention in 1911, when her nude dance in Munich led to a court proceeding. She was acquitted after Munich artists spoke on her behalf. See "Dancer is Acquitted: Munch Jury Defends 'The Higher Interests of Art,'" *New York Times*, 10 March 1912. See also Toepfer, *Empire of Ecstasy*, 23–24.

92. "La danse sans voiles," *Le Temps*, 14 December 1911. Quoted in *Adorée Villany: Phryné moderne devant l'Aréopage* (Munich, 1913).

93. Gabriel Mourey, "La danse et le nu," *Paris-Journal*, 4 January 1912.

94. Bastion, "Danse et danseuses," *Le Rappel*, 2 January 1912.

95. "To Repeat Dance in Public: Mlle. Villany in Trouble with Paris Police, Says She'll Defy Them," *New York Times*, 2 March 1913. See Toepfer on Villany's 1912 book *Tanz-Reform und Pseudo-Moral*, in *Empire of Ecstasy*, 23.

96. Françoise Labridy-Poncelet, "Imaginaires féminins et pratiques sportives: L'image de la femme bourgeoise et son usage des pratiques sportives: l'exemple de la revue *La femme française* (1902–1904)," in Arnaud, *Athlètes de la République*, 324–25.

97. Sally Banes, *Dancing Women: Female Bodies on Stage* (London, 1998), 76.

98. At some point, Colette wrote a vignette about one of Duncan's performances, published in a posthumous collection. See Colette, "Isadora Duncan," in Isadora Duncan, *La Danse de l'avenir, suivis de regards sur Isadora Duncan, par Elie Faure, Colette, et Andre Levinson*, ed. Sonia Schoonejans (Brussels, 2003), 125–28. Originally published in Colette, *Paysages et portraits* (Paris, 1958).

99. In not wearing a leotard, Colette joined Duncan, who pioneered the wearing of "loose and corsetless" costumes as a rejection of conventional restrictions and as an expression of "spiritual, moral, and political liberation." See Banes, *Dancing Women*, 79.

100. Pichois and Brunet, *Colette*, 127. She was obliged to add a leotard during performances in Belgium.

101. Curnonsky, "La Semaine 'Music-Hall'," *Paris qui chante*, 14 October 1906. Curnonsky (the pen name of Edmond Maurice Saillard) was one of Willy's ghostwriters.

102. Germain d'Esparbès, "Au Kursaal de Lausanne," *Genève mondain*, 2–3 July 1911. The first line of this discourse is verbatim from Colette's "Toby-Chien Parle," in *Dialogues des bêtes* (1904).

103. Em. T., "Colette Villy dans la Chair," *Genève mondain*, 25 June 1911.

104. Lambert was the author of *scénarios* at the Grand Guignol. See Rémy, *Georges Wague*, 71. Pichois and Brunet indicate that Wague and Impéria performed it in Paris in May 1907 as a series of "tableaux vivants" (*Colette*, 154).

105. *L'Illume* (Brussels), 30 November 1911.

106. Snob, *Le Rire*, 7 March 1908. Colette was performing in Monte Carlo.

107. One cartoon depicts Colette nude, holding the remnants of her dress. See *Théâtra* (Marseilles), 9 May 1911 and 8 June 1909.

108. See Armand Massard, "Ni 'Chair', ni poisson," *La Presse*, 5 November 1907.

109. *Nouveau Journal*, 21 February 1908; *Le Rire*, 7 March 1908; *La Petite République*, 2 April 1908.

110. *Cri de Marseille*, 8–16 October 1910. Colette linked the semiclothed body with the sexual pathologies of men like Willy and his fictional alter ego Maugis, who preferred "the deshabille to

the nude." From *Mes Apprentissages* (1936), quoted in Burgaud, *Colette: Romans, récits, souvenirs*, 2:1233.

111. Cians, *La Flèche de Triboulet*, 1908, newspaper clipping, Bibliothèque de l'Opéra, D412 (3).

112. *L'Album comique: Périodique illustré d'art théâtral*, October 1908.

113. Fernand Brulin, 16 November 1907, newspaper clipping, Bibliothèque de l'Opéra, D412 (3).

114. Marius Cevair, June 1909, untitled article, Bibliothèque de l'Opéra, D412 (3). Emphasis in original.

115. *Lyon Mondain*, 16 October 1909.

116. *La République*, 11 April 1908. This review also appeared in *La Vie Moderne*.

117. Louis Delluc, "La maison des danseuses," *Comoedia Illustré*, 5 January 1913. Quoted in Pichois and Brunet, *Colette*, 161.

118. *Journal des théâtres et concerts*, 16 November 1907.

119. Review of *The Flesh*, *Petit Havre*, 30 September 1911. Colette played Yulka's male lover.

120. Émile Vuillermoz (1878–1960) was a music critic and composer who once wrote under Willy's name. For more on the relationship between the two, see Michel Mercier, "Colette et Vuillermoz," *Cahiers Colette* 24 (2002): 7–63.

121. Émile Vuillermoz, "La Vie Théâtrale: Semaine Musicale," *Paris-Midi* and *L'Action*, 23 September 1911. Several reviews compared Colette to the ancient Greek courtesan Phryné, acquitted of impiety when her unveiled body disarmed the tribunal.

122. Léon Werth, "Ingres, Marquet, Colette Willy," *Paris-Journal*, 2 May 1911. On Werth, see Gilles Heuré, *L'Insoumis: Léon Werth, 1878–1955* (Paris, 2006), 20.

123. Werth, "Ingres, Marquet, Colette Willy."

124. Letter to Wague, September 1908, in *Lettres de la vagabonde*, 23. Emphasis in original.

125. "Nos auteurs et le cinéma: Mme Colette Willy," *Le Cinéma*, 18 October 1912.

126. Mary Louise Roberts explores this facet of interwar French fashion, promoted as more active and liberated, yet often still involving an elaborate bodily regime. See *Civilization Without Sexes: Reconstructing Postwar France, 1917–1927* (Chicago, 1994).

127. André du Fresnois, "Colette Willy," *Akadémos*, 15 February 1909.

128. See Colette's stories "The Accompanist" and "The Circus Horse" in *The Collected Stories of Colette*, trans. Matthew Ward, Antonia White, and Anne-Marie Callimachi (New York, 1983). Originally published in *Envers du music-hall* (1913).

129. *La Vagabonde*, 268.

130. *The Shackle*, 105.

131. Alain Corbin discusses the cultural imperative that sought to keep adolescent girls innocent of sex but notes that Colette presented "a very different image of what young ladies were like." See "Backstage," in *A History of Private Life* (vol. 4), ed. Michelle Perrot, trans. Arthur Goldhammer (Cambridge, MA, 1990), 494.

132. Colette, *Claudine in Paris*.

133. *Claudine Married*, trans. Antonia White, in *The Claudine Novels*, 420, 433. Originally *Claudine amoureuse* or *Claudine en ménage* (1902).

134. Colette, *Retreat from Love*, 19.

135. Colette, *L'Ingénue libertine* (Paris, 1956). Originally published in 1904 and 1905 as two novels, *Minne* and *Les Égarements de Minne*, and reworked as *L'Ingénue libertine* in 1909.

136. *Claudine and Annie*, trans. Antonia White, in *The Claudine Novels*, 497. Originally published as *Claudine s'en va*, 1903.

137. *La Vagabonde*, 265.

138. Ibid.

139. Martin-Fugier writes that from 1900 to 1925, the development of a more fit female body was accompanied by an appreciation of women's "right" to sexual pleasure (*La Bourgeoise*, 141–42).

140. See Rachel Mesch's discussion of *L'Ingénue libertine* in relation to other novels from the period detailing marriage and female orgasm. Mesch, *The Hysteric's Revenge*.

141. Colette, *L'Ingénue libertine*, 248–49.

142. *The Shackle*, 132, 139.

143. Ibid., 104.

144. Colette, *Retreat from Love*, 42.

145. Ibid., 17.

146. Guillaume Apollinaire, quoted in Kristeva, *Colette*, 100. Emphasis in Kristeva's text.

6

"THE PEOPLE'S MUSE"

Pantomime, Social Art, and the Vie intérieure

In the spring of 1911 two French performers engaged in a lively public disagreement that drew responses from well-known writers, artistes, and critics and lasted for several years. This heated war of words centered on the unconventional but wildly popular pantomime shows of Georges Wague. While some called Wague "a true innovator"[1] and one of the "prophets of a future religion,"[2] a mime named Bighetti claimed he was nothing more than the "Barnum of a dizzying attraction" who succeeded by appealing to "the little pig that sleeps in all men."[3] In 1916, so-called modern pantomime's defenders won out, when Paris's Conservatoire National established a program in pantomime led by Wague.

More than an internal quarrel about a "secondary art," the debate over pantomime gave form to elite concerns about the democratization of art. It also revealed the strong cultural appeal of an art form that was legible and that reflected exterior experience in a realistic way. Instead of fleeing the material world as the Decadent and Symbolist artists did, modern pantomime sought to render human emotion and movement with extreme precision, a sort of refurbished naturalism or realism. Mimes such as Georges Wague employed heightened observation to achieve a meticulous exteriorization of the interior life, a realm of thought and feeling that seemingly eluded such representation. Colette energetically defended this new brand of pantomime, and she employed a similar aesthetic approach to the links between observation and imagination in her belle époque popular fiction.

In this way, popular entertainment became one channel by which a new secular ordering of the senses gained cultural currency in the belle époque. Modern pantomime's specific formulation of artistic creation reflected the tense treatment of the imagination and the *vie intérieure* in turn-of-the-century republican culture. The new secularized public school system of the Third

Republic released the imagination of the child with the use of a dynamic new *méthode intuitive,* which sought to construct active but "wholesome" interior lives grounded in positivistic observation. Pedagogical directives to discipline student imagination were considered especially crucial for two problematic social targets of the secular revolution—women and workers. Belle époque debates about the performing arts bore the marks of this cultural and pedagogical framework, as well as the class and gender tensions that accompanied it. In a new "democratized" public sphere of mass spectacle, debates about pantomime engaged with an unprecedented cultural blending of artistic priorities and popular accessibility. At the same time, defenders of modern pantomime exposed the class limits of this democratized and accessible aesthetic by way of their own patent ambivalence about an initiative to bring free pantomime classes to young workingwomen.

The Art of the Mime

In the years before World War I, French mimes and their supporters attempted to gain status for pantomime as an art in its own right. The ensuing dispute over pantomime exposed the process by which new modern forms of art were defined during this period.[4] The central figure in these debates was Georges Wague, a determined proponent of a new brand of pantomime that broke with tradition and demanded recognition as more than street entertainment. A regular participant in Parisian artistic gatherings in the 1890s, Wague had been a member of the circle surrounding Léon Deschamps's literary journal *La Plume,* a Symbolist review that also drew substantial contributions from anarchism and naturisme, among others.[5] At the journal's weekly soirées, Wague mingled with the likes of Paul Verlaine, the anarchist Marc Legrand, and the musician Xavier Privas, and he became known for his cantomimes—a fusion of movement, song, and poetry.[6] By 1900 Wague had gained a reputation as the master of a new genre of pantomime that represented states of feeling with natural movement. He denounced the traditional mime's efforts to translate words through an arcane sign language of the body based on a pantomime alphabet.[7] Modern mimes, Wague proclaimed, were indifferent to such absurd translations and instead sought to express the truth of human experience through natural gestures.

Pantomime, in Wague's estimation, was an incomparable means of representing feeling and interior reflection in exact, material terms: "With a blazing of the eyes, a rhythm of the foot, a swaying of the torso, and a creasing of the features, a mime artist can characterize obscured thoughts of hate, remorse, desire, extreme pleasure or disgust, sentiments that the most warmly written sentences and most skillfully recited dramatic verse can only approximate."[8] Wague did not wish to, as he put it, "ape human language but to represent the movements of thought, struggles of conscience, and secret sensations," even more accurately than could words.[9] In a 1907 essay in *La Petite République*, the writer and socialist arts reformer Camille de Sainte-Croix agreed that modern mimes such as Wague sought to express the "subtlety of interior existence" and "to exteriorize the intimate being." In such performances, the interior life of man found "its admirable visualization perfectly represented by the infinite resources of pantomime" and its "physiognomic realism."[10] After Colette began taking lessons with Wague in 1905, she reiterated this artistic conviction about modern pantomime as an unrivaled expression of one's interior life. In an interview several years later, she defined pantomime as a means of "expressing *feelings*, by successful gestures, with all of the resources of an expressive physiognomy."[11]

Its defenders gave prominence to modern pantomime's ability to connect the metaphysical and the physical aspects of art—reflecting not only the popularity of *culture physique* in the music hall but also a broader artistic investment in joining the interior life with sensory experience. According to Wague, the new school of pantomime was "more sober and true" than traditional pantomime because it made "an effort to paint a feeling, a state of the soul, exclusively by the posture of the body and the play of the physiognomy."[12] Using a bodily metaphor, Wague insisted that traditional pantomime was dying in its "conventional corset," while modern pantomime was "broad, vast, human, and even a little revolutionary."[13] Camille de Sainte-Croix concurred that the "genius" of pantomime was achieved when the artist was able to "identify his exterior nature with all that his interior being perceives."[14] Art critic Gabriel Reuillard asserted that modern pantomime was "a living interpretation of eternal passions" and the "corporeal expression of the pain and joy of men."[15] Claude Valmont called Wague a "true innovator" who "knew how to find the movements and expressions of physiognomy that are in perfect harmony with the idea or feeling that he wants to translate."[16] The heightened physicality in such pantomime brought reproach from some. Attacking Wague in *Excelsior* in 1910, theater director Gabriel Boissy called pantomime "a bastard art" that was "unhealthy" [*malsain*] because it drew "excessive attention to clowneries that are solely physical."[17]

Boissy's criticism indicates the slightly polemical tone that crept into such discussions in the years before World War I, as pantomime became a trigger for impassioned arguments about the boundaries of popular culture and art. Many reviewers praised Wague's shows not simply as good entertainment but as an art form that transcended "high" cultural barriers. In his 1908 review of *The Flesh*, J.-B. Séguy wrote that "if the very delicate art of pantomime seemed to have been sleeping for some time . . . today, only its hardened detractors continue to obstinately proclaim its decline and to predict its impending death. . . . The magnificent success that 'The Flesh' has just won amply justifies our confidence in the future of pantomime."[18] Another journalist titled his positive review of *The Flesh* "The Renaissance of Pantomime."[19]

Pantomime became the subject of contentious discussion in this period because the question of popular entertainment itself had become tremendously fraught, beginning in the last years of the nineteenth century. Experimental avant-garde and government-subsidized initiatives to expose "the People" to the performing arts began to appear in the 1880s and 1890s with the naturalist Théâtre Libre of André Antoine and the solidarist People's Theater of Maurice Pottecher. In the first decade of the twentieth century, such efforts multiplied, with the social populist works of Romain Rolland, Gustave Charpentier's Fête de la Couronnement de la Muse du Peuple, the theatrical programs of the Universités Populaires, and the socialist popular theater proposals of Camille de Sainte-Croix (among many others).[20] All of these efforts shared a vibrantly secular, if not strictly republican, view of art's power to inspire social consciousness and reform. Such initiatives, writes historian Sally Charnow, sought to provide "a secular morality for 'the people'" that would lead either to "national regeneration and social integration" or revolution, depending on the goals of the organizers. These experiments, Charnow argues, embraced "legibility" and a cross-class public as an essential feature of modernism, making modernist theater at the turn of the twentieth century "one of the building blocks of Third Republican democracy."[21] This artistic innovation took place in the context of new mass cultural forms like those analyzed by Vanessa Schwartz which "offered a mass cultural equivalent to universal education" because, in principle, "everyone might consume the same product." I propose that, like mass education and mass spectacle, the belle époque controversy over pantomime grew out of this (in Schwartz's words) vexed "democratizing conception of culture."[22]

Throughout the debates about pantomime, artistic quality was associated consistently with a heterogeneous audience's understanding of the piece. Wague and his supporters contended that audience comprehension distinguished their modern pantomime from the sterile archaism of its traditional form. While classic pantomime was "absolutely incomprehensible and obsolete," wrote Wague, modern pantomime could be readily understood by all because it used natural movements and expressed common emotional truths.[23] While traditional pantomime's obscure signs would be "a foreign language" to the audience, modern pantomime was an inclusive art, made for the new public sphere of mass entertainment:

> Put an audience composed of well-read people, illiterates[,] . . . people of different nationalities, and diverse social situations all into one auditorium. The mime who succeeds in effecting the emotions . . . of all of the spectators at once, that will be the true mime. . . . [The mime] will not accomplish this with the conventional pantomime language, unknown to a mixed audience, but rather only with that [language] that always comes from the just expression of human feeling. Because men, no matter what their station, are joyful and sad, love, suffer, laugh, and cry all in the same manner.[24]

The modern pantomime artist envisioned by Wague was a hero of the democratized public sphere and a purveyor of an art for all people, regardless of class or national difference.

Supporters of modern pantomime used the facility of the audience's comprehension as a gauge of a performance's success and artistic value. Guillaume Livret, a participant in a public exchange of letters and articles on pantomime in 1907, defended Wague's novel style in just such terms. A mime like Wague, Livret wrote, "gave the audience unforgettable impressions and provoked intense emotion with a superior art that was nonetheless accessible to all, throughout thousands of performances."[25] Wague agreed in a letter to *Le Figaro* several days later; he held that the pantomime "in which the performer truly creates a work of art is that in which he translates feelings. . . . With the others, the conventional gestures lose the audience, who inevitably loses interest in the piece being performed."[26] Reviewers of Wague and Colette's shows recognized that they were witnessing a new kind of pantomime that combined artistic value and popular appeal. A 1912 review of *The Night Bird* in Geneva proclaimed that Colette and Wague had "attained the summit of mimed art and, without the least effort, the spectator could follow the action."[27] That same year, another critic remarked that Colette had discovered "the beauty of this mute art . . . this silent language that is without a doubt the only universally intelligible one."[28]

Reviewers also perceived the intelligibility of these shows as a socially beneficial process. Again and again, critics noted that Colette and Wague's pantomimes had an edifying effect on the popular venues in which they played. In 1911 *Comoedia* remarked upon the pair's appearance at a somewhat plebian *café-concert* on the rue de la Gaîté: "In the past, renowned artists only sang and performed in classy music halls or *cafés-concerts*. . . . Today . . . the best performers are going into all neighborhoods with their performances. . . . Decidedly, art has no borders."[29] Léon Vibert agreed that Wague and Colette raised the standards of the popular music hall with their shows. In his 1912 review of *The Night Bird* at the Ba-ta-clan, Vibert wrote that the music hall had "produced a genuine effort of art. If only those Parisians who were in raptures last year over a dense, incomprehensible German mimodrama . . . could realize that for some time now, there is something besides obscenities and foolishness in the music hall; there is true art."[30]

Some, by contrast, who applauded modern pantomime as a noble art nonetheless lamented the working-class venues that housed this new art form. Camille de Sainte-Croix, though a keen defender of Wague's modern pantomime and a fierce advocate of republican people's theater, was distressed that performances of such "sublime effort" should find their "unique refuge" in the music hall, where they were "nothing more than a season interlude, to fill holes in the program, between two scatological and successful leotard revues. . . . Music halls live off of an audience that is not that of the spectacle of ideas. . . . [This audience] needs its obscenities and foolishness." Still, Sainte-Croix insisted that their crude setting should not prohibit critics from seeing in the new pantomimes a "brilliant renaissance." "It is not a defect to come from the music halls!" de Sainte-Croix wrote. "It would be one to stagnate there!"[31]

Critic Francis Norgelet, who knew Wague as a young man in the 1890s, noted with dismay the popular limits of the talented mime's performances:

> The Georges Wague that we see now on stage is not the Georges Wague that we should see. His skills are greater than the pieces he performs. *The Flesh* and *Bat' d'Af*, for example, have a terribly coarse diction. In my opinion, he needs another milieu, another audience. . . . He needs the esteem of the elite. . . . The well-read bourgeoisie should know him, . . . If only he would not exclusively seek popular success; it demands concessions that are too disheartening. If only he would seek the other, that which animates more highly, more purely, and does not intoxicate, but satisfies.[32]

Norgelet complained that Wague was unfamiliar to bourgeois audiences, and he implied that his pantomimes were written expressly for more debased, popular tastes for the sake of monetary profit. A pantomime for the "well-read bourgeoisie" would be high and pure art, elevated beyond the "coarse diction" apparently so pleasing to Wague's mass audiences.

The mass success of Wague's pantomimes was, for his opponents, inextricably linked with the deficiency of modern pantomime as an art form. In April 1911 the classic Marseillais mime Bighetti used the commercial appeal of Wague's performances to denounce "modern" pantomime, this "sacrilegious profanation" of the art form. He declared that Wague's "modernism" was "not a formula of art" but rather "at the most, a recipe to bring in crowds."[33] It was not Wague's so-called artistic reforms that earned impressive box office receipts. Instead,

> The little pig that sleeps in all men feverishly dishes out [the big money] to this enchantress Polaire or to this delightfully feminine Christine Kerf. And then what becomes of Mr. Wague and his modern pantomime? He fades backstage with the props. . . . [Mr. Wague,] if you feel like it, be the Barnum of a dizzying attraction for those who love strong sensations and excessive realism. Make lovely sums. . . . That's fine, but do not pose yourself as the innovator of a genre.[34]

Bighetti's critique summarized one of the chief accusations leveled against Wague and Colette—that the duo was guilty of cynically creating marketable sensations designed for maximum commercial success, not art. While Colette and Wague defended the seminudity in *The Flesh* as an artistic decision in favor of natural expression, Bighetti charged that the pantomime had sacrificed art in order to appease the seedier, if more profitable, side of human character. He reduced Wague's so-called artistic innovation of pantomime to a savvy, commercialized circus act.

In his criticism, Bighetti attempted to distinguish the rarefied realm of art from popular entertainment—a distinction Wague and his defenders vehemently rejected. In a published response to Bighetti three weeks later, Wague countered that envy of his large box-office earnings was the principal source of his opponent's irritation with modern pantomime. Wague defended his broad appeal, declaring that pantomime should be "the universal form of expression and, as such, should remain artistic, human, and especially comprehensible to all, in any country and in front of audiences as diverse as possible." While Bighetti remained locked in arcane tradition, Wague proclaimed, "As for me, I prefer Electricity to the Candle," thereby specifically connecting his popularity to technological advancement and progress.[35] Proud of his box-office success, Wague embraced audience comprehension as a vital component of a modern art aesthetic. According to Wague, the heroes depicted in modern pantomime shows would come not solely from allegory and tradition, like Pierrot and Colombine; instead, they would be "the heroes of current life, from all different lands, either fictitious or real, characters that are less conventional and more human."[36] Wague's most popular mimodramas indeed featured ordinary figures from everyday modern life: colonial soldiers, thieves, bickering spouses, and peasants.

The use of more quotidian characters was not simply a nod to accessibility; modern pantomime was founded upon a scrupulous realism that linked the creative process with empirical observation of the natural world. When a journalist asked Wague in 1910 how his pantomime differed from the modern dance of Isadora Duncan, he responded that "Duncan's art is a sort of ascension toward the imprecise, an evasion toward the Dream; my art, on the contrary, is like an approximation of Life. It tends to approach daily reality as closely as possible."[37] He believed that pantomime should be made up of "precise" gestures, in which the acts being expressed had been thoroughly prepared through observation.[38] Wague praised the new technology of the cinema because it facilitated his careful attention to realistic, almost scientific detail in his pantomimes:

> Cinema permitted me to observe and, in some way, to find the materialized justification of ideas that I was advancing on pantomime. . . . The first demonstrations of cinema were the recording of the movements or vibrations of nature (wind in trees, flowers, streams, the movements of the ocean, the flight of birds, etc.). In the face of that, how can anything that moves away from natural expression not seem like nonsense?[39]

Colette was equally enthusiastic about film as a tool of observation for performers, claiming in 1912 that "the artist can benefit from seeing himself projected on the screen and studying his movements there."[40]

More than one critic commented upon the natural realism and exactness of Wague's performances with Colette. Claude Valmont wrote that, thanks to

Wague's innovation, pantomime had become "the most expressive of all the arts and the most easily comprehensible, since it reproduces nature itself in all its truth."[41] *Le Journal*'s Joe Bridge (the pen name of Jean Barrez) enthused that in the 1911 *Aux Bat'd'Af*, Colette rendered the "most subtle nuances, the most diverse sensations" with "a tremendous realism."[42] A press release for her ill-fated *Rêve d'Egypte* in 1906 claimed that the upcoming show would be "a very exact evocation of the morals of the Egypt of yesteryear. . . . It is staged . . . with a rigorous exactitude and Mme Colette Willy spent several entire days at the museum of the Louvre studying the mosaics of the era."[43] A journalist who reviewed *The Flesh* in Lyon applauded the mimes' "gestures, which are of such an exact accuracy that their comprehension is most easy."[44] One review of *The Night Bird* insisted that Wague and Colette "had altered pantomime" by seeking expression in "the truth of movement."[45]

The naturalness and "truth" of these performances were commended repeatedly by critics and performers alike as a key facet of an artistic "renaissance" and "revolution." Roger Ducos wrote that Wague's "guide, model, and goal" in his pantomime was always "life"; he taught his students "truth on stage, its transcription by natural gestures, ease, imagination—to say it all in one word: the theatrical liberty of the mind and body."[46] Colette gave lectures on her music-hall career in which she spoke of the "war on the old methods" of pantomime "led by Georges Wague, so enamored of the natural and the true."[47] She extolled the virtues of "modern pantomime" as "that which takes its inspiration from the sight of reality, of truth."[48]

Some were so impressed by the precision of modern pantomime that they attributed a national pedagogical role to this renovated art form. One critic declared that the music hall of Wague and Colette could serve as a "course in corporeal art" in which the nation could "contemplate the realization of linear and pictorial harmony, familiarize themselves with the play of light and color, and acquire an invaluable education of the eye."[49] Another critic called modern pantomime a veritable "science of bodily attitudes."[50] Wague too asserted that the pantomime lessons he gave to Parisian youth served a broader pedagogical purpose: "I would like to teach children the secret of graceful posture, but, from a point of view that no pedagogue could disdain, it also has to do with forcing those young minds to observe. I tell one of my students, 'Pretend to sew.' Having never reflected on it, the child makes some false gestures. I rectify this and little by little she watches herself in action and watches life."[51] More so than other art form, Wague maintained that modern pantomime provided performers from all disciplines with invaluable skills of agility, expression, and movement.

In the years just before the war, debates over the pedagogical and artistic worth of modern pantomime intensified with the proposal of a pantomime course at Paris's Conservatoire National, the venerable academic institution devoted to French performing arts.[52] In his defense of the proposed class in 1910,

Wague argued that changes in theater had made the skills that a pantomime course would teach invaluable: "Modern theater . . . demands of artists a deep knowledge of human gestures capable of translating all the author's thoughts and soundly bringing to life all the characters he imagines."[53] In the years that followed, Colette used her connections behind the scenes to pressure the administration of the Conservatoire on behalf of the possible class.[54] In an interview with *L'Intransigeant* in 1914, she advocated the class for those performers attempting to "live in another epoch" in their theatrical work, honing their attention to the details of that era—the stage thereby becoming a site of instruction rather than perilous artistic excess.[55]

In the months before the war broke out, debate about the proposed pantomime course reached a fever pitch when René Viviani, the socialist minister of public instruction and fine arts, took the unusual step of establishing the course by government decree. Rumors were spread in the press that Wague would be named the professor of this newly created course. The director of the Conservatoire, Gabriel Fauré, was reportedly so irked by this executive decision to create a course of study that he believed useless that he briefly tendered his resignation. Delayed by the outbreak of war, the course was finally established in January 1916, and Wague was named as professor.[56]

Why so much emotion over a class at the Conservatoire? Wague's biographer, Tristan Rémy, suggests that many at the Conservatoire saw pantomime as an art form too closely associated with a cross-class democratized audience. To his opponents, Wague was "not a mime" but "an actor, or else a ham [*cabotin*]" who had "no right to identify himself with pantomime. He uses it to his own profit, without contributing anything."[57] More traditional, entrenched professors discouraged their students from taking the pantomime course and, according to Rémy, sometimes reminded Wague with a "malicious tone of superiority" that he came from the music hall. In his first years at the Conservatoire, Wague also faced complaints from students and their parents surrounding his reputation as a troublingly realistic performer who took his cues from the more permissive culture of the music hall.[58]

Even those who supported Wague's course noted the weighty artistic import of his popular music-hall origins. In a review of productions at the Paris Opéra in February 1916, a writer for *Le Temps* mentioned Wague's appointment to the Conservatoire. This wartime critic spent much of the review applauding the efforts by some to renovate the Opéra, "this severely wounded man [*ce grand blessé*]" by way of "rehabilitation exercises meant to bring back its vigor and health," namely, the production of more realistic shows drawn from the stories of everyday life. The review ended with a tribute to Wague, who was performing in the Opéra's *Coppélia*: "The steadfast partisans of the fusion of genres will register a victory when they remark that the role of Coppélius . . . went to the mime Georges Wague, who was effortlessly elevated to the direction of a class at the Conservatoire by dint of the solid technique of the music hall. . . . This is a date to remember, a date of great importance." The reviewer implicitly linked Wague's ascension from the music hall with a rejuvenated Opéra opening itself once again to the "contemporary subjects" and "unsophisticated language" of naturalism.[59]

Though many contemporaries attempted to do so, elite artistic debates of this period cannot be separated from the popular entertainment of the music hall. In renovating traditional pantomime, performers such as Wague and Colette championed an artistic aesthetic that praised the accessibility of art and the realistic description of nature, bodily expression, and emotion. Thus, late nineteenth-century naturalism was adapted to arenas of popular entertainment, giving credence to musicologist Steven Huebner's assertion that "Symbolist art did not have the *sole* rights to musical modernism" at the dawn of the twentieth century, "nor even to the ineffability which (paradoxically) could be articulated within a naturalist aesthetic."[60] While some dismissed pantomime shows such as *The Flesh* for succeeding only because of their salacious content, many recognized that such seemingly trivial fare was founded on the tenets of an aesthetic modernity that fused the real, the observed, and the material with the most profound fluctuations of the soul. Colette's fiction in these years embraced this same version of the creative process.

Writing *la vie intérieure*

Colette came of intellectual age during the 1890s, in heady Symbolist and Decadent literary circles that prioritized the life of the dream and the disintegration of the self.[61] Though she prized the satisfactions of a rich interior life, she also carried with her a republican legacy that associated artistic liberation with worrisome immoderation. Indeed, as we have seen, she rarely categorized her work as art, more often representing writing and performance as skilled craft that highlighted her corporeal and moral health. Indeed, in those uncommon moments in her fiction, letters, and interviews when she did consider the imaginative life and artistic creation, Colette inevitably harnessed liberating fantasy to exterior observation and to physical work—falling back on the mental techniques of her laic intellectual formation and the aesthetics of republicanism. This in part explains her attraction to and public support of Georges Wague's particular brand of pantomime. It also helps decipher her treatment of the question of imagination and artistic creation in her belle époque fiction. While many in the avant-garde blurred the distinction between external experience and art and attempted to downplay the commercial aspects of creative production, Colette clung to external observation, labor, and commercial value as guide rails for her artistic endeavors.

Colette's rare fictional references to the artistic abandon of pantomime and dance are often hemmed in by narrative devices involving labor and physical effort. In her *Dialogues des bêtes* and *Sept dialogues des bêtes* (1904 and 1905, respectively), a bourgeois wife turned dancer (referred to only as "She") pronounces her newfound independence in a swirling monologue detailing the imaginative escape of performance: "I shall dance naked or clothed for the sheer pleasure of dancing, of suiting my gestures to the rhythm of the music and spinning round ablaze with light, blind as a fly in a sunbeam. . . . I shall invent beautiful slow dances with a veil. . . . I shall be a statue, a vase that comes to life, a leaping animal, a tree swaying in the wind, a drunken slave. . . . Never have I felt more true to myself!"[62] Here, a middle-class woman asserts her autonomous selfhood by way of Decadent tropes of the oriental and the exotic (seminude veil dances, animals, enchanted ceramics, slaves). The narrator is alternately "blind," "ablaze with light," and "drunken," lost in the imaginative spell of her dance. And yet in the very next line, she is called back from the disorderly extravagance of the dance: "Sometimes when I've taken refuge in that stern retreat that I've made for myself in the depths of my being, I'm wakened by the jolly voice of an Italian ballet-master: 'You there, my honey, what d'you think you're doing?'"[63] Though she finds release and self-knowledge in this inspired bodily expression, the narrator describes her interior world as a "stern retreat," and she is anchored to reality by the discipline of a ballet lesson.

Colette regularly girded descriptions of artistic expression in this way, with reminders about the effort and labor of such expression. In *Retreat from Love* (1907), Claudine witnesses a pantomime rehearsal in which the mimes "expend fantastic amounts of energy": "they make the same gesture fifteen times over, and gradually it becomes uncluttered and precise, it stands out as something luminous and perfect."[64] In the short story "The Bad Morning," Colette describes a stage rehearsal led by a fictionalized version of Wague, in which she notes the "multiple attempts and failures" and the "effort" of this process. Having thus disciplined their bodies and minds, the performers are liberated in the act of creation: "Words, less and less urgent, detach from us like fragments of a rough outer crust. . . . We are eager to strike from our mute dialogues all words, the crude obstacle that separates us from perfect, rhythmic, limpid silence, silence that proudly expresses and recognizes no other support . . . than Music alone."[65] This creative release is permitted only after bodily effort.

When *The Vagabond*'s Renée Néré performs at an elegant *soirée*, she is initially reluctant to dance half naked before her bourgeois acquaintances from the years of her first marriage. The potency of Renée's interior world, however, enables her to rise above their critical gaze. As she dances, she imagines that "a beautiful serpent winds itself along the Persian rug, an Egyptian amphora tips forward, spilling out a wave of perfumed hair, a stormy blue cloud rises and takes flight, a feline beast pounces . . ." As in the passage from *Dialogue des bêtes*, Colette reappropriates the orientalist exotic dancer to stage a moment of radical female autonomy. As she dances, Renée thinks, "I have pulled myself together. . . . Do these people in front of me exist? . . . No, no, there is nothing real but dance, light, freedom, music . . . There is nothing real but giving rhythm to one's thoughts and translating them into beautiful movement."[66] Like republican instructional manuals urging students to control their imaginations, Renée forces her imagination into her service, allowing her to transcend an awkward *déclassement*. Significantly, Renée leaves the soirée "joyfully clasping" the francs that comprise her payment for the dance. Colette thus reasserts the material function of the dance; the flight of fancy is also profitable labor.[67]

Colette's representations of artistic creation often joined sensual abandon and intellectual fulfillment with honest labor. *The Vagabond*'s Renée asserts time and again that writing involves labor, excavating one's interior reflections "so rapidly that at times one's hand struggles and recoils, overworked by the impatient god that guides it." Yet this effort is contradicted by her references to writing as "a divine fever" and "the pleasure and pain of the idle." Renée remarks that the life of writing she once enjoyed is nearly impossible when combined with the necessities of earning a living: "The fragile tale that I am erecting falls to pieces when the tradesman rings, or the bootmaker presents his bill."[68] In this way Colette articulated the difficulty of fusing a life of work with artistic creation. I argue that in framing the creative process in this way, Colette revealed her own uneasiness about the disruptive aspects of imaginative expression.

In addition to tempering artistic rebellion with signs of physical labor, Colette often restrained moments of creative expression in her fiction with detailed observation of the natural world—self-directed *leçons des choses* that grounded the imagination. Indeed, the first words of Colette's first novel, *Claudine at School*, find the heroine quoting her *Manual of Departmental Geography* and then proceeding with a loving and meticulous description of the landscape and natural beauty of her *pays natal*.[69] Numerous literary scholars have noted Colette's extraordinary earthiness and sensuality—indeed, her love of nature and attention to sensual and sensory delights became one of the central components of her literary persona.[70] Her third husband, Maurice Goudeket, recalled that Colette's "way of making contact with things was through all her senses." He wrote,

> It was not enough for her to look at them; she had to sniff and taste them. When she went into a garden she did not know, I would say: "I suppose you are going to eat it, as usual." And it was extraordinary to see her setting to work. . . . She separated the sepals of flowers, examined them, smelled them for a long time, crumpled the leaves, chewed them, licked the poisonous berries and the deadly mushrooms, pondering intensely over everything she had smelt and tasted.[71]

Such tales became a stock element of Colette's increasingly mythologized public image as the most French and the most womanly of Frenchwomen. This amplified sensitivity to the natural world was manifested in the vivid descriptions that made her novels famous.

I argue that this remarkable sensory engagement was generated in part by a distinctive approach to the exterior world that Colette imbibed as a student in the *école laïque*. It was the outward expression of a mental technique and moral structure that prized sensory observation as a means of adorning the soul—and of controlling the disquieting excesses of the imagination. When republican pedagogues in the 1880s sent students out on *promenades scolaires* and taught them to feed their imaginations with a secular miraculous made up of the minutia of the natural world, they intended such methods as a wholesome antidote to Catholic superstition. In Colette's hands, observation of and imaginative connection to the natural world became an endlessly replenishable source of artistic delight that valorized her flight from her *pays natal* and from bourgeois conventions.

In her numerous fictionalized self-portraits, Colette often characterizes her mind or that of her heroines as an active physical being exploring the natural world. In one story the narrator's thoughts run wild "like a seagull whose feet are held and who frees itself by flapping its wings."[72] In *The Vagabond* Renée envisions the physical activity of her mind, these "gymnastics of the solitary," in which, though she tries not to think, her mind is an animate creature that "rebels, breaks away, runs off along a ray of sunlight that has opened up to her on the balcony, then she is off over there to a mosaic roof made of green tiles, where she pauses capriciously to play with a reflection, the shadow of the clouds."[73] In a similar fashion, the protagonist "She" of *Dialogue des bêtes* mentally roams the natural world even as she daydreams: "You think She's asleep; but at this very moment She's in the kitchen garden, picking the white strawberries that smell like squashed ants. . . . She's on every lawn and close to every tree and flower. . . . Her spirit courses like a subtle blood along the veins of all the leaves, strokes the velvet of the geraniums and the varnish of the cherries."[74] Her dream is not a fantastic escape but a magnified physical occupation of the exterior world. The liberation and escape of this daydream is firmly grounded in the corporealization of her thoughts, as well as the near-scientific observation of the botanical world, from the "veins" of the foliage to the "strawberries that smell like squashed ants."

In "Gray Day" (1908), Colette's ailing narrator endures an overcast afternoon at the seaside by withdrawing, in a kind of dream state, not to a world of decadent fantasy but to the botanical minutiae of her natal countryside. At the outset of the story, the narrator announces that this leaden day by the ocean "pains me! I no longer have in me a secret place, a sheltered corner. . . . Naked, swept away, scattered, in vain I gather the fragments of my thought."[75] To combat this mental and physical malaise, the daydreaming narrator conjures up the forests, fruit, flowers, and valleys of her youth—sensory evocations of the landscape and vegetation of the Yonne. Heartened by her imaginative excursion, and physically fortified, the narrator throws off the blanket covering her and sets out to explore the now sunlit seascape, applying the same scrutiny to sensory and botanical details that characterized her daydream. Generally speaking, Colette's elaborate descriptions of flora and fauna, as well as her persistent valorization of visual perception, all echoed the observation-based instruction "by the eyes" so touted in early Third Republic schools.

Often in Colette's oeuvre this engagement with the natural world and heightened sense of observation signal the health of the *vie intérieure*. In "The Recovery" (1908), Colette assures a grieving friend that her "suffering soul" will gradually heal and that this healing of her interior life will be announced by a renewed sensory attention to the exterior world: "One fine spring day, or even a wet autumn morning . . . you will feel something inexpressible and alive in your heart stretching out voluptuously. . . . You will discover, with a newfound naïveté, that the light is pink though the lace of the curtain, and the rug is soft under your bare feet,—the scent of flowers and that of ripe fruit are exalting, instead of overwhelming."[76] This internal recuperation is manifested in the revived enjoyment of external pleasures and the keen perception of sensory information: the tone of the light, the texture of a carpet, the scent of ripening fruit.

The ability to observe and record appears in Colette's fiction as a primal need to possess and be possessed by the natural world. *The Vagabond*'s Renée admits that since putting aside her pen for a career in the music hall, she occasionally feels compelled to write, "an acute need, like thirst in summer, to note, to describe."[77] Several times over the course of the novel, Renée refers to her detailed observations of the sensory world as an act of mutual possession, in which she takes in the exterior world and leaves behind a piece of herself. Relaxing at a seaside restaurant while on tour, Renée senses a union with the landscape, "her changeable kingdom": "Everything here belongs to me and possesses me. . . . It seems as if a shadow of myself, detached from me like a leaf, will remain here."[78] Elsewhere in the novel, Renée again refers to mentally engaging the ever-changing scenery on tour: "some part of me cleaves to everything I pass—new countryside, clear or cloudy skies, the sea pearl gray under the rain—and clings there so ardently that it seems that I leave behind me a thousand little phantoms that look like me, rocked by the waves, cradled on a leaf, lifted in a cloud." Amongst all of these imagined shades of herself, Renée recognizes one that most resembles her, a child sitting by the fireplace, "dreaming and well behaved," bent "over a book that it forgets to read."[79] Thus, Renée's truest representation is mentally engaged, lost in reverie, and yet, significantly, obedient. This passionate engagement with the exterior world is grounded in an ordered interior life, and vice versa.

This drive to observe, engage, and record leads Renée directly to her decision to reject the marriage proposal of her persistent suitor Max—a proposal whose acceptance will mean the end of her career as a traveling performer. While voyaging by train on a theatrical tour, Renée has an epiphany about her relationship with Max in an occasion of intense, irresistible observation of the natural world:

"Salt-pans filed past, edged with grass glittering with salt, and sleeping villas, white as salt, between their dark laurels. . . . Half asleep, like the sea . . . I thought I was skimming the waves, so close at hand, with a swallow's cutting flight." Once again, Colette's heroine explores the natural world while she daydreams. It is in this moment that she realizes that she has, for the first time, forgotten Max, "as though I had never known his gaze . . . as if the one dominating anxiety in my life were to seek for words, words to express how yellow the sun is, how blue the sea . . . as if the only urgent thing in the world were my desire to possess through my eyes the marvels of the earth."[80] These are not casual musings but active description and possession. By prioritizing engaged observation and an immersion in the life of the mind, Renée is able to reconsider the bourgeois comfort offered by Max's proposal. At last, she resolves: "I refuse to contemplate the earth's most beautiful lands, reflected back, ever so small, in the amorous mirror of your eyes."[81] Thus, Colette justifies her heroine's surprising rejection of a respectable marriage by elevating expansive sensory experience. This triumph of the interior and sensory life, however, is also a means of subjugating desire. Addressing Max, Renée reflects: "I shall desire you as I desire in turn the fruit that hangs out of reach, the far-off water. . . . In each place where my desires have strayed, I leave thousands and thousands of shadows in my own shape, shed from me: one lies on the warm blue rocks of the combes in my own country, another in the damp hollow of a sunless valley, and a third follows a bird, a sail, the wind and the wave."[82] This is the third time during the course of the novel that Renée describes a virtual engagement of the landscape. Such a process allows Renée to experience the transgressive joys of travel, flight, and sexual desire, but ultimately only in her imagination, as her physical body continues to labor diligently.

In a farewell letter to Max, Renée explains that she has become like a kind of "old maid," those women "who fend off all sentimental misalliances and return to sit before a window, bent over their needles, alone with their incomparable, vain imaginations."[83] Colette here depicts an "old maid" devoted wholly to her mental, creative world, *and* to the most feminine of manual tasks, thereby reconciling two potent elements of the republican ideal: the idealization of labor and the cultivation of the inner life. Both elements are elevated at the expense of the one role most intended for the Republic's ideal *citoyenne:* marriage. While Renée admits that she may at times yearn for the comfort Max offered, her desire for immersion in a vital interior life, made honorable by honest labor, is dominant. She rejects Max's attempt to infiltrate the "secret pagoda of my thoughts. I have closed it off to everyone."[84] Her return to writing represents not only a decisive turn from bourgeois conjugality but also the triumph of the *vie intérieure*. Colette's vagabond willfully makes her home in an ordered Bohemia of her own creation, a Bohemia that abides by ideals of work and artistic satisfaction.

In squaring artistic satisfaction with social order in her adult life as a music-hall performer and writer, Colette relied on modes of apprehension acquired in

the laic school of the People. Her pantomime performances and her fiction negotiated the tense relationship between artistic expression and exterior order using
the intellectual strategies of the republican *morale laïque*. Despite and perhaps
because of her unconventional life in these years, Colette seems to have taken
comfort in pantomime as an artistic realm that valued an ordered version of the
imaginative life—a far cry from the Decadent circles of her early years in Paris,
in which writers and poets sought just that "evasion toward the Dream." There is
even a hint of defensiveness in her frequent denials of artistic vocation in favor
of phlegmatic workmanship. This posture reveals a profound unease with a life
devoted to imaginative creation—an unease, I argue, that stemmed from republican France's own paradoxical engagement with this question.

Further evidence of Colette's culturally coded unease with the imagination
was that she shared the Republic's suspicion of providing an artist's liberated
selfhood to women and workers, two problematic categories of republican citizen. Indeed, Colette's many representations of the music hall sometimes qualify
the wonders of the interior life according to class. Working-class performers in
Colette's fiction have the honor and discipline of their labor, yet they seldom
appear to share in the transformative imaginative release that Colette and her
(middle-class) fictional narrators experience. In *The Vagabond* Renée refers to
music-hall performers as "rudimentary beings" who "scarcely think at all."[85] At
times, Colette and her fictional middle-class alter egos are soothed by the absence
of thought in this working-class milieu. In the story "We arrive, we rehearse," the
narrator and her fellow performers are "dull-witted and happy, without intuition
or forethought."[86] By and large, in all of Colette's music-hall literature, only she,
her fictional alter egos, and her middle-class coach Wague/Brague are depicted
as creative artists, subtly set apart from the music-hall proletariat. This aspect of
Colette's music-hall fiction indicates not only the author's personal discomfort
with opening up the higher realms of the creative process to all classes but also
a culture-wide anxiety about this same democratization. Many of the social theater endeavors of the belle époque, while designed to expose the working classes
to the performing arts, were plagued by a similar ambivalence. When one such
project began to offer workers training as actual performers rather than simply
as an attentive public, the response from social reformers, writers, and theatrical
professionals exposed significant cracks in the façade of cross-class *solidarité* trumpeted by Third Republican social philosophy.

The Mimi Pinsons

In June 1910, while continuing to perform and to publish stories, Colette decided
to report on a novel pedagogical endeavor led by Georges Wague. Wague was
teaching a free weekend course in pantomime to young Parisian workingwomen

as part of Gustave Charpentier's Conservatoire Populaire de Mimi Pinson (founded in 1902 and named for the seamstress heroine of an 1845 story by Alfred de Musset).[87] Charpentier's students performed all over France in ambitious laic festivals that celebrated work and art through the allegorical crowning of the "the People's Muse," Mimi Pinson, usually represented by a local female laborer elected by her coworkers.[88] Wague was prominently featured in these festivals, playing the mimed part of "Human Suffering." In December 1909 the Conservatoire Populaire added to its curriculum Wague's modern pantomime course, which met at ten o'clock on Sunday mornings at a girls' public schoolhouse in Paris. In contrast to the resistance to Wague's course at the elite Conservatoire National, initial enrollments in the free class were reportedly so high that organizers were obliged to make a selection from the pool of applicants.[89]

The Parisian press was captivated by the idea of teaching performing arts to the city's seamstresses and female day laborers, and sizeable articles describing Wague's classes became a forum for discussing the merits of popular performing arts education. In all cases, both critics and supporters of the popular conservatory expressed anxiety that artistic liberation might upset the social order if placed at the disposal of working-class women. Some notion of artistic liberation was, at least ostensibly, part of the Conservatoire Populaire's curriculum. In discussing Wague's course, one journalist quoted Charpentier himself: "our *midinettes* . . . should be allowed to know the pleasures of art, before now reserved to the privileged, so that they can ornament their naturally keen and open minds with a thousand lights of life."[90] Nevertheless, such proclamations of art were few and far between in discussions of the Mimi Pinsons. Most of the press on the Conservatoire Populaire was devoted to warning of the dangers the initiative might bring, or to demonstrating how such dangers were assiduously prevented by its organizers. Many expressed concern that Wague's class might impel honest, hardworking girls toward less than honorable careers in the music hall. A 1910 editorial in *Gil Blas* fretted that in opening working-class girls' minds to the performing arts, well-meaning *artistes* such as Wague were sowing the seeds of class discontent:

> We would render a proud service to our sweet, industrious *Parisiennes* if we would be willing to leave them alone. These different *arts d'agrément*, instilled in these good children for whom life has been modest and simple, strike a violent contrast with the rest. They learn just enough to more sharply feel that which they lack. . . . They will necessarily head toward a lamentable life of ham acting [*cabotinage*], composed of exaggerations, vanity, ambitious illusions, and brutal disappointments.[91]

Here, simplicity and industriousness are placed in "violent" opposition to a life of artistic expression. This unnamed critic continued that many of these girls would be needlessly pulled from their "sweet and healthy obscurity" by classes such as those offered by Wague. *Gil Blas* suggested that these young working-women "would be less inclined to consider taking a skewed path if we did not mark it out for them with unexplored temptations and if we did not open danger-ous avenues to them." These young women would be better advised to "exit their obscurity by upright paths, by their intellect, by their ingenuity in their métier, by their marriage."[92] Marriage and (a presumably nonartistic) métier were the ap-propriate paths to prosperity for these women, and theatrical performance only a deleterious fantasy. Jacques d'Halmont, writing for *Le Nouveau siècle*, agreed that Wague's lessons could be exceedingly harmful to industrious working-class girls, "ignorant of Bohemia": "Are we right to let [these girls] dream? . . . The theater is encumbered enough with the untalented and the *'théâtreuses'* of fortune . . . without making these nice little girls, who have other amusements besides this Sunday morning distraction, drop their needles."[93] Here once again, artistic sat-isfaction is depicted as incompatible with hard work.

Even passionate supporters of the pantomime course were quick to reassure the public that Wague was not grooming workingwomen for careers in the the-ater. Writer and music critic Georges Jean-Aubry insisted that Wague's lessons were nothing more than "an intelligent and healthy distraction" for workers, "not a preparation for the theater."[94] René Simon averred that the Conservatoire Populaire "does not produce *déclassées.*"[95] Another journalist stressed that the class did not "push [the Mimi Pinsons] toward the theater"; rather, the students were "serious young girls who love to make music or recite verse after work. The evenings at home are long, but at class they are short."[96] Albert Acremant, the secretary general of the Conservatoire Populaire (and later a playwright), assured readers that no *mère de famille* would abandon her family to come to the Conser-vatoire. In addition, he continued, any Mimi Pinson who became engaged to be married promptly discontinued her lessons, leaving in order to assure the "hap-piness of a hardworking husband."[97] The left-wing newspaper *Le Radical* wistfully imagined the Mimi Pinsons performing "little plays within their families, in or-der to occupy Sunday leisure hours with art."[98]

While Wague himself was not distressed by the idea of some of his working-class students pursuing a stage career, he confirmed that his goal was not to create declassed women: "do not make the common error of accusing me of misdirecting future housewives toward the theater. All we are doing here is some *culture physique* and, if I dare say, *culture artistique.* . . . Our initiative cannot push women toward the stage who should be watching over the *pot-au-feu.*"[99] Though he admitted that he was teaching these young women just as he would "female stage professionals," he sought only to provide his working-class students with "a very wholesome and gracious artistic distraction that will occupy them on Sundays."[100]

To this end, Wague and his supporters consistently framed the goals of the initiative not as art but as feminine *arts d'agrément*, essentially, in this context, lessons in graceful comportment. One commentator insisted that Wague was not teaching the Mimi Pinsons "in order to turn them into mimes in their own right, but to make their smallest gesture more delicate, to render their lovely movements more ideal, to give their supple forms more expression, and to make all of their sweet, amiable person more graceful."[101] The art critic André Warnod assured readers that Wague had "taken great care to instruct" his students "only in that which befits honest and simple girls":

> [This course] develops and augments the charm of these beaming little *ouvrières* of Paris by distracting them and occupying them in a pleasant manner. . . . This initiative could become quickly harmful and perverse if these little students, quitting their fiancé, family, and workshop, went off to display their new talent on the stage of some lowly *café-concert*, taking as a métier that which should remain an agreeable pastime. . . . Georges Wague and the course's organizers understand this very well.[102]

Again and again, in similar passages, the natural grace of the working-class Mimi Pinsons is extolled and protected by the middle-class men who offer them some innocent recreation after their grueling workweek. The pantomime classes of the Conservatoire Populaire endeavored to make these young women more pleasant in their daily lives as manual laborers, rather than provide them with moments of transcendent imaginative liberation. In its review of the pantomime class, *Fantasio* addressed Mimi Pinson, saying, "Whereas others learn to excavate the recesses of their complicated soul, you, Mimi, learn to smile."[103] This understanding of the course as lessons in poise seems supported by the fact that this was an initiative aimed only at female workers.

The mimodrama that Wague rehearsed with his working-class students, *Pierrot marie ses filles* (Pierrot Marries Off His Daughters), served as proof to several journalists of the moral soundness of the venture. Jean-Aubry asserted that this mimodrama was a moral piece whose "gracious simplicity . . . will be a delicate spectacle that will console us after the luxurious stupidity of music-hall ballets. . . . Here we will not see two or three hundred suggestive extras marching by."[104] Another commentator called the pantomime a "little play . . . of the highest morality."[105] The mimodrama was indeed quite different from those Wague performed with Colette. While his critically acclaimed shows involved forceful scenes of violence, betrayal, and nudity, the piece he taught the Mimi Pinsons was a moralistic pantomime featuring Pierrot and his five daughters (the youngest being Mimi Pinson). Though the older daughters all suffer from some character flaw, "a glutton, a dreamer, and a coquette," Mimi Pinson is faultless and is devoted to her father. The story is a morality tale in which filial piety is challenged and ultimately triumphs.

By way of a response to the critics of the initiative, supporters of the pantomime class often noted the impeccable behavior of the students in Wague's class. Many of the articles on the course began with a reference to its location: the classroom of a girls' public school. This setting allowed several journalists to equate the workingwomen with well-behaved primary schoolgirls. In proclaiming its approval of the class, *Le Radical* remarked, "You had to have seen Wague yesterday morning, standing in the middle of his students, who are docilely lined up around him, just like on the benches of the school they recently left."[106] The title of Colette's article, "Mimi Pinson at School," not only played on that of her famous memoir of the laic school; it also highlighted the pedagogical element of Wague's pantomime. Colette's account was unique among the articles on Wague's mime class in that she specified that the school at which the lesson was held was a "laic" one.

The respectful comportment of Wague's working-class students was remarked in almost all of the articles on the course. One journalist assured readers that he had seen no "effrontery on [the Mimi Pinsons'] faces, nothing of the bad kind in their *toilette*. There were certainly no ulterior motives and no hint of theatrical histrionics in the depths of their little amused brains."[107] Several commentators employed descriptions of the Mimi Pinsons' modest comportment as a way of distinguishing them from workers who spent their free time in less respectable ways. One journalist insisted that the Mimi Pinsons "are not those exuberant young girls who only leave the workshop to go to dances, ice rinks, or theaters. [The Mimi Pinsons] are serious. Their gaiety is genuine. Their coquetry is of the most acceptable kind, with its desire to learn to sing well, to recite beautiful verse, and to dance graceful dances, which have been adapted to their youth by a skillful teacher."[108] A column in *Gil Blas* noted approvingly that the Mimi Pinsons in Wague's mime class had "nothing of the slightly noisy, let us say, somewhat plebeian exuberance, that one might suppose. I was struck by the good tone, by the simplicity . . . of all of these gracious young girls." After attending Wague's class, this journalist went as far as to call the Conservatoire Populaire "a school of good behavior and virtue" for the young women of Paris.[109]

By insisting upon this distinction between the Mimi Pinsons and less worthy women, whether workers or actresses, commentators on both sides of the debate demonstrated that the mixing of art and work was a troublesome enterprise. Frequently, the charm and modesty of the Mimi Pinsons were linked directly to their ability to work. An ideal alternative to the slovenly music-hall cocotte, the women of the Conservatoire Populaire represented the best of the working classes, according to Albert Acremant:

> The fact that they come, in the evening, after the fatigue of a workday, to attend classes that are not always amusing says enough in their favor. Sometimes it snows or rains, and it would be nice to stay at home or to go to the music hall to spend money earned at the workshop, but Mimi Pinson prefers to come to the schoolroom,

humming a couple of notes while tapping the rhythm with an arm that does not remember having operated a needle all day.[110]

In this depiction, the pantomime class is an agreeable complement to the daily grind of manual labor, primarily because it supplants less worthy pastimes. Three times in this brief passage, Acremant makes reference to the labor of these young women, as if to more sharply accentuate the social stakes involved in regulating their leisure hours.

Acremant's contention that in Wague's classroom these workingwomen's bodies can forget the monotonous labor of the day ("an arm that does not remember having operated a needle all day") illustrates the important if delusive social remedy proponents and critics alike hoped to find in the Conservatoire Populaire. Many journalists described the pantomime lessons with a similarly wistful tone, evidently relishing the notion that such lessons were a pleasant and socially beneficial curative for the hardship of these women's laboring lives. Jean-Aubry confessed that he was charmed by the Mimi Pinsons: "In merry groups . . . these young women . . . devote themselves to their pleasurable labor with conviction and liveliness, without intending to eclipse the professional stars who, oftentimes, they dress during the week." He complimented the course for providing a healthy "distraction" that "releases Mimi Pinson from the worries and fatigues of the working life."[111] Whatever "worries and fatigues" result from the Mimi Pinsons' socially necessary labor are smoothed away by a simple weekly mime class, and Jean-Aubry can guiltlessly take pleasure in their youthful prettiness. *Le National's* "J.-H." admitted, "it leaves me dreamy, all these little seamstresses and milliners who come here to forget the gestures of the trade that earns their daily bread, and to learn others that could never be remunerated by anyone."[112] Like Jean-Aubry and Acremant, this journalist finds something enchanting in the notion that workingwomen can "forget" their labor and still remain pleasingly removed from professional artistic aspirations.

In the eyes of its supporters, the Conservatoire Populaire offered the attractive vision of a social remedy in which working-class girls found an edifying pastime to ease the unmentionable hardship of their workweek. This remedy involved the very attentive leadership of a middle-class professor, who, within a chaste pedagogical setting, provided the girls with just enough art to amuse them, but not so much that they would leave their needles idle. The initiative's proponents were eager to believe that free art classes, not a radical restructuring of economic relationships, had the power to rectify grim social inequities. This eagerness exposes the uneven and ambivalent place of women, workers, and art in the Third Republic's social program.[113]

The Conservatoire Populaire's defenders plainly perceived a connection between this performing arts initiative and the construction of a laic, democratic society. René Simon exclaimed, "Are there any bourgeois left who are oblivious enough to protest this *oeuvre* of Art and Beauty for the people? . . . The talent and devotion of several has done more for the 'education of the democracy' than twenty dead-end projects of our good-for-nothing politicians."[114] Wague spoke of this issue when interviewed about the class: "In former times, women knew only religious art, because of the attention of Church patronage. . . . Young girls learned to sing canticles. . . . Today we teach them the splendid choruses of the Couronnement de la Muse. . . . Do you think she has lost in this?"[115] He thus explicitly tied the teaching of art to working-class women to the laic revolution of the Third Republic. According to this ideal, inspired teacher-artists such as Wague would train the young imaginations of the female working population in a salutary direction and provide them with a spiritual, if secular, release from labor on their weekly day of rest. Still, even if many accepted the theoretical notion that all citizens had a right to art and beauty, the practical implementation of such an enterprise clearly was rife with difficulties from the perspective of social order.

* * *

Like many other commentators on the Mimi Pinsons, Colette expressed approval of the young women's upright behavior and tidiness. In her article for *Paris-Journal* she noted the "discreet chatter" of the girls, "neat in their Sunday best." They were, she noted with apparent surprise, "very civilized little girls, in truth."[116] As with the other journalists who covered the Mimi Pinsons, Colette's attention to the behavior of the young women sometimes assumed a tone of parental condescension. As the Conservatoire Populaire was attended by women ranging from fifteen years old to late middle age, the frequent use by Colette of the term "little girls" to describe the students makes an exaggerated point of their youth. She declared that the lesson she had witnessed seemed to pass quickly because "these little girls interest me as much as animals—intelligent and very civilized animals."[117]

Like many of those observing Wague's classes, Colette found the girls' working abilities particularly important. She noted with relief that when the lesson began, "these children, who, all week long gather ribbons, quilt cloth, and hem linens, demonstrate that they know how to work. They know the price of time; they listen, obey, and do not grumble." Specifically, she noted the manual and orderly nature of their labor, as well as their physical vigor. The girl who demonstrated the most aptitude for pantomime was "hardy" and had "a flawless body." Another gifted student was "strong[,] . . . nimble, and straight," and she jumped to her feet easily when Wague called her.[118]

As with her own experience as a mime and writer, Colette saw a tension between disciplined training and imaginative release in the pantomime lessons of the Mimi Pinsons. She described Wague's class as tiring work, not liberated inspiration: "The lesson is arduous; it takes all the patient authority of the teacher.

His novice students apply themselves to it with surprised modesty. They 'hold back' their physiognomy as one holds back a burst of laughter or a sob. They do not dare to carry a gesture all the way through, and the radiant expression, the divine light, only spreads across their young faces in timid nuances."[119] Their pantomime, though gradually producing the "divine light" of art, is bounded by a process of trial and error.

Colette reproached the Mimi Pinsons for lacking the naturalness that Wague's genre of modern pantomime so highly prized: "The natural . . . that's what is missing from this demi-quateron of *pinsonnes* [finches]. They are, from birth, theatrical and schooled." When Wague asks one of the girls to pretend to sew, Colette notes: "The student, an authentic seamstress of seventeen, sits and pretends to sew like the clowns at the circus, fifty stitches per minute . . . hastily pulling each needle stroke out a meter. She has forgotten a professional gesture and seems to have never held a needle."[120] Though Colette's music-hall fiction lionized actresses and dancers who sew in between acts, this "authentic seamstress" makes the mistake of moving in the opposite moral direction.

Though approving of Wague and his efforts, Colette seems at best amused, at worst irritated by the *embourgeoisement* of these working-class girls through the classes of the Conservatoire Populaire. She relates some of the "astonishing" bits of conversation she overhears from the Mimi Pinsons attending the class:

—Are you doing fencing this year?
—No, the doctor has forbidden it. But I started singing again: I am wild about classical music.

Colette is surprised, and possibly even disappointed, that these young working-women "speak of sport and art with the negligent self-assurance of *mondaines;* the general tone, it seems to me, aims for a somewhat affected simplicity."[121] She appears to believe, not unlike many of the commentators discussed above, that these young women spoil their innate working-class purity by taking on the accoutrements of idle, upper-class women. In an inversion of Colette's own experience, the art of pantomime is the vehicle of this corrupting *embourgeoisement.* While Colette found an antidote for the strictures and contradictions of bourgeois femininity in pantomime, the Mimi Pinsons, already at the moral level of honest laborers, are diminished by their withdrawal from the world of work and toward the theatrical world.

Still, Colette did not completely dismiss the possibility that, through hard work, these young women could learn the craft of pantomime and move toward art. As she approvingly notes, all of the Mimi Pinsons know how to work: "these tenacious and sensible Parigotes understand quickly. . . . Their progress is of a rapidity that rewards all the efforts of their master." Given Colette's formulation of work and reward in her own life, it is interesting that here it is the master

(Wague) who will have his "efforts" rewarded, not the Mimi Pinsons. Colette was confident that after several months of training with her former teacher, "guided by that demanding and indulgent will, they will know how to express wordlessly gaiety, anxiety, sadness; they will know how to captivate and fire the attention of the spectator by a raising of the eyebrows, a tensing of the mouth; they will know how to smile without silliness, cry without ridicule, listen without effort."[122]

The patronizing tone of Colette's essay on the Mimi Pinsons was mirrored in a short piece she wrote in February 1914 about an evening lecture at the Université Populaire. She praised the "sensible" working-class audience who waited for a presentation by orators and actors, much like the obedient girls in Wague's class: "It is truly the intelligent elite of the People that assembles here, respectful of the texts that one reads them, courteous to the point of reserve. . . . They wear upon them, men and women alike, pieces of thread, flakes of ground metal, stains of varnish or acid. . . . There is not a single man who has had 'one too many.'"[123] Echoing her description of the Mimi Pinsons, Colette praised the reasonable, well-behaved workers who enjoyed the art presented to them and who, quite literally, wore the marks of their labor. To be sure, Colette publicly defended Charpentier's popular conservatory and published fiction and essays that at times evinced a judicious recognition of the dark underside of the republican idealization of work, particularly for women. Yet she seems to have found the economic hardship of music-hall *artistes* compelling only inasmuch as their working-class austerity served to highlight her own flight from bourgeois idleness. Celebrating the labor of music-hall performers became significant for her only as far as it served her internal need to temper artistic expression with order, honorable work, and meticulous observation of the exterior world.

Her work thus typifies the social naïveté and even hypocrisy of a republican *morale* that sought to repair tensions between labor and capital by means of a rather utopian (and manipulative) ideology of work. In the end, Colette's ambivalence about workingwomen as inspired artists reflected the same anxieties about artistic expression with which she struggled as a writer and performer. Drawn to the intellectual satisfaction of artistic production, Colette found a means of reconciling art's appealing liberation with cultural strictures that warned against its excesses, by binding imagination to observation and labor. By way of resolving these concerns, Colette insisted throughout her work and long life that all artistic expression involve a truthful rendering of the exterior world and be bound by the canon of manual work. That she even sought a resolution to this issue in both a public and personal way speaks to the wider import of this enterprise for the cultural history of the belle époque.

Like Colette's descriptions of working-class performers "shunning thought" in her music-hall stories, her treatment of the Mimi Pinsons and other such initiatives demonstrates that, on the practical level, the question of art and class became considerably more ambiguous in practice than it appeared in debates over modern pantomime or in primary school readers. Wague and his supporters made popular appeal and working-class venues crucial components of an aesthetic and philosophy of modern art. In a general way, many of these critics and performers were sincerely devoted to bringing the performing arts to "the People." They agreed that, in a democratic society, the popular classes had a right to enjoy art as consumers. What was less clear was *whether* and *how* a democratic society should open the realm of artistic production to the working classes. While the worker as spectator was somewhat problematic, the worker as liberated artist was far more troublesome. If a rich interior life of artistic expression was indeed to be provided to the people, it was with the assurance that art would be inextricably connected to a life of work. For society itself to remain ordered and functioning, art, particularly if produced by the working classes, must necessarily be bound by the dictates and practice of diligent labor.

Notes

1. Claude Valmont, "La Pantomime rénovée," *La Revue Moderne,* 10 June 1913.

2. Émile Vuillermoz, "La Vie théâtrale: Semaine musicale," *Paris-Midi* and *L'Action,* 23 September 1911.

3. "Le populaire Bighetti répond à Georges Wague," *Théâtra* (Marseilles), 4 April 1911.

4. Sophia Rosenfeld's *A Revolution in Language: The Problem of Signs in Late Eighteenth-Century France* (Stanford, CA, 2001), discusses debates over pantomime in the eighteenth century.

5. See Pierre Aubery, "L'anarchisme des littérateurs au temps du symbolisme," *Le Mouvement Social* 69 (October 1969): 21–34.

6. Rémy, *Georges Wague,* 20–23; Storey, *Pierrots,* 313.

7. At least one contemporary decried Wague's misrepresentation of traditional pantomime: Léon Uhl in "Pantomime classique ou pantomime moderne," *Arts et Sciences,* November 1912.

8. Wague quoted in Rouzier-Dorcières, "La Pantomime à notre époque," January 1908, Bibliothèque de l'Opéra, D412 (3), 60–61. Wague was quoting Camille de Sainte-Croix.

9. Georges Wague, "La Pantomime moderne," *Le Monde Théâtral,* June 1914.

10. Camille de Sainte-Croix, "Les Grands Mimes," *La Petite République,* 18 September 1907. Wague quoted this portion of de Sainte-Croix's article in his own essay "La Pantomime moderne," *Paris-Journal,* 19 November 1910. For more on Camille de Sainte-Croix (1859–1915), see David James Fisher, "The Origins of French Popular Theatre," *Journal of Contemporary History* 12, no. 3 (July 1977): 461–97.

11. "Nos auteurs et le Cinéma: Mme Colette Willy," *Le Cinéma,* 18 October 1912. Emphasis in original. Colette and Wague probably met in the 1890s at the *soirées* at the Café du Procope, where Willy was a regular.

12. Rouzier-Dorcières, "La Pantomime à notre époque."

13. Wague quoted in ibid.

14. de Sainte-Croix, "Les Grands Mimes," *La Petite République,* 18 September 1907.

15. Gabriel Reuillard, "La Pantomime," *Les Hommes du Jour,* 17 January 1914.

16. Claude Valmont, "La Pantomime rénovée," *La Revue Moderne,* 10 June 1913.

17. Gabriel Boissy, "Une Classe de pantomime au Conservatoire: La Pantomime n'est qu'un art secondaire," *Excelsior,* November 1910.

18. J.-B. Séguy, "A propos de 'La Chair," *La Rampe,* 11 April 1908.

19. "La Renaissance de la pantomime," *Le Tout-Élégant Illustré* (Bordeaux), 15 September 1908.

20. For more on Romain Rolland, see David James Fisher, *Romain Rolland and the Politics of Intellectual Engagement* (Los Angeles, 1988) and Venita Datta, "Romain Rolland and the Theatre de la Révolution: A Historical Perspective," *Clio* 20, no. 3 (1991): 213–222. Fisher points out that reformers such as de Sainte-Croix and Rolland represented a French left "sympathetic to socialism for moral and aesthetic reasons only, regarding the organized movement as a contemporary extension of the French Revolution's social programme and ethical ideas" ("French Popular Theatre," 490). For more on Pottecher and Antoine, see Charnow, *Theatre, Politics, and Markets*. Beach's *Staging Politics and Gender* examines the political stakes of theater in this period. On the Universités Populaires, see Elwitt, *Third Republic Defended*, and Lucien Mercier, *Les Universités populaires, 1899–1914: Education populaire et mouvement ouvrière au début du siècle* (Paris, 1986).

21. Charnow, *Theatre, Politics, and Markets*, 155, 94, 208. Others in the avant-garde looked down on more "mimetic" art forms such as cinema. See Staller, "Méliès' 'Fantastic' Cinema."

22. Schwartz, *Spectacular Realities*, 202.

23. Wague, "La Pantomime moderne," *Le Monde Théâtral*, June 1914.

24. Ibid.

25. Letter from Guillaume Livret to *Le Figaro*, 9 September 1907.

26. Letter from Georges Wague to *Le Figaro*, 12 September 1907.

27. "'L'Oiseau de Nuit' à Apollo," *Genève Mondain*, 26 October 1912.

28. "Nos auteurs et le Cinéma: Mme Colette Willy," *Le Cinéma*, 18 October 1912.

29. "La vogue des sketches," *Comoedia*, 4 November 1911. The rue de Gaîté in Montparnasse was home to several popular, rather bawdy, working-class *café-concerts*.

30. Léon Vibert, *Music Hall* (Paris), 1 October 1912.

31. Camille de Sainte-Croix, "Les Grands Mimes," 18 September 1907.

32. Francis Norgelet, "La Mimique," *La Société Nouvelle*, November 1911. *Bat'd'Af* was a mimodrama that Colette performed with Wague.

33. "Le populaire Bighetti répond à Georges Wague," letter in *Théâtra* (Marseilles), 4 April 1911. The letter was a response to Wague's "La Pantomime moderne," *Théâtra*, 28 March 1911, in which he attacked the Marseillais style of pantomime that Bighetti exemplified.

34. "Le populaire Bighetti répond à Georges Wague," 4 April 1911. He is referring to Colette as Polaire.

35. Letter from Wague, *Théâtra*, 25 April 1911. Bighetti replied that Wague's shows sold well because he bowed to the trend of including "la Femme" to please the audience, referring primarily to *The Flesh*. The exchange of letters continued into May.

36. Wague, "La Pantomime moderne," *Le Monde Théâtral*, June 1914.

37. Joseph Gravier, "Les Idées de Georges Wague, Prince du Geste," *La Presse Sportive et Littéraire* (Lyon), 31 December 1910.

38. Letter from Georges Wague to *Le Figaro*, 12 September 1907.

39. Georges Wague, "Beaucoup de mimique! Pas de gestes!" *Le Film*, 22 April 1916. In 1923 Gustave Fréjaville wrote that the belle époque music hall was the "berceau du cinéma" (*Au Musichall* [Paris, 1923]), 276. Charles Rearick refers to the music hall as the purveyor of a truly modern art form because of the discontinuity that characterized varied artistic programs (*Pleasures of the Belle Epoque*, 153).

40. "Nos Auteurs et le Cinéma: Mme Colette Willy," *Le Cinéma*, 18 October 1912.

41. Claude Valmont, "La Pantomime rénovée," *La Revue Moderne*, 10 June 1913.

42. Joe Bridge, "Colette Willy et Georges Wague à Ba-ta-clan," *Le Journal*, 28 August 1911. Bridge was the pen name of the illustrator and journalist Jean Barrez (1886–1967). The show, an adaptation of a novel by Aristide Bruant, featured Colette as a dancer in a Saharan bar whose clientele are "the soldiers of the African Penal Battalion." After a fight, the dancer's lover is killed, and Colette

"in a fit of despair . . . strangled the farmer and went mad." See Francis and Gontier, *Creating Colette*, 1:303.

43. *L'Evénement*, December 1906. This piece appeared verbatim in *Le Figaro* that same month.

44. *Lyon-Mondain*, October 1909.

45. "'L'Oiseau de Nuit' à Apollo," *Genève mondain*, 26 October 1912.

46. Roger Ducos, "Les Classes à coté: La Classe de Georges Wague," *La Rampe*, 7 February 1918.

47. *L'Avenir*, 23 June 1919. This may refer to a lecture at the Trianon-Lyrique that included a mimodrama by Wague.

48. Pierre Humble, *L'Indicateur des Spectacles*, 25 June 1919. Untitled newspaper clipping, Bibliothèque de l'Opèra, Coupures sur Colette et George Wague, D. 412 (5).

49. Vuillermoz, "La Vie théâtrale: Semaine musicale," *Paris-Midi* et *L'Action*, 23 September 1911.

50. François de Nion, "La Pantomime," *L'Éclair*, 11 June 1914.

51. Wague quoted in an interview by Hautfort, "L'école des mimes," *La France* (Bordeaux), July 1910.

52. Opponents of the Conservatoire class held that pantomime was a superfluous category of instruction. See Gabriel Boissy, "Une classe de Pantomime au Conservatoire," *Excelsior*, 1910. Wague responded to Boissy in *Paris-Journal*. Also see "Pierrot professeur," *Paris-Midi*, 27 May 1914.

53. Wague, "La Pantomime Moderne," *Paris-Journal*, 19 November 1910.

54. Colette defended the course in Maurice Montabré's "Pierrot ressuscite," *L'Intransigeant*, 28 May 1914. Also see an unpublished letter to Wague, October–November 1918, BNF vol. 3, #144, and unpublished letter to Wague, BNF vol. 3, #194.

55. Maurice Montabré, "Pierrot ressuscite," *L'Intransigeant*, 28 May 1914.

56. Rémy, *Georges Wague*, 112, 116. The new minister of public instruction and fine arts, Paul Painlevé, signed off on the proposition of the undersecretary of fine arts, Albert Dalimier. Wague taught his first class on 15 January 1916. By this time, the new director at the Conservatoire was Henri Rabaud.

57. This is a summary of critiques by Rémy in *Georges Wague*, 107–8.

58. Ibid., 121. One student's mother complained when she heard her daughter would have to disrobe when playing a nymph. When two students kiss on the mouth in one of Wague's shows, there were protests from some (122).

59. V., "Chronique: À l'Opéra," *Le Temps*, 22 February 1916. The author references the work of Émile Zola and Alfred Bruneau. For more on Zola and Bruneau's operatic collaborations in the 1890s, see Steven Huebner, "Naturalism and supernaturalism in Alfred Bruneau's *Le Rêve*," *Cambridge Opera Journal* 11, no. 1 (March 1999): 77–101.

60. Huebner, "Naturalism and supernaturalism," 100.

61. On Symbolism, see Henri Peyre, *What Is Symbolism?* trans. Emmett Parker (University, AL, 1980); and Robert Goldwater, *Symbolism* (New York, 1979). Colette's literature also shares many of the tenets of *naturisme*. For a discussion of *naturisme* see Patrick L. Day, *Saint-Georges de Bouhélier's Naturisme: An Anti-Symbolist Movement in Late-Nineteenth-Century French Poetry* (New York, 2001).

62. Colette, *Creatures Great and Small*, trans. Enid McLeod (New York, 1951), 129. This publication includes both of Colette's *Dialogues* works.

63. Colette, *Creatures Great and Small*, 129.

64. Colette, *Retreat from Love*, 115.

65. Colette, "Un mauvais matin," in *L'Envers du music-hall*, 177–78.

66. *La Vagabonde*, 254.

67. Ibid., 255.

68. Ibid., 226–27.

69. *Claudine à l'école*, 17.

70. Kristeva writes that for Colette, "the barriers among the five senses, like the threshold between intimate perception and external reality that lies behind them, are posited only to be transcended" (*Colette*, 195).

71. Maurice Goudeket, *Close to Colette*, trans. Enid McLeod (London, 1957), 15. Originally published as *Près de Colette* in 1956.

72. Colette, "Jour gris," in *Les Vrilles de la vigne* (1908; Paris, 1934), 43–44.

73. *La Vagabonde*, 376.

74. Colette, "Music-Hall," in *Creatures Great and Small*, 120.

75. Colette, "Jour gris," 43–44.

76. Colette, "La Guérison," in *Les Vrilles de la vigne*, 183.

77. *La Vagabonde*, 227.

78. Ibid., 373.

79. Ibid., 276. The last phantom is "rêveur" and "sage" in the original French.

80. *The Vagabond*, 207.

81. *La Vagabonde*, 399.

82. *The Vagabond*, 223.

83. *La Vagabonde*, 397–98.

84. Ibid., 399.

85. Ibid., 241.

86. "On arrive, on repète," in *L'Envers du music-hall*, 175.

87. Mary Ellen Poole offers a concise history of the Conservatoire Populaire in "Gustave Charpentier and the Conservatoire Populaire de Mimi Pinson," *Nineteenth-Century Music* 20, no. 3 (Spring 1997): 231–252.

88. Pomfret provides an analysis of the Couronnement de la Muse du Peuple in "A Muse."

89. "Pierrot Professeur: Au Conservatoire de Mimi-Pinson," *Paris-Journal*, 11 April 1910.

90. Jean-Aubry, "Mimi Pinson silencieuse," *Madame et Monsieur*, 10 May 1910.

91. "Les Professeurs de Mimi Pinson," *Gil Blas*, 14 June 1910. The editorial was signed "Gil Blas."

92. Ibid.

93. J. d'Halmont, "La Pantomime chez les Midinettes," *Le Nouveau Siècle*, 6 February 1910.

94. Jean-Aubry, "Mimi Pinson silencieuse."

95. René Simon, "Chronique musicale: Le Conservatoire de 'Mimi-Pinson'," *L'Aéro*, 20 August 1911.

96. *La République de l'Oise* (Beauvais, Oise), 20 January 1911.

97. Albert Acremant, "Le Conservatoire Populaire de Mimi Pinson: à Paris et en vogage," *Comoedia Illustré*, 1 May 1910.

98. "L'Art du geste: L'Éducation de Mimi Pinson—le mime Wague lui enseigne la pantomime," *Le Radical* (Paris), 21 February 1910.

99. Hautfort, "L'école des mimes," *La France* (Bordeaux), July 1910.

100. Wague quoted in ibid. and in H. de F.'s "Première leçon de pantomime au Conservatoire de Mimi Pinson," *Les Nouvelles*, 11 January 1910.

101. "L'Art du geste," *Le Radical*, 21 February 1910.

102. André Warnod, "Un cours de pantomime: Colombine et Mimi Pinson," *Comoedia*, 27 April 1910.

103. "Pierrot, professeur de Mimi Pinson," *Fantasio*, 4 January 1910.

104. Jean-Aubry, "Mimi Pinson silencieuse," 10 May 1910.

105. Hautfort, "L'école des mimes," July 1910.

106. "L'Art du geste, " *Le Radical*, 21 February 1910.

107. H. de F. "Première leçon de pantomime ," 11 January 1910.

108. "Gustave Charpentier et Mimi Pinson," *La Revue Septentrionale*, April 1910.

109. "Autour de la vie féminine . . ." *Gil Blas*, 2 January 1910.

110. Acremant, "Le Conservatoire Populaire de Mimi Pinson . . ."

111. Jean-Aubry, "Mimi Pinson silencieuse," 10 May 1910.

112. J.-H., *National*, June 1910. Untitled newspaper clipping, Bibliothèque de l'Opéra, Coupures sur Colette et George Wague, D. 412 (4).

113. Poole writes, "Charpentier's efforts . . . represent a complicated attempt to confine [Mimi Pinson's] behavior even as he aimed to expand her sphere of action" ("Gustave Charpentier," 231).

114. Simon, "Chronique musicale," 20 August 1911.

115. Hautfort, "L'école des mimes," July 1910.

116. Colette Willy, "Mimi Pinson à l'école," *Paris-Journal,* 13 June 1910.

117. Ibid. Colette, it should be noted, was an animal lover and was known to the public as such.

118. Ibid.

119. Ibid.

120. Ibid.

121. Ibid.

122. Ibid.

123. Colette, Contes des mille et un matins, 84.

Epilogue

⚜

When Colette died in August 1954, she was honored with a state funeral, the first ever for a woman in the French Republic.[1] Her coffin was draped in the tricolor flag, set in the cour d'honneur of the Palais-Royal, and attended by a military honor guard. Wreaths lined the coffin, representing condolences from, among many others, the French government, the queen of Belgium, the Co-médie Française, the author's "compatriots" in Saint-Sauveur, and her music-hall comrades.[2] The twenty-five hundred invited quests were joined by more than six thousand mourners who silently filed past throughout the day. The actress Mar-lene Dietrich, in attendance that day, recalled that "a wind in the courtyard gave a fluttering life to the great tricolor folds which draped the catafalque. . . . The flag seemed to live and breathe as it enveloped the coffin."[3] Thus, with one last laic ceremony, the *ingénue libertine* who had indulged in the gamut of transgres-sive behavior throughout her long life was laid to rest draped in the Republic's supreme symbol. Certainly, this apotheosis smoothes over the rutted terrain that was Colette's relationship with the French Republic. But it also signals the ulti-mate rapprochement between this state and this individual.

The French government was represented at the funeral by the minister of education, Jean Berthoin, who had paid private condolences to Colette's family a week before.[4] In his eulogy, Berthoin described Colette's work as "dionysiac" and "full of rustic health in the midst of the feverish chills of human misery." Her writing, he said, in a phrase that evoked her style, "avoided darkness and pre-ferred the blue of vibrant atmosphere, the green of shimmering foliage, the red of palpitating blood."[5] The minister of education's presence at the ceremony was especially appropriate, since, by 1954, Colette was not only a national treasure and an icon of French joie de vivre but also a prominent part of the country's national educational curriculum. Indeed, as early as the 1930s, when antholo-gies of her work designed specifically for young readers were first published, more than 40 percent of the public school system's *manuels scolaires* included excerpts or stories by Colette; this figure rose to 72 percent by the 1960s.[6] A study in 1981 found that Colette was the third most recognized author by French sixth graders, behind only Camus and Sartre.[7] Her strongest presence was in the primary school curriculum—in part because of the forceful connections, biographical and otherwise, that pedagogues and the public drew between Colette and the republican *école primaire* and *école primaire supérieure*. Marie-Odile André points out that from the 1930s through the 1980s, Colette, despite her evident exceptionality, was incorporated into the primary curriculum as "the representative of all those boys and girls who, like her, had attended or were attending primary schools . . . the model of the excellence and the success that was possible in the School."[8] André also notes that Colette, while transformed into a contemporary classic even during her lifetime, remained a "minor classic" and one who until only fairly recently was employed exclusively in the primary school system. Colette's oeuvre, admired for its style but somewhat dismissed as a *littérature féminine* that lacked intellectual substance, seemed at once to suggest the possibilities of democratized, popular education and its limits.[9]

By the time she was eulogized by the minister of education in 1954, Colette had been seen as a cherished, if at times controversial, image of France for decades. Critics, celebrities, admiring readers, and the republican curriculum itself waxed romantic about her feminine sensitivity to flora and fauna, her rustic good sense, and her earthy contentment, and saw no irony in the laic sacralization of a rather apolitical woman who had first become famous lampooning the laic revolution. Many concurred with Pierre Mazars, who, upon Colette's death, unintentionally echoed belle époque descriptions of her work: "it is a hymn to sight and nature without anguish about the hereafter or metaphysical interrogations. But it is neither an impure nor immoral oeuvre. It is an oeuvre that is often modest."[10] Jean Cocteau, Colette's friend and neighbor, wryly noted the scrubbing of the author's reputation in her later years: "One scandal after another—then everything changes and [Colette] becomes an idol. She ends her life of music halls, beauty parlors, old lesbians, in an apotheosis of respectability."[11]

And yet, by opposing Colette's early career as music-hall bohemian and her later status as a sanitized icon, Cocteau missed the essential inseparability of these two identities. To be sure, Colette somewhat distanced herself from the scandals of her youth as she aged. She once denied to the painter Boldini that she had ever appeared nude on stage, reinforcing his notion of her as a "bonne petite bourgeoise!"[12] She arguably employed the same tactic as a young writer by casting music-hall performance as punishing manual labor when in reality she was often traveling first class and being pampered by her wealthy lovers. Yet, more than simply a whitewashing of her past, such a perspective also harmonized with Colette's lifelong dedication to work, to a distinct code of honorability, to bodily health, and to artistic production. It was this curious celebration of *morale laïque*, this particular version of French femininity, that inspired the public's affection for and even mythologization of Colette as an author and woman. In *Mémoires d'une jeune fille rangée* (1958), Simone de Beauvoir recalled Colette's Claudine as one of the rare exceptions to the "idiotic young women or futile society ladies" who passed for "heroines" in the literature of her youth, and, in *La Deuxième sexe* (1949), she used *La Vagabonde* as an example of early twentieth-century Frenchwomen's important efforts to balance femininity and métier.[13]

* * *

This study ends with the outbreak of World War I—a caesura in both the historical narrative and in Colette's life. In the two years before the war broke out, Colette married Henry de Jouvenel, stopped performing in the music hall, and gave birth to her first and only child, Colette Renée de Jouvenel. And so, it would seem, the bourgeois girl temporarily enamored with the subversive honor of the working world returned to the leisure class, married the rich nobleman, and bore his child. And yet she continued to write, prolifically, voraciously, and profitably, through her pregnancy, her brief stint as a republican socialite, her divorce from Jouvenel in 1925, and both world wars. Most important for this project, she continued to formulate her literary endeavors as an honorable manual craft that provided moral and physical soundness.

In the decades that followed her music-hall career, interviews with Colette often adhered to a predictable narrative: a rather awestruck journalist arrives at Colette's apartment and immediately is swept into the vigorous rhythm of her workday. This was true of press accounts of "the Baronne de Jouvenel" in the 1920s and remained so of interviews with "Madame Colette" in the 1950s. In this way, journalists, biographers, friends, and family helped promote the author's reputation of workmanlike diligence. By the 1950s, though she was paralyzed by arthritis and confined to her apartment in the Palais-Royal, reporters granted an audience were still inevitably caught up in the productive commotion of Colette's daily routine. In one such interview from 1926, Colette claimed, typically, "If I do not have passion, I have the honor of my métier. . . . I work very honestly, as well as I can, with severity."[14] Her daughter later recalled Colette's familiar description of her writing method: "slowly, with difficulty, like the oxen of my region who heavily mark out their furrows. . . . I see an enormous block of blank paper, and I think: 'In six months, all of those sheets must be filled with black marks.' . . . It is so painful and discouraging to tell oneself this!"[15] When Jean Parmentier asked in a 1930 interview whether writing was a sacrifice that Colette made for her readers, she responded: "Yes, but a necessary sacrifice, a sacrifice that I enjoy. . . . We cannot escape from this idea that we deserve a reward for our labor. It is only after having worked hard that we find complete pleasure in seeing, hearing, and living."[16] Writing was, then, even in Colette's later years, a burden—but somehow an essential and rewarding burden.

Well after she had established herself as a prestigious author with numerous literary laurels and financial comfort, Colette persisted in categorizing her work as necessary craft labor and took a shopkeeper's glee in profits and savings. In the

1920s, when offering her services to a friend opening a couture business, Colette exclaimed: "Make use of me . . . my physical solidity, my good head, which isn't crazy, my desire for work, my good old bourgeois work ethic, which compels me to succeed at whatever task is entrusted to me."[17] Colette's third husband, Maurice Goudeket, her companion for more than twenty-five years, declared that "a manual trade would have given her the greatest pleasure. It was not a more noble activity to write, than, for example, to make a pair of sabots. . . . She had all the virtues of the French artisan—humility, patience, self-exaction, pleasure in a well-finished article."[18]

The craft of writing, Colette repeated throughout her life, was difficult but imperative. Reading through her vast correspondence from the beginning of the century until her death in 1954, work is a common refrain even in brief letters to friends, publishers, and acquaintances: "I work. I live—in that is everything"; "I am working hard"; "I have been working with such severity"; "I'm working like I am an entire plantation!"; "I'm working like a female convict."[19] Particularly after arthritis made physical activity impossible, Colette relied on work as a moral outlet. She explained to a friend in 1945 that she had reduced her personal correspondence in order to work more, "so as to keep myself in honorable activity."[20] She also took up the "rhythmic labor"[21] of crewelwork in these years: "My women friends say that I amuse myself thereby; my best friend knows that I find it restful. Simply, I've found my aim therein . . . a satisfying occupation."[22] In her 1946 memoir *The Evening Star*, Colette claimed that while she could not cease working completely in her final years, she had at least found a peaceable union of personal desire and work: "I continue to work. . . . On a resonant road the trotting of two horses harnessed as a pair harmonizes, then falls out of rhythm to harmonize anew. Guided by the same hand, pen and needle, the habit of work and the commonsense desire to bring it to an end become friends, separate, come together again . . . Try to travel as a team, slow chargers of mine: from here I can see the end of the road."[23]

In this way, Colette often expressed a bemused resignation toward her involuntary impulse to work. In her last full work, *The Blue Lantern* (1949), she wrote once more of this unremitting drive to work, that "insurrection of the spirit" that throughout her life she had "often rejected, later outwitted, only to accept it in the end, for writing leads only to writing": "For me there is no other destiny. . . . I used to think that it was the same with the completed book as with other finished ploys, you put down tools and raise the joyful cry, 'Finished!', then you clap your hands only to find pouring from them grains of sand you believed to be precious."[24] The ubiquity, fervor, and at times palpable frustration of such statements suggest not merely that Colette was adopting an attractive public persona but rather that such fierce productivity and commitment to métier held a powerful sway over the author. These values were fundamental to her perception of the world, and to some degree affected even her most primary emotions and bodily sensations. What is more, given Colette's popularity, these values were evidently attractive to the public at large, suggesting that such a formulation of labor and art responded in some intuitive fashion to the culture in which Colette lived and wrote.

In a like manner, Colette's approach to the body, first noted in reviews of her seminude pantomime performances in *The Flesh*, became an enduring characteristic of her literary legend and broad appeal. As part of a special issue of *Le Capitole* devoted to Colette in 1925, Paul Réboux penned an essay titled "La Vertu de Colette" in which he mused, "when one takes up one of Colette's books, it is quite difficult to feel one's senses troubled, because the admirable writer that is this woman knows so well how to express the riskiest things in new and healthy terms."[25] Upon her death, Maurice Martin du Gard wrote that Colette was "indeed the representative type of our Third Republic. Among other things, she has discovered a sensuality which is not strictly speaking Latin. . . . And the great art of this born writer is that, while she admits a rather plebeian taste for flesh, she has imposed on it a rank among the most delicate masterpieces."[26] This "plebeian" robustness sprang from a deep-rooted mental structure, a way of ordering the world that differed drastically from the moral proscriptions of Catholicism. Rather than denigrating the flesh in favor of immaterial spiritual growth, Colette privileged her body as the most efficient conduit of her *vie intérieure*, once telling a friend, "As for me, it's my body which thinks. It's more intelligent than my mind. When my body thinks, all my flesh has a soul."[27]

Finally, for Colette, the guides of republican discourse inspired (and regulated) an intense lifelong plundering of the exterior world in the service of *la vie intérieure*. Honorable labor, physical exertion, immersion in the self—even in her fifties, Colette's heroines would repeat this winning combination. When the narrator of her semi-autobiographical 1928 novel *The Break of Day* [La Naissance du jour] ends her relationship with a young lover, she combats her solitude with a thirst for natural observation and possession that echoes *The Vagabond's* Renée Néré: "From yesterday's rain, in the shade, a new perfume is born; or is it I who am once again going to discover the world and apply new senses to it?" While love had once again offered her "a little shriveled treasure," she resolves: "In future I shall gather nothing except by armfuls. Great armfuls of wind, of colored atoms, of generous emptiness that I shall dump down proudly on the threshing floor."[28] Here, in one short passage, Colette connected heady but precise observation of the natural world with the richness of her interior life (and did so using a metaphor of manual labor)—a stylistic approach that became synonymous with her work in general. When Émile Vuillermoz reviewed *Break of Day* in 1928, he situated the "perpetual miracle" of Colette's art in her ability to possess the natural world with a keen sense of observation that illuminated the spirit. He wrote that Colette, "this *observatrice* of life and love," knew better than anyone how to "commandeer that which is the most robust and the most delicate in the vegetable, mineral, and animal kingdoms," transforming "the most humble terms into talismans."[29] *Break of Day* also saw Colette once more seeking that reconciliation of work, art, and femininity that she had attempted fictionally in *The Vagabond*. Yet by the late 1920s Colette had the social, emotional, and financial security necessary to make such a reconciliation durable.

In responding to Colette, French audiences and readers were responding in part to this pleasing rapprochement of the Republic's most fundamental contradictions. Colette would undoubtedly have concurred with Boldini that she was a "good little bourgeoise," but her definition of goodness owed its peculiar hues to the exhortations and contradictions of her republican youth. This study has probed what it meant for a belle époque woman such as Colette to be "respectable" and, more importantly, to consider herself as such.

Colette's reimagining of the *morale laïque* was part of a wider artistic engagement with bourgeois values in France that had its root in the early nineteenth century but acquired a new insistency and social breadth with the Third Republic. This was a negotiation that had marked French Bohemia and the European avant-garde since their inception. But the Republic's *morale laïque* complicated this relationship by not only trumpeting values of frugality, hard work, and class cooperation but also by attempting to change the very way French men and women saw, the way they imagined, and the way they envisioned and ornamented their selfhood. Thus Bohemian *artistes* and music-hall audiences alike inherited ready associations between a revulsion for idleness and the observation of the natural world, between the fortification of the body and the primacy of craft labor. It was this associative power, rather than the discursive messages alone, that produced the unusual secular habits of mind that took on such grand cultural proportions in the decade before World War I. The belle époque was raucous not simply because radicals were tearing at the edges of traditional moral and artistic standards but also because broad swaths of society had adopted a new secular moral code. Indeed, the secular morality of the republican schools of the 1880s before long became, in the words of sociologist Jean Baubérot, "the morality of 'la plus grande majorité des Français.'"[30]

The meaning of secularization, then, was more than political, or at least, it was political in the most expansive sense of the word. If the Republic's *morale laïque* was designed by a rather elite ensemble of bourgeois politicians and academics, this design was not drafted or executed in a vacuum. The values of the laic Republic developed over time, through vigorous exchanges between intellectual elites and the quotidian experience of republicanism by shopkeepers, teachers, artisans, and schoolchildren. In this way, official republican discourse was no more significant than how this discourse was reiterated and transformed by French men and women who grew to adulthood within republican institutions. Exhorting men and women to work diligently was not a novel pedagogical plea. However, when strung together with calls to cultivate an externally attentive imagination and bodily strength, lessons of wage-paying manual labor could provide a remarkable range of both options and constraints for students. By binding her exceptional artistic liberation to the exterior world and to manual work, Colette exposed the imperfect nature of the republican morale and its essential flexibility, particularly for women.

As Colette's life and work make plain, the complex of laic ideas available to women regarding work, femininity, and individual expression during the Third Republic was not confined to those narrow models prescribed by republican discourse. Colette became a mother in 1913, amidst sharp demographic anxieties that saddled the blame for depopulation on, among others, the New Woman and trumpeted the maternal devotion of the *vraie femme*. Given the puissance of such rhetoric in the belle époque, it is notable that Colette's own formulation of motherhood fit only awkwardly into the period's pronatalist ideal of the *mère*. Colette resolutely rejected the notion of motherhood as a tender, biologically ordained fulfillment of her feminine destiny. In 1946 she imagined her long-deceased mother, Sido, telling her: "You'll never be more than a writer who has produced a child."[31] Her uneasy relationship with her daughter Colette de Jouvenel is ground well trod by biographers. Most relevant for the purposes of this study is that Colette was able to compose a respected, feminine, and secular identity that scarcely acknowledged her role as a mother.

By 1914, where this study ends, French women were still, in the most evident political way, marginal members of the Republic—they could not vote. The sluggish arrival of French women's suffrage in 1944 has proved somewhat confounding to scholars working in the field of French gender history. Many follow Joan Scott in laying the responsibility for this tardy emancipation at the feet of French liberalism's paradoxes, namely, the exclusionary necessities of universalist discourse. The preceding study spells out more precisely how this exclusion functioned at the individual and the cultural levels. Historian James Lehning argues that suffrage, despite its centrality to republican discourse at the turn of the twentieth century, "held little attraction" for those "for whom the vote did not seem to bring about the Republic they wished," such as workers, and "for those who were not allowed to vote—women, foreigners, colonial subjects."[32] Indeed, Colette herself was untroubled by her inability to take an active part in French politics for much of her life, and she took scant interest in the suffrage question. Yet even if most members of the marginal groups described by Lehning were blocked from engaging in republican electoral politics in a direct fashion, many nonpolitical realms of French civil society nonetheless absorbed in some measure the language and moral codes of political republican practice—and in absorbing them, transfigured them.

The Third Republic, then, fashioned with its *morale laïque* a sort of suprapolitical citizenship, which made the vote only one of a panoply of actions and *modes de vie* that qualified one as a member of the laic sodality. Women such as

Colette could, with good reason, feel themselves integrated participants in the Republic by way of their labor and fitness. Such a sentiment was not simply a convenient compensation for the blank of suffrage but the most basic expression of a tremendously effectual social bond. For those raised in the first flush of pedagogical laicization, the Republic seemed held together by this bond—a shared understanding of the redemptive grace of labor, a shared intuition of the links between the exterior world and the self, a shared attentiveness to the physical body. This foundational bond held out the promise that layers of political discord and economic inequity could be stripped away, leaving a perfectly solidarist *Patrie*. In numerous ways this social identity echoed the prerepublican bonds of Catholic community in France, but in the Third Republic, they were divested of their ecclesiastical meaning, so that only the nation remained. To be sure, this was an imagined cohesion, shot through with contradictions at every turn and capable of inducing a degree of complacency and even hostility toward the question of women's political rights. But, like religious faith, such imaginings also had the power to seep into and pigment the self, both to rouse and to restrain social change, and even to penetrate the most intimate bodily experiences of pain and pleasure.

The language of labor, imagination, and fitness that marked belle époque popular culture did not disappear in the summer of 1914. Indeed, the peculiar accents of Third Republican discourse have often resurfaced in cultural rhetoric in the century that has followed, across the political spectrum. Léon Blum spoke in 1936 of reviving in his exhausted country the "taste for work" ("goût du travail").[33] Marshall Pétain made *Travail* one of the three pillars of his Vichy France. In 2007 Nicholas Sarkozy came to power as the standard-bearer of a new political program that would stand up for "the France that gets up early" ("la France qui se lève tôt") Such political rhetoric, however dissimilar in content and intent, must be understood not only in the context of contemporary debates but also as a language with a special republican genealogy. Sarkozy was responding to very Fifth Republic concerns about the thirty-five-hour workweek, immigration, and globalization; but he also took rhetorical cues from the cultural and social inheritance of the republics that went before. Certainly, Blum, Pétain, and Sarkozy are figures of radically different historical moments and political programs. Yet they all were obliged to grapple with the legacy of the Third Republic's laic revolution, explicitly or not.

The profound convictions and emotions stirred in France by *l'affaire de foulard* from 1989 to this day are a useful gauge of *laïcité*'s enduring cultural currency beyond the political sphere. In the debates over the headscarves, public schoolgirls have once again taken center stage in nationwide discussions of the meaning and limits of the laic Republic. As in the 1880s, some seem to believe that the future of the nation itself rests on *laïcité*'s ability to draw women (and alienated youths) away from their familial and religious affiliations.[34] If the permutations of the *morale laïque* engendered by the Third Republic's laic revolution are any indication, these early twenty-first-century battles over *laïcité* may, at the very least, produce results far different from those envisaged by today's most vocal supporters of the *morale laïque*.

Notes

1. Thurman, *Secrets of the Flesh*, 499.
2. See Sarde, *Colette: Free and Fettered*, 425; Francis and Gontier, *Creating Colette*, 2:248.
3. Richardson, *Colette*, 229.
4. Ibid., 228, 230.
5. Quoted in Francis and Gontier, *Creating Colette*, 2:248.
6. Marie-Odile André, *Les Mécanismes de classification d'un écrivain: Le cas de Colette* (Metz, 2000).
7. Rambach, *Colette, pure et impure*, 359.
8. André, *Les Mécanismes*, 158–59, 160.
9. Ibid., 353.
10. Pierre Mazars, "Colette ou la Fraîcheur," *Revue de la Pensée Française*, October 1954, Bibliothèque historique de la ville de Paris (BHVP), Bouglé, Série 30.
11. Quoted in Francis and Gontier, *Creating Colette* 2:221.
12. Mazars, "Colette ou la Fraîcheur."
13. Simone de Beauvoir, *Mémoires d'une jeune fille rangée* (Paris, 1958), 111; *La Deuxième sexe, II: L'expérience vécue* (Paris, 1949), 615. See Éliane Lecarme-Tabone, "Témoignages: Simone de Beauvoir et Colette," *Cahiers Colette* 20 (1998): 119–25.
14. Frédéric Lefèvre, "Une Heure avec Colette," *Les Nouvelles Littéraires*, 27 March 1926.
15. "Colette évoquée par sa fille Colette de Jouvenel," BNF NAF 18718, micro 3319, #210.
16. Jean Parmentier, "Colette, sa fille, et l'ennemi," *Bravo*, 3 January 1930. Bibliothèque de l'Arsenal (BA) Rf 55.239(45).
17. Letter to Germaine Patat, quoted in Thurman, *Secrets of the Flesh*, 324.
18. Goudeket, *Close to Colette*, 13–14. Colette married Goudeket at the age of sixty-two, after a long relationship.
19. Letter to Marie-Thérèse Montaudry, 8 June 1937; letter to Eugène Rey, 28 November 1928; letter to Mme. Henri de Regnier, 1923; letter to Marie-Thérèse Montaudry, 15 January 1929; undated letter to the Comtesse de Polignac. BNF NAF 18707 and 18718.
20. Letter to Marie-Thérèse Montaudry, 29 June 1945, BNF NAF 18707.
21. Francis and Gontier, *Creating Colette*, 2:214.
22. Colette, *The Evening Star*, 142.
23. Ibid., 144.
24. Colette, *The Blue Lantern*, trans. Roger Senhouse (London, 1963), 161. Originally *Le Fanal bleu*, published in 1949.
25. Paul Réboux, "La Vertu de Colette," *Le Capitole*, Numéro consacré à Colette, 1925.
26. Maurice Martin du Gard, in his *Impertinences . . .*, quoted in Richardson, *Colette*, 239.
27. Related by Claude Chauvière and quoted in Richardson, *Colette*, 238.
28. Colette, *Break of Day*, trans. Enid McLeod (New York, 1961), 141. Originally *Naissance du jour* (Paris, 1928).
29. Émile Vuillermoz, review of *Naissance du Jour*, in *Excelsior*, 19 April 1928. Reprinted in *Cahiers Colette* 24 (2002): 48–51, quotation at 50.

30. Jean Baubérot, "Laïcité and Its Permutations at the Fin(s) de Siècle(s)," in *New Perspectives on the Fin de Siècle in Nineteenth- and Twentieth-Century France*, ed. Kay Chadwick and Timothy Unwin (Lewiston, ME, 2000), 21–42.

31. Colette, *The Evening Star*, 138.

32. Lehning, *To Be a Citizen*, 184, 185.

33. Quoted in *Léon Blum: chef du gouvernement, 1936–1937*, ed. Pierre Renouvin and René Rémond (Paris, 1967), 258.

34. See, for example, *Matériaux pour l'histoire de notre temps* 78. (April-June 2005), a special issue devoted to "La laïcité: un enjeu sur la voie de l'émancipation humaine," including Elisabeth Badinter's "La laïcité, un enjeu pour les femmes," 50–53.

BIBLIOGRAPHY

Archival Collections

Archives nationales de France (AN). Série AJ/71/19–81, F/17/1477-F/17/12544.
Archives départementales de la Yonne (ADY). Série T (Instruction Publique, Sciences, et Arts). Auxerre, France.
Bibliothèque de l'Opéra, Paris (BO). Series D 412 (3, 4, 5).
Bibliothèque historique de la ville de Paris (BHVP). Bouglé Collection (Des Archives Marie-Louise Bouglé): Biographie-Actualités, Série 30: Colette.
Bibliothèque de l'Arsenal (BA), Paris. Dossier Colette. RF 55. 239 (9).
Bibliothèque Nationale de France (BNF). Manuscrits. Colette, Correspondence: NAF 18706, 18707, 18708.
Bibliothèque Littéraire Jacques Doucet, Paris (BLJD).
Bibliothèque Marguerite Durand (BMD).
Musée Colette, Saint-Sauveur-en-Puisaye, Yonne.
Centre d'études Colette, Conseil général de l'yonne.

Published Primary Sources

Periodicals

Alouette: Revue de l'Yonne et du Centre de la France Littéraire, Artistique, Pédagogique [Auxerre], 1886–87
Artistique Revue—Musicale et Littéraire [Nice]
Cahiers Colette (Société des amis de Colette, Presses Universitaires de Rennes)
Comoedia (Comedia Illustré)
La Culture Physique, 1904–5
L'Echo de Paris
L'Echo du Lycée: Bulletin de l'Association Amicale des Anciennes Élèves du Collège et Lycée de Jeunes Filles d'Auxerre, 1895–1906
Excelsior
Fantasio
La Femme Nouvelle & La Jeune Française: Revue bi-mensuelle illustrée, 1904–6
Le Fin de Siècle
La Jeune Province: Revue mensuelle, didactique et littéraire illustrée
Le 'Music-Hall' [Marseilles]
Paris-Journal
La Revue Pédagogique, 1878–82

Instructional Material and Writings on Pedagogy

Barrau, Théodore. *Livre de Morale pratique, ou choix de préceptes et de beaux exemples destinés à la lecture courante dans les écoles et dans la famille.* Paris: Hachette, 1857.

Bentzon, Thérèse [Marie-Thérèse de Solms Blanc], and A. Chevalier. *Causeries de morale pratique.* Paris: Hachette, 1899.

Bérillon, Louis-Eugène. *La Bonne Ménagère agricole, ou simples notions d'économie rurale et d'économie domestique: livre de lecture à l'usage des jeunes filles des écoles primaires.* Auxerre: Imprimerie A. Gaillot, 1874.

Bert, Paul. *La cléricalisme, questions d'éducation nationale avec une préface de A. Aulard.* Paris: Armand Colin, 1900.

———. *Discours prononcé par M. Paul Bert à l'occasion du banquet, qui lui offert; par les instituteurs et les institutrices de France, le 18 septembre 1881 suivi de la liste des souscriptions au banquet . . .* Paris: Picard-Bernheim, 1881.

———. *L'Instruction civique à l'école (notions fondamentales).* Paris: Picard-Bernheim, 1882.

———. *L'Instruction religieuse dans l'école conférence faite au cirque d'hiver . . . le 28 août 1881 sous la présidence de M. Gambetta.* History of Education Series, fiche 28, 747. Paris: Picard-Bernheim, 1882.

———. *Leçons, discours, et conférences.* Paris: G. Charpentier, 1881.

———. *Rapport présenté à la Chambre des députés sur la loi de l'enseignement rimaire.* History of Education Series, fiche 17, 451–17, 455. Paris: G. Masson, 1880.

———. *La cléricalisme, questions d'éducation nationale avec une préface de A. Aulard.* Paris: Armand Colin, 1900.

Bentzon, Thérèse [Marie-Thérèse de Solms Blanc] and Chevalier, A. *Causeries de morale pratiques.* Paris: Hachette, 1899.

Bruno, G. *Francinet: Principes généraux de la morale, de l'agriculture.* Paris: Belin, 1869.

Buisson, Ferdinand, ed. *Dictionnaire de pédagogie et d'instruction primaire.* 4 vols. in 2 parts. Paris: Hachette, 1882, 1887.

Burdeau, Auguste. *Instruction morale à l'école: devoir et la Patrie.* Paris: Picard-Bernheim, 1884.

Carraud, Zulma. *Contes et historiettes à l'usage des jeunes filles qui commencent à savoir lire.* Paris: Librairie Hachette, 1862.

———. *Maurice ou le travail.* Paris: Librairie Hachette, 1853.

———. *La Petite Jeanne, ou le Devoir: Livre de lecture courante spécialement destiné aux écoles primaires de filles.* Paris: Librairie Hachette, 1853.

Caumont [Anne-Marie-Louise Lardenois de Caumont, also Mme. Alfred Mézières]. *Lectures courantes des écoliers français.* Paris: Librairie Ch. Delagrave, 1884.

Compayré, Gabriel. *L'Éducation intellectuelle et morale.* Paris: Librairie Classique Paul Delaplane, 1908.

———. *Éléments d'instruction morale et civique.* Paris: Librairie Classique Paul Delaplane, 1882.

———. *Lectures on Pedagogy: Theoretical and Practical.* Translated by W. H. Payne.Boston: D. C. Heath & Co., 1889.

———. *The History of Pedagogy.* London: Swan, Sonnenschein, Lowrey & Co., 1888. Translated by W.H. Payne. Originally *Histoire critique des doctrines de l'éducation en France depuis le seizième siècle* (1879), later just *Histoire de la pédagogie.* Paris: Librairie Classique Delaplane, 1888.

Defodon, Charles and Vallée, J. *Petites dictées pour les écoles rurales: textes et explications.* Paris: Hachette, 1880.

———. Defodon, Charles. *Cours de dictées: adaptés à la grammaire des écoles primaires.* Paris: Hachette, 1867.

Defodon, Charles, and J. Vallée. *Petites dictées pour les écoles rurales: Textes et explications.* Paris: Hachette, 1880.

Delon, Charles. *Lectures expliquées: Tableaux et récits, accompagnés de nombreuses vignettes*. Paris: Hachette, 1875.

Descieux, Dr. *Leçons élémentaires d'hygiène*. Paris: Ch. Fouraut et fils, 1875.

De Solenière, Eugène. *Willy*. Paris: Librairie P. Sevin et E. Rey, 1913.

Didon, Le P. *L'Éducation présente: discours à la jeunesse*. Paris: Librairie Plon, 1898.

Durand-Gréville, Alice. *L'Instruction morale et civique des jeunes filles*. Paris: E. Weil and G. Maurice, 1882.

École et écoliers d'autrefois. Archives Départementales de l'Yonne, Brochure No. 16. Auxerre: Service Éducatif des Archives.

L'Éducation des jeunes filles: il y a cent ans. Rouen: Exposition Inaugurale de la Maison des Quatre Fils Aymon, Musée National de l'Education, 1983.

Garrigues, M. *Simples lectures sur les Sciences, les Arts et l'Industrie, à l'usage des écoles primaires*. Paris: Librairie Hachette, 1877.

Jost, Guillaume. *Annuaire de L'Enseignement élémentaire en France et dans les pays de langue française*. Publié sous la direction de M. Jost, délégué dans les fonctions d'Inspecteur général de l'Instruction publique. Armand Colin: Paris, 1885.

Jost, Guillaume, and Frédéric Braeunig. *Lectures pratiques, (éducation et enseignement, instruction morale et civique), destinées aux élèves des cours moyen et supérieur*. Paris: Hachette, 1881 and 1899.

Jost, Guillaume, and V. Humbert. *Lectures pratiques: Destinées aux élèves du cours élémentaire*. Paris: Hachette, 1881.

Juranville, Clarisse. *Le Premier livre des petite filles: nouvelles lectures graduées*. Paris: Aug. Boyer et Cie, 1880.

———. *Premiers sujets de style avec sommaires raisonés: Méthode intuitive, mise à la portée des plus jeunes enfants*. Paris: Aug. Boyer et Cie, 1869.

———. *Le Savoir-Faire et le Savoir-Vivre dans les diverses circonstances de la vie: Guide pratique de la vie usuelle à l'usage des jeunes filles*. Paris: Aug. Boyer et Cie, Libraires-Éditeurs, 1879.

———. *Le Style enseigné par la practice: Méthode nouvelle*. Paris: Aug. Boyer et Cie, 1869.

Labbé, J. *Morceaux choisis des classiques français (prose et vers, à l'usage des écoles municipales)*. Paris: Librairie Hachette et Cie, 1884.

Lacharrière, Marie. "Les récréations dans les Lycées de jeunes filles." *Bulletin Mensuel de l'Association des Élèves de Sèvres*, November 1888, 2–5.

Legrand, Emile-Albert. "Étude de pédagogie théorique: L'Imagination.—Son rôle à l'école primaire." *L'Alouette: Revue de l'Yonne et du Centre de la France, Littéraire, Artistique, Pédagogique* 6 (April 1887): 89–92.

Louis, Antonin. *Chants et exercices de gymnastiques pour les jeunes filles, suivis de la chanson des jeux, avec paroles*. Paris: Désiré Ikelmer, 1885.

Mabilleau, Léopold. *Cours de morale (cours élémentaire)*. Paris: Hachette, 1883.

———. *Cours d'instruction civique: cours élémentaire et moyen*. Paris: Hachette, 1883.

Marion, Henri. *Leçons de morale*. Paris: Armand Colin, 1884.

———. *Leçons de psychologie: Appliquées à l'éducation*. Paris: Armand Colin, 1882.

Messin, Jules. *Les Lectures quotidiennes de l'école et de la famille: Recueil de morceaux choisis à l'usage des cours moyens et supérieurs*. Paris: Gedalge Jeune, 1877.

Mézières, Alfred. *Éducation morale et instruction civique à l'usage des écoles primaires (cours moyen et supérieur)*. Paris: Librairie Ch. Delagrave, 1883.

———. *La Société francaise: Études morales sur le temps présent*. Paris: Didier et Cie, 1869.

Ministère de l'Instruction Publique. *Manuel de gymnastique à l'usage des écoles primaires et secondaires de filles et des écoles normales primaires d'institutrices*. Paris: Imprimerie Nationale, 1881.

Payot, Jules. *Aux Instituteurs et aux institutrices: Conseils et directions pratiques*. Paris: Armand Colin, 1897.

———. *Cours de morale*. 1904; Paris: Armand Colin, 1930.

———. *L'Éducation de la démocratie*. Paris: Armand Colin, 1895.

Pellissier, Augustin. *La Gymnastique de l'esprit (méthode maternelle), 1e partie: Observations des choses et des êtres*. Paris: Librairie Hachette, 1873.

———. *La Gymnastique de l'esprit (méthode maternelle), 2e partie: Jugements et raisonnements sur les choses et les êtres*. 1874; Paris: Hachette, 1893.

———. *La Gymnastique de l'esprit (méthode maternelle), 3e partie: Directions pour la mémoire et l'imagination*. 1875; Paris: Hachette, 1887.

———. *La Gymnastique de l'esprit (méthode maternelle), 4e partie: Éducation du sens moral et religieux*. 1875; Paris: Librairie Hachette, 1883.

———. *La Gymnastique de l'esprit (méthode maternelle), 5e partie: Éducation du goût*. Paris: Librairie Hachette, 1876.

Regodt, Henri. *Notions d'histoire naturelle: Applicables aux usages de la vie*. Paris: Imprimerie Jules Delalain, 1874.

Rousselot, Paul. *L'École primaire: Essai de pédagogie élémentaire*. Paris: Librairie Ch. Delagrave, 1880.

———. *Leçons de choses et lectures*. Paris: Librairie Ch. Delagrave, 1881.

———. "La Pédagogie dans les écoles de filles, à propos du concours d'admission aux fonctions de directrice d'école normale." *Revue Pédagogique* (July-December 1879): 552–69.

Saucerotte, Constant. *Petite hygiène des écoles: Simples notions sur les soins que réclame la conservation de la santé*. Paris: Jules Delalain et fils, 1876.

Schuwer, Charles. *L'École civique: Les droits & les devoirs de l'enfant, de l'homme, du citoyen*. Orange, Vaucluse: Chez l'Auteur, 1879.

Steeg, Jules. *Instruction morale et civique: l'homme, le citoyen, à l'usage de l'enseignement primaire*. Paris: F. Nathan, 1890.

Vergnes, Charles-Charlemagne. *Manuel de gymnastique, à l'usage des écoles primaires, des écoles normales primaires, des lycées et des collèges*. Paris: Hachette, 1869.

Other Published Primary Sources

Adorée Villany: Phryné moderne devant l'Aréopage. Munich: F. Bruckman, 1913.

Barney, Natalie Clifford. *Souvenirs indiscrets*. Paris: Flammarion, 1960.

Bès, Guillaume. *Souvenir de ma visite à L'Exposition Universelle de 1878: Mémoire adressée à mes collègues du canton*. AN F/17/9388.

Bodin, Marguerite. *Les Psaumes d'amour*. Paris: Eugène Figuière & Cie, 1915.

———. *Les Surprises de l'école mixte*. Paris: Librairie Universelle, 1905.

Burgaud, Françoise, ed. *Colette: Romans, récits, souvenirs—1900–1919*. Paris: Robert Laffont, 1989.

Colette. *Le Blé en herbe*. Paris: Flammarion, 1923.

———. *Break of Day*. Translated by Enid McLeod. New York: Farrar, Straus and Cudahy, 1961. Originally published as *Naissance du jour* (Paris: Flammarion, 1928).

———. *Ces Plaisirs . . .* Paris: Ferenczi, 1932. Later rereleased as *Le Pur et l'impur* and translated as *The Pure and the Impure* by Herma Briffault (New York: Penguin, 1966).

———. *Chéri*. Paris: A. Fayard, 1925.

———. *Claudine à l'école*. Paris: Ollendorff, 1900.

———. *Claudine à Paris*. Paris: Ollendorff, 1901.

———. *Claudine en ménage*. Paris: Mercure de France, 1902. First published as *Claudine amoureuse* (Paris: Ollendorff, 1902).

———. *The Claudine Novels*. Translated by Antonia White. New York: Penguin, 1987.

———. *Claudine s'en va*. Paris: Ollendorff, 1903.

———. *The Collected Stories of Colette*. Translated by Matthew Ward, Antonia White, and Anne-Marie Callimachi. New York: Farrar, Straus and Giroux, 1983.

———. *Contes des mille et un matins*. Paris: Flammarion, 1970.

———. *Creatures Great and Small*. Translation by Enid McLeod of *Dialogues des bêtes* (1904) and *Sept dialogues des bêtes* (1905). New York: Farrar, Straus and Giroux, 1951.

———. *Dans la foule*. Paris: G. Crès, 1918.

———. *Dialogues des bêtes*. Paris: Mercure de France, 1904.

———. *Earthly Paradise*. Edited by Robert Phelps. New York: Farrar, Straus and Giroux, 1966.

———. *Les Égarements de Minne*. Paris: Ollendorff, 1905.

———. "Enquête sur les devoirs de vacances," *Nos Loisirs*, 1 August 1923. Reproduced in *Cahiers Colette* 12 Archipel (1990).

———. *L'Entrave*. Paris: Librairie des lettres, 1913. Translated as *The Shackle* by Antonia White (London: Secker and Warburg, 1964).

———. *L'Envers du music-hall*. Paris: Flammarion, 1913.

———. *The Evening Star (Recollections)*. Translated by David Le Vay. London: Peter Owen, 1973. Originally published as *L'Étoile vesper (souvenirs)* (Paris: Éditions du Milieu du monde, 1946).

———. *Le Fanal bleu*. Paris: Ferenczi, 1949. Translated as *The Blue Lantern* by Roger Senhouse (London: Secker and Warburg, 1963).

———. *La Fin de Chéri*. Paris: Flammarion, 1926.

———. *Gigi*. Paris: Ferenczi, 1945.

———. *Les Heures longues*. Paris: A. Fayard, 1917.

———. *L'Ingénue libertine*. Paris: Ollendorff, 1909; Albin Michel, 1956. Reworking of *Minne* (1904) and *Les Égarements de Minne* (1905).

———. *Julie de Carneilhan*. Paris: A. Fayard, 1941.

———. *Letters from Colette*. Translated by Robert Phelps. New York: Farrar, Straus and Giroux, 1980.

———. *Lettres à sa fille, 1916–1953*. Paris: Gallimard, 2003.

———. *Lettres à ses pairs*. Paris: Flammarion, 1973.

———. *Lettres de la Vagabonde*. Edited by Claude Pichois and Roberte Forbin. Paris: Flammarion, 1961.

———. *Looking Backwards*. Translated by David Le Vay. London: Peter Owen, 1975. Originally *Journal à rebours* (1941) and *De ma fenêtre* (1942).

———. *Mes Apprentissages*. Paris: Ferenczi, 1936. Translated as *My Apprenticeships* by Helen Beauclerk (London: Secker and Warburg, 1957).

———. *Mes vérités: Entretiens avec André Parinaud*. Paris: Éditions Écriture, 1996.

———. *Minne*. Paris: Ollendorff, 1904.

———. *My Mother's House*. Translated by Roger Senhouse. London: Secker & Warburg, 1953. Originally *La Maison de Claudine* (1922) and *Sido* (1929).

———. *Oeuvres complètes de Colette*. 16 vols. Paris: Flammarion, 1973.

———. *Paysages et portraits*. Paris: Flammarion, 1958.

———. *Sept dialogues des bêtes*. Paris: Mercure de France, 1905.

———. *Retreat from Love*. Translated by Margaret Crosland. New York: Bobbs-Merrill, 1974. Originally published as *La Retraite sentimentale* (Paris: Mercure de France, 1907).

———. *La Seconde*. Paris: Bernard Grasset, 1929.

———. *Sido: Lettres à sa fille—précédé de lettres inédites de Colette*. Artigues-près-Bordeaux: Des Femmes, 1984.

———. *La Vagabonde*. Paris: Ollendorff, 1911. Translated as *The Vagabond* by Enid McLeod (London: Secker and Warburg, 1954).

———. *Le Voyage égoïste*. Paris: Helleu et Sargent, 1922. Translated as *Journey for Myself: Selfish Memories* by David Le Vay (New York: Bobbs-Merrill, 1972).

———. *Les Vrilles de la vigne*. Paris: Éditions de 'La Vie Parisienne,' 1908; Ferenczi, 1934.

Colette. Paris: Exposition de la Bibliothèque Nationale de France, 1973.

De Beauvoir, Simone. *La Deuxième sexe, II: L'expérience vécue*. Paris: Gallimard, 1949.

———. *Mémoires d'une jeune fille rangée*. Paris: Gallimard, 1958.

De la Hire, Jean. *Willy et Colette*. Paris: Adolphe d'Espie, 1905.

Dubief, F. *La Question du vagabondage*. Paris: Bibliothèque-Charpentier, 1911.

Du Fresnois, André. "Colette Willy." *Akadémos*, 15 February 1909.

Duncan, Isadora. *La Danse de l'avenir, suivis de regards sur Isadora Duncan, par Elie Faure, Colette, et Andre Levinson*. Edited by Sonia Schoonejans. Brussels: Éditions Complexe, 2003.

Dupanloup, Félix. *De l'éducation: tome troisième, Les Hommes d'éducation*. Paris: Ancienne Maison Charles Douniol, P. Téqui, Successeur, 1897.

———. *La Femme Chrétienne et Française, dernière réponse à M. Duruy et à ses défenseurs par Mgr l'Évêque d'Orléans*. Paris: Charles Douniol, 1868.

———. *La Haute éducation de la jeunesse, conférence faite au Cercle catholique du Luxembourg, le 22 janvier 1874*. Paris: Typographie Lahure, 1874.

Fildier, André, ed. *Colette: Sa famille, ses amis à Chatillon-Coligny—des documents inédits*. Paris: Fildier-Cartophile, 1992.

Flat, Paul. *Nos Femmes de lettres*. Paris: Perrion et cie, 1909.

Forestier, Henri, ed. *L'Yonne au XIXe siècle, 3e partie, 1848–1870*, Archives du département de l'Yonne, Documents et inventaires complémentaires. Auxerre: Imprimerie Universelle, 1967.

Fréjaville, Gustave. *Au Music-hall*. Paris: Éditions du Monde Nouveau, 1923.

Goudeket, Maurice. *Close to Colette*. Translated by Enid McLeod. London: Secker & Warburg, 1957. Originally published as *Près de Colette* (Flammarion, 1956).

Lefèvre, Frédéric. "Une Heure avec Colette." *Les Nouvelles littéraires*, 27 March 1926.

Martin, Georges. "Une Interview de Colette Willy." *La Renaissance Contemporaine*, 10 January 1913.

Mirabaud, A. *Un Match sensationnel: Fantaisie sportive en un acte et deux tableaux*. Paris: Librairie théatrale Georges Ondet, 1913.

Musidora. "Conférence de Musidora." *Cahiers Colette* 14 (1992): 30–51.

Polaire. *Polaire par elle-même*. Paris: Éditions Eugène Figuière, 1933.

Prost, Yvette. *Catherine Aubier*. Paris: A. Colin, 1912.

———. *Salutaire orgueil*. Paris: Librairie des Annales politiques et littéraires, 1905. Translated as *The Saving Pride* by Frank Alvah Dearborn (New York: Dodd, Mead and Company, 1912).

Querlin, Marise. "L'École de Claudine." *Marianne*, 19 January 1938.

"Souvenirs inédits de deux condisciples de Claudine." *La Grive*, July-September 1960.

Renouvin, Pierre, and René Rémond, eds. *Léon Blum: Chef du gouvernement, 1936–1937*. Paris: Presses de la fondation nationale des sciences politiques, 1967.

Réval, Gabrielle. *Un Lycée de jeunes filles: Professeurs-femmes*. Paris: Ollendorf, 1901.

———. *Les Lycéennes*. Paris: P. Ollendorff, 1902.

———. "Preface" in *Pour bien connaître ses droits*, Femina-Bibliothèque. Paris: Pierre Lafitte & Cie, 1913.

———. *Les Sévriennes*. Paris: P. Ollendorff, 1900.

Rolland, Romain. *The People's Theatre*. Translated by Barrett H. Clark. New York: Henry Holt and Company, 1918.

Rondeau-Luzeau, Lucie. *Chants de la nature, poèmes*. Paris: René Helleu, 1938.

———. *Le Livre d'une étudiante*. Serialized in *Le Temps*, 20 May 1914 to 17 June 1914.

———. *La Porte du rêve, poèmes*. Paris: René Helleu, 1946.

———. *Les Voix du mystère, poèmes*. Paris: René Helleu, 1935.

Schwaeblé, René. *Dans la peau: Roman de moeurs de café-concert*. Paris: Librairie Artistique, 1907.
Verne, Maurice. *Aux Usines du plaisir: La vie secrète du music-hall*. Paris: Éditions des Portiques, 1929.
Villars, Meg. "Chorus-Girl." *L'Indiscret*, May 1912.
Willy [Henri Gauthier-Villars]. *Claudine: Operette en trois actes, d'après les romans de Willy et Colette Willy*. Paris: Heugel et Cie, 1910.

Secondary Sources

Accampo, Elinor. *Blessed Motherhood, Bitter Fruit: Nelly Roussel and the Politics of Female Pain in Third Republic France*. Baltimore: Johns Hopkins University Press, 2006.
Accampo, Elinor, Rachel G. Fuchs, and Mary Lynn Stewart, eds. *Gender and the Politics of Social Reform in France, 1870–1914*. Baltimore: Johns Hopkins University Press, 1995.
Agulhon, Maurice. *Marianne into Battle: Republican Imagery and Symbolism in France, 1789–1880*. Translated by Janet Lloyd. London: Cambridge University Press, 1981.
———. "Le Parti républicain." In *Les Opportunistes: Les débuts de la République aux républicains*, edited by Léo Hamon, 1–14. Paris: Les Entretiens d'Auxerre, Éditions de la Maison des Sciences de l'Homme, 1986.
Aisenberg, Andrew. *Contagion: Disease, Government, and the "Social Question" in Nineteenth-Century France*. Stanford, CA: Stanford University Press, 1999.
Alaimo, Kathleen. "Adolescence, Gender, and Class in Education Reform in France: The Development of *Enseignement Primaire Supérieur*, 1880–1910." *French Historical Studies* 18, no. 4 (Fall 1994): 1025–55.
———. "The Authority of Experts: The Crisis of Female Adolescence in France and England, 1880–1920." In *Secret Gardens, Satanic Mills: Placing Girls in European History, 1750–1960*, edited by Mary Jo Maynes, Birgitte Søland, and Christina Benninghaus, 149–63. Bloomington: Indiana University Press, 2005.
Albisetti, James. *Schooling German Girls and Women: Secondary and Higher Education in the Nineteenth Century*. Princeton, NJ: Princeton University Press, 1988.
André, Marie-Odile. *Les Mécanismes de classification d'un écrivain: Le cas de Colette*. Metz: Université de Metz, 2000.
Andrieu, Gilbert. "A propos d'un livre: 'Pour devenir belle . . . et le rester', ou, La culture physique au féminin avant 1914." In *Histoire du sport féminin, tome 2: Sport masculine—sport féminin: éducation et société*, edited by Pierre Arnaud and Thierry Terret, 27–39. Paris: L'Harmattan, 1996.
———. "La gymnastique de plancher: Une pratique pour une bourgeoisie se preparant à prendre pouvoir?" *Stadion* 11, no. 1 (1985): 49–60.
———. *L'homme et la force*. Joinville-le-Pont: Éditions Actio, 1988.
———. "L'influence de la gymnastique suédoise sur l'éducation physique en France." *Stadion* 14, no. 2 (1988): 163–80.
———. "Les médecins culturistes à la fin du XIXème siècle en France." *Stadion* 12–13 (1986–1987): 311–16.
Apter, Emily. "Acting Out Orientalism: Sapphic Theatricality in Turn-of-the-Century Paris." In *Performance and Cultural Politics*, edited by Elin Diamond, 15–34. New York: Routledge, 1996.
———. "Sexological Decadence: The Gynophobic Visions of Octave Mirbeau." In *The Decadent Reader: Fiction, Fantasy, and Perversion from Fin-de-Siècle France*, edited by Asti Hustvedt, 962–78. New York: Zone Books, 1998.
———. "Splitting Hairs: Female Fetishism and Postpartum Sentimentality in the Fin-de-Siècle." In *Eroticism and the Body Politic*, edited by Lynn Hunt, 164–90. Baltimore: Johns Hopkins University Press, 1991.

Arnaud, Pierre, ed. *Les Athlètes de la République: Gymnastique, sport, et idéologie républicaine, 1870/1914.* Paris: L'Harmattan, 1997.

Arnaud, Pierre, and Thierry Terret, eds. *Histoire du sport féminin, tome 2: Sport masculine—sport féminin: éducation et société.* Paris: L'Harmattan, 1996.

———.*Les Sports et ses espaces, XIXe-XXe siècles.* Paris: Éditions du CTHS, 1998.

Aubery, Pierre. "L'Anarchisme des littérateurs au temps du symbolisme." *Le Mouvement Social* 69 (October 1969): 21–34.

Auspitz, Katherine. *The Radical Bourgeoisie: The Ligue de l'Enseignement and the Origins of the Third Republic, 1866–1885.* Cambridge: Cambridge University Press, 1982.

Badinter, Elisabeth. "La laïcité, un enjeu pour les femmes." *Matériaux pour l'histoire de notre temps* 78 (April-June 2005): 50–63.

Banes, Sally. *Dancing Women: Female Bodies on Stage.* London: Routledge, 1998.

Baubérot, Jean. "Laïcité and Its Permutations at the Fin(s) de Siècle(s)." In *New Perspectives on the Fin de Siècle in Nineteenth- and Twentieth-Century France,* edited by Kay Chadwick and Timothy Unwin, 21–42. Lewiston, ME: Edwin Mellen Press, 2000.

Baxandall, Michael. *Painting and Experience in Fifteenthth-Century Italy.* New York: Oxford University Press, 1972.

Beach, Cecilia. *Staging Politics and Gender: French Women's Drama, 1880–1923.* New York: Palgrave Macmillan, 2005.

Beaumont, Germaine, and André Parinaud. *Colette, par elle-même.* Paris: Éditions du Seuil, 1958.

Benstock, Shari. *Women of the Left Bank: Paris, 1900–1940.* Austin: University of Texas Press, 1986.

Bentley, Toni. *Sisters of Salome.* New Haven, CT: Yale University Press, 2002.

Berenson, Edward. *The Trial of Madame Caillaux.* Los Angeles: University of California Press, 1992.

Berlanstein, Lenard R. *Daughters of Eve: A Cultural History of French Theater Women from the Old Regime to the Fin de Siècle.* Cambridge: Cambridge University Press, 2001.

———. "Selling Modern Femininity: *Femina,* a Forgotten Feminist Publishing Success in Belle Epoque France." *French Historical Studies* 30, no. 4 (Fall 2007): 623–49.

Bernstein, George and Lottelore. "The Curriculum for German Girls' Schools, 1870–1914." *Paedogogica Historica* 18, no. 2 (1978): 275–95.

Bistis, Marguerite. "Creating Cultural Space: Paris Lectures at the Turn of the Century." *Proceedings of the Annual Meeting of the Western Society for French History* 27 (1999): 111–17.

Bordeau, Catherine. "Animal Attractions: The Question of Female Authority in Zola, Rachilde, and Colette." Ph.D. dissertation, University of Michigan, 1993.

Boustani, Carmen. *L'Écriture-corps chez Colette.* Bordeaux: Bibliothèque d'Études féminines, 1993.

Brown, Gregory S. *A Field of Honor: Writers, Court Culture, and Public Theater in French Literary Life from Racine to the Revolution.* New York: Columbia University Press, 2005.

Caradec, François. *Feu Willy: Avec et sans Colette.* Paris: Carrère, 1984.

Caspard, Pierre. "De l'horrible danger d'une analyse superficielle des manuels scolaires." *Histoire de l'éducation* 21 (1984): 67–74.

Chalon, Jean. *Colette, l'éternelle apprentie.* Paris: Flammarion, 1998.

Charlet, Jean-Claude. *Colette, La Vagabonde.* Précy-sous-Thil: Éditions de l'Armançon, 1994.

Charleux-Leroux, Elisabeth. "Gabrielle Colette à l'école élémentaire." *Cahiers Colette* 12 (1990): 143–54.

———. "Réalité et fiction dans *Claudine à l'école.*" *Bulletin de la Société des sciences historiques et naturelles de l'Yonne* 113 (1981): 121–64.

Charleux-Leroux, Elisabeth, and Marguerite Boivin. *Avec Colette, de Saint-Sauveur à Montigny.* Saint-Sauveur-en-Puisaye: Société des Amis de Colette, 1995.

Charnow, Sally Debra. *Theatre, Politics, and Markets in Fin-de-Siècle Paris.* New York: Palgrave Macmillan, 2005.

Charvet, P. E. A Literary History of France. Volume V, The Nineteenth Centuries, 1870–1940. London: Ernest Benn Limited, 1967.

Chauveau, Philippe, and André Sallée. Music-hall et café-concert. Paris: Bordas, 1985.

Chenut, Helen Harden. The Fabric of Gender: Working-Class Culture in Third Republic France. University Park: Pennsylvania State University Press, 2005.

———. "The Gendering of Skill as Historical Process: The Case of French Knitters in Industrial Troyes, 1880–1939." In Gender and Class in Modern Europe, edited by Laura L. Frader and Sonya O. Rose, 77–107. Ithaca, NY: Cornell University Press, 1996.

Citti, Pierre. Contre la Décadence: Histoire de l'imagination française dans le roman, 1890–1914. Paris: Presses Universitaires de France, 1987.

Clark, Linda L. Schooling the Daughters of Marianne: Textbooks and the Socialization of Girls in Modern French Primary Schools. Albany: State University of New York Press, 1984.

Clark, T. J. The Painting of Modern Life: Paris in the Art of Manet and His Followers. Princeton, NJ: Princeton University Press, 1984.

Coffin, Judith G. The Politics of Women's Work: The Paris Garment Trades, 1750–1915. Princeton, NJ: Princeton University Press, 1996.

Collado, Mélanie E. Colette, Lucie Delarue-Mardrus, Marcelle Tinayre: Émancipation et résignation. Paris: L'Harmattan, 2003.

Corbin, Alain, ed. "Commercial Sexuality in Nineteenth-Century France: A System of Images and Regulations." In The Making of the Modern Body, edited by Thomas Laqueur and Catherine Gallagher, 209–219. Berkeley: University of California Press, 1987.

———. Histoire du corps: Tome 2, De la Révolution à la Grande Guerre. Edited by Alain Corbin, Jean-Jacques Courtine, and Georges Vigarello. Paris: Éditions de Seuil, 2005.

———. Women for Hire. Cambridge, MA: Harvard University Press, 1990.

Cornec, Jean, and Michel Bouchareissas. L'heure laïque. Paris: Clancier Guénaud, 1982.

Cottington, David. Cubism in the Shadow of War: The Avant-Garde and Politics in Paris, 1905–1914. New Haven, CT: Yale University Press, 1998.

Covington, Elizabeth Ercell. "Egotistical spectator: Rachilde (1860–1953) and the Fin-de-siècle novel." Ph.D. dissertation, University of California, Los Angeles, 1998.

Crosland, Margaret. Colette: A Provincial in Paris. New York: British Book Centre, 1954.

———. Madame Colette. London: Peter Owen Limited, 1953.

Cross, Máire. "1890–1914: A 'Belle Epoque' for Feminism?" In A 'Belle Epoque'? Women and Feminism in French Society and Culture, 1890–1914, edited by Carrie Tarr and Diana Holmes, 23–36. Oxford: Berghahn Books, 2007.

———. "Women Teachers in Control? Findings on Expansion of Primary Education in Nineteenth-Century France." European History Quarterly 27, no. 3 (1997): 417–20.

Datta, Venita. "Romain Rolland and the Theatre de la Révolution: A Historical Perspective." Clio 20, no. 3 (1991): 213–222.

Davies, Margaret. Colette. London: Oliver and Boyd, 1961.

Dawkins, Heather. The Nude in French Art and Culture, 1870–1910. New York: Cambridge University Press, 2002.

Day, Patrick L. Saint-Georges de Bouhélier's Naturisme: An Anti-Symbolist Movement in Late-Nineteenth-Century French Poetry. New York: Peter Lang, 2001.

Defrance, Jacques. L'Excellence corporelle: La formation des activités physiques et sportives modernes, 1770–1914. Rennes: Presses Universitaires de Rennes, 1987.

Del Castillo, Michel, ed. Colette: Destins de femmes. Paris: Le Toit de la Grande Arche, 1999.

Desvignes, Dominique. "L'École et la lecture dans le Pas-de-Calais entre 1880 et 1914." Revue du Nord 72, no. 288 (1990): 841–60.

Diamond, Elin, ed. Performance and Cultural Politics. New York: Routledge, 1996.

Dormann, Geneviève. *Amoureuse Colette*. Paris: Éditions Herscher, 1984.

Downs, Laura Lee. *Childhood in the Promised Land: Working-Class Movements and the Colonies de Vacances in France, 1880–1960*. Durham, NC: Duke University Press, 2002.

Dubreuil, Léon. "Le Brevet de Colette." *Le Cerf Volant* 18 (July 1957).

———. *Paul Bert*. Paris: F. Alcan, 1935.

Dupont, Jacques. *Physique de Colette*. Toulouse: Presses Universitaires du Mirail, 2003.

Ehrenpreis, David. "Cyclists and Amazons: Representing the New Woman in Wilhelmine Germany." *Women's Art Journal* 20, no. 1 (Spring-Summer 1999): 25–31.

Eisinger, Erica Mendelson, and Mari Ward McCarty, eds. *Colette: The Woman, the Writer*. University Park: Pennsylvania State University Press, 1981.

Elwitt, Sanford. "Education and the Social Questions: The Universités Populaires in Late Nineteenth Century France," *History of Education Quarterly* 22, no. 1 (Spring 1982): 55–72.

———. *The Third Republic Defended: Bourgeois Reform in France, 1880–1914*. Baton Rouge: Louisiana State University, 1986.

Epstein, William, ed. *Contesting the Subject: Essays in Postmodern Theory and Practice of Biography and Biographical Criticism*. West Lafayette, IN: Purdue University Press, 1991.

Erber, Nancy. "Colette: The Making of a Writer." Ph.D. dissertation, Cornell University, 1988.

Evans, Martha Noel. *Masks of Tradition: Women and the Politics of Writing in Twentieth-Century France*. Ithaca, NY: Cornell University Press, 1987.

Faulk, Barry J. *Music Hall and Modernity: The Late Victorian Discovery of Popular Culture*. Athens, OH: Ohio University Press, 2004.

Febvre, Lucien. *Le Problème de l'incroyance au XVIe siècle: La religion de Rabelais*. Paris: Albin Michel, 1947.

Feschotte, Jacques. *Histoire du Music-Hall*. Paris: Presses Universitaires de France, 1965.

Fisher, David James. "The Origins of French Popular Theatre." *Journal of Contemporary History* 12, no. 3 (July 1977): 461–97.

———. *Romain Rolland and the Politics of Intellectual Engagement*. Los Angeles: University of California Press, 1988.

Flieger, Jerry Aline. *Colette and the Fantom Subject of Autobiography*. Ithaca, NY: Cornell University Press, 1992.

Forth, Christopher. *The Dreyfus Affair and the Crisis of French Manhood*. Baltimore: Johns Hopkins University Press, 2004.

Foucault, Michel. *The History of Sexuality: An Introduction, Volume 1*. Translated by Robert Hurley. New York: Vintage Books, 1978.

Frader, Laura L., and Sonya O. Rose, eds. *Gender and Class in Modern Europe*. Ithaca, NY: Cornell University Press, 1996.

Fraisse, Geneviève, and Michelle Perrot, eds. *A History of Women in the West: IV—Emerging Feminism from Revolution to World War*. Cambridge, MA: Belknap Press, 1993.

Francis, Claude, and Fernande Gontier. *Creating Colette. Volume 1—From Ingenue to Libertine, 1873–1913; Volume 2—From Baroness to Woman of Letters, 1912–1954*. South Royalton, VT: Steerforth Press, 1998. Originally published as *Colette* (Paris: Librairie Académique Perrin, 1997).

Fulcher, Jane F. *French Cultural Politics and Music: From the Dreyfus Affair to the First World War*. New York: Oxford University Press, 1999.

Furet, François. *Jules Ferry, fondateur de la République*. Colloquium organized by l'École des Hautes Études en Sciences Sociales, presented by François Furet. Paris: Éditions de l'École des Hautes Études en Sciences Sociales, 1985.

Furet, François, and Jacques Ozouf. *Lire et écrire: L'alphabétisation des français de Calvin à Jules Ferry*. 2 vols. Paris: Éditions de minuit, 1977.

Gemie, Sharif. "Institutional History, Social History, Women's History: A Comment on Patrick Harrigan's 'Women Teachers and the Schooling of Girls in France.'" *French Historical Studies* 22, no. 4 (Autumn 1999): 613–23.

———. *Women and Schooling in France, 1815–1914: Gender, Authority and Identity in the Female Schooling Sector*. Keele: Keele University Press, 1995.

Genet-Delacroix, Marie-Claude. "L'Enseignement artistique au XIXe siècle." *Historiens et Géographes* 83, no. 338 (1992): 213–26.

———. "Esthétique officielle et art national sous la Troisième République." *Le Mouvement Social* 131 (April-June 1985): 105–20.

Gildea, Robert. *Education in Provincial France, 1800–1914: A Study of Three Departments*. Oxford: Clarendon Press, 1983.

———. *France, 1870–1914*. New York: Longman, 1996.

Ginzburg, Carlo. *The Cheese and the Worms: The Cosmos of a Sixteenth-Century Miller*. Translated by John and Anne Tedeschi. 1976; New York: Penguin Books, 1982.

Giolitto, Pierre. *Histoire de l'enseignement primaire au XIXe siècle*. 2 vols. Paris: Nathan-Université, 1983.

Giry, Jacqueline. *Colette et l'art du discours intérieur*. Paris: La Pensée universelle, 1980.

Goldstein, Jan. *The Post-Revolutionary Self: Politics and Psyche in France, 1750–1850*. Cambridge, MA: Harvard University Press, 2005.

Goldwater, Robert. *Symbolism*. New York: Harper and Row, 1979.

Goodwin, James. *Autobiography: The Self Made Text*. New York: Twayne, 1993.

Gordon, Rae Beth. "Natural Rhythm: La Parisienne Dances with Darwin: 1875–1910." *Modernism/modernity* 10, no. 4 (2003): 617–56.

———. *Why the French Love Jerry Lewis: From Cabaret to Early Cinema*. Stanford, CA: Stanford University Press, 2001.

Green, Andy. *Education and State Formation: The Rise of Education Systems in England, France, and the USA*. London: Macmillan, 1990.

Green, Nicholas. "'All the Flowers of the Field': The state, Liberalism, and Art in France Under the Early Third Republic." *Oxford Art Journal* 10, no. 1 (1987): 71–84.

Grew, Raymond, and Patrick J. Harrigan. "The Catholic Contribution to Universal Schooling in France, 1850–1906." *Journal of Modern History* 57 (June 1985): 211–47.

———. *School, State, and Society: The Growth of Elementary Schooling in Nineteenth-Century France—A Quantitative Analysis*. Ann Arbor: University of Michigan Press, 1991.

Grosclaude, Pierre. *Une Femme de science et poète*. Paris: Nouvelles Éditions Latines, 1958.

Guiney, M. Martin. *Teaching the Cult of Literature in the French Third Republic*. New York: Palgrave Macmillan, 2004.

Hamon, Léo, ed. *Les Opportunistes: Les débuts de la République aux républicains*. Paris: Éditions de la Maison des Sciences de l'Homme, 1991.

Harrigan, Patrick J. "Church, State, and Education in France from the Falloux to the Ferry Laws: A Reassessment." *Canadian Journal of History* (April 2001): 51–83.

———. "Women Teachers and the Schooling of Girls in France: Recent Historiographical Trends." *French Historical Studies* 21, no. 4 (Autumn 1998): 593–610.

Harris, Ruth. *Lourdes: Body and Spirit in the Secular Age*. New York: Penguin Press, 1999.

———. *Murder and Madness: Medicine, Law, and Society in the Fin de Siècle*. New York: Oxford University Press, 1989.

———. "The 'Unconscious' and Catholicism in France." *Historical Journal* 47, no. 2 (2004): 331–54.

Hayat, Pierre. *La passion laïque de Ferdinand Buisson*. Paris: Éditions Kimé, 1999.

Hecquet, Michèle. "Colette: Femmes au Travail." *Cahiers Colette* 15 (1993): 40–41.

Hemmings, F. W. *The Theater Industry in Nineteenth-Century France*. New York: Cambridge University Press, 1993.

Herbert, Robert L. *Impressionism: Art, Leisure, and Parisian Society*. New Haven, CT: Yale University Press, 1988.

Heuré, Gilles. *L'Insoumis: Léon Werth, 1878–1955*. Paris: Viviane Hamy, 2006.

Hobsbawm, Eric. *The Age of Empire, 1875–1914*. New York: Vintage Books, 1989.

Holmes, Diana. *Colette*. New York: St. Martin's Press, 1991.

Holmes, Diana, and Carrie Tarr, eds. *A 'Belle Epoque'? Women in French Society and Culture, 1890–1914*. Oxford: Berghahn Books, 2007.

Holt, Richard. *Sport and Society in Modern France*. London: Macmillan, 1981.

Huebner, Steven. "Between Anarchism and the Box Office: Gustave Charpentier's 'Louise.'" *Nineteenth-Century Music* 19, no. 2 (Autumn 1995): 136–60.

———. "Naturalism and Supernaturalism in Alfred Bruneau's *Le Rêve*." *Cambridge Opera Journal* 11, no. 1 (March 1999): 77–101.

Huesca, Roland. "Succès des ballets russes à Paris: 1900–1911—Renouveau technique et fusion des arts." In *Les Sports et ses espaces, XIXe-XXe siècles*, edited by Pierre Arnaud and Thierry Terret, 349–64. Paris: Éditions du CTHS, 1998.

Huffer, Lynne. *Another Colette: The Question of Gendered Writing*. Ann Arbor: University of Michigan Press, 1992.

Hughes, H. Stuart. *Consciousness and Society: The Reorientation of European Social Thought, 1890–1930*. New York: Vintage Books, 1961.

Hunt, Lynn. *The Family Romance of the French Revolution*. Berkeley: University of California Press, 1993.

Hustvedt, Asti. "The Art of Death: French Fiction at the Fin de Siècle." In *The Decadent Reader: Fiction, Fantasy, and Perversion from Fin-de-Siècle France*, edited by Asti Hustvedt, 10–29. New York: Zone Books, 1998.

Jelavich, Peter. *Berlin Cabaret*. Cambridge, MA: Harvard University Press, 1993.

Johnson, Douglas. *Guizot: Aspects of French History, 1787–1874*. Toronto: Toronto University Press, 1963.

Kennedy, Katherine. "Domesticity (*Hauswirthschaft*) in the *Volksschule*: Textbooks and Lessons for Girls, 1890–1914." *Internationale Schulbuchforschung* 13 (1991): 5–21.

Kershaw, Angela. "Proletarian Women, Proletarian Writing: The Case of Marguerite Audoux." In *A 'Belle Epoque'? Women in French Society and Culture, 1890–1914*, edited by Diana Holmes and Carrie Tarr, 253–269. Oxford: Berghahn Books, 2007.

Koritz, Amy. *Gendering Bodies/Performing Art: Dance and Literature in Early Twentieth-Century British Culture*. Ann Arbor: University of Michigan Press, 1995.

Kristeva, Julia. *Colette*. Translated by Jane Marie Todd. New York: Columbia University Press, 2004.

Lacy, Cherilyn. "From Caregivers to Consumers: Domestic Medicine and the Transformation of Medical Practice in the Third French Republic, 1871–1914." Ph.D. dissertation, University of Chicago, 1997.

———. "Science or Savoir-Faire? Domestic Hygiene and Medicine in Girls' Public Education." *Proceedings of the Annual Meeting of the Western Society for French History* 24 (1997): 25–37.

Ladimer, Bethany. *Colette, Beauvoir, Duras: Age and Women Writers*. Gainesville: University Press of Florida, 1999.

Lamberti, Marjorie. *State, Society, and the Elementary School in Imperial Germany*. Oxford: Oxford University Press, 1989.

Landes, Joan. *Women and the Public Sphere in the Age of the French Revolution*. Ithaca, NY: Cornell University Press, 1988.

Larnac, Jean. *Colette, sa vie, son oeuvre*. Paris: Simon Kra, 1927.

Lecarme-Tabone, Éliane. "Témoignages: Simone de Beauvoir et Colette." *Cahiers Colette* 20 (1998): 119–25.

Lehning, James. *To Be a Citizen: The Political Culture of the Early French Republic*. Ithaca, NY: Cornell University Press, 2001.

Lejeune, Dominique. *La France de la Belle Époque, 1896–1914*. Paris: Armand Colin, 1991.

Lejeune, Philippe. *On Autobiography*. Minneapolis: University of Minnesota Press, 1989.

Levin, Miriam R. *Republican Art and Ideology in Late Nineteenth-Century France*. Ann Arbor, Michigan: UMI Research Press, 1986.

Linton, Derek S. "Reforming the Urban Primary School in Wilhelmine Germany." *History of Education* 13, no. 3 (1984): 207–19.

Lucey, Michael. *Never Say I: Sexuality and the First Person in Colette, Gide, and Proust*. Durham: Duke University Press, 2006.

Maingueneau, Dominique. *Les Livres d'école de la République, 1870–1914: Discours et idéologie*. Paris: Le Sycomore, 1979.

Mansker, Andrea. "'Mademoiselle Arria Ly Wants Blood!' The Debate Over Female Honor in France." *French Historical Studies* 29, no. 4 (Fall 2006): 621–647.

———. "'The Pistol Virgin': Feminism, Sexuality and Honor in Belle Époque France." Ph.D. dissertation, University of California, Los Angeles, 2003.

Margadant, Jo Burr. *Madame le Professeur: Women Educators in the Third Republic*. Princeton, NJ: Princeton University Press, 1990.

———. *The New Biography: Performing Femininity in Nineteenth-Century France*. Berkeley: University of California Press, 2000.

Marks, Elaine. *Colette*. New Brunswick, NJ: Rutgers University Press, 1960.

Martin-Fugier, Anne. *La Bourgeoise: Femme au temps de Paul Bourget*. Paris: Bernard Grasset, 1983.

———. *Comédienne: De Mlle Mars à Sarah Bernhardt*. Paris: Éditions du Seuil, 2001.

Mayeur, Françoise. *L'Éducation des filles en France aux XIXe siècle*. Paris: Hachette, 1979.

———. *L'Enseignement secondaire des jeunes filles sous la Troisième République*. Paris: Presses de la Fondation Nationale des Sciences Politiques, 1997.

———. "La femme dans la société selon Jules Ferry." in *Jules Ferry, fondateur de la République: Actes du colloque organise par l'École des Hautes Études en Sciences Sociales*, edited by François Furet, 79–87. Éditions de l'École des Hautes Études en Sciences Sociales: Paris, 1985.

Maynes, Mary Jo. *Schooling in Western Europe: A Social History*. Albany: State University of New York Press, 1985.

———. *Taking the Hard Road: Life Course in French and German Workers' Autobiographies in the Era of Industrialization*. Chapel Hill: University of North Carolina Press, 1995.

Maynes, Mary Jo, Birgitte Søland, and Christine Benninghaus, eds. *Secret Gardens, Satanic Mills: Placing Girls in European History, 1750–1960*. Bloomington: Indiana University Press, 2005.

Mazón, Patricia M. *Gender and the Modern Research University: The Admission of Women to German Higher Education, 1865–1914*. Stanford, CA: Stanford University Press, 2003.

McCarty, Mari. *Colette: A Study of the Short Fiction*. New York: Twayne, 1995.

McCormick, John. *Popular Theaters of Nineteenth-Century France*. New York: Routledge, 1993.

McMillan, James F. *France and Women, 1789–1914*. New York: Routledge, 2000.

Mercier, Lucien. *Les Universités populaires, 1899–1914: Education populaire et mouvement ouvrière au début du siècle*. Paris: Les Éditions ouvrières, 1986.

Mercier, Michel, "Colette et Vuillermoz." *Cahiers Colette* 24 (2002): 7–63.

Mesch, Rachel. *The Hysteric's Revenge: French Women Writers at the Fin de Siècle*. Nashville: Vanderbilt University Press, 2006.

Mester, Terri A. *Movement and Modernism: Yeats, Eliot, Lawrence, Williams, and Early Twentieth-Century Dance*. Fayetteville: University of Arkansas Press, 1997.

Miller, Nancy K. *Subject to Change: Reading Feminist Writing*. New York: Columbia University Press, 1988.

Mitchell, Yvonne. *Colette: A Taste for Life*. New York: Harcourt Brace Jovanovich, 1975.

Munholland, John Kim. "Republican Order and Republican Tolerance in Fin-de-Siècle France: Montmartre as a Delinquent Community." In *Montmartre and the Making of Mass Culture*, edited by Gabriel P. Weisberg, 15–36. New Brunswick, NJ: Rutgers University Press, 2001.

Murard, Lion, and Patrick Zylberman. *L'hygiène dans la République: La santé publique en France, ou l'utopie contrariée, 1870–1914*. Paris: Librairie Arthème Fayard, 1996.

Nique, Christian, and Claude Lelièvre. *La République n'éduquera plus: La fin du mythe Ferry*. Paris: Plon, 1993.

Nord, Philip. *The Republican Moment: Struggles for Democracy in Nineteenth-Century France*. Cambridge, MA: Harvard University Press, 1995.

Nye, Robert. *Crime, Madness, and Politics in Modern France: The Medical Concept of National Decline*. Princeton, NJ: Princeton University Press, 1984.

———. *Masculinity and Male Codes of Honor in Modern France*. Los Angeles: University of California Press, 1993.

Offen, Karen. "French Women's History: Retrospect (1789–1940) and Prospect." *French Historical Studies* 26, no. 4 (Fall 2003): 727–67.

———. "The Second Sex and the Baccalauréat in Republican France, 1880–1924." *French Historical Studies* 13 (1983): 252–86.

Ognier, Pierre. *L'École républicaine française et ses miroirs: L'idéologie scolaire française et sa vision de l'école en Suisse et en Belgique à travers la Revue Pédagogique, 1878–1900*. New York: Peter Lang, 1988.

O'Hara, Patricia. "'The Woman of To-Day': The Fin de Siècle Woman of The MusicHall and Theatre Review." *Victorian Periodicals Review* 30, no. 2 (1997): 141–56.

Ozouf, Jacques, and Mona Ozouf. *La République des instituteurs*. Paris: Éditions du Seuil, 1992.

Ozouf, Mona. *Women's Words: Essays on French Singularity*. Translated by Jane Marie Todd. Chicago: University of Chicago Press, 1997.

Paret, Peter. *The Berlin Secession: Modernism and Its Enemies in Imperial Germany*. Cambridge, MA: Belknap Press, 1980.

Pedersen, Jean. *Legislating the French Family: Feminism, Theater, and Republican Politics, 1870–1920*. New Brunswick, NJ: Rutgers University Press, 2003.

Pedley-Hinson, Catherine. "Jane Avril and the Entertainment Lithograph: The Female Celebrity and Fin-de-siècle Questions of Corporeality and Performance." *Theatre Research International* 30, no. 2 (2005): 107–23.

Peebles, Catherine M. *The Psyche of Feminism: Sand, Colette, Sarraute*. West Lafayette, IN: Purdue University Press, 2004.

Périllon, Marie-Christine. *Vies de femmes: Les travaux et les jours de la femme à la Belle Époque*. Roanne: Éditions Hovarth, 1981.

Perrot, Michelle, ed. *A History of Private Life, Vol. 4: From the Fires of Revolution to the Great War*. Translated by Arthur Goldhammer. Cambridge, MA: Belknap Press, 1990.

Peyre, Henri. *What Is Symbolism?* Translated by Emmett Parker. University: University of Alabama Press, 1980.

Pichois, Claude, and Alain Brunet. *Colette*. Paris: Éditions de Fallois, 1999.

Pichois, Claude, and Vincenette Pichois. *Album Colette*. Paris: Gallimard, 1984.

Pickering, R. S. E. "Colette's Two Claudines: Problems in Writing the Divided Self." *Romance Quarterly* 42, no. 3 (Summer 1995): 133–42.

Poole, Mary Ellen. "Gustave Charpentier and the Conservatoire de Mimi Pinson." *Nineteenth-Century Music* 20, no. 3 (Spring 1997): 231–252.

Pomfret, David M. "'A Muse for the Masses': Gender, Age, and Nation in France, Fin de Siècle." *American Historical Review* 109, no. 5 (December 2004): 1439–1474.

Poskin, Anne. "Colette et 'l'Argus de la presse.'" *Études Françaises* 36, no. 3 (2000): 113–26.

Price, Roger. *A Concise History of France*. London: Cambridge University Press, 1993.

Prost, Antoine. *Histoire de l'Enseignement en France, 1800–1967*. Paris: Armand Colin, 1968.

Pujade-Renaud, Claude. *L'école dans la littérature*. Paris: Les Éditions ESF, 1986.

Quartararo, Anne T. *Women Teachers and Popular Education in Nineteenth-Century France: Social Values and Corporate Identity at the Normal School Institution*. Newark: University of Delaware Press, 1995.

Rambach, Marine. *Colette, pure et impure: Bataille pour la postérité d'un écrivain*. Paris: Éditions gaies et lesbiennes, 2004.

Rauch, André. "Mises en scène du corps à la belle époque." *Vingtième siècle* 40 (1993): 33–44.

———. *Le Souci du corps: Histoire de l'hygiène en éducation physique*. Paris: Presses Universitaire de France, 1983.

Rearick, Charles. *Pleasures of the Belle Époque: Entertainment and Festivity in Turn-of-the-Century France*. New Haven, CT: Yale University Press, 1985.

Reddy, William. *The Invisible Code: Honor and Sentiment in Postrevolutionary France, 1814–1848*. Los Angeles: University of California Press, 1997.

Rémy, Tristan. *Georges Wague: Le Mime de la belle époque*. Paris: Georges Girard, 1964.

Resch, Yannick. *Corps féminin, corps textuel: Essai sur le personnage féminin dans l'oeuvre de Colette*. Paris: Librairie C. Klincksieck, 1973.

Richardson, Joanna. *Colette*. London: Methuen, 1983.

Roberts, Mary Louise. "Acting Up: The Feminist Theatrics of Marguerite Durand." *French Historical Studies* 19 (Fall 1996): 1103–38.

———. *Civilization Without Sexes: Reconstructing Postwar France, 1917–1927*. Chicago: University of Chicago Press, 1994.

———. *Disruptive Acts: The New Woman in Fin-de-Siècle France*. Chicago: University of Chicago Press, 2002.

Rocher, Jean-Pierre. "Auxerre pendant la première moitié du XIXe siècle." In *Histoire d'Auxerre des origines à nos jours, éducation*, edited by Jean-Pierre Rocher and Alain Bataille, 338–39. Le Coteau-Roanne: Horvath, 1984.

———. "La presse bourguignonne." In *Les Opportunistes: Les debuts de la République*, edited by Léo Hamon, 83–104. Paris: Entretiens d'Auxerre; Editions de la Maison des Sciences de l'Homme, 1986.

Rogers, Juliette. *Career Stories: Belle Epoque Novels of Professional Development*. University Park: Pennsylvania State University Press, 2007.

———. "Claudine's Peers: Social and Historical Expectations for Colette's First Heroine." *Symposium* 50, no. 4 (Winter 1997): 224–237.

———. "The 'Counter-Public Sphere': Colette's Gendered Collective." *MLN* 111, no. 4 (1996): 734–46.

———. "Educating the Heroine: Turn-of-the-Century Feminism and French Women's Education Novels." *Women's Studies* 23, no. 4 (1994): 321–34.

———. "Feminist Discourse in Women's Novels of Professional Development." In *A 'Belle Époque'? Women in French Society and Culture, 1890–1914*, edited by Diana Holmes and Carrie Tarr, 183–196. Oxford: Berghahn Books, 2007.

Rogers, Rebecca. *From the Salon to the Schoolroom: Educating Bourgeois Girls in Nineteenth-Century France*. University Park: Pennsylvania State University Press, 2005.

Rosanvallon, Pierre. *Le Moment Guizot*. Paris: Gallimard, 1985.

Rosenfeld, Sophia. *A Revolution in Language: The Problem of Signs in Late Eighteenth-Century France*. Stanford, CA: Stanford University Press, 2001.

Roth, Michael S. "Introduction." In *Rediscovering History: Culture, Politics and the Psyche*, edited by Michael S. Roth, 1–7. Stanford, CA: Stanford University Press, 1994.

Rudelle, Odile. "Les elections en Bourgogne, 1877–1885." In *Les Opportunistes: Les débuts de la République aux républicains*, edited by Léo Hamon, 59–77. Paris: Les Entretiens d'Auxerre, Éditions de la Maison des Sciences de l'Homme, 1986.

Rudorff, Raymond. *Belle Époque: Paris in the Nineties*. London: Hamilton, 1972.

Salomon, Hélène. "Le corset: Entre la beauté et la santé (1880–1920)." In *Histoire du sport féminin, tome 2: Sport masculine—sport féminin: éducation et société*, edited by Pierre Arnaud and Thierry Terret, 11–26. Paris: L'Harmattan, 1996.

Sánchez, Gonzalo J. "Hephaistos in the New Athens: Design-Art Industries in Republican France, Between Politics and the Museum, 1871–1894." *Nineteenth Century Studies* 11 (1997): 51–69.

Sarde, Michèle. *Colette: Free and Fettered*. Translated by Richard Miller. New York: William Morrow, 1980. Originally published as *Colette: Libre et entravée* (Paris: Éditions Stock, 1978).

Schmidt, Vivien. *Democratizing France: The Political and Administrative History of Decentralization*. Cambridge: Cambridge University Press, 1990.

Schorske, Carl S. *Fin-de-Siècle Vienna: Politics and Culture*. New York: Vintage Books, 1981.

Schwartz, Vanessa. *Spectacular Realities: Early Mass Culture in Fin-de-Siècle Paris*. Los Angeles: University of California Press, 1998.

Scott, Joan Wallach. *Gender and the Politics of History*. New York: Columbia University Press, 1988.

———. *Only Paradoxes to Offer: French Feminists and the Rights of Man*. Cambridge, MA: Harvard University Press, 1996.

Seigel, Jerrold. *Bohemian Paris: Culture, Politics, and the Boundaries of Bourgeois Life, 1830–1930*. New York: Penguin, 1985.

Sevran, Pascal. *Le Music hall français: De Mayol à Julien Clerc*. Paris: Oliver Orban, 1978.

Sewell, William H. *Work and Revolution in France: The Language of Labor from the Old Regime to 1848*. New York: Cambridge University Press, 1980.

Sherman, Daniel. "Art Museums, Inspections, and the Limits to Cultural Policy in the Early Third Republic." *Historical Reflections/Réflexions Historiques* 15, no. 2 (1988): 337–59.

Silverman, Debora. *Art Nouveau in Fin-de-Siècle France: Politics, Psychology and Style*. Los Angeles: University of California Press, 1989.

———. "The 'New Woman,' Feminism, and the Decorative Arts in Fin-de-Siècle France." In *Eroticism and the Body Politic*, edited by Lynn Hunt, 144–63. Baltimore: Johns Hopkins University Press, 1991.

———. *Pilgrim's Progress and Vincent Van Gogh's Métier*. London: Barbican Art Gallery, 1992. In conjunction with the exhibition "Van Gogh in England: Portrait of the Artist as a Young Man."

———. *Van Gogh and Gauguin: The Search for Sacred Art*. New York: Farrar, Straus and Giroux, 2000.

Slawy-Sutton, Catherine. "Colette's Correspondence, or 'Ceci n'est pas une lettre, c'est un petit bulletin sanitaire.'" *Pacific Coast Philology* 34, no. 1 (1999): 1–17.

Smith, Bonnie G. *Ladies of the Leisure Class: The Bourgeoises of Northern France in the Nineteenth Century*. Princeton, NJ: Princeton University Press, 1981.

Smith, Sidonie. *The Poetics of Women's Autobiography: Marginality and the Fictions of Self-Representation*. Bloomington: Indiana University Press, 1987.

Spivak, Marcel. "Quelques aperçues de la recherche en histoire de l'éducation physique et des sports en France." *Histoire de l'Éducation* 10 (1981): 1–19.

Staller, Natasha. "Méliès' 'Fantastic' Cinema and the Origins of Cubism." *Art History* 12, no. 2 (June 1989): 202–32.

Stewart, Joan Hinde. *Colette*. New York: Twayne Publishers, 1996.

Stewart, Mary Lynn. *For Health and Beauty: Physical Culture for Frenchwomen, 1880s-1930s*. Baltimore: Johns Hopkins University Press, 2001.

Stock-Morton, Phyllis. *Moral Education for a Secular Society: The Development of Morale Laïque in Nineteenth-Century France*. Albany: State University of New York Press, 1988.

Storey, Robert. *Pierrots on the Stage of Desire: Nineteenth-Century French Literary Artists and the Comic Pantomime*. Princeton, NJ: Princeton University Press, 1985.

Strand, Dana. *Colette: A Study of the Short Fiction*. New York: Twayne Publishers, 1995.

Strumingher, Laura S. *What Were Little Girls and Boys Made Of? Primary Education in Rural France, 1830–1880*. Albany: State University of New York Press, 1983.

Taithe, Bertrand. "Should the Third Republic Divide Us Least?" *French History* 18, no. 2 (2004): 222–33.

Thibault, Jacques. "Les origines du sport féminin." In *Les Athlètes de la République: Gymnastique, sport, et idéologie républicaine, 1870/1914*, edited by Pierre Arnaud, 331–40. Paris: L'Harmattan, 1997.

Thompson, Christopher. "Controlling the Working-Class Sports Hero in Order to Control the Masses? The Social Philosophy of Sport of Henry Desgrange." *Stadion* 27 (2001): 139–51.

———. "Un troisième sexe? Les bourgeoises et la bicyclette dans la France fin de siècle." *Le Mouvement Social* 192 (2000): 9–40.

Thurman, Judith. *Secrets of the Flesh: A Life of Colette*. New York: Alfred A. Knopf, 1999.

Tiersten, Lisa. *Marianne in the Market: Envisioning Consumer Society in Fin-de-Siècle France*. Los Angeles: University of California Press, 2001.

Tilburg, Patricia. "Wholesome imaginations—Pedagogy in the Early Third Republic," *Proceedings of the Western Society for French History*. Vol. 29, Spring 2003.

———. "Earning her Bread: Métier, Order, and Female Honor in Colette's Music Hall, 1906–1913," *French Historical Studies*. Summer 2005 (vol. 29, no. 3).

———. "'The Triumph of the Flesh': Women, Physical Culture, and the Nude in the French music hall, 1904–1914," *Radical History Review*. Vol. 98. (Spring 2007).

———. "Colette: The New Woman Takes the Stage in belle époque France," *The Human Tradition in Modern Europe, 1750 to the Present*. Eds. Cora Granata and Cheryl A. Koos. (New York: Rowman & Littlefield Publishers, Inc., 2007).

Toepfer, Karl. *Empire of Ecstasy: Nudity and Movement in German Body Culture, 1910–1935*. Los Angeles: University of California Press, 1997.

Van Slyke, Gretchen. "Monsters, New Women and Lady Professors: A Centenary Look Back at Gabrielle Reval." *Nineteenth-Century French Studies* 30, nos. 3 and 4 (Spring-Summer 2002): 347–62.

Vigarello, Georges. *Concepts of Cleanliness: Changing Attitudes in France Since the Middle Ages*. Translated by Jean Birrell. New York: Cambridge University Press, 1988.

———. *Le corps redressé: Histoire d'un pouvoir pédagogique*. Paris: Armand Colin, 2001.

———. "Hygiène du corps et travail d'apparences." In *Histoire du corps: Tome 2, De la Révolution à la Grande Guerre*, edited by Alain Corbin, Jean-Jacques Courtine, and Georges Vigarello, 299–312. Paris: Éditions de Seuil, 2005.

———. *Le Sain et le Malsain: Santé et mieux-être depuis le Moyen Âge*. Paris: Éditions du Seuil, 1993.

Vigarello, Georges, and Richard Holt. "Le corps travaillé: Gymnastes et sportifs au XIXe siècle." in *Histoire du corps: Tome 2, De la Révolution à la Grande Guerre*, edited by Alain Corbin, Jean-Jacques Courtine, and Georges Vigarello, 313–321. Paris, Éditions de Seuil, 2005.

Waelti-Walters, Jennifer. *Feminist Novelists of the Belle Époque: Love as Lifestyle*. Bloomington: Indiana University Press, 1990.

Waelti-Walters, Jennifer, and Steven C. Hause, eds. *Feminisms of the Belle Époque: A Historical and Literary Anthology*. Lincoln: University of Nebraska Press, 1994.

Walker, Cheryl. "Persona Criticism and the Death of the Author." In *Contesting the Subject: Essays in Postmodern Theory and Practice of Biography and Biographical Criticism*, edited by William Epstein, 109–21. West Lafayette, IN: Purdue University Press, 1991.

Weber, Eugen. *France, Fin de Siècle*. Cambridge: Belknap Press, 1986.

————. "Gymnastics and Sports in Fin-de-Siècle France: Opium of the Classes?" *American Historical Review* 76 (February 1971): 70–98.

————. *Peasants into Frenchmen: The Modernization of Rural France, 1870–1914*. Stanford, CA: Stanford University Press, 1976.

Weisberg, Gabriel, ed. *Montmartre and the Making of Mass Culture*. New Brunswick, NJ: Rutgers University Press, 2001.

Whatley, Janet. "Colette and the Art of Survival." In *Colette: The Woman, The Writer*, edited by Erica Mendelson Eisinger and Mari Ward McCarty, 32–39. University Park: Pennsylvania State University Press, 1981.

Wilson, Michael. "'Sans les femmes, qu'est-ce qui nous resterait?' Gender and Transgression in Bohemian Montmartre." In *Body Guards: The Cultural Politics of Gender Ambiguity Education*, edited by Julia Epstein and Kristina Straub, 195–222. New York: Routledge, 1991.

Winock, Michel. *La Belle Époque: La France de 1900 à 1914*. Paris: Perrin, 2002.

Wlassikoff, Michel, and Jean-Pierre Bodeux. *La fabuleuse et exemplaire histoire de bébé Cadum*. Paris: Syros Alternatives, 1990.

Wohl, Robert. *Generation of 1914*. London: Weidenfeld and Nicolson, 1980.

Wright, Gordon. *France in Modern Times: From the Enlightenment to the Present*. New York: W. W. Norton, 1995.

Zeldin, Theodore. *France, 1848–1945*. Oxford: Oxford University Press, 1973.

INDEX

CPSIA information can be obtained
at www.ICGtesting.com
Printed in the USA
BVHW040738121121
621389BV00006B/22